MURDER INCORPORATED

empire \ genocide \ manifest destiny

A Three Book Series

BOOK ONE:

"Dreaming of Empire"

BOOK TWO: **"America's Favorite Pastime"**

BOOK THREE: **"Perfecting Tyranny"**

Mumia Abu-Jamal & Stephen Vittoria

PRISON RADIO
San Francisco
2018

Published by Prison Radio
San Francisco

First Published in 2018

Prison Radio, P.O. Box 411074, San Francisco, CA 94141

Edited by Justin Lebanowski

Cover Design by Robert Guillory

Interior Design by Rocco Melillo

First Edition Hardcover / February 2018

LIBRARY OF CONGRESS CATALOGING-IN-PUBLICATION DATA

Abu-Jamal, Mumia – Vittoria, Stephen. Murder Incorporated: Empire, Genocide, and Manifest Destiny/Book One—1st ed. p. cm.

Includes bibliographical references and index.

1.History—American Empire.
2. History—Genocide—Slavery.
3.History—Manifest Destiny.

ISBN: 978-0-9989600-1-2

Printed in the USA

To the Reverend Malcolm Boyd—the quiet man with the heart of a lion, the espresso priest who found his groove (and all of ours) in the smoky dreck of sixties nightclubs like San Francisco's *hungry i*—this sweet dear man who took his last breath as we typed our last words, our 91-year-old friend who was so damn excited about this book ("our book" he lovingly called it, as his story indeed closes this series).

We dedicate this work to his revolutionary spirit, one that now soars through the cosmos like a high-octane comet.

—MAJ & SV

If we're going to anoint the canvas of America, then we must acknowledge the stains on that canvas. We must prophetically and courageously admit where the stains are rather than lie through our teeth. We must confess sins. But it's never enough to confess sins. That's cheap grace. We must change the direction. Repentance means changing direction.

—Rev. Malcolm Boyd (City of Angels, 2014)

ACKNOWLEDGMENTS

Who births a book? Who gives it blood, sinews, limbs, brain, and spine? Books are born, more often than not, by other books, which light flames in the psyche, passing light to those flung far into the river of time.

When I think of great books, it is hardly or ever the official Canon. It is often little known people who wrote against the storm, their minds ablaze by fires from another era—like J.A. Rogers, a self-taught historian who appeared in a slew of Black newspapers, like the *Pittsburgh Courier*, the *Afro American*, and who also wrote numerous books, filled not only with texts, but photographs to affirm his theories. He traveled across continents to salvage some tidbit, some morsel of knowledge that would amaze readers, of Black names, Black nations, Black princes who emerged in worlds we had never known.

This work, therefore, was sparked when a curious teenager found more fun in a bookstore than on a baseball diamond. For, there he read Yosef Ben-Jochannon, Ivan Van Sertima, Herbert Aptheker, C.L.R. James, George Nash, Ishakamusa Barashango, Runoko Rashidi, Ward Churchill, DuBois, et al.

Often the works of these historians were emblazoned with deftly drawn dark figures in majestic poses, speaking to us across eons, saying softly, almost imperceptibly: "I am Here. I am Here."

Many, if not most of these historians were (a term few would use themselves) "outlaw" historians—rebels, who turned their backs on the Guild, for their work was so disruptive of the accepted Canon.

They searched and searched and unearthed Canons from Antiquity that preceded the works of Europe by centuries. For example, who knows that the phrase "Black is Beautiful!" so evocative of the proverbial '60s, was echoed in spirit more than a thousand years before that era? As a man of that era (really, a teen), I thought we were breaking new ground, speaking thoughts that bubbled in our breasts for the first time.

Well, Dr. Ben (as Yochannon was affectionately known by his students) certainly knew, for in many of his typewritten texts, he cited Al-Jahiz's *Book of the Glory of the Black Race*, written by a Black Arab of Basra, Iraq, decades after Islam's founding. This work, written between 776-868 A.D., reads as if it were written at the height of the Black Power Movement, circa 1968!

These writers dared to break new ground, and to not only learn new things, but to unlearn old canonical verities that were as traditional as they were misleading.

Of course, this work is inspired by the remarkable Howard Zinn, who, burned by the savagery of World War II, and inspired by the true courage of civil rights activists (many of whom were his students, like the acclaimed novelist, Alice Walker), learned not from the classics, but from his students, among them men and women who marched on the front lines of history.

This work is dedicated to all of them, who, by their works, made this one possible.

Mumia Abu-Jamal

The idea for this project emerged from dust during a late evening conversation I had with Gore Vidal in the parlor of his home in the Hollywood Hills. His grasp of history, all history, was only surpassed by his grasp of the evils unleashed by the ruling elite that he knew so well, the robber barons who own the club—own it lock, stock, and smoking barrel. Our back and forth tête-à-tête jumped from TR to FDR, Caesar to Camelot, Foggy Bottom to Langley, and of course from Italian to California wine. And in the crevices and fissures, feeling wholly out of my league with this legendary mind, I stumbled upon the genesis of *Murder Incorporated*—some rudimentary concept that I actually verbalized aloud (thinking, of course, what gibberish did I just set free). But to my great surprise Gore acknowledged the idea with that devious twinkle he sometimes offered and then consecrated my embryonic suggestion by pronouncing "Exactly." That's all I needed.

This project started as a feature documentary film. But after thirty-plus hours of filmed interviews, I slowly realized that it was near insanity to try and tell the five-hundred-year saga of the American Empire in an hour and a half. That's when I turned to my brother with an amazing mind and rock solid will to tell the truth, the whole truth, and nothing but the truth, Mumia Abu-Jamal, and said, "Mu, whaddaya say we..." His immediate fire jettisoned our ship into orbit.

There are a few other writers and soothsayers that delivered me to that night with Mr. Vidal, starting with Dick Gregory (a prophet), Muhammad Ali (the people's champion), Jim Bouton (fire-balling right-hander and unheralded revolutionary), Hunter S. Thompson (with those "right kind of eyes"), Arthur George Rust, Jr., Howard Zinn and Noam Chomsky, Norman Mailer and Bob Dylan, Stanley Kubrick and Dalton Trumbo, George Carlin and Lenny Bruce, the Man in Black, as well as the man wearing white linens and seersucker, Samuel Langhorne Clemens.

There are some folks who helped immensely with stewarding this project along the way: our savage editor Justin Lebanowski, who I still feel like punching every now and then (and then hugging because he was usually right); literary agent Morty Mint who never stopped supporting this project; Jim Kelch who read every word and offered invaluable counsel; Robert Guillory remains a constant pillar of strength and designed killer covers; Rocco Melillo and Julia Sarno-Melillo for their inspired hand and eye designing the interior of these books; Riva Enteen for her tireless work clearing all the potent voices we weaved throughout;

proofreader Jennifer Grubba for making sure everything was punctuated and sppellled correctly, and that at least something from our grade school teachers/grammaticians sunk in to Messrs. Abu-Jamal and Vittoria; and to Catherine Murphy for her invaluable help on Che and Cuba.

And, of course, to Noelle Hanrahan of Prison Radio for her ongoing heroic and Herculean efforts of producing thousands of broadcasts, delivering Mumia Abu-Jamal's voice around the world... and for embracing this book series and the authors with unbridled enthusiasm.

And finally, to a mother and father who didn't teach their son hate... to my daughter Shannon, art historian extraordinaire and a woman who continues to amaze me every moment of every day, offering great hope for the future... and to my lifelong partner and BFF, Ellen Mary Vittoria, whose love keeps my blood pumping for all these sunrises.

Stephen Vittoria

EDITOR'S NOTE

The book series you have in your hand, be it paper or pixels, is the result of an unusual collaboration between two men who met in unusual fashion, but who communed as we always have, since the origin of thought yielded not only "like-mindedness" but the deeper affinities of friendship, solidarity, and love. When filmmaker Stephen Vittoria set out to make a documentary about the "500 year Euro-American march of Empire," he made two valuable discoveries: first, that such a story could not be properly told in a feature length film; second, that one of his interviewees could be, in fact would be, the subject of his next film. *Long Distance Revolutionary* (2013) tells the life story of journalist and imprisoned dissident Mumia Abu-Jamal, whose fascinating life both before and after incarceration had been largely backgrounded by the publicity of his case and its connection to the Death Penalty debate that raged in the late 1990s.

The kinship kindled during the making of that film has yielded this book, written collaboratively through correspondence between Vittoria and Abu-Jamal, the former composing on a MacBook in Los Angeles and the latter composing on a Swintec clear cabinet electronic typewriter (manufactured especially for prisoners) in the Pennsylvania State Correctional Facility at Mahanoy. (*Murder Incorporated: Empire, Genocide, and Manifest Destiny,* will in fact be the ninth volume penned solely or in collaboration by Abu-Jamal from within prison.) It's worth noting that since the life of this book began as a film, a number of interviews were already conducted (with the likes of Gore Vidal, Noam Chomsky, Tariq Ali, Michael Parenti, and others), excerpts of which you'll find peppered throughout. And much like a documentary film, this book includes a colorful choir of trenchant voices, many of them an inspiration to the authors, underscoring that history must be told by the many and, often, the many unheard, and not by the few armed with bullhorn and bully pulpit.

Some readers may take affront at this book, as they might others like it that seek to stridently criticize the American nation, or perhaps more pointedly, the American government and its position and conduct in the world, throughout its brief and productive history. But for the muted and muffled to be heard, their gestures must be bold and their voices loud. Some may take affront at the ironic humor and fiery, sometimes vulgar characterizations. But what is a vulgar word employed to describe vulgar acts of treachery, thievery, slavery, and murder? And ultimately, this book is intended to be informative, insightful, inspiring, and compelling. And if it pisses you off, I can tell you—it's meant to.

J. Alan Lebanowski, Editor

Winter, 2017
New York City

CHAPTERS

FOREWORD

The historian James W. Loewen calls American history a "landscape of denial." The struggles of the radicals and populists, who as Howard Zinn pointed out were the real engines of social change in the United States, are ignored or minimalized. Our history includes vast areas of historical amnesia, especially about slavery, race, class struggle, radical movements such as the anarchists and communists, and the many crimes of empire. American history is often more myth than history.

History, like most scholarly pursuits in academia, is dominated by the banal and the trivial. The mantra of disinterested scholarship and the obsession with data collection add up, as the historian Howard Zinn wrote, "to the fear that using our intelligence to further our moral ends is somehow improper." Historians are rewarded for buttressing the ruling social structure, producing heavy tomes on the ruling elites and ignoring the underlying social forces that have been the true engines of social and political change in the United States. Most historians are complicit in masking the inconvenient facts that tarnish the myth, facts about genocide, slavery, class, repression, and the lies told by the ruling elites, the mass media, and powerful institutions to justify their power. Historians who are apologists for the past are rewarded and promoted. Truth tellers are marginalized.

Murder Incorporated provides an historical framework for understanding our past and thereby understanding out present. It is a comprehensive overview of historical events that is in stark contrast from the myths perpetuated in most high school and college textbooks. Mumia Abu-Jamal and Stephen Vittoria compile a collection of documents and interviews with distinguished historians, such as Gary Nash and the late Howard Zinn, to revive the central importance of the radical tradition.

The authors begin with the foundations of white supremacy, tracing the origins of the imagined "Aryan prototype." "It's clear to see, with even a cursory read of American history, that this white supremacist ideology of civilization chasing the sun west has its legendary claws buried deep inside the foundation of American expansionist rationale," the authors write. They point to an illuminating quote from Theodore Roosevelt in 1906: "The world would have halted had it not been for the Teutonic conquests in alien lands."

Abu-Jamal and Vittoria urge us to reexamine our founding myths, including the Revolutionary War. Was the upheaval that followed the Stamp Act a united resistance against the British? Or was it the result of deep inequality? Food riots, slave uprisings, and tenant rebellions, they point out, plagued the colonies. "These people didn't hate the taxes because they came from 'Mother England,'" Abu-Jamal and Vittoria write. "They hated the taxes because they were often desperately poor and could ill afford to pay them...Popular rebellions weren't so much against Britain as they were against the wealthy...When the chances presented themselves, they were more rebellious, more radical than most of us were ever taught."

Abu-Jamal and Vittoria illustrate that a grassroots American opposition has, for centuries, resisted and continues to resist the tentacles of U.S. colonial imperialism and capitalism. They remind us that radical activism is deeply rooted in our country's past. "Many of us tend to think that the radical days are isolated to the 1960s, but...Americans of every stripe and fashion were always a pretty radical bunch," the authors write. In 1745, thirty years before the American Revolution, farmers in New Jersey repeatedly broke into prisons to help their unjustly incarcerated friends break out. Gary Nash in *The Unknown American Revolution* writes:

> In mid-September 1745, about 150 New Jersey farmers armed with "clubs, axes, and crow bars" descended on the jail in Newark, the capital of the royal colony of New Jersey. They demanded that the sheriff release Samuel Baldwin, who had been arrested for cutting down trees on lands claimed by Governor Lewis Morris, a man of great wealth and the owner of scores of slaves. When the sheriff refused, the crowd mobbed him. They tore the jail door off its hinges and set Baldwin free. Triumphantly making their way out of town, they vowed to mobilize again and bring "fighting Indians" with them on the next occasion that one of their own was imprisoned.
>
> Fourteen weeks later, when the sheriff followed orders from the royal governor to arrest three of the farmers involved in the September jailbreak, the defiant yeomen assembled again. Armed with clubs, they freed one of the prisoners as he was being transferred from one jail to another. Trying to uphold royal authority, the sheriff called out thirty militiamen to surround the Newark jail and prevent further breaks. Undaunted, three hundred determined farmers, marching under a pennant, confronted the militia. "Those who are under my list, follow me," shouted Amos Roberts,

> a yeoman leader. With that, the farmers overpowered the militiamen, thrashed the sheriff, freed their friends and marched out of town...
>
> Other similar events followed. In July 1747, two hundred men marched into Perth Amboy in East New Jersey and vowed that if they were challenged "there should not have been a man left alive, or a house standing." Springing open the town jail, they freed one of their imprisoned leaders."

Murder Incorporated elevates the numerous slave rebellions and resistance of African-Americans, usually washed out of historical accounts, to show that Blacks have a long and proud tradition of defying their white masters. And Blacks were often crucial to the victories celebrated as iconic moments in our history. Quoting from authors Fred Jerome and Rodger Taylor, Abu-Jamal and Vittoria remind us of the Black soldiers who were vital to the victory of several American Revolution battles:

> A part of the story most people haven't heard is that black colonial Americans in the community of Princeton and beyond played a significant role in this critical victory. Several colonial African Americans, including many from the elite all-black First Rhode Island Regiment [*see endnote] fought in the battle. Black Revolutionary War veteran Oliver Cromwell recalled in the spring of 1852, at the age of one hundred, how Washington's army "knocked the British about lively." Some of the fighting took place in Princeton's African American community. "Nineteen Hessian soldiers were killed on Witherspoon Street. For years after the battle residents spoke of being terrorized by a ghost of a Hessian soldier who was killed in the fight."

The Union Army was able to begin to push back the Confederate forces in the south when some 200,000 African-American troops were conscripted to fight. The Confederate monuments that dot the south, Eric Foner has written, mostly erected between 1890 and 1920 by the Daughters of the Confederacy, were designed to negate not only Black heroism, but to bury the brief period of equal rights for Blacks during Reconstruction. General Nathan Bedford Forrest, one of the largest slave traders in the south, a vicious racist, the founder of the Ku Klux Klan and the commander who oversaw the massacre of Black Union soldiers after their surrender at Fort Pillow, has his image in statues, markers, and busts throughout the former Confederate states. He was, in the eyes of white racists, worth memorializing. But there are no statues of Confederate commanders such as General James Longstreet or General James Fleming Fagan because they supported Black rights after the war. There are few memorials to slavery or lynching. And the great Black leaders of Reconstruction have been disappeared.

"Public monuments are built by those with sufficient power to determine which parts of history are worth commemorating and what version of history ought to be conveyed," Foner writes.

Abu-Jamal and Vittoria expose the racism of well known writers and figures such as L. Frank Baum, who wrote *The Wizard of Oz.* Baum, along with iconic leaders such as George Washington and Thomas Jefferson, championed the genocide of Native Americans. Abu-Jamal and Vittoria quote Baum's article in South Dakota's *Aberdeen Saturday Pioneer*:

> The nobility of the Redskin is extinguished, and what few are left are a pack of whining curs who lick the hand that smites them. The Whites, by law of conquest, by justice of civilization, are masters of the American continent, and the best safety of the frontier settlements will be secured by the total annihilation of the few remaining Indians. Why not annihilation? Their glory has fled, their spirit broken, their manhood effaced; better that they should die than live the miserable wretches that they are.

"History does not merely refer to the past..." James Baldwin wrote. "History is literally the present in all we do."

It is only when we face our own darkness, and in particular the fact that this nation was founded and perpetuated to this day on the myth of white supremacy, that we can begin to understand and solve the most pressing evils of our time.

"Think of the racial strife that continues to plague American society today; the injustices amidst the vast silences," Abu-Jamal and Vittoria write. "We act, frankly, as if we do not see what we see, and so it gets progressively worse because we have internalized and normalized what would be unspeakable injustices if it happened to us."

We continued to view our own history through the lens of sanitized words such as "settlers" and "pioneers" instead of "murderers" and "land thieves." The word "savage" evokes images of Native Americans. Loewen, describes the lingering stereotypes:

> Our textbooks do not teach against the archetypes of the savage Indian that pervades popular culture. On the contrary, textbooks give very little attention of any kind to Indian wars. As a result, my college students still come up with "savage" when I ask them for five adjectives that apply to Indians. Like much of our "knowledge" about Native Americans, the "savage" stereotype comes particularly from Western movies and novels, such as the popular "Wagons West" series by Dana Fuller Ross. These paperbacks, which have sold hundreds of thousands of copies, claim boldly, "The general outlines of history have been faithfully followed." Titled with state names—Idaho!, Utah!, etc—the novel's covers warn that "marauding Indian bands are spreading murder and mayhem among the terror-stricken settlers." In the Hollywood Old West, wagon trains were invariably encircled by savage Indian hordes. In the real West, among 200,000 whites and blacks who journeyed across the Plains between 1840 and 1860, only 362 pioneers (and 426 Native Americans) died in all the recorded battles between the two groups. Much more commonly, Indians gave the new settlers directions, showed them water holes, sold them food and horses, bought cloth and guns, and served as guides and interpreters. These activities are rarely depicted in movies, novels, or our textbooks. Inhaling the misinformation of the popular culture, students have no idea that natives considered European warfare far more savage than their own.

Yet, when it came to the savagery of war, it is clear who the true savages are. Abu-Jamal and Vittoria write:

> The Indian way of war was profoundly different from the Anglo-American way. The Indians, as did many indigenous peoples, considered war a kind of sport among men, where the object (or even intention) was rarely death—and the killing of noncombatants was virtually unheard of. There was no honor in a warrior slaying a woman or a child. Many Indian tribes developed a kind of warfare called counting coup, where a brave would ride or run up his opponent, and strike him, or some other minor interplay. This demonstration of his braveness was considered a way of proving his honor, and though men left such wars with wounded pride, they often left it alive. If wounded, this was considered a badge of honor, for it brought luster to the warrior's legend.

Empires founded on genocide and slavery that refuse to take responsibility for their crimes and continue to revel in mythical beliefs about their greatness and moral superiority ultimately lose touch with reality. The authors write:

> It took the epic French Revolution and two massive military debacles to bring down Louis XVI, Napoleon, and the First French Empire. One hundred and fifty years later, in 1954, history reminded the French once again about the follies of empire-building when their more recent attempt at overt colonialism was thrashed at Dien Bien Phu by General Vo Nguyen Giap and his Viet Minh forces, sending the French back to Paris with their tail between their legs.
>
> The Spanish Empire was on the ropes for what seems like forever until they were finally undone by a number of wars, revolutions, and battles—like the whooping they took at Trafalgar when Lord Nelson and the British Royal Navy wiped out the combined fleets of Spain and France off the coast of the Iberian Peninsula.
>
> ...Has the American Empire crossed the Rubicon? Like Julius Caesar's army crossing the River Rubicon, has the empire now headquartered in Washington passed the point of no return? Has its assault on any semblance of democracy and the rights of man finally swallowed hope whole? In 49 BC, standing on the banks of the famed river in northern Italy, Caesar articulated his bottom-line: Alea iacta est or "the die is cast." He was referring to his impending march across Italy and a civil war against Roman leader Pompey the Great—but Caesar's spirit travels to the here and now and aptly underscores the world's first lone superpower—a global sheriff with heretofore-unequaled power and domain.

The decay of our empire has spawned internal rot—militarized police forces, mass incarceration, and modern mass surveillance technologies, a condition that Abu-Jamal and Vittoria describe as "the insane growth of a surveillance state beyond imagination—one so ambitious and universal that it makes the dystopian predictions by Orwell look mild by comparison."

Like all empires, the harsh and violent forms of control that have been used on the "wretched of the earth," have migrated back to the homeland in a time of decay to keep the population in check. The tyranny we have imposed on others is now being imposed on us.

Former chief economist John Perkins described the CIA's role, one that will become familiar to us at home, in *Murder Incorporated*:

> The CIA has played a very, very active role in spreading this empire and most Americans don't understand this at all—but the CIA is everywhere...They're constantly feeding information to the economic hit men. They're feeding information to the corporations all the time. And when all else fails, they're the ones that step in. But it's usually not CIA employees who step in. The CIA hires contracted people. You can't place the blame on the CIA because you can't find anything. It's not there, in the same way that economic hit men don't work directly for the government. I never did. We work for private firms that are paid by the government. These "jackals" that work for the CIA as assassins, or those overthrowing governments, providers of information, they're usually not on a government payroll. They're working for somebody else. They're called "security analysts" or "international marketing specialists," or maybe "executive recruiters." But they're out there collecting this information—tremendous amounts of information about what's going on in other countries, and it's all coming in through the CIA and their operatives. They're using all these means to help business and the military—help spread the empire. And it's been a very efficient system from the standpoint of the emperors, from the standpoint of the corporatocracy.

Culture and literacy, in the final stage of imperial decline, are replaced with noisy diversions and empty clichés. The Roman statesman Cicero inveighed against their ancient equivalent—the arena. Cicero, for his honesty, was hunted down and murdered. His severed head and his right hand were nailed onto the speaker's platform in the Forum. The roaring crowds were gleefully told he would never speak or write again.

Today, we are infected with a toxic, mindless cacophony, our own version of spectacle and gladiator fights, of bread and circus, pumped out over the airwaves in endless cycles. Political life has fused into celebrity worship. Education is primarily vocational. Intellectuals are cast out and despised. Artists cannot make a living. Few people read books. Thought has been banished, especially at universities and colleges, where timid pedants and careerists churn out academic drivel. "Although tyranny, because it needs no consent, may successfully rule over foreign peoples," Hannah Arendt wrote in *The Origins of Totalitarianism,* "it can stay in power only if it destroys first of all the national institutions of its own people." And because ours have been destroyed, the imbecilic utterings of our degraded culture is tweeted daily in incoherent sound bites from the Oval Office.

There will come a moment of implosion, the authors warn us. Empires finally reach a point where they push too far and demand too much. They exhaust their resources, as we are doing, in endless wars and economic folly. No one can predict when this will happen or what will trigger the revolt. But the tinder is there.

"Revolutions are funny things," Abu-Jamal and Vittoria go on to write. "When they begin, no one really knows where they will end, for the forces unleashed thereby can run in many and sundry directions, often far afield from those who claim to have started them."

Chris Hedges
Princeton, New Jersey

PROLOGUE

Don't trust anyone who isn't angry.

—John Trudell, American Indian Movement

Let's drop the pretense.

To hell with "In fourteen hundred and ninety two, Columbus sailed the ocean blue."

To hell with the safe or guild historian.

To hell with John Gast's 1872 painting "American Progress," the allegorical representation of hegemony run amok.

To hell with the notion of "American exceptionalism" as crafted by Governor John Winthrop in 1630 when he called the Massachusetts Bay Colony "a city upon a hill"—a nifty little piece of primitive propaganda spit-shined a few hundred years later when Ronald Reagan called America "a shining city on a hill."

To hell with the 19th century editor and writer, John O'Sullivan, and his treatise declaring divine sanction for American expansionism—at any and all costs—and, of course, with god on their side. And therein exists the power: astral rationale and spurious moral sanction for any horrific act that might move the Anglo expansion further west—including trivial oh-by-the-way events along the Yellow Brick Road like genocide, pillage, enslavement, and subjugation. Here's a slice from O'Sullivan's sweet xenophobic pie:

> The fulfillment of our manifest destiny to overspread the continent allotted by Providence for the free development of our yearly multiplying millions.

To hell with Manifest Destiny.

Ask an American Indian how he or she feels about Manifest Destiny ("if you can find one...you gotta locate an Indian first; we've made 'em just a little difficult to find"—George Carlin; his sword sorely missed). It was an American holocaust.

Ask an African slave how she feels about Manifest Destiny—you can still do this by visiting the living words of Harriet Tubman, who like many others, rebelled against her barbarous oppression. The whitewashed history written about American slavery portrays the African slave population as timid, docile, and meek—submissively accepting their horrific plight while singing sweet spirituals waiting for Jesus to wave a magic wand. But if you dig beneath the commercial spin (lies) written in American textbooks by public relation scribes masquerading as historians, you will discover firsthand accounts by slaves and abolitionists that tell a much different story; a gut-wrenching narrative that corroborates beyond a shadow of a doubt that there was never a time when Africans blindly or obediently accepted their fate: they poisoned their captors; they burned down houses and barns; they escaped to freedom, leaving the chains of hate and economics behind. Africans fought in every way possible against their inhuman fate.

Ask a Mexican circa 1850, or a Filipino circa 1898 how they feel about Manifest Destiny. Or ask a Japanese mother of five on the morning of 6 August 1945 when "Little Boy" came tumbling down from a crystal clear blue sky, raining instant annihilation and murder upon thousands and thousands and tens of thousands of souls... another brutal example of The Empire making the *unthinkable normal*—and always with the guild historians and various apologists helping to philosophize disgrace. Ask that mother how she feels about Manifest Destiny.

Ask a Haitian circa 1915, a Salvadoran, a Nicaraguan, or anyone in Latin America during the whole of the so-called American Century, especially in the 1980s, when the neoconservatives emerged from the gates of hell, loaded for bear with the full wherewithal of the Central Intelligence Agency, not to mention the American president and his arsenal of weapons and his minions of economic hit men. Ask them all how they feel about Manifest Destiny.

Ask Iraqis or Afghanis today how they feel about Manifest Destiny. Ask Mamana Bibi—a 68-year old grandmother and midwife who delivered hundreds of babies in her Pakistani community. Actually that might be a problem because we can't. Not since 24 October 2012 when she was picking okra in the family field and an American hellfire missile hit her flush on. In that sorrowful instant, Mamana Bibi became another bloody victim of Manifest Destiny.[1] Your tax dollars hard at work.

In fact, ask an American about Manifest Destiny—although you'll probably have to explain it first. And then pick an atrocity, any atrocity. John Q. Patriot won't like it, but as Douglas Popora writes in *How Holocausts Happen–The United States in Central America*: "Although the American people disapproved of what was going on, they did not much care about it either."

The American version of the "Corporation" (herein referred to by its charter name, "Murder Incorporated") counts on the masses to continue their lock-step impersonation of ghouls meandering through the abyss—not unlike the black and white zombies in George Romero's *Night of the Living Dead* meandering through a foggy Pennsylvania countryside. Gore Vidal renamed the sleepwalking American populace: "The United States of Amnesia." Ultimately, journalist Chris Hedges nails them to the cross:

> The collective retreat into self-delusion has transformed huge swaths of the American populace into a peculiar species of adult-children who live in a Peter Pan world of make believe where reality is never permitted to be an impediment to desire.[2]

Empire complete.

Historical Framework

From page one to the last, *Murder Incorporated* examines the myth and reality of American history—a history founded in genocide, nurtured through slavery, and perpetuated by endless war. We reveal American historical myths as folly, replacing the widely accepted legends regarding liberty with the unfortunate and ugly meat-hook realities that paint a much different picture—one of violence and misery. Political historian Michael Parenti:

> This enormous gap between what US leaders do in the world and what Americans think their leaders are doing is one of the great propaganda accomplishments of the dominant political mythology.[3]

The term may have been coined in 1845, but the seeds of Manifest Destiny arrived with Christopher Columbus when he stumbled onto the shores of North America—the self-styled "New World." Since then, the death grip of its ideology has been the operating principle of the American Empire—a fervent, fanatical, at times religious mandate to carry out economic and geo-political acts that will always benefit the chosen few, which, in today's parlance is the "one percent." In fact, this Draconian gospel of exceptionalism has been the all-powerful dogma fueling American imperialism and free-market fundamentalism at the core of U.S. armed atrocities—both domestic and foreign. Writer and cabinetmaker Charles Sullivan offers this allegory: "It is the unquestioned religion of America that also bears a strange resemblance to the ideology of the cancer cell."[4]

Murder Incorporated views these ignoble moments not as a series of isolated incidents but rather as an uninterrupted continuum that runs through American history like a main circuit cable. Here again, Charles Sullivan gets to the heart of the matter:

> Endless war is necessary to feed the insatiable engine of capitalism. The assumption of moral superiority and therefore greater worth is dangerous, because it sanctions and rationalizes the slaughter of innocent people and the theft of their land. Under such religious authority these atrocities are, in effect, the will of God and therefore right and just.[5]

This insatiable drive for power and dominion is the underlying motivation for these odious and destructive actions. Manifest Destiny, as embodied in American exceptionalism, employs racism, hypocritical religiosity, and derisive politics to drive the relentless and sadistic aims of The Empire. Every new campaign is positioned and sold like toothpaste—polished with well-oiled Madison Avenue slickness. It is unabashed American machismo: the virile cowboy mythology complete with gunslingers and six-shooters blasting their way to glory. It's Clint Eastwood painting the town red and then riding off into a mirage, vanishing into thin air. Hence those would-be cowboys Cheney and Bush with their "Shock and Awe," and of course the wannabe strongman Trump with his "Make America ~~Great~~ White Again." Manifest Destiny...sloganized.

Beyond unmasking the insidiousness of calling this use of raw power "right and just," *Murder Incorporated* details how the Corporation has managed to place (and continues to place) the responsibility for the atrocities on the victims themselves. The most popular myth used is the "myth of the savage," an ENORMOUS LIE that justifies all the pain and suffering brought down on the innocents by the Corporation as the unavoidable march of civilization (in this case the Euro-American civilization) in the name of a superior strain of humanity. This ENORMOUS LIE sets forth the idea that the inferior "savages" (who are not only dehumanized but demonized) have no rights to life, liberty, or the actual land they live on and usually have lived on for thousands of years.

In fact, the cruelties of Manifest Destiny have been historically cloaked in various ways, as in Rudyard Kipling's famous 1899 poem "White Man's Burden," where he championed the idea that the United States—following in the footsteps of Great Britain—had the burden to help the lesser peoples of the world adjust to the canons of Christianity. Kipling's exhortations to the U.S. with regard to taking up the responsibility of empire (in this case in the Philippine Islands when, in a bloodbath, American forces killed more than 600,000 Filipinos) became the "racialized" hymn to U.S. imperialism.

> **White Man's Burden**
> *Take up the White Man's burden–*
> *Send forth the best ye breed–*
> *Go bind your sons to exile*
> *To serve your captives' need;*
> *To wait in heavy harness,*
> *On fluttered folk and wild–*
> *Your new-caught, sullen peoples,*
> *Half-devil and half-child.*

The ENORMOUS LIE continues... deepens... and goes something like this: these inferior creatures cannot utilize the land and resources like the Anglo-Saxons, so they essentially have no right to them. Savages have no civilization (that these invaders recognize) and therefore no political institutions (worthy of mention). Rather these are people who suffer as a consequence of their inferior state.

Now, if that codicil to the ENORMOUS LIE doesn't finish the job, the Corporation rolls out this one: "We will free the world of tyranny, dictatorship, and despotism"—and the walking dead buy this one almost every time. Manifest Destiny becomes the "white knight" spreading freedom and liberty to the Philistines. Author Thomas Jimson in his essay "Reflections on Race & Manifest Destiny" offers this lampoon: "The march of conquest was not genocide, slavery, and dispossession; it was the Peace Corps of the 19th Century."[6]

Power, Piety, and Profit

At the heart of Manifest Destiny—at the heart of all American imperialist adventures—is a ravenous three-headed monster, a Cerberus-on-Earth—built of Power, Piety, and Profit. In fact, the totalitarian behavior of this beast has fueled the march of U.S. history since a warm and idyllic Caribbean day in October of 1492—and continues to fuel the march of empire through every one of America's drone strikes. Dr. Cornel West offers his own troika of "free-market fundamentalism... aggressive militarism... and escalating authoritarianism"[7] as the fuel for hegemony abroad and destructive, anti-democratic forces at home.

Murder Incorporated unravels and dissects this unholy trinity of militarism (power), religion/authoritarianism (piety), and big business (profit) to reveal how it gnaws at the collective soul. Michael Parenti sketches out the destructive path of empire this way:

> The history of the United States has been one of territorial and economic expansionism, with the benefits going mostly to the U.S. business class in the form of growing investments and markets, access to rich natural resources and cheap labor, and the accumulation of enormous profits. The American people have had to pay the costs of empire, supporting a huge military establishment with their taxes, while suffering the loss of jobs, the neglect of domestic services, and the loss of tens of thousands of American lives in overseas military ventures. The greatest costs, of course, have been borne by the peoples of the Third World who have endured poverty, pillage, disease, dispossession, exploitation, illiteracy, and the widespread destruction of their lands, cultures, and lives.[8]

To be an American also means that one is related to all peoples in the Americas: like the Cubans, the Venezuelans, the Nicaraguans, the Brazilians—in fact all brothers and sisters in Central and South America. As a group, they have experienced the wrath of their North American cousins. These citizens of sovereign states do not embrace the idea that it's even remotely the business of the CIA or the American military—or any other agency operating out of Washington—to destroy the leaders or popular organizations of their states, neighboring states or even distant ones. The innocents massacred on 11 September 1973 by the Pinochet thugs in Chile (orchestrated by the American thugs, Richard Nixon and Henry Kissinger) will painfully attest to this. They do not believe that it is the inherent right, or the "manifest destiny" of the Norteaméricano rule over them.

From the embryonic beginnings of empire in 1492 through the current jack-booted "New World Order," our reassessment of the American narrative underscores the transmutation from old world empire to the "New Rome" or "Manifest Destiny Rides Again." Thomas Jimson concludes:

> A philosophy such as Manifest Destiny once internalized in the culture, is never really abolished, it merely adapts to the present conditions and transforms itself into a suitable logic for the times.[9]

Murderer of Men (and Women)

In trying to wordsmith a wrap-up for this prologue, we stumbled into perfection, written, oddly enough, by South Dakota Republican Senator Richard Pettigrew in 1898:

> Throughout all recorded time manifest destiny has been the murderer of men. It has committed more crimes, done more to oppress and wrong the inhabitants of the world than any other tribute to which mankind has fallen heir. Manifest destiny has caused the strong to rob the weak and has reduced the weak to slavery. Manifest destiny built the feudal castle and supplied the castle with its serfs. Manifest destiny impelled republics that have heretofore existed and perished to go forth and conquer weaker races and to subject their people to slavery, to impose taxation against their will, and to inflict governments odious to them. Manifest destiny is simply the cry of the strong in justification of their plunder of the weak.[10]

And in the wake of Manifest Destiny we find bodies—lots of them. What's palpable when you unravel the myths sanctified over the centuries is that murder stands as the unrivaled byproduct of empire. Not food, education, science, medicine, liberty, or freedom. Murder. *Top of the Charts. The Big Kahuna. Numero Uno.* It's the Corporation's number one negotiating tool in its pursuit of power, the protection of Christendom, and the procurement of wealth and natural resources.

And, unfortunately, it's not afraid to use it—hence the title of this book.

The struggle against unfettered conquest and murder began in the late 15th century, as chronicled in the diaries of Christopher Columbus (aka Cristoforo Colombo, aka Cristóbal Colón, aka Cristóvão Colombo—considered armed and dangerous) as transcribed by Dominican priest Bartolomé de las Casas, as well as in Las Casas' own work, including *In Defense of the Indians* written in 1550. The inimitable Howard Zinn and the Dominican friar from Seville, Spain offer this glimpse:

> What the Spaniards did to the Indians is told in horrifying detail by Bartolomé de las Casas, whose writing gives the most thorough account of the Spanish-Indian encounter... [he] spent forty years on Hispaniola and nearby islands, and became the leading advocate in Spain for the rights of the natives. Las Casas, in his book *The Devastation of the Indies,* writes of Arawaks: "...of all the infinite universe of humanity, these people are

the most guileless, the most devoid of wickedness and duplicity... yet into this sheepfold... there came Spaniards who immediately behaved like ravening beasts... Their reason for killing and destroying... is that Christians have an ultimate aim which is to acquire gold..."[11]

Murder Incorporated is committed to breaking through the seemingly impenetrable walls of mythical Euro-American history that have been erected over the past 500 years—storybook fables about the demon-savage as well as the ensuing American chronicle that deftly replaced clear-cut imperial designs with racism and Social Darwinism. Today, we might call this toxic poison "tribalism." As journalist Glenn Greenwald writes:

> Western victims are mourned and humanized, while victims of Western violence are invisible and thus dehumanized. Aside from being repugnant in its own right, this formula, by design, is deeply deceptive as propaganda: It creates the impression among Western populations that we are the victims but not the perpetrators of heinous violence, that terrorism is something done to us but that we never commit ourselves, that "primitive, radical and inhumanely violent" describes the enemy tribe but not our own. [12]

❖ ❖ ❖

We dedicate this narrative to our fellow terrestrial space travelers whose true birthright of human liberty and personal freedom have been commandeered over the centuries by Murder Incorporated—robber barons who take without asking and will literally kill you if you dare stand-up and say:

Hey, what the fuck?

—Mumia Abu-Jamal & Stephen Vittoria
Parts Unknown

1 With God On Our Side

Well, you see Willard...In this war, things get confused out there... power, ideals, the old morality, and practical military necessity. But out there with these natives it must be a temptation to be god. Because there's a conflict in every human heart between the rational and the irrational, between good and evil. And good does not always triumph. Sometimes the dark side overcomes what Lincoln called the better angels of our nature. Every man has a breaking point. You and I have one. Walt Kurtz has reached his. And very obviously, he has gone insane.

—General Corman to Captain Willard, *Apocalypse Now*

When Francis Ford Coppola adapted Joseph Conrad's seminal work, *Heart of Darkness,* for his Vietnam War epic *Apocalypse Now,* he found in the 1903 novella a searing attack on the cruelties of colonialism and the toxic seeds of empire. In Conrad's story, as in the world he lived in, European occupiers exercised a brutal exploitation of the working class. In *Heart of Darkness* it was specifically the African working class. Clearly for Coppola, this was a fitting parallel to the American Empire's savage assault on the people of Southeast Asia. Conrad recognized the oppressive operational apparatus of the white European ruling class: social Darwinism combined with a muscular belief in the Carlylean work ethic, which Conrad underscores throughout *Heart of Darkness.* Of course the occupier's embrace of these two Victorian standards is their era's justification of the perennial exploitation of an "inferior" indigenous population presupposed to be in desperate need of the "superior" scientific and spiritual knowledge offered so graciously by white Europeans to the "Dark Continent." But like most occupations throughout human history, just the act of occupation is corrupt and sadistic. Conrad demonstrates this historic truth as the European's piggish thirst for wealth and power devastates the land and the people of Africa without sorrow and without regret.

> *The conquest of the earth, which mostly means the taking it away from those who have a different complexion or slightly flatter noses than ourselves, is not a pretty thing when you look into it too much.*
>
> —Joseph Conrad, *Heart of Darkness*

No doubt that it's murder and plunder for fortune. Capitalism 101. But there's more than just meat chunks of avarice in this colonial stew. There is also madness—the warped embrace of human exceptionalism, of being God's chosen people, allowed to behave like brutes and then dance like angels.

Translatio Imperii, which translates from the Latin as "transfer of rule" or "transfer of empire," is a concept rooted in the Middle Ages describing the movement of history as a transfer of power from one imperium to the next. It's the idea that one nation or empire will be the dominant political and cultural influence across the globe until the power shifts to another state over the passage of time; Rome, Great Britain, America (with apologies to all the Empires not mentioned).

Social Darwinism: Imperial Justification

The concept of "Social Darwinism" has been a useful and convenient tool in the march of empire. Even before Charles Darwin published *On the Origin of Species* in 1859, the progenitors of conquest were well acquainted with the paradigm later coined as "survival of the fittest" by English philosopher Herbert Spencer. Then, as always, the power elites were very good at unleashing the dogs of war or swinging the scythe of economic terrorism in their bloody pursuit of conquest, meticulously ensuring the ends justified the means. According to the canon of social Darwinism, those with strength—be it economic, physical, or technological—flourish, and those without are destined for extinction. War on the weak is "survival of the fittest" fueled by greed, characterized by bloodlust, infused with a superiority complex and, when stripped of its pretenses, little more than a business model cashing in on another civilization. And this has been true, even if it's meant eradicating or beating the tar out of an already-in-place population. Africans. American Indians. Mexicans. Filipinos. Latin Americans. Asians. Iraqis. Afghanis. Hell, any brown, yellow, or red skinned group of "inferior beings" fits the bill. Let's roll. It's arrogance on steroids. Imperial hubris loaded in a warhead. Or as anthropologist Wade Davis concludes:

> Other cultures are not failed attempts to be like you. They are unique manifestations of the human spirit.

So as we revisit *Heart of Darkness* for the illustrative purposes of deconstructing the merciless tentacles of colonialism, as practiced (in this case) by the Europeans, it becomes clear that Conrad presents a very valuable side-by-side comparison: the harmony between the native Africans and their indigenous environment as opposed to the white "civilized" imperialists who brutishly take without asking and then reign over the wealth and resources without any regard to human dignity, liberty, and of course the basic tenets of sovereignty. In fact this malicious trek up the channel for riverboat captain Charles Marlow shines a bright light on the sinister nature of imperial hubris—the blatantly racist disruption of indigenous cultures for power and profit. Throughout the novella, Conrad calls into question the accepted history of colonial conquest and underscores the moral bankruptcy of Europe. In fiction, as in the harsh light of reality, the occupiers' ruthless treatment of the natives rips open and reveals the true heart of darkness.

> *It was very simple, and at the end of that moving appeal to every altruistic sentiment it blazed at you, luminous and terrifying like a flash of lightning in a serene sky: "Exterminate all the brutes!"*
>
> —Joseph Conrad, *Heart of Darkness*

Whether it's a work of thinly veiled fiction or the grim realities born in the foggy shadows of unfathomable acts of evil perpetrated during the American Holocaust over the last five hundred years, Darwin's model of "natural selection"—later manipulated by Spencer to become "survival of the fittest"—was never intended to be a model for the practiced and accepted behavior used against nations and races of people. American labor leader and author Sidney Lens describes it this way in his classic work, *The Forging of the American Empire*:

> The 1880's and 1890's were a period in which conservative intellectuals invariably used the Darwinian theory of natural selection as justification for their political goals. Nothing should be done for the poor, Herbert Spencer and other Social Darwinists proclaimed, because they had been destined for the scrap heap by the immutable laws of nature. On the other hand, the preeminent Anglo-Saxons were clearly selected for world domination and should accept their assignment with dignity.[1]

But Social Darwinism was only the modern, nouveau scientific argument for a psychotic self-image of superiority that had been brewing for centuries, with its corruptive tendrils reaching back to a convoluted and inherently dubious myth of racial apotheosis.

The Aryan Prototype

The growth of civilization and all subsequent empires has forever been tied to the mythical but powerful tale that civilization follows the sun. The fable (read: lie) went something like this: Herculean and heroic white Christian males appeared silhouetted on the eastern horizon (like Shaolin monk Kwai Chang Caine portrayed by white actor David Carradine in the old American television show *Kung Fu*) eager to civilize inferior races. In fact, this myth eventually declared the white Christian male as king of the jungle, top dude on the human evolutionary hierarchy, and, via infiltration of lesser foreign peoples, arbiter of all the great feats of human history. In his compelling historic narrative, *The Imperial Cruise* (which we will cite numerous times), author James Bradley details the Aryan myth that would come to dominate White Western consciousness:

> ONCE UPON A TIME, the story went, an "Aryan race" sprang up in the Caucasus Mountains north of what is now Iran. (The word Iran derives from the word Aryan.) The Aryan was a beautiful human specimen: white-skinned, big-boned, sturdily built, blue-eyed, and unusually intelligent. He was a doer, a creator, a wanderer, a superior man with superior instincts, and, above all, a natural Civilizer. In time, the Aryan migrated north, south, east, and west. The ancient glories of China, India, and Egypt indeed, all the world's great civilizations–were the product of his genius... It was the myth that "civilization follows the sun." The roots of this belief could be found in a concoction of history, fable, and fantasy.[2]

The Aryan myth continued to take shape throughout the first millennia after Christ, but all did not progress as planned. The Aryan male warriors made the near fatal mistake of mixing their blood with non-whites: Asian, Indian, as well as Egyptian women. The result, according to this myth, was the weakening of the race as miscegenation created a mongrelized crossbreed. James Bradley continues:

> Not all was lost, though. A group of Aryans had followed the sun westward from the Caucasus to the area of northern Europe we now call Germany. This Aryan tribe did not make the mistake of their brethren. Rather than mate with lesser-blooded peoples, these Aryans killed them. By eradicating the Others, the Aryans maintained the purity of their blood.[3]

It was here, in the uncharted German hinterlands, that the Aryan prototype evolved into "the Teuton"—a superman conqueror who appeared to have no equal. As the legend grew, the Teutons developed into an even more advanced race—a race chock-full of white civilizing heroes. Bradley describes this mythic growth of the Teutons' political and social shrewdness:

> The clever Teuton demonstrated a unique genius for political organization. He paid no homage to kings or emperors. Instead, the Teuton consulted democratically among his own kind and slowly birthed embryonic institutions of liberty that would later manifest themselves elsewhere.[4]

At the end of the first century AD, Roman historian Tacitus recorded this account: "The peoples of Germany were a race untainted by intermarriage with other races, a peculiar people and pure, like no one but themselves... with a high moral code and a profound love of freedom and individual rights; important decisions were made by the whole community."[5] So as the sun traveled west across the ages, the Teutons—representing civilization as it ought to be—dramatically drove history forward. James Bradley continues the fable:

> Eventually the Teuton—with his Aryan-inherited civilizing instinct spread out from the German forests. Those who ventured south invigorated Greece, Italy, and Spain. But these Teuton tribes made the same mistake as the earlier Aryans who founded China, India, and Egypt: instead of annihilating the non-White women, they slept with them, and the inferior blood of the darker Mediterranean races polluted the superior blood of the White Teuton. Thus the history of the Mediterranean countries is one of dissolution and nondemocratic impulses.[6]

In time, the Teutons crossed the English Channel and settled on what are today the British Isles. Again, as the story goes, they succumbed to temptation and began procreating with non-Aryans, their blood debased by these lesser beings. All hope for humankind may have been teetering on the brink, but "luckily for world civilization, these Teutons obeyed their instincts. By methodical slaughter of native men, women, and children, they kept themselves pure. As these Germanic tribes spread westward and northerly, they gradually became known as Anglo-Saxons."[7]

By the sixteenth century, the great myth of white supremacy was cemented as gospel in many quarters and, when English King Henry VIII split from Pope

Clement VII and the authority of the Roman Catholic Church, he founded the new Anglican Church of England as a beacon of the true Anglo-Saxon tradition—a tradition that existed before the Norman conquest of 1066. So as the sun rose and guided the 1600s west toward the so-called "New World," the accepted history of the British Empire was framed by three laws regarding civilization: the white race established all civilizations; when the white race preserves its "whiteness," civilization is sustained; when the white race suffers defeat or the purity of its blood is overly diffused, civilization is lost.[8]

Even a superficial look at history supports the necessary elements of the "whiteness" line of reasoning. Bradley writes:

> The Anglo-Saxons were a liberty-loving people who spawned the Magna Carta, debated laws in Parliament, produced exemplars like Shakespeare, and tinkered the Industrial Revolution to life. But woe to those who ignored civilization's rules and went south to Africa or east to Egypt, India, and China. The Anglo-Saxon in those benighted countries were but small rays of light overwhelmed by the more populous dark races. There were just too many Africans, Indians, and Chinese to slaughter in order to establish superior civilizations. The best that could be hoped for was an archipelago of White settlement and the exploitation of local primitives in order to produce greater European riches.[9]

Although this paradigm for Anglo-Saxonism produced great riches, it also meant significant limitations on their ultimate growth and unrelenting expansion. So, once again, as the sun passed overhead, they heard the sacred call. Bradley concludes:

> Progress sailed across the Atlantic with the White Christians who followed the sun west to North America. And once again—emulating their successful Aryan and Teuton forebears—the American Aryans eliminated the native population. From Plymouth Rock to San Francisco Bay, the settlers slaughtered Indian men, women, and children so democracy could take root and civilization as they understood it could sparkle from sea to shining sea.[10]

It's clear to see, with even a cursory read of American history, that this Aryan supremacist ideology of civilization chasing the sun west has its legendary claws buried deep inside the foundation of American expansionist rationale. Never one to let down the gods of empire and Anglo-Saxon supremacism, blustery Theodore

Roosevelt barked in 1906, "The world would have halted had it not been for the Teutonic conquests in alien lands."[11]

Toward a New Jerusalem: America as the New Israel

> *You are the light of the world. A city set on a hill cannot be hid. Nor do men light a lamp and put it under a bushel, but on a stand, and it gives light to all in the house. Let your light so shine before men, that they may see your good works and give glory to your Father who is in heaven.*
>
> —Jesus Christ, The Sermon on the Mount, Matthew 5:14-16

> *When he shall make us a praise and glory, that men shall say of succeeding plantations: the lord make it like that of New England: for we must Consider that we shall be as a City upon a Hill, the eyes of all people are upon us; so that if we shall deal falsely with our God in this work we have undertaken and so cause him to withdraw his present help from us, we shall be made a story and a byword through the world, we shall open the mouths of enemies to speak evil of the ways of God and all professors for Gods sake...*
>
> —John Winthrop (Governor, Massachusetts Bay Colony), "City Upon A Hill," 1630

> *I have been guided by the standard John Winthrop set before his shipmates on the flagship Arbella three hundred and thirty-one years ago, as they, too, faced the task of building a new government on a perilous frontier. "We must always consider", he said, "that we shall be as a city upon a hill—the eyes of all people are upon us". Today the eyes of all people are truly upon us—and our governments, in every branch, at every level, national, state and local, must be as a city upon a hill—constructed and inhabited by men aware of their great trust and their great responsibilities.*[12]
>
> —President-Elect John F. Kennedy, 1961

> *I've spoken of the shining city all my political life, but I don't know if I ever quite communicated what I saw when I said it. But in my mind it was a tall proud city built on rocks stronger than oceans, wind-swept, God-blessed, and teeming with people of all kinds living in harmony and peace, a city with free ports that hummed with commerce and creativity, and if there had to be city walls, the walls had doors and the doors were open to anyone with the will and the heart to get here. That's how I saw it and see it still.*[13]
>
> —President Ronald Reagan, 1989

> *Americans know that our future is brighter and better than these troubled times. We still believe in the hope, the promise and the dream of America. We still believe in that shining city on the hill.*[14]
>
> —Presidential Candidate Mitt Romney, 2012

Almost four hundred years have passed since John Winthrop wrote the words "we shall be as a City upon a Hill, the eyes of all people are upon us" —words that have come to define and bolster the myth known as American exceptionalism. And like any giant lie, this fiction is responsible for the massive bloodstains splattered across the canvas of American history: centuries of holocaust and enslavement, accompanied by centuries of the always-in-vogue reality of perpetual state-sanctioned terror, also known as the murder and mayhem of war.

American leaders have been invoking this mythical city upon a hill since Winthrop paraphrased the Sermon on the Mount to justify the land-grab about to take place with its subsequent atrocities heaved upon the Pequot and Narragansett Indians—brutal massacres often launched against noncombatants. Governor Winthrop even declared the colony a "vacuum," concluding that the indigenous inhabitants had no legal right or standing to their land.

It was as if the existent population simply did not exist. And soon that would be fact.

Winthrop and all the latter-day propagandists envisioned America as Shangri-La—a mystical and harmonious place, almost supernatural, where liberty, justice, democracy, and peace (not to mention affordable electronics) were the guiding principles. Well, like any good fairytale, this American rhetoric sounds good, even sounds great, but has no basis in reality. There's no Easter bunny, no Santa Claus, and there's definitely no utopian city upon a hill, protected by a special sky god who represents American exceptionalism over all nations and cultures. Just like with James Hilton's novel *Lost Horizon,* once you put down the fictitious and make-believe fable, there's no Shangri-La hidden at the western end of the Kunlun Mountains.

American mythology preaches that John Winthrop and his Puritan brothers left England in pursuit of religious tolerance and freedom. But in fact, Winthrop, the de facto father of American exceptionalism, was no proponent of religious tolerance or democracy in any way, shape, or form. "If we should change from a mixed aristocracy to mere democracy," Winthrop wrote, "we first should have no warrant in scripture for it: for there was no such government in Israel... A democracy is, amongst civil nations, accounted the meanest and worst of all forms of government. [To allow it would be] a manifest breach of the 5th Commandment."[15]

The colony he helped create did not hesitate to execute Quakers or go medieval on those considered to be witches. Slavery was cool, too... and according to the Puritan ethic of the time, slavery was condoned in the professed Holy Book and not perceived as a slight against God—just a few extra hands around the house. Sure, Africans were already enslaved in the neighborhood when Winthrop showed up, but he clearly supported the practice as governor, writing the very first law on the American continent sanctioning the enslavement of Africans. In fact, Winthrop enjoyed wheeling and dealing in the slave trade, especially after the Pequot War (1634-1638) when the Massachusetts Bay Colony, led by Winthrop, enslaved many of the captured Pequot Indians. But the captured warriors, who weren't taking this shit lying down, were still freaking out the good church folk, so Winthrop traded these 'insurgents' for "cotton, and tobacco and Negroes." Now the Winthrops, who wanted to keep up with the Joneses, also needed some help around the house, so they kept three Pequot slaves for themselves. American exceptionalism and Christendom at its absolute best... indeed, a shining city on a hill.[16]

Vacuum Domicilium or No Man's Land

Anders Stephanson, Professor of History at Columbia University and the author of a remarkable discourse on the foundation of American Empire entitled *Manifest Destiny: American Expansion and the Empire of Right,* makes a powerful case regarding the molten core of Europe's religious drive to conquer and colonize the Americas:

> For Europeans, land not occupied by recognized members of Christendom was theoretically land free to be taken. When practically possible, they did so. The Christian colonizers of the Americas—including the Spanish and the Portuguese—understood theirs as sacred enterprises; but only the New England Puritans conceived the territory itself as sacred, or sacred to be... This, then, was the New Canaan, a land promised, to be reconquered and reworked for the glory of God by His select forces, the saving remnant in the wilderness.[17]

Charged with the dominion of Providence, the European settlers (read: occupiers) engaged in a practice known as *vacuum domicilium,* also known by another Latin term, *terra nullius,* which is derived from Roman law and translates to "land belonging to no one" or "no man's land." Initially, many of the first colonists attempted to acquire the title to the land they occupied, but quickly abandoned this weak attempt to respect sovereignty and instead embraced the notion that "law is politics by other means," embarking on an all-out land grab via *vacuum domicilium*: if the property is not in active use then it's simply free for the taking. So if the terrain was used seasonally by the indigenous population for farming, hunting, or fishing and appears barren—too bad—the occupiers can simply claim the land. In fact, the colonizers made a straightforward, God-inspired rule: the rights of civilized Christians superseded the rights of the hunter-gatherers, heathens, and savages.

The Protestant Reformation, Christianity's 16th century schism between the Roman Catholic Church and early Protestant reformers led by John Calvin and Martin Luther, laid the necessary foundation for Biblical prophecy to be used as the spiritual motivation for the occupation of this "New Israel" as well as the eventual removal of—as Jefferson and Franklin later defined them—*savages.*[18] Stephanson suggests:

> The Book of Revelation, in short, made sense to English Protestants in general and Puritans in particular. It allowed the Reformation to be interpreted as either a moment on the way to Armageddon or even as the battle itself... Surely, it could not have been an accident either that God had unveiled this New World, this new continent, hidden for so many ages, precisely at the moment when the process of purification had begun in the Old World.[19]

And this process of purification was happening everywhere in the Americas. Stephanson continues, "Every activity, personal and communal, was irreducibly part of the holy war against Satan and his infidels. The aristocracy of saints had to work ceaselessly at this critical moment to make the present world as solemnly and gloriously Christian as it could be."[20] The Puritans, true to their name, placed tremendous weight on always defining who was "inside" and who was "outside" when it came to their communal existence. "The message to the heathens outside was in this respect as radical as St. Paul's: see the light or perish in eternal damnation!"[21]

In the Virginia colony at this time, John Rolfe—when he wasn't busy cultivating and exporting tobacco and then marrying Pocahontas, Christianizing her, and changing her name to Rebecca—fortified the English occupiers of Virginia as "a peculiar people, marked and chosen by the finger of God."[22]

From John Winthrop through Benjamin Franklin almost two hundred years later, American exceptionalism went viral, providing the necessary pretext and justification to exterminate the indigenous population at will until every last uncivilized-bestial-nonliterate-undomesticated-feral-vicious-and-barbaric savage was road kill. First let's hear from Winthrop regarding a smallpox epidemic that had wiped out the area's Indian population in the 1630s—something Winthrop viewed as divine intervention:

> God hath consumed the natives with a miraculous plagey.[23]

Next, from the City of Brotherly Love, we hear from Ben Franklin regarding how rum was being utilized by God Almighty to help soften up the savages for the big kill:

> ...the appointed means (by which) the design of Providence to extirpate these savages in order to make room for the cultivators of the earth.[24]

This escalating myth of being the "Chosen People," cultivators of a new "Promised Land"—a new "Israel"—became an integral premise in America's bloated self-interpretation. Samuel Langdon, colonial American clergyman and president of Harvard University from 1774 until 1780, was a typical cheerleader for American exceptionalism during the twilight years of the 18th century when he preached at Concord, New Hampshire:

> We cannot but acknowledge that God hath graciously patronized our cause and taken us under his special care, as he did his ancient covenant people.[25]

Ezra Stiles, another colonial theologian and president of Yale University, also stoked the xenophobic fires of America's mushrooming opinion of itself when he waxed poetic about the recently concluded Revolutionary War: "Never was the possession of arms used with more glory, or in a better cause, since the days of Joshua, the son of Nun," with, of course, George Washington cast in the role of the American Joshua.[26]

Shortly after the colonial cry for independence reached King George back in the home office, rogue middle managers Franklin and Jefferson lobbied for bold "Promised Land" imagery to grace the new nation's Great Seal. Franklin suggested Moses dividing the Red Sea with the Pharaoh's armed forces ready to be swallowed up by the rising tide. Jefferson pushed for a representation of the

Israelites being led through the wilderness by a pillar of fire. Jefferson held this sense of divine election close as he wrote in his second inaugural address in 1805:

> I shall need, too, the favor of that Being in whose hands we are, who led our forefathers, as Israel of old, from their native land, and planted them in a country flowing with all the necessaries and comforts of life.[27]

American Holocaust

In his in-depth and exhaustive work on the American Holocaust entitled *A Little Matter of Genocide,* author and political activist Ward Churchill distills the narrative of the embryonic American Empire:

> In his 1782 plan, Washington advanced the unequivocal belief that, after all was said and done, the objective of federal policy should be to force the entire indigenous population east of the Mississippi River into the "illimitable regions of the west" to which the United States was not yet pressing claims. Those who physically resisted such a fate in any way would have to be broken by force, or, as Thomas Jefferson bluntly put it, "exterminated." This "removal policy" was in keeping with a sense of "Manifest Destiny"—an outlook founded in precisely the same matrix of virulent Anglo-Saxon supremacism that would later give rise to Nazi Aryanist ideology—already pronounced among American leaders and citizens alike.[28]

As the fledgling America grew, it seemed as if the country was drunk on the elixir "Manifest Destiny." The culture at the time bristled with constant references. Poet Walt Whitman was typical. Here he weighs in on the march of civilization, clearly following the sun as it roared to the west, in his poem "Facing West from California's Shores:"

> *FACING west from California's shores,*
> *Inquiring, tireless, seeking what is yet unfound,*
> *I, a child, very old, over waves, towards the house of maternity,*
> *the land of migrations, look afar,*
> *Look off the shores of my Western sea, the circle almost circled;*
> *For starting westward from Hindustan, from the vales of Kashmere,*
> *From Asia, from the north, from the God, the sage, and the hero,*

From the south, from the flowery peninsulas and the spice islands,
Long having wander'd since, round the earth having wander'd,
Now I face home again, very pleas'd and joyous...

White supremacy was well entrenched in almost every aspect of 19th century American life. The foundation was deep and well-rooted, having started with Columbus hacking his way around the Caribbean, followed by the religious zeal oozing out of the Massachusetts Bay Colony, and then it became official when "the best and the brightest" of colonial America made it gospel. There was no doubt, the sun of civilization was moving again—this time across a land mass made up of many nations with names like Shawnee, Choctaw, Cherokee, Apache, Sioux, Pawnee, Cheyenne, Crow, Blackfoot, Shoshone, Ute, Navajo, and Paiute—among many others. The Indian nations could not have known nor calculated what was about to hit them—but it would have a name: The American Holocaust.

From the screenplay to the 1990 film *Dances With Wolves,* directed by Kevin Costner and written by Michael Blake:

Kicking Bird and Dances With Wolves are alone. Each man is preoccupied with his own thoughts.

DANCES WITH WOLVES
You have asked me many times about the white people...
you always ask how many more are coming.
(long pause as they exchange glances)
There will be a lot my friend... more than can be counted.

KICKING BIRD
Help me to know how many.

DANCES WITH WOLVES
Like the stars.

This is what Kicking Bird wanted to know. And it hits him like a rock. Kicking Bird bows his head in thought while Dances With Wolves raises his. He never wanted to say this, he wishes it wasn't true.

DANCES WITH WOLVES
It makes me afraid for all the Sioux.

Flash-forward to the end of the 19th century: Once the extermination and removal policy wrapped up on the North American continent, America began to look beyond her shores, across the peaceful shining sea to the west, where the Philippines and their guileless people lay waiting for conquest—and the ugly formula for its destiny remained the same. "Any difference of culture or language will do," writes historian Reginald Horsman, "and the power of racism to facilitate the worst sorts of human behavior is well established."[29] Horsman continues with a bare-naked look at a United States Senator's guide to colonial adventures:

> Senator Albert J. Beveridge (R., Indiana) offered the Senate his own divinely guided rationale for war on the Philippines: "God has not been preparing the English-speaking and Teutonic peoples for a thousand years for nothing but vain and idle self-contemplation and self-admiration. No! He has marked the American people as His chosen nation to finally lead in the redemption of the world."[30]

Linguist, philosopher, and historian Noam Chomsky looks back on the march of Manifest Destiny and its iron-fisted colonial conquests and sums it up this way:

> Most imperialist countries leave the population there and try to rule over them and exploit them. Settler colonialism, the most savage kind, exterminates them.[31]

Mark Twain also recognized the savageness of America's imperial nature. In fact, he was so moved by "The Battle Hymn of the Republic," he felt compelled to write additional lyrics in 1901:

> *Mine eyes have seen the orgy of the launching of the Sword;*
> *He is searching out the hoardings where the stranger's wealth is stored;*
> *He hath loosed his fateful lightnings, and with woe and death has scored;*
> *His lust is marching on.*

Follow the Money

> *This European opulence is literally scandalous, for it has been founded on slavery, it has been nourished with the blood of slaves and it comes directly from the soil and the subsoil of that under-developed world. The well-being and the progress of Europe have been built up with the sweat and the dead bodies of Negroes, Arabs, Indians, and the yellow races.*
>
> —Frantz Fanon, *The Wretched of the Earth*

There is no doubt that religious fervor combined with the moral imperative to "civilize" a "new" continent "infested with savages" was a major force behind the European modus operandi responsible for the occupation, settlement, and subsequent genocidal maelstrom unleashed in the titular New World. But one doesn't need to dig too deep to find the profit motive rumbling like rolling thunder just below the surface. In fact in all things geo-political, it's like what Deep Throat tells Bob Woodward in *All The President's Men*: "Follow the money."

The same pretext and justification used to exterminate the indigenous population was also used to validate and defend the enslavement of Africans in the young and growing nation—a nation founded in genocide and built by slavery (complete discussion in Chapter 5). Many tend to dismiss the horrors and murderous brutality of American slavery as an isolated, antebellum Southern "thing," or a misguided tributary of American history, but as Dr. James Horton of George Washington University sums up America's economic growth (which at the time was the envy of the world):

> Slavery was not a sideshow. It was the main event.[32]

The power centers in Europe—families, governments, and companies—created, organized, and controlled slavery throughout the Americas, and as the 17th and 18th centuries unfolded in the American colonies, slavery became a time-honored American institution. Current critics of historians and writers who position slavery as a gruesome cancer central to American history—as well as a disgrace for its chiseled-in-stone heroes—usually camouflage their protection of the benevolent and kindly apostles of American exceptionalism as humans caught up in the realities of their time. Let's repeat that for emphasis: "caught up in the realities of their time." Here's a classic explanation (read: historical delusion) by a mainstream academic historian from Rutgers University in a 2004 *U.S. News and World Report* article: "Other scholars believe the Founding Fathers can best be seen squarely within their time. 'To contextualize is not to excuse,' says Rutgers University historian Jan Lewis, who concludes, 'It's to show the complexity.' Understanding the early leaders' severe lapse in judgment over slavery, say Lewis and other historians, makes their ability to found a new and democratic nation all the more incredible."[33]

But it's not enough to simply contextualize and vindicate, some push beyond mythmaking toward erasure.

Let's now hear from a spokesman for the Tennessee Tea Party. This group attempted to remove references of American slavery (and the fact that the vast majority of the country's founders were long-standing slave owners) from school textbooks. "My name is Hal Rounds, R-O-U-N-D-S, like .45 caliber rounds. I teach the Constitution coast-to-coast for Tea Parties… [History textbooks contain] an awful lot of made-up criticism about, for instance, the founders intruding on the Indians or having slaves or being hypocrites in one way or another. The thing we need to focus on about the founders is that, given the social structure of their time, they were revolutionaries who brought liberty into a world where it hadn't existed, to everybody — not all equally instantly — and it was their progress that we need to look at."[34] Interesting to see and good to know that esteemed historians like Jan Lewis from Rutgers University (who is typical of the centurions standing guard over the status quo) and bat-shit crazy tea baggers agree on the contextualization of the terrorism that was American slavery for almost 400 years.

Richard Pryor also offers some insight on the contextualization of American slavery:

> *Niggers be holding them dicks too, Jack. And white people go, "Why you guys hold your things?" Say you done took everything else, motherfucker!*[35]

Unfortunately, as civilization "followed the sun," many were—

Blinded by the Light

Slavery for us is defined by two concepts—one is straightforward economics and the other has to do with flesh, blood, and terror—not the usual framing of American slavery that exists in the abstract. First, the economic definition: the imperialist conversion of humans into instruments for the production of goods. With this definition, slavery is a practical exercise in the commercial world, similar to any capitalist endeavor: cheap labor (very cheap labor) coupled with the distribution of product. At the time it was perfectly legal, morally acceptable, and great for business: what a windfall—you get your work force for free. *Jesus, the good old days!*

In fact, guys like James Madison jumped all over this great opportunity, boasting to a British friend that he made about $257 a year on every Negro slave he owned and he only had to spend about $13 bucks on his keep.[36] Other founding fathers took a real hands-on approach with their slaves, like old hot head Patrick Henry and his good buddy, signer of the Declaration of Independence, Richard Henry Lee, both of whom actively traded and whipped their slaves. These guys were really involved. They took pride in their small business ownership. Also, it's encouraging when the boss visits. Employees yearn to have their hard work affirmed.[37]

> *No defender of slavery, I concede that it has its benevolent aspects in lifting the Negro from savagery and helping prepare him for that eventual freedom which is surely written in the Book of Fate.*
>
> —Thomas Jefferson

The second definition centers on slavery as physical and psychological terrorism—perpetrated not by (as history would have us believe) munificent and caring paternal white father figures like Jefferson, with his hope of civilizing these savages (savages that Jefferson had no problem fucking and fathering children by), but rather perpetrated by psychotic purveyors of violence for profit who were then exonerated by scribes then and now, absolved of any real crimes. It's just another classic case in the history of mankind of when the power elites make–

The Unthinkable Normal

> *They blame everything on us, had nerve enough to even blame slavery on us. They said, "We didn't bring 'em over here, we went to Africa to get some elephants, niggers just jumped on the ship—'take me, take me'—'nigger, we don't want you, get back boy'—'oh come on, take me!'—'alright, boy, we'll take you, what else you you wanna do?'—'put a chain on my leg so I don't slip off!'"*
>
> —Dick Gregory

The myth remains safe and the whitewash of history not only pardons these scoundrels for crimes against humanity, it actually vindicates their evil actions. If the reality were actually contemplated to its core, the force of this terror would shake every foundation this nation rests on. One would be forced to come face-to-face with a reality that would include the following highlights:

- The theft of human beings from their home—mothers, fathers, brothers, sisters, husbands, wives... who were then shackled and transported on slave ships that can only be described as beyond shocking, where conditions would make a maggot vomit. Pure and unadulterated horror.

- When this journey through hell ended on the pristine shores of America, these so-called animal savages (in reality, the brave and resilient human beings lucky enough not to have been clubbed to death and tossed in the Atlantic) then began the multi-generational nightmare of misery and anguish; human bondage...bought and sold away from your family on a master's whim...whippings, beatings, bludgeoning, vicious rapes, tarring and feathering, castration, the removal of limbs for what were called "minor infractions," forced to fight human cock fights, hangings, more hangings, and of course executions on demand. And then you wake up the next day and do it all over again.

- Now, in case we forget the real and lasting terrorism of slavery, let's add the psychological hell to the physical hell. W.E.B. Du Bois was one of the most prolific advocates of exposing the long-term psychological toll caused by slavery and its monstrous practices—practices like "selective breeding," which helped to ensure that the master had an ongoing supply of strong slaves capable of performing superhuman feats. "Look, up in the sky...it's a bird, it's a plane, it's Super Mandingo!" The sheer terrorism that was American slavery is another clear-cut horror that runs unbridled through American history, responsible for devastating an incalculable number of families—their structure and value debased and obliterated well into the future, into the present.

This befouling and malignant behavior begs the rhetorical question: What was the base motivation to terrorize a people for centuries? W.E. Burghardt Du Bois reminds us once again... for it can never be overstated:

> [B]oth Europe and the earlier colonists themselves regarded this land as existing chiefly for the benefit of Europe, and as designed to be exploited, as rapidly and ruthlessly as possible, of the boundless wealth of its resources. This was the primary excuse for the rise of the African slave-trade to America.[38]

Paradox of Liberty

Lest we forget, this chapter is about the great white Aryan Anglo-Saxon civilization's commitment to follow the sun, civilize the world, and help all the unfortunate savages find Jesus. One of those civilizing Anglos was, of course, Thomas Jefferson. In fact, the Smithsonian installed an exhibit dedicated to the "Greatest Gentleman Slave Owner of the United States" entitled "Slavery at Jefferson's Monticello: Paradox of Liberty." Author Leah Caldwell writes after visiting the exhibit, "It doesn't bode well that if you entered the Jefferson exhibit not knowing what slavery was, you might come out thinking it was an intensive training program for highly-skilled craftsmen."[39]

Nevertheless, Edward Rothstein's review in *The New York Times* is a classic example of the establishment's "fourth estate" protecting the status quo ("sit down, don't rock the fucking boat") when he actually criticizes the exhibit for stating that Jefferson's Declaration of Independence "did not extend 'life, liberty, and the pursuit of happiness' to African-Americans, Native Americans, indentured servants, or women." Rothstein wrote that this "pushed too far," and that "each of those cases needs different qualifications and examinations. They distract from the subject."[40]

In his autobiography, *Narrative of the Life of Frederick Douglass,* the great social reformer remembers his first thoughts regarding his condition. In fact, his reflections on his own experiences offer an appropriate response to Jefferson's cheerleaders:

> *Why am I a slave? Why are some people slaves, and others masters? Was there ever a time when this was not so? How did the relation commence?*...Once... engaged in the inquiry, I was not very long in finding out the true solution of the matter. It was not *color,* but *crime,* not *God,* but *man,* that afforded the true explanation of the existence of slavery; nor was I long in finding out another important truth, viz: what man can make, man can unmake.[41]

Here's another answer for those who like to contextualize about those masters who own, subjugate, and crush other human beings: it's never been considered "okay" to own another soul, unless of course you're modeling yourself after Satan; remember, this wasn't during the Lower Paleolithic period—it was during the so-called "Age of Enlightenment." In his essay "Jefferson's Crime: Not Mitigated by the Standards of Time," journalism professor Robert Jensen frames Jefferson's blameworthiness:

> Certainly Jefferson was familiar with Paine and the arguments against slavery. Certainly Jefferson was aware of the existence of the idea that all humans had an equal claim to liberty and the argument that Africans should be considered human in these matters. Certainly there were many different ideas about the institution of slavery and racism in play at the time. So, we are not judging Jefferson by the standards of our time when we point out the way in which he employed racism to justify the barbarism of slavery. We are acknowledging that others in Jefferson's time—including such notable figures as Paine—articulated anti-slavery and anti-racist principles, at the same time that Jefferson was in 1781 writing in his "Notes on the State of Virginia" about the natural inferiority of blacks.[42]

Discussing the nightside of Jefferson's legacy in the radio documentary *American Icons: Monticello,* American artist Maira Kalman suggests, "If you want to understand this country and what it means to be optimistic and tragic and wrong and courageous you need to go to Monticello."[43] Tragic and wrong for sure.

Monticello

Jefferson's neoclassical Virginia brick villa stoically perches above 5,000 acres of rolling green hills—his plantation once tended to by hundreds of African slaves. From Jefferson's divine resting place, vistas stretch forever and the Blue Ridge Mountains loom to the west. Monticello is a popular tourist attraction where Jefferson's slavery component is, for the most part, whitewashed down the hillside where it flows to the Rivanna River, which connects to the James River, past other sprawling Virginia estates that should rightly be categorized as America's colonial terrorist camps, also known as plantations. "It's as if we've been erased," observed one African American visitor.[44]

The iconic architectural element of Monticello is the dome structure that towers above all else on his celestial home. Many believe the dome to be nothing more than a stately aesthetic element. But factoring in Jefferson's obsession with African slaves, actual testimony from his slaves, and an architectural concept called the "Panopticon," a darker, more deviant purpose emerges.

> *All along the watchtower princes kept the view, while all*
> *the women came and went, barefoot servants too.*
> —Bob Dylan

Lucia Cinder Stanton, Monticello's Senior Historian, envisions Monticello "as a Panopticon with Jefferson the all seeing at the top. He could see everything that was going on."[45] Jefferson's library contained a copy of a book called "Panopticon" that outlined a new and controversial prison design that called for circular cells surrounding a central watchtower. Inmates would be unaware if they were being watched. "At least two former slaves talk about Jefferson with his telescope, watching enslaved people at work," Stanton reports. "So this whole concept of surveillance from his central place on the apex of the mountain came through the oral tradition. He could see out but nobody could see in."[46] Equipped with his telescope, this warden in a powdered wig would gaze down from his heavenly dome tracking his enslaved labor force on Mulberry Row, or in the fields, or wherever forced labor took them.

The "enlightened" Jefferson kept meticulous records of almost everything associated with his life. Two subjects stand out: vegetables and slaves. Novelist and professor Jamaica Kincaid, with regard to lettuce, cabbage, carrots, cucumbers, and peas:

> The "Garden Book" has details of the things he planted, the food he planted, but it looks as if it just falls magically at the table. So he'll say peas were planted... six weeks later peas appear at the table. There's no involvement of labor, there's no...soil at all. It's as if it's Eden. It doesn't have any evil in it.[47]

But when it comes to the checklist of "Negroes owned" as calculated by Jefferson, Kincaid says, "The 'Farm Book' on the other hand, is all evil."[48] Very similar to his book about peas, corn, beets, and other vegetables, the Farm Book is a painstaking record of the human beings Jefferson owned. "Betty...Martin...Thenia...Critta... Sally...Johnny...Daniel...Molly..." And so forth.

Sinister? Yes. Evil? Absolutely. More fairytales about America's founders? Of course. Here's how the Monticello website heralds the bullshit:

> Monticello was home not only to the Jefferson family, but
> to workers, black and white, enslaved and free.

Workers? Jesus Christ, American bullshit runs deep.

Jefferson historian Joseph Ellis underlines Monticello Tom's warped sense of his Teutonic responsibility:

> Jefferson argued that one of the reasons that he couldn't free his slaves was that once freed the blacks would intermarry with the whites and would dilute the pure Anglo-Saxon race. Well, he's fathering children by Sally Hemings, and some of them look almost purely white and, again, you get a Faulknerian scene: he's eating dinner and he's being served by a slave who happens to be his own son![49]

Political satirist Stephen Colbert piles on another pound of truth regarding Jefferson's sadistic history of slavery, especially his love/lust/rape relationship with Sally Hemings:

> One of our greatest presidents, our greatest Founding Father, is also the one we've got the goods on in terms of being a jerk...In the Declaration of Independence, Jefferson declared all men's inalienable rights to Life, Liberty and the Pursuit of Sally Hemings' sweet apple-cheeked booty...I don't think there's anything sort of sacred about his relationship with Sally Hemings. It still seems like an abusive power relationship, especially when he talks so much about power relationships in what he wrote about—whether it was about power of the state to the church, or one state to another state, or the government over man.[50]

Quite simply, those who contextualize American slavery and want to excuse the wickedness unleashed from hell are doing nothing more than–

Philosophizing Disgrace

Throughout mankind's history, the same elite mindset that terrorizes with slavery terrorizes with war. Terrorism is terrorism: genocide, holocaust, war, slavery, poverty, denial of healthcare, denial of education, wanton destruction of the planet's resources—it's all the same witch's brew: terrorize the flesh, terrorize the spirit. As the *soi-disant* "civilized" Anglo-Saxons followed the sun, venturing west with their insatiable desire to expand and take possession, war on demon-savages was the operating principle of imperial conquest—ultimately a common practice that remains so to this day.

Europeans often used the fact that slavery also existed in various African states at the time as a way to further justify their own slave trade, even beyond the warped divine notion of civilized master ruling the savage slave. In fact, to this day, there are segments of the ruling class and their errand boys who continue to perpetuate this perverted point of view. In *A People's History of the United States,* Professor Howard Zinn distinguishes American slavery from African slavery of the same period:

> Slavery existed in the African states, and it was sometimes used by Europeans to justify their own slave trade. But, as [Basil] Davidson points out [in his book *The African Slave Trade*], the "slaves" of Africa were more like the serfs of Europe—in other words, like most of the population of Europe. It was a harsh servitude, but they had rights which slaves brought to America did not have, and they were "altogether different from the human cattle of the slave ships and the American plantations."[51]

Zinn goes on to note that in the Ashanti Kingdom, which was located on the western coast of Africa, a slave could marry, own property, swear an oath, be a witness, and even become a beneficiary to his master. Zinn concludes:

> African slavery is hardly to be praised. But it was far different from plantation or mining slavery in the Americas, which was lifelong, morally crippling, destructive of family ties, without hope of any future. African slavery lacked two elements that made American slavery the most cruel form of slavery in history: the frenzy for limitless profit that comes from capitalistic agriculture; the reduction of the slave to less than human status by the use of racial hatred, with that relentless clarity based on color, where white was master, black was slave.[52]

Absolute power corrupts absolutely. Madness eats away at the soul of men who play God—like Kurtz in *Heart of Darkness* (as well as Walt Kurtz in the jungles of Indochina). The temptation to play God becomes the bad acid trip that triggers savage barbarity. In the same fashion, the cancer of American Slavery also devoured the hearts and minds of the slave-owner. Frederick Douglass explains how his "mistress"—his owner, Mrs. Auld—was summarily transformed from a kind and compassionate woman to a malevolent tyrant:

> The fatal poison of irresponsible power was already in her hands, and soon commenced its infernal work. That cheerful eye, under the influence of slavery, soon became red with rage; that voice, made all of sweet accord, changed to one of harsh and horrid discord; and that angelic face gave place to that of a demon.[53]

Capitalism & Slavery

Between Columbus' arrival and the end of the U.S. Civil War, nearly twelve million slaves were viciously ripped from their homeland and transported to the Americas, with approximately one half million arriving in the U.S., leaving almost eleven million landing south of the U.S. border.[54] The dead—and there were countless souls lost on these murderous voyages along the Middle Passage—were not counted but rather tossed overboard. In fact many Africans who suffered from disease or were driven insane by deplorable and shocking conditions were either thrown overboard alive or first clubbed to death and then thrown overboard. It is against this backdrop of a macabre and low-down slave trade, along with wanton murder, that the European powers and the British Empire fueled and maintained their vaunted industrial revolution, moving dramatically from mercantilism to the corporate god of capitalism. It is no wonder that Karl Marx writes in *Capital* of European capitalism rising out of the "bloody womb" of African slavery.

Looking back over Marx's influential work as a philosopher, economist, and historian, it becomes clear that he identified the enslavement of Africans in America as an essential force behind mounting capitalism, not only in the "New World," but in Europe as well. In the late 1840s, Marx wrote a prescient observation regarding American slavery as it relates to the American Empire's financial wherewithal:

> Direct slavery is just as much the pivot of bourgeois industry as machinery, credits, etc. Without slavery you have no cotton; without cotton you have no modern industry. It is slavery that has given the colonies their value; it is the colonies that have created world trade, and it is world trade that is the pre-condition of large-scale industry. Thus slavery is an economic category of the greatest importance.[55]

In 1944, Eric Williams' *Capitalism and Slavery* challenged the secure, mythical tenets of European and American history. Williams, who later became the prime minister of Trinidad and Tobago, makes a powerful case that the African slave trade propelled Europe's rise to global economic dominance and that the massive profits from the triangular slave trade (Europe to Africa to the Americas and back again) helped to finance and bolster the Industrial Revolution. Williams contends that the occupation and subsequent takeover of the so-called "New World" was reliant upon the enslavement and exploitation of the African slaves held captive in the Americas. Williams examines this economic history by focusing on the British slave trade with the West Indies:

> The triangular trade thereby gave a triple stimulus to British industry... The profits obtained provided one of the main streams of that accumulation of capital in England which financed the Industrial Revolution. Sir Josiah Child estimated that every Englishman in the West Indies, "with the ten blacks that work with him, accounting what they eat, use and wear, would make employment for four men in England." By Davenant's computation one person in the islands, white or Negro, was as profitable as seven in England.[56]

England was by far the dominant force in the triangular slave trade throughout the 17th, 18th, and 19th centuries. A powerful navy coupled with seemingly unlimited capital enabled the British to flourish when it came to human trafficking, although the French, Portuguese, Dutch, and Americans were vigorous competitors. Among many others, Karl Marx suggests that all capitalist societies, in their formative years, require "the primitive accumulation of capital." The slave trade provided a mother load of this necessary early wealth to help launch the French, Dutch, and British capitalist models.[57]

The "triangular slave trade" refers to the approximate shape of the shipping routes on a map of the Atlantic. The first stage involved transporting goods from Europe to Africa to expand colonial empires and acquire more slaves; the second stage, or the Middle Passage, was the export of slaves to the Americas; and the third stage was the return of the fruits of slave labor to Europe—primarily cotton, tobacco, sugar, molasses, and rum. This sadistic cycle worked like a charm for the booming economies of Europe and, later, America. For instance, prior to the U.S. Civil War, one crop—slave grown cotton—provided more than 50% of all American export earnings. *Fifty percent.* In fact, for decades, American slaves cultivated more than 60% of the world's cotton.[58] This major windfall in the textile industry laid the foundation for America's vast economic growth throughout the 19th century. For two hundred years, American historians and propagandists have conveniently tried to frame slavery as "pre-capitalist" when in fact this horrific chapter in Europe and America's history is inherent to wealth building in the modern era.

At the time (and to this day) there were widely held claims that the collapse of slavery in the West Indies was brought about by British humanitarianism. Williams dismisses this claim, arguing that abolition was driven instead by the changing financial conditions and new economic demands that arose as the British Empire transitioned from a mercantile model to a capitalist system. Williams reasoned that it was only after slavery became an economic hindrance that abolitionists in Europe and then in the United States actually succeeded in curbing the slave trade and finally abolishing slavery. Historian, journalist, and social theorist C.L.R. James (whose seminal work on the African Diaspora, *The Black Jacobins,* greatly influenced Eric Williams), like any good investigative journalist, asked the hard and necessary questions: *What turned the tide on the British slave trade? Was it the intellectual and moral climate of the Enlightenment? Or was it the changing economic climate?* James passionately concludes:

> The loss of the slave-holding American colonies took much cotton out of the ears of the British bourgeoisie. Adam Smith and Arthur Young, heralds of the industrial revolution and wage-slavery, were already preaching against the waste of chattel-slavery. Deaf up to 1783, the British bourgeois now heard, and looked again at the West Indies. Their own colonies were bankrupt. They were losing the slave trade to French and British rivals. And half the French slaves that they brought were going to San Domingo, the India of the eighteenth century. Why should they continue to do this? In three years, the first abolitionist society was formed and Pitt [British Prime Minister] began to clamor for the abolition of slavery—"for the sake of humanity, no doubt," says Gaston-Martin [slave trade historian], "but also, be it well understood, to ruin French commerce."[59]

James argues that there were two central reasons. First, that despite the theatrics in Britain's Parliament about the immorality of slavery, it was the economic pressure that brought about their sudden change of heart. But there was another even more responsible historic groundswell that forced the captors' hand and that was the actual resistance and rebellions of the African slaves themselves. One of the great myths perpetrated on the world in general, and the American people in particular, is that of the submissive and obedient African slave. C.L.R. James dispels this lie:

> The Negro's revolutionary history is rich, inspiring, and unknown. Negroes revolted against the slave raiders in Africa; they revolted against the slave traders on the Atlantic passage. They revolted on the plantations. The docile Negro is a myth.[60]

Myth indeed, for we only need to investigate the names Denmark Vesey, Nat Turner, Gabriel Prosser, Harriet Tubman, Toussaint L'Ouverture, and a Missouri slave named Celia who was executed by the state for fighting back against her master for his ongoing penchant for rape.

Shoot Out on the Plantation

The Anglo-Saxon's march to destiny was not, as advertised, a divinely inspired walk in the clouds. It was orchestrated with deviant, stone-cold calculations and carried out by a long litany of repugnant actors. And, unbeknownst to most, this march was impeded by righteous rebellions that have been relegated to the back of the historic bus. Here we give them their rightful due. As Feste the clown reminds

Malvolio in *Twelfth Night*, "the whirligig of time brings in his revenges." Below are some of the more dramatic victories and defeats by slave rebels: :

- San Miguel de Gualdape Revolt on Sapelo Island, Georgia in 1526 (victory)
- Gaspar Yanga's Revolt at Veracruz, Mexico in 1570 (victory)
- New York City Slave Revolt of 1712 (defeat)
- Stono or Cato's Rebellion of 1739 (defeat)
- Haitian Revolution from 1791 through 1804 (victory)
- Gabriel's Revolt outside Richmond, Virginia in 1800 (defeat, conspiracy leaked prior to rebellion)
- Igbo Slave Revolt on Ebos Landing, St. Simons Island, Georgia in 1803 (defeat)
- Chatham Manor Revolt in Virginia where George Washington was a frequent visitor (defeat)
- German Coast Uprising in the Territory of Orleans in 1811 (defeat)
- Denmark Vesey's Revolt in Charleston, South Carolina in 1822 (defeat, conspiracy leaked prior to rebellion)
- Nat Turner's Rebellion in Southampton County, Virginia in 1831 (defeat)
- The Amistad Ship Revolt of 1839, near Cuba (victory at sea and victory in the U.S. Supreme Court, which found that the Africans on board were "unlawfully kidnapped, and forcibly and wrongfully carried on board a certain vessel on the coast of Africa"[61])
- Black Seminole Rebellion in Florida, 1835-1838 (partially victorious, largest revolt in U.S. history)
- African Slave Revolt from the Cherokee Nation in 1842, Southern U.S. (defeat)
- John Brown's Raid on Harper's Ferry in 1859 (defeat)

Clearly, slavery as an institution was on shaky ground primarily because of decades upon decades of resistance by African slaves who were anything but submissive. In fact, this ongoing counteroffensive—which was defined by waves of insurgencies that battled the horrors of oppression on cotton and sugar plantations all over the Americas—was forcing major breakthroughs in the late 18th century and through the first sixty years of the 19th century. Nothing crystallized this reality of rebellion more than the insurrection on the island of San Domingo in 1791.

The Haitian Revolution, a struggle that lasted for twelve brutal years, is the only successful slave rebellion in human history. The foundation of murder, hatred, and gross exploitation cracked under the weight of heroic human resistance.

There is no doubt that when you move a civilization west, you need money, BIG MONEY, to finance the trip...as well as the eventual occupation and long-term settlement of the new and occupied lands. Not only were the white Christian civilizers following the sun, they were following the money—and nothing underscores that more than their complete embrace of slavery. It was a very practical approach—a good, solid business decision... if you're a heartless psychopath. In fact, the 1% made a king's ransom.

> *It's called the American Dream because you have to be asleep to believe it.*
>
> —George Carlin

In 1726, English bishop, George Berkeley, penned a paean to the ideals of *translatio imperii* entitled *Verses on the Prospect of Planting Arts and Learning in America.* Colonial Americans embraced with great passion this testament to the superiority of Anglo-Europeans over all other peoples. If Bruce Springsteen's critical "Born in the USA" was misappropriated in the 1980s as the jingoistic Reaganite anthem, Berkeley's earnest poem was generously offered two hundred years earlier to the glory of empire:

> *Westward the course of empire takes its way*
> *The first four acts already past*
> *A fifth shall close the drama of the day*
> *Time's noblest offspring is the last*

Warmed by the Aryan Sun

The megalomaniacal spirit that infused the march of Anglo-Saxon civilization saturated colonial America. The fledgling republic, its institutions, as well as the general public, were steeped in and exhilarated by the ongoing occupation and expanding settlement. Andrew Burnaby, a British clergyman, wrote about his travels through America during the colonial period and experienced early American exceptionalism first hand:

> An idea, strange as it is visionary, has entered into the minds of the generality of mankind, that empire is traveling westward; and everyone is looking forward with eager and impatient expectation to that destined moment when America is to give law to the rest of the world.[62]

Burnaby keenly identified the spirit of exceptionalism that was alive and well in America. As historian James Bradley writes, "Thomas Jefferson—who persuaded the trustees of the University of Virginia to offer the nation's first course in the Anglo-Saxon language—justified Colonial America's breaking its ties with Mother England as a return to a better time when his Aryan ancestors had lived in liberty."[63] Bradley continues his excavation of Jefferson's imagined Aryan roots:

> In 1774, he wrote *A Summary View of the Rights of British America,* a series of complaints against King George, which foreshadowed by two years his 1776 Declaration of Independence. Jefferson refers to "God" twice, but invokes England's "Saxon ancestors" six times. In calling for a freer hand from the king, Jefferson writes of their shared "Saxon ancestors [who] had... left their native wilds and woods in the north of Europe, had [taken] the island of Britain ... and had established there that system of laws which has so long been the glory and protection of that country." Jefferson argued that since the original Saxons were ruled by "no superior and were [not] subject to feudal conditions," the king should lighten his hold on his American colonies.[64]

Bradley concludes that Jefferson "envisioned a new country warmed by the Aryan sun." Jefferson postulates the rock-solid foundation of Anglo-Saxon rule and tradition:

> Has not every restitution of the ancient Saxon laws had happy effects? Is it not better now that we return at once into that happy system of our ancestors, the wisest and most perfect ever yet devised by the wit of man, as it stood before the 8th century?[65]

On 4 July 1776 the Continental Congress asked Franklin, Adams, and Jefferson to suggest images to grace the Great Seal of the United States. Let's hearken back to our earlier example of Jefferson's penchant for mythic pomposity when he invoked the biblical Israelites. This time Tom goes straight to his passion for Anglo-Saxonism and spit-balls this gem about two tough Teuton brothers named Hengst and Horsa, "the Saxon chiefs from whom we claim the honor of being descended, and whose political principles and form of government we have assumed."[66]

As the 19th century continued, American exceptionalism and its Aryan Anglo-Saxon roots were evolving and maturing—a perfect rationale and rallying cry for the predetermined march to the Pacific, even if it meant the murder and removal of those "merciless savages" Jefferson wrote so eloquently about in his Declaration thirty years before.

After he died (having amassed more than 600 slaves, just in case you were counting), Jefferson was followed by a devout clique that included Missouri senator Thomas Hart Benton—an architect and strong advocate of westward expansion at all costs. "All obey the same impulse—that of going to the West; which, from the beginning of time has been the course of heavenly bodies, of the human race, and of science, civilization, and national power following in their train," Benton wrote. "In a few years the Rocky Mountains will be passed, and the children of Adam will have completed the circumambulation of the globe, by marching to the west until they arrive at the Pacific Ocean, in sight of the eastern shore of that Asia in which their first parents were originally planted."[67]

At its base, Manifest Destiny provided the necessary rationalization for manipulation, greed, selfishness, and violence (as always read: murder). In his 1850 novel *White-Jacket,* American novelist Herman Melville drank a healthy dose of 19th century Manifest Destiny-flavored Kool Aid and presented the case for America's infallibility:

> And we Americans are the peculiar, chosen people—the Israel of our time; we bear the ark of the liberties of the world. Seventy years ago we escaped from thrall; and, besides our first birth-right—embracing one continent of earth—God has given to us, for a future inheritance, the broad domains of the political pagans, that shall yet come and lie down under the shade of our ark, without bloody hands being lifted. God has predestinated, mankind expects, great things from our race; and great things we feel in our soul. The rest of the nations must soon be in our rear. We are the pioneers of the world; the advance-guard, sent on through the wilderness of untried things, to break a new path in the New World that is ours. In our youth is our strength; in our inexperience, our wisdom. At a period when other nations have but lisped, our deep voice is heard afar. Long enough have we been skeptics with regard to ourselves, and doubted whether, indeed, the political Messiah has come. But he has come in us, if we would but give utterance to his promptings. And let us always remember that with ourselves, almost for the first time in the history of the earth, national selfishness is unbounded philanthropy; for we can not do a good to America but we give alms to the world.

Stick to whales Herm.

American intellectuals of the time, like "individualist" and "Transcendentalist" Ralph Waldo Emerson, were as James Bradley writes "also under the Aryan spell." Emerson posits: "It is race, is it not? that puts the hundred millions of India under the dominion of a remote island in the north of Europe. Race avails much... Race is a controlling influence in the Jew, who for two millenniums, under every climate, has preserved the same character and employments. Race in the Negro is of appalling importance... I chanced to read Tacitus 'On the Manners of the Germans...' and I found abundant points of resemblance between the Germans of the Hercynian forest, and our Hoosiers, Suckers, and Badgers of the American woods."[68]

The 19th century also witnessed the rise of the social sciences. "Not surprisingly, they validated Aryan supremacy," James Bradley concludes. "One after another, White Christian males in America's finest universities 'discovered' that the Aryan was God's highest creation, that the Negro was designed for servitude, and that the Indian was doomed to extinction."[69]

In mid-century, just about the same time John L. O'Sullivan coined the term "Manifest Destiny" in an 1845 issue of the *United States Magazine and Democratic Review,* physician Josiah Nott and Egyptologist George Giddeon wrote *Types of Mankind,* a textbook that used "science" to support a hierarchy of races and the suppression of Blacks through slavery. This 19th century bestseller would focus its "science" on Native Americans, boasting that, "He can no more be civilized than a leopard can change his spots."[70] Nott, the proud owner of nine African slaves, would later declare that "the negro achieves his greatest perfection, physical and moral, and also greatest longevity, in a state of slavery."[71]

And then just for kicks, let's tune in to the father of American anthropology, one Lewis Henry Morgan, who adapted Darwinian theory during the 19th century to conclude that the various races were in different stages of physical and cultural evolution. "For Gilded Age American anthropologist Lewis Henry Morgan... the black man was inferior to the white and was falling behind every year," writes law professor Herbert Hovenkamp. "Morgan named the three stages of human cultural achievement: savagery, barbarism, and civilization." Morgan—who was president of the American Association for the Advancement of Science—went on to speculate that "the Aryan family represents the central stream of human progress, because it has produced the highest type of mankind, and because it has proved its intrinsic superiority by gradually assuming the control of the earth."[72]

> *Today, democracy, liberty, and equality are words to fool the people. No nation can progress with such ideas. They stand in the way of action. Therefore, we frankly abolish them. In the future, each man will serve the interest of the State with absolute obedience. Let him who refuses beware! The rights of citizenship will be taken away from all Jews and other non-Aryans. They are inferior and therefore enemies of the state. It is the duty of all true Aryans to hate and despise them.*
>
> —Minister of the Interior Garbitsch
> From Charlie Chaplin's *The Great Dictator (1940)*

"Following the sun" sounds so damn romantic. It conjures up images in the mind's movie making machine, such as Chaplin's enduring tramp walking away arm-in-arm with Paulette Goddard into a life of bliss at the end of *Modern Times*—although the sunset is in black and white. And maybe that's the point. You expect sunsets to be in color, just like "following the sun" yearns to be in the glorious saturation of Technicolor. But as you dig beneath the surface of a diabolical historical spin that involves large doses of enforced Christianity, murder, terrorism, white supremacy, and of course ill-begotten financial gains beyond calculation, it becomes painfully transparent that there is no beauty associated with this enterprise. The truth is found, understood—and must then be acknowledged—in the grim, black and white meat-hook of reality.

❖ ❖ ❖

2 Lamenting the Corruptions of Empire

When I was a girl, the idea that the British Empire could ever end was absolutely inconceivable. And it just disappeared, like all the other empires.
—Doris Lessing, British Novelist, Poet, Playwright

Look back over the past, with its changing empires that rose and fell, and you can foresee the future, too.
– Marcus Aurelius, Roman Emperor, Philosopher

One of the persistent cycles of history is that of empires ruling the majority of the world's population. The word itself—*empire*—and the underlying foundational concept is derivative from the Latin defining power and authority. But when a ruling entity is designated an empire by the intelligentsia in charge of such definitions, there are some basic rules adhered to and criteria that must be met by the candidate in question.

A ruling government is classified an "empire" if the entity dominates and holds sway over significant landmasses populated in large numbers, especially if this population is culturally and ethnically divergent from the imperial power. As well, a sovereign must rule the empire or the ruling regime must be an oligarchy.

Much of the population living throughout present day Massachusetts Commonwealth live in fear and loathing of what they term "The Evil Empire." No, it's not a historical reference to the old Soviet Union but rather a derogatory slam on the baseball club that hails from, as Arthur George Rust Jr. wrote, "the big ball orchard in the Southern Bronx," otherwise known as the New York Yankees—the

National Pastime's true oligarchic franchise. Now, this paranoid tendency by the good folks of Red Sox Nation is instructive in two ways.

First of all "evil"—even as hyperbole—is being completely misused by the Beantown Bashers because what the Yanks are being accused of actually sits at the heart of what makes mom and apple pie tick. The men in pinstripes are not evil by American standards but instead are just really good at capitalism—wasting billions of dollars fielding ballplayers that don't win as much as their financial power would indicate. It's also clear that the "evil" connotation flies in the face of America's inherent embrace of capitalism. In fact, the vast majority of Americans are willing to finance—and many are willing to bear arms and slaughter people they don't know—to help the U.S. government protect America's corporate masters and their associated business interests and various takeovers.

So in both words and in deeds, these folks actually realize that unbridled capitalism—as practiced by the New York Yankees, Incorporated—is a wicked and "evil" system. It proves once again that the elixir of blind nationalism, supplemented by an educational system selling myths and fables, have the masses bamboozled. They are walking talking contradictions.

Secondly, the choice of the word "empire" is equally disturbing because it's clearly used as a pejorative to describe something they despise—this evil Yankees' Empire. Yet, with every iota of red, white, and blue blood pulsing through their veins, they believe in and support the largest most violent empire to ever rule the third planet from the sun. In fact, it is the first empire to create a doomsday scenario that threatens the very existence of the human species. American dissident Noam Chomsky, in his recent masterwork, *Hegemony or Survival: America's Quest for Global Dominance,* traces the two choices facing the world's population:

> One can discern two trajectories in current history: one aiming toward hegemony, acting rationally within a lunatic doctrinal framework as it threatens survival; the other dedicated to the belief that "another world is possible."[1]

This is empire, American style: adhere to American Exceptionalism and U.S. global dominance or face the firing squad. It's pretty clear-cut.

There is also one additional distinctive occurrence or characteristic common to all empires throughout history: each and every one of them disappeared—and what's left behind? Crumbling ruins and stained monuments depicting rulers who turned to dust.

For many, the term "empire" evokes recollections of ancient Rome, probably the most recognized and longest-lasting empire in human history. For well over a thousand years, and through various manifestations, the Roman Empire has impacted Western culture like no other entity in history. European language and culture, jurisprudence, architecture, as well as religious foundations, are deeply rooted in Roman legacy. Of course the Roman Empire was also an orgy of slavery, religious persecution, and brutal-bloody-deadly games of sport—animals ripping each other apart, ripping humans apart, and humans as gladiators ripping each other apart. Rome was characterized by ruthless emperors whose behavior defined madness—men who ordered political and social suicides; and if the victim eschewed their responsibility, they would then be murdered anyway. Death was everywhere as evidenced by emperors issuing general public decrees for the killing of a rival, complete with reward and bounty.

As with our planet's most recent empire, death and destruction was an essential component of the imperial machinery.

The Groom's Still Waiting at the Altar

Rome's authority and dominion over millions lasted more than a millennia, and as the empire expanded dramatically throughout the Mediterranean world and beyond, the sovereignty and political structure of this colossal entity changed drastically. The relative stability and vast prosperity of Pax Romana was trampled by massive colonial expansion, stretching the limits of Roman power during the 3rd and 4th century Anno Domini (or Common Era if you prefer). Responding to this classic overextension of empire, Emperor Diocletian designed a split in power between the eastern and western worlds of the empire, transferring authority over the Greco partition to Byzantium, later known as Constantinople and now Istanbul. This moment in time also witnessed the adoption of Christianity as the state religion of the Roman Empire, incorporated into Rome's imperial rule by political necessity and Constantine's thirst for power. The once illegal faith of Christianity was officially decriminalized by the Edict of Milan in 313, which read in part:

> Let this be so in order that the divine grace which we have experienced in such manifold ways, may always remain loyal to us and continue to bless us in all we undertake, for the welfare of the empire.

Behold... the wedding of empire and Christianity.

This force—triggered by Emperor Constantine the Great in the first decades of the 4th century—roared through the past seventeen centuries like a runaway freight train. "Constantinian Christianity"—the marriage of elite power and wealth with the sacrificial blood of Christ—was a marriage of political expediency, a marriage that for almost two millennia exemplified ruthless pragmatism in the drive for dominion and imperial supremacy. In fact, at the time, Rome was so desperate for power that they simply could not tolerate the prophetic teachings of Jesus Christ and his mushrooming hoard of followers. "When the growth of the religion couldn't be stopped," writes Dr. Cornel West, "the Roman empire co-opted it."[2] When Constantine saw the light and fell to his knees at the feet of his savior, "a terrible co-joining of church and state was institutionalized from which the religion and many of its victims, especially Jews, have suffered ever since."[3] West goes on to frame this unholy alliance of church and state, one that has never looked back: "Constantine... proceeded to use the cloak of Christianity for his own purposes of maintaining power."[4] West concludes by drawing a straight line to the American experience:

> This same religious schizophrenia has been a constant feature of American Christianity... [Constantinian Christian leaders] sell their precious souls for a mess of imperial pottage based on the false belief that they are simply being true to the flag and the cross. The very notion that the prophetic legacy of the grand victim of the Roman empire—Jesus Christ—requires critique of and resistance to American imperial power hardly occurs to them.[5]

This is the essence of "Prophetic Christianity," a chorus apart, speaking from the shadows of Constantinian Christianity, which today continues to co-opt the liberating ethos of compassion in favor of political control and social dominion. But the prophetic and social compassion necessary to stand up to empire has been historically trampled by the oppressive weight and thrust of empire itself. Dr. West, one of those prophetic voices fighting in the trenches, has instinctively pushed back against this 1,700-year-old force of empire. He understands its destructive path and warns of those "who sit comfortably at the table of imperial elites and downplay social justice." West indicts those that "highlight individual piety" and then have "very little to say about the ways in which the structures and institutions in our society actually scar and wound" vast populations.[6]

But voices do join the chorus apart: David Walker's antislavery document *Appeal.* William Sloane Coffin and the Berrigan brothers' potent and uncompromising response to America's vicious war in Southeast Asia. Ida B. Wells-Barnett, who alerted the world to that unique form of American terrorism known as lynching. Frederick Douglass. Martin Luther King. Dorothy Day. The Catholic Worker Movement. The list of fighters, those who have stood up and said "no" to empire, is long and always growing but the onslaught of empire rides in on a tsunami and leaves little in its wake. Constantinian Christianity, with its promulgation of and adherence to a material world—one that's protected by imperial and militaristic fervor—has been and continues to be a fundamental weapon in the arsenal of empire.

The Twilight of Rome

In the 5th century, the once thought to be invincible Roman Empire finally collapsed under the weight of its own colossus—overreaching itself in almost every geo-political endeavor, especially along its "barbarian" frontiers as Germanic clans such as the Angles, Saxons, Vandals, and Goths migrated in vast numbers throughout the Roman realm. Various schools of thought posit differing explanations responsible for the fall of the Roman Empire. Some identify rampant moral decay and the subsequent rise of Christianity as the root cause; others stand firm on the abovementioned massive migration of humanity that stretched the Roman complex to the outer limits, forcing the walls to come tumbling down; still others believe that Rome didn't so much fall but rather morphed, after a period of decline, into the Frankish Empire with Charlemagne carrying the torch as the first Holy Roman Emperor. Finally, many cite Rome's demise as an inevitable result of the turmoil spurred on by many factors, the most damaging of which was the debilitating taxation necessary to support a mammoth military budget, allowing for the collapse of commerce and industry, sounding the death knell for Roman rule as Europe and the world passed into the Middle Ages.

Nevertheless, American forefathers—the architects of this elite republic (read: oligarchy)—embraced Rome as the blueprint for their fledgling nation, and now, interestingly enough, the fate of Rome offers a primer on the current accelerating decline of the American Empire. In fact, this "government by the few" has either devoured the Roman primer as the playbook for their final death wish for the American republic or they're completely delusional and/or blind to the striking and sinking similarities between the two apocalyptic empires—similarities that go beyond mere parallel comparison and resemble something more like a high-gloss, four-color Xerox copy:

- The desire, drive, and ability to exert economic and forceful authority over nations and populations.

- The sensual love affair with military might and the very real bloodlust hankering to use it.

- The suicidal use of treasure and human lives to fund their military madness at the fatal expense of the people's needs and the common good.

- The absolute shock corridor paranoia as evidenced by the insane growth of a surveillance state beyond imagination—one so ambitious and universal that it makes the dystopian predictions by Orwell look mild by comparison.

These historic characteristics—not unlike the seven revelatory trumpets blaring inside the head of John the Divine, exiled by the Romans on the island of Patmos—should send chills down all of our spines. In fact, this forewarning should once and for all drive a stake into the heart of the myth called American democracy... reminding us of Gore Vidal's admonishment:

> We should stop going around babbling about how we're the greatest democracy on earth, when we're not even a democracy. We are a sort of militarized republic. The founding fathers hated two things: one was monarchy and the other was democracy. They gave us a constitution that saw to it we will have neither.[7]

Give 'Em Bread and Circuses

With history as our witness, are we correct in writing this requiem for the decline and expected fall of the American Empire? Can we hear the New Orleans jazz funeral dirges and hymns as we trudge from the church of America to the graveyard of empires? "The last days of empire are carnivals of folly," argues Chris Hedges. "We are in the midst of our own, plunging forward as our leaders court willful economic and environmental self-destruction. Sumer and Rome went down like this. So did the Ottoman and Austro-Hungarian empires."[8] Hedges goes on to skewer America's own corruptions of empire:

> The final days of empire give ample employment and power to the feckless, the insane and the idiotic. These politicians and court propagandists, hired to be the public faces on the sinking ship, mask the real work of the crew, which is systematically robbing the passengers as the vessel goes down. The mandarins of power stand in the wheelhouse barking ridiculous orders and seeing how fast they can gun the engines. They fight like children over the ship's wheel as the vessel heads full speed into a giant ice field. They wander the decks giving pompous speeches. They shout that the SS America is the greatest ship ever built. They insist that it has the most advanced technology and embodies the highest virtues. And then, with abrupt and unexpected fury, down we will go into the frigid waters.[9]

And what about the people? Cannot the mass American population fight back? Cannot the government of, by, and for the people clutch a populist victory from the jagged jaws of autocratic defeat? Hedges offers grave doubts:

> The populations of dying empires are passive because they are lotus-eaters. There is a narcotic-like reverie among those barreling toward oblivion. They retreat into the sexual, the tawdry and the inane, retreats that are momentarily pleasurable but ensure self-destruction.[10]

Hedges, the Pulitzer Prize-winning journalist, weaves an unnerving exploration of a degenerate and hallucinating American populace mesmerized by "absurd promises of hope and glory" that are "endlessly served up by the entertainment industry, the political and economic elite, the class of courtiers who pose as journalists, self-help gurus like Oprah and religious belief systems that assure followers that God will always protect them. It is collective self-delusion, a retreat into magical thinking." [11]

Fantasy becomes reality.

First century Roman poet Juvenal (Decimus Iunius Iuvenalis) was highly critical of how the leaders of his day were manipulating the masses by diversion, distraction, and amusement: buy their vote *and their complacency* with "panem et circenses."

> Already long ago, from when we sold our vote to no man, the People have abdicated our duties; for the People who once upon a time handed out military command, high civil office, legions—everything, now restrains itself and anxiously hopes for just two things: bread and circuses.[12]

The poet came down hard on his fellow citizens who were abandoning their civic responsibilities to their own birthright. Juvenal also viewed it as outright bribery—and it worked... then and now. Acclaimed film director and writer Barry Levinson knows a thing or two about American society and echoes the ancient poet, warning that America has now become a "Roman Circus."

> The goal is to quiet the populace. Silence the voices of outrage. And it works. The protests are small, the voices of opposition muffled... the Romans ruled for centuries. They understood the mission: Feed the masses bread and circus.[13]

Hedges agrees: "Culture and literacy, in the final stage of decline are replaced with noisy diversions and empty clichés."[14] If this doesn't define American society in the 21st century, nothing does. The cultural noise machine rants at decibels well above eardrum bursting levels. The captains of empire tingle with joy as an anesthetized population remains distracted by consumer toys, mindless social media, empty celebrity worship—and all of it undergirded by a foundation built on the belief that *ignorance is bliss.* All is good, no worries, we're number one.

In fact, this avalanche of avarice coupled with boldface corruption began rolling downhill with increasing speed and a deafening roar during the so-called Reagan Revolution and continued unabated through the Wall Street-fueled CEO presidencies of Clinton, Bush, and Obama, finally culminating in what Hedges terms "a mafia state," with the election of Donald J. Trump—the crowning glory of barbarism masquerading as electoral politics and democracy.

> *Throughout the world what remains of the vast public spaces are now only the stuff of legends: Robin Hood's forest, the Great Plains of the Amerindians, the steppes of the nomadic tribes... Rousseau said that the first person who wanted a piece of nature as his or her own exclusive possession and transformed it into the transcendent form of private property was the one who invented evil. Good, on the contrary, is what is common.*[15]
>
> – Antonio Negri & Michael Hardt, Philosophers (from their book *Empire*)

Imperium Sine Fine

Translated from the Latin: "empire without end." The British variation on the Roman aspiration was (is!) "Where the Sun Never Sets." Unfortunately for the proponents of Pax Romana and Pax Britannica (*but fortunately* for the peoples of the world), "empire without end" and "the sun never sets," while bold ambitions, were not preordained destiny, despite the fate Roman poet Virgil prescribed for his Trojan hero Aeneas and, by inference, for Rome itself in his narrative poem *Aeneid*:

> *He was to be ruler of Italy,*
> *Potential empire, armorer of war;*
> *To father men from Teucer's noble blood*
> *And bring the whole world under law's dominion.*[16]
>
> *Think of your expectations of your heir,*
> *Iulus, to whom the whole Italian realm, the land*
> *Of Rome, are due.*[17]

Virgil saw it as the certain fate of Rome to claim and exert dominion over mankind. And there's no doubt that Rome clearly saw it as fate—destiny, and providence—guiding their glory. But a funny thing happened on the way to the Forum—the same funny thing that happens to all empires on their way to a world without end: they all prove to be built on quicksand, sinking and crumbling in the famous final act.

> *Humpty Dumpty sat on a wall*
> *Humpty Dumpty had a great fall*
> *All the king's horses and all the king's men*
> *Couldn't put Humpty together again*

The crumbling remains consistent. Recent empires reached their breaking point and like our anthropomorphic egg above, they all experienced "a great fall."

It took the epic French Revolution and two massive military debacles to bring down Louis XVI, Napoleon, and the First French Empire. One hundred and fifty years later, in 1954, history reminded the French once again about the follies of empire-building when their more recent attempt at overt colonialism was thrashed at Dien Bien Phu by General Vo Nguyen Giap and his Viet Minh forces, sending the French back to Paris with their tail between their legs.

The Spanish Empire was on the ropes for what seems like forever until they were finally undone by a number of wars, revolutions, and battles—like the whooping they took at Trafalgar when Lord Nelson and the British Royal Navy wiped out the combined fleets of Spain and France off the coast of the Iberian Peninsula. (Talk about pitching a shutout: Nelson, aboard his *HMS Victory*, destroyed thirty-three vessels while the Royal Navy did not lose a single ship.)

The British Empire had two distinct periods: their first imperial articulation centered on the settler colonies, especially the thirteen American colonies; the second empire took root during the entire 19th and early 20th centuries and is usually defined by its Victorian qualities. The British Empire's colonial ambitions were heavy-handed as evidenced by their oppressive rule over India. In various configurations, as well as dramatically growing and shrinking in geographic size, this aggressive and truly global empire lasted roughly 500 years—beginning with its colony in Newfoundland in 1497 and finally ending in 1997 when Great Britain relinquished control of Hong Kong. Similar to America's hallucinatory ability to view its own violently imperial sledgehammer as benevolent and necessary, Britain—for centuries (and up to today)—has viewed its vicious adventures as prudent, judicious, as well as being the ultimate contribution to the history of man.

When surveying empire's historic field of battle, pastures littered with the corpses of what British historian Mark Curtis calls the "unpeople," it becomes clear that the corruptions of empire (the elite rulers enslaving, plundering, and often killing those under their imperial decree) callously destroy the hopes, dreams, and possibilities of "actual" people—human beings processed like ground chuck under the tread of a giant inhuman and insatiable machine. In *Web of Deceit,* Curtis' scathing book chronicling the twilight of the British Empire, he underscores this harsh reality:

> The reality is that British governments bear significant responsibility for global poverty—not only as a former colonial power that shaped many of the current unjust structures, but in their championing of a world trade system and economic ideology that enriches the few and impoverishes many more...Yet I do not think I have ever seen a media article that mentions that Britain might in some way systematically contribute to poverty in the world. Is this not extraordinary?[18]

Great Britain's mendacious yet archetypal view of history (as written by the rulers) also highlights another consistent truth found in the DNA of every empire since the ancient Semitic rule of the Akkadian Empire (circa 2330 BC, Mesopotamia)—and that is the GIANT and often told LIE that goes something like this: ruling entities are burdened with the responsibility of civilizing and controlling the lesser beasts; the superior colonial saviors instinctively know what's better for these wretched souls; always on a mission from God, the advanced redeemers should be at the helm because they can better utilize and manage resources; and in an ironic twist on Greek tragedy, the empire positions itself as a *deus ex machina,* saving the day and cradling the masses from inevitable ruin.

It's Manifest Destiny roaring through the ages.

Now, the obvious piece of the puzzle that is conveniently left out of empire's central fantasy is that these imperial rulers exerting power, violence, and control over foreign people and lands have no prior or legal sovereignty whatsoever. It is hegemony galloping like a bull through a china shop—only this bull is not only graceless but also coercive and cruel as it pilfers and ransacks everything in sight. It's about the accumulation of wealth and the accrual of power that will continue to protect the wealth—and every empire since Homo sapiens spread out from their African homeland has followed this path of corruption.

History details how various empires "dress-up" their behavior in a multitude of ways. Like individuals, empires have personalities. The British Empire appears much different than the Third Reich. The Ottoman and Austro-Hungarian Empires went about their business in a distinctly different manner than the seafaring Portuguese Empire and its far-reaching colonial conquests. The meteoric rise of Genghis Khan and his crusading Mongol Empire, with its staggering death count, was markedly different from the more sophisticated albeit still brutal Roman Empire. Different still was the isolated and secretive Japanese Empire that lasted less than a hundred years. But what lies at the dark heart of empire—especially modern empire—remains the same:

- perpetual war in the name of perpetual peace
- the elimination (or impossibility) of republican government
- widespread mendacity on the part of officialdom
- economic collapse[19]

Empires and their "mythologists" will project themselves "as benign, wise and essentially truthful, even a gift to humanity," writes journalist John Pilger. America and Great Britain have been particularly adept at spinning this lie. Pilger offers this additional insight:

> That the opposite is true may shock some people. "A truth's initial commotion," wrote the American sage Dresden James, "is directly proportional to how deeply the lie was believed. It wasn't the world being

> round that agitated people, but that the world wasn't flat. When a well-packaged web of lies has been sold to the masses over generations, the truth will seem utterly preposterous and its speaker a raving lunatic."[20]

As we witness everyday, the brave truth-tellers of the current age are ridiculed, scorned, and marginalized as "raving lunatics." Some are eliminated. When the Empire is questioned or undressed, the noise machine beholden to the elite cries "conspiracy theorist... traitor... apostate"—all of which quickly smears and deprecates this newly crowned "public enemy," one who is unafraid to speak the unspeakable truth.

Drunk with Power

Many dissenters in the crumbling Roman Empire suffered a similar, though often more brutal, fate. Marcus Tullius Cicero was one such victim.[21] When he wrote and delivered the fourteen *Philippics* that harshly castigated the tyranny of Rome and called for the restoration of the Republic, he quickly became an enemy of the state as deemed by his adversary Mark Antony, who unleashed proscription (sort of like Nixon's enemies list), after which Cicero was brutally murdered. Beheaded with his hands hacked off, the targeted truth-teller's body parts were nailed up and publically displayed. Antony's wife, Fulvia (in an act that Ann Coulter probably dreams about), spit on the severed head, grabbed her hairpins and began stabbing Cicero's tongue—the very same tongue that so eloquently damned his beloved Rome, an empire drunk with power, its vices out of control. (Ms. Coulter wakes up in ecstasy: *Take that, you motherfucker...*)

Flash-forward to America, circa right now—look closely... Fulvia plunging hairpins into a severed head is not far from the naked truth. Instead, as a slight variation on the theme, the American Empire more resembles a giant dissatisfied infant with its finger on the trigger of a Glock 9mm. (Don't worry, America, accidental suicide is painless.)

Although Americans remain blinded by the light, bamboozled by fables of liberty, goodness, Jesus, frankincense and myrrh—all hell breaks loose around them. In her book, *Haunted by Empire,* anthropologist Ann Laura Stoler writes that, "Global events have placed empire under new scrutiny, helping to remind us that 'exceptionalism' is a shared self-description of imperial forms and that *every empire imagines itself as exception.*"[22] [Emphasis added]

George Walker Bush, the unelected 43rd President of the United States, had this to say about America as empire during his 2004 State of the Union teleprompting session:

> America is a nation with a mission, and that mission comes from our most basic beliefs. We have no desire to dominate, no ambitions of empire. Our aim is a democratic peace, a peace founded upon the dignity and rights of every man and woman.[23]

The hubris with which this statement can be uttered in public with a straight face is astounding. It's also an insight into how deep the American population has been seduced by this fairytale myth of American history—one that immortalizes beyond rational thinking the fable of democracy, liberty, and (drum roll) justice for all. It is an exploitation that flies in the face of an ongoing historic tempest that literally defines the polar opposite. The manipulation is brazen and baseline scary in how cavernous this river runs.

Empire's Final Chapter?

Has the American Empire crossed the Rubicon? Like Julius Caesar's army crossing the River Rubicon, has the empire now headquartered in Washington passed the point of no return? Has its assault on any semblance of democracy and the rights of man finally swallowed hope whole? In 49 BC, standing on the banks of the famed river in northern Italy, Caesar articulated his bottom-line: *Alea iacta est* or "the die is cast." He was referring to his impending march across Italy and a civil war against Roman leader Pompey the Great—but Caesar's spirit travels to the here and now and aptly underscores the world's first lone superpower—a global sheriff with heretofore-unequaled power and domain.

Chalmers Johnson, former CIA consultant to Allen Dulles and one of the preeminent scholars on America's evolution into a global empire, in his trilogy of books on America's enforcement of hegemony, offers a prophetic warning regarding the corruptions of empire. Johnson chose the title for one of these books, *Nemesis: The Last Days of the American Republic,* because "Nemesis was the ancient Greek goddess of revenge, the punisher of hubris and arrogance in human beings... she is the one that led Narcissus to the pond and showed him his reflection, and he dove in and drowned... it seems to me that she's present in our country right now, just waiting to carry out her divine mission."[24]

Johnson, who taught for thirty years at the University of California and was a foundational and memorable interview in Eugene Jarecki's documentary *Why We Fight*, offers a stark appraisal of U.S. foreign policy and its corrosive effects on the commonwealth:

> [T]he political system of the United States today, history tells us, is one of the most unstable combinations there is—that is, domestic democracy and foreign empire... A nation can be one or the other, a democracy or an imperialist, but it can't be both. If it sticks to imperialism, it will, like the old Roman Republic, on which so much of our system was modeled... lose its democracy to a domestic dictatorship.[25]

Interestingly enough, the British Empire, when faced with a post-World War II decision of either continuing their empire via tyrannical means or giving up their empire in order to save their democracy, chose the later. "It became apparent to the British quite late in the game that they could keep the jewel in their crown, India, only at the expense of administrative massacres," Chalmers Johnson points out. In fact, he says, Great Britain was already carrying out this totalitarian, violent, and bureaucratic logic throughout India.[26]

With London's last viceroy, Lord Louis Mountbatten at the helm, the British Empire finally withdrew from India leaving great sectarian violence in its colonial wake. But it didn't stop there. "There were tremendous atavistic fallbacks in the 1950s," Johnson stresses, including the Anglo, French, and Israeli attack on Egypt as well as the "savage repression" of the Kikuyu/Bantu people in Kenya. But "the most obvious and weird atavism of them all," Johnson emphasizes, was Tony Blair's recent and conspicuous "enthusiasm for renewed British imperialism in Iraq." Even with the continued stains on the Union Jack canvas of a dying empire, Johnson admires the fact that Britain actually "gave up its empire in order to remain a democracy." Chalmers Johnson goes on to assess Washington: "I believe this is something we should be discussing very hard in the United States."[27]

Investigative journalist and historian Nick Turse calls this rock that revolves around the sun, "The Pentagon's Planet of Bases," tersely summing up how American military might covers every continent except Antarctica. "In a world of statistics and precision, a world in which 'accountability' is now a Washington buzzword, a world where all information is available at the click of a mouse," writes Turse, "there's one number no American knows. Not the president. Not the Pentagon. Not the experts. No one."[28]

And that number would define how many U.S. military bases dot the worldwide landscape. But defining the exact number, or even achieving a consensus ballpark figure is difficult to say the least. It depends on who's counting as well as semantics—distinguishing between bases that are "bases" and bases that are "sites." There's also the clandestine factor to consider as bases throughout war-torn areas like Iraq and Afghanistan are shrouded in secrecy, and the same is true throughout many Middle Eastern countries where the host government fears anti-American sentiment among their populations.

If you count using public government documents, the Pentagon maintains approximately 760+ bases or sites. But other documents list higher totals, bringing the official count to 971. Some documents suggest additional bases. "There are more than 1,000 U.S. military bases dotting the globe," Turse writes of his own research. "To be specific, the most accurate count is 1,077. Unless it's 1,088. Or, if you count differently, 1,169. Or even 1,180."[29] Frankly, Bud Abbott and Lou Costello could have a "Who's on First?" field day with this routine.

In fact, the actual number could even be higher if you factor in bases "rented" or "utilized" by Pentagon and CIA operations around the globe, especially when it comes to drone warfare.

Space... The Final Frontier

> *And if your head explodes with dark forebodings too*
> *I'll see you on the dark side of the moon*
>
> —Roger Waters

Add to this massive global footprint, American military might floating above the planet in space, like the Air Force's secretive X-37B drone space shuttle. At first a NASA project, the furtive drone flying machine was then developed by Darpa, the Pentagon's R&D division, and finally by the Air Force's own secretive rapid capabilities division.[30] Add this giant "eye in the sky" to the already hovering bank of U.S. spy satellites (like the NROL-67) gathering "intelligence" from hundreds of miles above the Earth's surface, and then imagine a chunky spider web encircling the planet. The Roman gods could only dream about an empire this massive and this suffocating: call it "full spectrum dominance." (The U.S. government does.) You can also call it reality.

Then reality gets really scary—weapons in space scary.

Darpa and other U.S. military planners are busy spending your money researching, designing, and testing weapons for space. It's like doing brain salad surgery on a bunch of Hollywood geek brains, only this shit is deadly serious, not some Star Trek aberration.

The race for space began during the Cold War and reached its zenith when Ronald Reagan and his brain trust launched the Strategic Defense Initiative—better known as "Star Wars." In his infamous 1983 speech regarding the U.S. militarization of space, Raygun said in what can only be defined as the quintessential Dr. Strangelove moment: "I call upon the scientific community who gave us nuclear weapons to turn their great talents to the cause of mankind and world peace..." Sure, let's turn to the bomb makers for world peace.

A few years before, in 1958, with the U.S. lagging behind in the Cold War space race (the Soviets had launched Sputnik in 1957), the United States Air Force concocted a top-secret plan (Project A119) to detonate a nuclear weapon on the moon—as a fucking commercial. "It was clear the main aim of the proposed detonation was a PR exercise and a show of one-upmanship," reveals Dr. Leonard Reiffel, a physicist who worked on the project. "The Air Force wanted a mushroom cloud so large it would be visible on earth."[31] Clearly, the horrific mass murder and genocide of Hiroshima and Nagasaki wasn't enough for the U.S. military desk-jockeys. At the time, Dr. Reiffel expressed his ecological concern about destroying the pristine lunar environment, "but the US Air Force were mainly concerned about how the nuclear explosion would play on earth."[32]

Raygun's aggressive (and some say technologically far-fetched) "Star Wars" plan was interpreted by the Soviets—and rightfully so—as a first-strike noose hanging over their head. The program never came to fruition but that hasn't stopped the Pentagon from exploring and tinkering with new space toys. History tells us that the powers in place are just itching to "engage Photon torpedoes."

In 2002, the United States Space Command—charged with the commandeering and annexation of space—released a snazzy pamphlet entitled "Vision for 2020" that outlines the themes and requirements for the U.S. to become "stewards for military space."[33] In accordance with the policies set forth by Secretary Donald Rumsfeld, Chair of the Commission to Assess U.S. National Security Space Management, the two main themes of the report were:

- Dominating the space dimension of military operations to protect US interests and investment
- Integrating space forces into warfighting capabilities across the full spectrum of conflict[34]

Now part of United States Strategic Command (USSTRATCOM), the Space Command blueprint defined the vision for "Full Spectrum Dominance" in three easy steps:

- Control of space
- Global engagement (world-wide situational awareness; defense against ballistic and cruise missiles, and the capability to hold at risk from space a small number of high value targets)
- Full force integration (the integration of space forces with air, land, and sea forces, enabling warfighters to take full advantage of space capabilities as an integral part of special, joint and combined warfare)[35]

The mission statement is crystal clear: the United States of America will become "masters of space." Why? Well, the answer is the same motivation for everything an empire wants to do. Open up the *Vision for 2020* pamphlet. They even announced it in giant yellow letters in a cheese ball graphic that pays homage to the opening crawl from Star Wars:

> US Space Command—dominating
> the space dimension of military operations
> to protect US interests and investment.
> Integrating Space Forces into warfighting
> Capabilities across the full spectrum
> of conflict.[36]

Check it out. It looks like a bad junior high science report. It would be embarrassingly funny if it weren't so clearly the work of madmen. They even start out with a quaint history lesson, drawing a straight line from "westward expansion" of the dawning empire (read: genocide) to their current grand scheme—to be masters of the universe.

> Historically, military forces have evolved to protect national interests and investments -- both military and economic. During the rise of sea commerce, nations built navies to protect and enhance their commercial interests. During the westward expansion of the

> continental United States, military outposts and the cavalry emerged to protect our wagon trains, settlements, and railroads.[37]

Making the case for the necessity to spend untold billions of taxpayer dollars is also part of their entire strategy. The U.S. government "is spending billions of dollars to research and eventually deploy anti-satellite and bombardments weapons in space," writes one study on the military blueprint. "In addition to aspirations to explore innovations and extend defense planning horizons, as stated in the Plan, another justification for this expansion—Secretary of Defense Donald Rumsfeld's invocation of a 'space Pearl Harbor'—appears a thin argument for such expenditures of treasure and good will."[38]

The architects of this heavenly distribution of Buck Rogers weaponry and death rays also expose their leanings regarding the sanctity of capitalism and the need to protect ongoing class oppression when they write: "The globalization of the world economy will also continue, with a widening between 'haves' and 'have-nots.'"[39] *Vision for 2020* continues to make their case, this time combining some bravado as the neighborhood bully but still concerned about the threat of terrorism and possible rogue elements when they write: "Although unlikely to be challenged by a global peer competitor, the United States will continue to be challenged regionally."[40] In fact the concept of "challenged regionally" is the perfect portal into the dark soul of the American Empire and its foundational creed that–

WE OWN THE WORLD.

Noam Chomsky has made this argument brilliantly for decades:

> If we own the world, then the only question that can arise is that someone else is interfering in a country we have invaded and occupied.

With regard to Iraq:

> [I]f you look over the debate that took place and is still taking place about Iranian interference, no one points out this is insane. How can Iran be interfering in a country that we invaded and occupied? It's only appropriate on the presupposition that we own the world. Once you have that established in your head, the discussion is perfectly sensible.

With regard to the public discourse of American politicians and the so-called Fourth Estate:

> [It is a] largely vigorous debate between the hawks and the doves, all on the unexpressed assumption that we own the world.

And finally, in the skewed Orwellian world of white is black and up is down:

> [S]ince we own the world U.S. forces cannot be foreign forces anywhere. So if we invade Iraq or Canada, say, we are the indigenous forces.[41]

So in the parlance of the Empire—

WE OWN SPACE.

Author David Foster Wallace was writing about the thuggish brute force of a tornado, observing that they are "omnipotent and obey no law." Then this powerhouse: "Force without law has no shape, only tendency and duration."[42]

He could have been describing empire.

Rods from Gods

NASA's Voyager 1 unmanned spacecraft completed its primary mission of exploring Earth's solar system in 1990 and, just before continuing on into deep space, the craft turned around at the behest of the preeminent astrophysicist and astronomer, Carl Sagan, and took a photograph of Earth. There were no human witnesses, only the stark image. Sagan (as only Sagan could) then reflected on the image, one he called *The Pale Blue Dot...*

> From this distant vantage point, the Earth might not seem of any particular interest. But for us, it's different. Consider again that dot. That's here. That's home. That's us. On it everyone you love, everyone you know, everyone you ever heard of, every human being who ever was, lived out their lives. The aggregate of our joy and suffering, thousands of confident religions, ideologies, and economic doctrines, every hunter and forager, every hero and coward, every creator and destroyer of civilization, every king and peasant, every young couple in love, every mother and father, hopeful child, inventor and explorer, every teacher of morals, every corrupt politician, every "superstar," every "supreme leader," every saint and sinner in the history of our species lived there – on a mote of dust suspended in a sunbeam.

Looking at our immediate solar system, the galaxies near and far, the mind-boggling immensity of the universe, the possible multiverse and omniverse, we could be crushed under the weight of our seeming insignificance. "Small" does not do it justice. Mathematically speaking, we almost don't exist. And yet, as Carl Sagan suggests, this speck, this wisp of matter we call home is the entirety of all we know. It's everything.

And this is how your government wants to proceed with your "everything." They want to expand their already-failed war pig mentality into the cosmos, the firmament, into empyrean.

As we touched on above, the powers that be are agog and just plain itching to "engage Photon torpedoes." They look to the heavens and they don't see awe-inspiring beauty but rather they see nothing more than another launching pad for their killer toys and omnivorous hegemony.

Here are just a few of their ideas as the 21st century unfolds.

Darpa is working on something appropriately called "MAHEM" or Magneto Hydrodynamic Explosive Munition that is based on a weapon conjured up by the science fiction mind of Arthur C. Clarke. "Using magnetic fields," writes David Hambling from *New Scientist,* "it will propel either a narrow jet of molten metal or a chunk of molten metal that morphs into an aerodynamic slug during flight."[43] Tanks and other missiles are the intended targets.

File this next space weaponization technology under "hard to believe they're even contemplating this shit." Roland Dante at *Cracked* explains:

> There's an urban legend about a woman killed by a shaft of frozen urine fallen from a plane's leaking toilet. Then there's the one about pennies dropped from the top of the Empire State Building, passing through pedestrians' skulls like bullets. Then there's the one about telephone pole-sized tungsten rods dropping from an orbital weapons platform at 36,000 feet per second to impact the earth below with the force of a meteor strike.
>
> Guess which one you won't find on Snopes under "stupid bullshit?"[44]

That's right—the last one: *rods from gods.* The Pentagon won't confirm or deny the research or even the conceptual existence of these "enormous Swords of Damocles" but in 2003, according to *Popular Science* and *The New York Times,* the U.S. Air Force discussed the idea as a "future systems concept" in their "Transformation Flight Plan" report where the technology is called "hypervelocity rod bundles."[45]

The uranium or tungsten rods would be placed in orbit on a weapons platform satellite, and then with "the wrath of Zeus" would be hurled to earth with an onboard guidance system at more than 7,000 miles per hour—kinetic energy "with the force of a tactical nuke."[46] Best of all for the politicos worried about the bad PR usually associated with nuking people, these non-radioactive weapons would fall (pun intended) outside of various nuclear non-proliferation treaties with the exception of the 1967 Outer Space Treaty, which also bans certain conventional weapons in space. These falling telephone poles from space are envisioned as a way to destroy deeply buried targets, especially what U.S. military minds categorize as rogue nuclear programs. Reporter Jonathan Shainin in *The New York Times* reports:

> Even if Thor will not be hurling tungsten thunderbolts at suspected bunkers in Iran any time soon, the military has accelerated its pursuit of space weaponry; one study of nonclassified budgets released earlier this year indicated that spending on space-weapons research has grown by more than a billion dollars each year since 2000, with an eye toward establishing uncontestable "space superiority."[47]

Chomsky asks: "Could we stop the militarization of space?" Maybe. The entire world is against it for obvious reasons. "[T]here are several treaties, which are in fact already in place, that are supported literally by the entire world and that the U.S. is trying to overturn," Chomsky notes. The 1967 Outer Space Treaty was ratified by almost every country and it bans nuclear weapons as well as weapons of mass destruction in space. "In 1999, the treaty came up at the UN General Assembly," Chomsky reports, "and the vote was around 163 to 0 with 2 abstentions, the U.S. and Israel, which votes automatically with the U.S."[48] A second major agreement was the 1972 Anti-Ballistic Missile Treaty that prohibits anti-satellite weapons. "That's something they (the U.S.) want to get rid of," Chomsky predicted in 2001, "they want to be able to destroy satellites, communication, and surveillance by anybody else. The rest of the world is supporting the ABM Treaty."[49] Well, Chomsky the prognosticator was correct because in 2002 the Bush Administration withdrew the U.S. from the ABM Treaty saying, "Treaties? We don't need no stinkin' treaties!"

Or at least that was the spirit.

John Rhinelander was one of the lawyers who negotiated the ABM Treaty back in 1972. In a press conference following the 2002 U.S. withdrawal he was clear in his opposition, stressing that "we'll be in a world without effective legal constraints in terms of nuclear nonproliferation" and "withdrawal from the ABM Treaty is really a fatal blow over the long term to the NPT (Nuclear Nonproliferation Treaty)."[50] The Arms Control Association called the withdrawal "neither necessary nor prudent."[51]

Of course it wasn't prudent if your agenda was peace and survival of the species. But if your agenda was lone superpower dominion over everything that moves, then dangerous and irresponsible decisions like this make perfect sense.

The Numbers Don't Lie: Part One—Economics

Part of any discourse regarding empire, specifically the American Empire, must include dialogue about war and peace; it must incorporate a discussion of the religious crusade component (aka Manifest Destiny); and of course there must be an exchange of ideas about control and the affects and influence of Social Darwinism. But, let's never lose sight that everything associated with empire and everything unleashed by empire—everything—is about money. Call it what you want—wealth, capital, treasure, fortune, assets, riches, or resources—every move by empire is to acquire, protect, and expand the pot of gold at the end of the rainbow. Everything.

> *The enemy has many faces but only one name: Capitalism.*
>
> —Indian Rights Movement, Mexico

Since the fall of Rome, the Anglo-Saxon empire, now led by Washington, has been conquering and colonizing people, lands, and resources for the benefit of the powerful. Many times the Empire grows through overt violence and massive war, and many other times the Empire grows through covert violence and targeted war—usually brutal and out of sight. And still other times the Empire grows through targeted economic stratagem; think of it as financial skullduggery.

John Perkins penned two remarkable books on the machinations of the American Empire—books written from his experiences on the inside (*Confessions of an Economic Hitman* and *The Secret History of the American Empire*). Perkins' work shines a bright light on this dark and ugly tendency of the American government to wreak economic havoc on international entities in support of American corporate interests—the backbone of empire. Through his life as an "Economic Hit Man," his research, interviews, and travels thereafter as a committed whistleblower on this specific aspect of empire building, Perkins—along with students at a number of universities—formulated this overall definition of empire. It's one that's worth repeating here:

> **Empire:** nation-state that dominates other nation-states and exhibits one or more of the following characteristics: 1) exploits resources from the lands it dominates, 2) consumes large quantities of resources—amounts that are disproportionate to the size of its population relative to those of other nations, 3) maintains a large military force that enforces its policies when more subtle measures fail, 4) spreads its language, literature, art, and various aspects of its culture throughout its sphere of influence, 5) taxes not just its own citizens, but also people in other countries, 6) imposes its own currency on the lands under its control.[52]

"Almost without exception," Perkins reports, "the students arrived at the following conclusion: The United States exhibits all the characteristics of a global empire." Perkins agrees and we agree. The U.S. embodies less than 5% of the global population yet consumes at least 25% of the planet's resources. "This is accomplished," Perkins writes, "through the exploitation of other countries, primarily in the developing world."[53] *Points 1 and 2—CHECK.*

The U.S. has built and continues to build (with no end in sight) the largest and most dangerous military ever... and it's a weapon the Empire never ceases to use. "Although this empire has been built primarily through economics," Perkins reminds us, "world leaders understand that whenever other measures fail, the military will step in."[54] *Point 3—CHECK.*

There's no doubt that American culture—led by Hollywood propaganda and Madison Avenue marketing wherewithal—dictates public opinion, buying trends, and personal desire. With regard to language, *The New York Times* reports that, "Riding the crest of globalization and technology, English dominates the world as no language ever has, and some linguists are now saying it may never be dethroned as the king of languages."[55] *Point 4—CHECK.*

At first glance, many folks would argue that the U.S. doesn't tax foreign countries or citizens and that the U.S. dollar hasn't replaced anything—in fact the dollar has stiff competition from other currencies. But Perkins (and many others) argue that the American corporatocracy does indeed impose a global taxation and that the U.S. dollar remains the prevailing currency in world markets. "This process began at the end of World War II when the gold standard was modified," Perkins explains, "dollars could no longer be converted by individuals, only by governments."[56] Here's how it worked:

> During the 1950s and 1960s, credit purchases were made abroad to finance America's growing consumerism, the Korean and Vietnam Wars, and Lyndon B. Johnson's Great Society. When foreign businessmen tried to buy goods and services back from the United States, they found that inflation had reduced their dollars—in effect, they paid an indirect tax. Their governments demanded debt settlements in gold. On August 15, 1971, the Nixon administration refused and dropped the gold standard altogether.[57]

After that economic tap dance, the United States used heavy influence and pushed hard on world markets to "continue accepting the dollar as standard currency."[58] Perkins reveals an economic mission he was personally involved with that helped to cement the dollar's world position as king of the hill:

> Under the Saudi Arabian Money-laundering Affair (SAMA) I helped engineer in the early seventies, the royal House of Saud committed to selling oil for only U.S. dollars. Because the Saudis controlled petroleum markets, the rest of OPEC (Organization of Petroleum Exporting Countries) was forced to comply. As long as oil reigned as the supreme resource, the dollar's domination as the standard world currency was assured—and the indirect tax would continue.[59]

Points 5 and 6—CHECK.

Perkins begins his bestselling exposé, *Confessions of an Economic Hit Man,* with this description of how Washington surreptitiously operates in the shadows:

> *Economic hit men (EHMs) are highly paid professionals who cheat countries around the globe out of trillions of dollars. They funnel money from the World Bank, the U.S. Agency for International Development, and other foreign "aid" organizations into the coffers of huge corporations and the pockets of a few wealthy families who control the planet's natural resources. Their tools include fraudulent financial reports, rigged elections, payoffs, extortion, sex, and murder. They play a game as old as empire, but one that has taken on new and terrifying dimensions during this time of globalization.*
>
> *I should know; I was an EHM.*[60]

Unlike any other empire since the beginning of time, the American Empire has been "built primarily through economic manipulation," testifies Perkins, "through cheating, through fraud, through seducing people into our way of life, through the economic hit men. I was very much a part of that."[61] EHMs, like Perkins, usually working for the CIA or in conjunction with the CIA, slither into a country, usually a third-world country or one vulnerable to manipulation. The individual in charge, Mr. Big—a banker, chief economist, or the like—represents a financial lending conglomerate and offers a massive loan. The country (or big fish) on the hook is typically in dire need of a major money infusion and therefore dives in headfirst, agreeing to all the jacked-up loan terms. The country on the hook also has no realistic means of being able to repay the loan. Mr. Big and his patrons know this going in. This is predatory capitalism at its worse—sordid, vile, ignoble.

The loans all have specific conditions. "Let's say (it's) a $1 billion loan to a country like Indonesia or Ecuador," Perkins explains, "and this country would then have to give ninety percent of that loan back to a U.S. company, or U.S. companies, to build the infrastructure," companies like Halliburton or Bechtel. These powerful and connected entities—basically extensions of the U.S. government—would then embark on the construction of expensive projects like roadways, ports, or energy systems, "and these would basically serve just a few of the very wealthiest families in those countries," Perkins continues. "The poor people in those countries would be stuck ultimately with this amazing debt that they couldn't possibly repay."[62]

Now it's time to lower the boom since the victim has no choice. Perkins details how the vultures go in for the kill:

> So, when we want more oil, we go to Ecuador and say, "Look, you're not able to repay your debts, therefore give our oil companies your Amazon rain forest, which is filled with oil." And today we're going in and destroying Amazonian rain forests, forcing Ecuador to give them to us because they've accumulated all this debt. So we make this big loan, most of it comes back to the United States, the country is left with the debt plus lots of interest, and they basically become our servants, our slaves. It's an empire. There's no two ways about it. It's a huge empire. It's been extremely successful.[63]

Does this paradigm sound familiar? It should if you're a fan of *The Godfather* or were a weekly visitor to *The Sopranos*, or were actually unfortunate to owe a real-life loan shark an inexhaustible "vig." Whether the loan shark was the notorious Mad Sam DeStefano from Chicago, or Nicky Cigars from the Bonnano crime family, or a front man for U.S. government in Latin America—the business model is identical.

We interviewed John Perkins for this project in the quiet, upstairs lair of City Lights Books in San Francisco's North Beach neighborhood. His insight at the height of the Iraq and Afghanistan invasions and subsequent occupations was startling. Perkins is casually blunt in his assessment of how this modern empire was built by exploiting the poor and disenfranchised around the world. He's equally blunt about how "in the dark" the American people are regarding their government's behavior. Perkins is clearly aware of this boldface reality: that for Americans to live comfortable lives, millions upon millions pay an extremely harsh price. He also expresses the inherent dangers of an empire running hog wild in the Middle East, Africa, and elsewhere:

> Attacking other countries gives us territory. It gives us access to resources—to oil and so on. And it increases terrorism tenfold because anybody who lives in a country that's attacked—or even their neighbors—become sympathizers with the dispossessed and are tempted to oppose the invading source. Just the same as early Americans were inspired to rebel back in the 1770s and clash with the invading forces of the British Empire. It triggers that sort of response. It's natural, survival. Attacking another country doesn't accomplish anything nor does it do away with terrorism—it encourages it. All it does is give you territory and access to someone else's resources.[64]

We interviewed political theorist and historian Michael Parenti for this project as well. We sat with Michael in his backyard in Berkeley, surrounded by his tomato plants and other well cultivated vegetation. Gregarious and feisty as ever, Michael started swinging away:

> Imperialism is the process of empire—that's what empires do: they do imperialism. The ruling interests of one country expropriate the land, the labor, the wealth, the natural resources, and the markets of another country. In ancient imperialism, they also expropriated the population as slaves, who were a source of great wealth. You get richer from their labor. And that continued deep into the history of the United States.[65]

In fact, the U.S. was the last imperial slave power. Parenti then turned his sharp eye on the Central Intelligence Agency: "The CIA is an instrument of imperialism. It is an instrument working overtime for ruling class interests." Perkins echoes Parenti's political evaluation: "The CIA has played a very, very active role in spreading this empire and most Americans don't understand this at all—but the CIA is everywhere." Perkins then pays it forward with his on-the-ground personal experience:

> They're constantly feeding information to the economic hit men. They're feeding information to the corporations all the time. And when all else fails, they're the ones that step in. But it's usually not CIA employees who step in. The CIA hires contracted people. You can't place the blame on the CIA because you can't find anything. It's not there, in the same way that economic hit men don't work directly for the government. I never did. We work for private firms that are paid by the government. These "jackals" that work for the CIA as assassins, or those overthrowing governments, providers of information, they usually are not on a government payroll.... They're working for somebody else. They're called "security analysts" or "international marketing specialists," or maybe "executive recruiters." But they're out there collecting this information—tremendous amounts of information about what's going on in other countries, and it's all coming in though the CIA and their operatives. They're using all these means to help business and the military—help spread the empire. And it's been a very efficient system from the standpoint of the emperors, from the standpoint of the corporatocracy.[66]

In his garden, Parenti contemplates another thought as he inspects a tomato... and then drives home this reality:

> The CIA has a role of making the world safe for the Fortune 500. That's the ultimate goal.[67]

The Numbers Don't Lie: Part Two—Murder

"We're #1"

A recent Gallup International poll queried 68 countries and found that the United States of America was voted the number one threat to world peace. In fact, the U.S. was voted *three times more dangerous* than the next country—Pakistan, followed by China.[68] Gallup found that Americans viewed their own nation as the fourth greatest threat. American students, ages 18 to 24, voted their nation the number one threat as well.[69]

Is it possible that the closer you are to education the clearer the truth becomes?

"We're #1"

Unfortunately, the numbers back up the analytical fear detected by the pollsters as well as the very real fear of the victims and potential victims living in smaller, weaker, and often times defenseless countries. The historical tally of governments overthrown by U.S. actions remains light years ahead of any other power. William Blum—historian, author, former U.S. State Department employee, and now a full time critic of American foreign policy—has written extensively about the dark history of Washington's ongoing toppling of foreign governments. In fact he was nice enough to compile a comprehensive list that represents his incredibly well researched history of these actions. His long list documents America's number one standing in this category:

> *Instances of the United States overthrowing, or attempting to overthrow, a foreign government since the Second World War.*[70]
> *(* –indicates successful ouster of a government)*

- China 1949 to early 1960s
- Albania 1949-53
- East Germany 1950s
- Iran 1953 *
- Guatemala 1954 *
- Costa Rica mid-1950s
- Syria 1956-7
- Egypt 1957
- Indonesia 1957-8
- British Guiana 1953-64 *
- Iraq 1963 *
- North Vietnam 1945-73
- Cambodia 1955-70 *
- Laos 1958 *, 1959 *, 1960 *
- Ecuador 1960-63 *
- Congo 1960 *
- France 1965
- Brazil 1962-64 *
- Dominican Republic 1963 *
- Cuba 1959 to present
- Bolivia 1964 *
- Indonesia 1965 *
- Ghana 1966 *
- Chile 1964-73 *
- Greece 1967 *
- Costa Rica 1970-71
- Bolivia 1971 *
- Australia 1973-75 *
- Angola 1975, 1980s
- Zaire 1975
- Portugal 1974-76 *
- Jamaica 1976-80 *
- Seychelles 1979-81
- Chad 1981-82 *
- Grenada 1983 *
- South Yemen 1982-84
- Suriname 1982-84
- Fiji 1987 *
- Libya 1980s
- Nicaragua 1981-90 *
- Panama 1989 *
- Bulgaria 1990 *
- Albania 1991 *
- Iraq 1991
- Afghanistan 1980s *
- Somalia 1993
- Yugoslavia 1999-2000 *
- Ecuador 2000 *
- Afghanistan 2001 *
- Venezuela 2002 *
- Iraq 2003 *
- Haiti 2004 *
- Somalia 2007 to present
- Libya 2011*
- Syria 2012
- Yemen 2015

And that's just since 1945. Before that, the list also includes but is not limited to: Hawaii, Cuba, Puerto Rico, the Philippines, Nicaragua, Honduras, Iran, and Guatemala.

And before that, lest we forget, the young country and budding empire rubbed out an entire race of indigenous people who called the North American continent home for about 25,000 years.

Looking back over this "impressive" list through the lens of the recent U.S. invasions, overthrows, and occupations of Iraq and Afghanistan, David Swanson—author of *War is a Lie*—writes that, "We've replaced democracy with dictatorship, dictatorship with chaos, and local rule with U.S. domination and occupation. In no case have we clearly reduced evil. In most cases, including Iran and Iraq, U.S. invasions and U.S.-backed coups have led to severe repression, disappearances, extra-judicial executions, torture, corruption and prolonged setbacks for the democratic aspirations of ordinary people."[71]

In 1987, Washington Post correspondent Coleman McCarthy reported on a group of former CIA officials—mostly covert operators—who were driven by guilt to reveal details from their past horrors. The group estimated that since the end of World War II "at least six million people have died as a consequence of U.S. covert operations."[72]

This group of CIA counterintelligence specialists and operators also made clear how shallow Washington's so-called "case" was against these countries and the subsequent six million dead. They said the historical record was:

> [R]eplete with accounts of U.S. covert operations that killed, wounded and terrorized millions of people whose countries were not at war with the United States nor possessed the capabilities to do remarkable physical hurt to the United States, who themselves bore the United States no ill will nor cared greatly about the issues of "communism" or "capitalism."[73]

McCarthy reports that former CIA Director Stansfield Turner spoke publically about the CIA's tendency toward murder and numerous "things we should be ashamed of as a country... They were generally errors of excessive enthusiasm to get the job done, to protect the country." McCarthy then asks, "To protect it from what—6 million people who needed to be rubbed out because a Casey, Richard Helms, William Colby, Allen Dulles or some other unaccountable director ruled them a threat?"[74]

Once again, American mandarins—dressed in suits and ties—knee-deep in gore.

"We're #1"

In 2014, the American Public Health Association released an in-depth report identifying militarism as a major health threat to the people of the world. Their findings are terrifying to say the least. Released in the *American Journal of Public Health*, the APHA established:

> Since the end of World War II, there have been 248 armed conflicts in 153 locations around the world. The United States launched 201 overseas military operations between the end of World War II and 2001, and since then, others, including Afghanistan and Iraq.[75]

201 foreign military incursions in sixty years—an astonishing reality. The APHA then reported that, "During the 20th century, 190 million deaths could be directly and indirectly related to war—more than in the previous 4 centuries."[76] Let's also be very clear here: there is an enormous amount of guilt to spread around and a long register of guilty countries. The United States—*regrettably*—is a major player on this list.

David Swanson explains that the release of these figures is vital "in the face of the current academic trend in the United States of proclaiming the death of war."[77] The death statistics associated with war have been dramatically skewed lower by the entities doing the killing. They spin and re-categorize "war" under other headings. In many instances, the American public remains in the dark when it comes to U.S. proxy wars, covert CIA operations, the utilization of U.S. "advisors" and military hardware and technology, as well as the economic pressures, threats, and actions as revealed by whistle-blowers like John Perkins—actions that have grave consequences but no official triggers. Swanson writes that this rosy repositioning of war is skewed even further by "minimizing death counts, and viewing deaths as proportions of the global population rather than of a local population or as absolute numbers." Swanson then chides these academics that "have tried to claim that war is vanishing."[78] Clearly, it is not.

And who dies during these wars for profit and dominion? Civilians. The APHA reports:

The proportion of civilian deaths and the methods for classifying deaths as civilian are debated, but civilian war deaths constitute 85% to 90% of casualties caused by war, with about 10 civilians dying for every combatant killed in battle.[79]

The utilization of landmines is especially heinous.

> Seventy percent to 90% of the victims of the 110 million landmines planted since 1960 in 70 countries were civilians.[80]

"We're #1"

The United States would not be the Empire they are today without the type of grandiose military spending that befits the owner of the world. *The New Yorker* reports that, "The United States spends more on defense than all the other nations of the world combined."[81] NBC reports that the U.S. spends more on defense than the next ten highest budgets combined. *The Washington Post* called the U.S. military budget "staggering" and reported a dramatic spike in spending since 11 September 2001. Obviously, the numbers and estimates are all over the place depending on who's counting and what they're counting. The APHA reports the massive spending this way:

> The United States is responsible for 41% of the world's total military spending. The next largest in spending are China, accounting for 8.2%; Russia, 4.1%; and the United Kingdom and France, both 3.6%.[82]

Regardless of the shell-game details, the bottom line is clear: the treasure spent and the ensuing human heartache associated with this absolute waste of resources is deplorable and downright criminal. Again, the numbers don't lie as America claims the number one spot in yet another (insane) category: setting off nuclear explosions since the detonation of "Trinity"—the code name given to the New Mexico nuclear test by the U.S. Army and the Manhattan Project in 1945. In fact, the U.S. is in first place by a wide margin: 1,032 detonations. The old Soviet Union is a distant second at 727, followed by the usual suspects.[83]

After the Trinity test, along with Hiroshima and Nagasaki, it was clear that the fucking thing worked. Did the lunatics in the halls of power really need to set off thousands more?

Empire as Rogue State?

In 1985, Ronald Reagan stood before the American Bar Association and discussed international terrorism. He lumped Libya, North Korea, Nicaragua, and, of course Cuba together, calling this foursome "The new international version of Murder Incorporated." He warned of their "fanatical hatred" of America, the American people, "and our way of life" (the juvenile rallying cry heard so often after 9/11). Reagan then pulled out all the stops: "And we are not going to tolerate these attacks from outlaw states run by the strangest collection of misfits, Looney Tunes and squalid criminals since the advent of the Third Reich."[84] There it is—the all-important Hitler reference, which always comes in handy when drawing lines in the sand, especially when defining outlaws and rogue states.

The definition of a rogue state is straightforward: *A nation or state regarded as breaking international law and posing a threat to the security of other nations or world peace.* Noam Chomsky, a scholar who has written and spoken extensively on the subject, defines it this way: "A 'rogue state' is a state that defies international laws and conventions, does not consider itself bound by the major treaties and conventions, World Court decisions—in fact, anything except the interests of its own leadership, the forces around the leadership that dominate policy."[85]

The term either has a straightforward or "literal" meaning or the term can be manipulated as propaganda. When Reagan framed rogue states, or anyone in the U.S. government echoes those sentiments to motivate policy and action, it's clearly propaganda because the entity using the term has the power and wherewithal to determine its definition and framework. "Cuba's a 'rogue state' because it does not submit to U.S. domination," Chomsky elaborates. "That's a different usage entirely. As I use the term 'rogue state,' the leading 'rogue state' in the world is the United States. That's the neutral term."[86]

A cursory glance at American history is enough to make this definition rock-solid: Preemptive wars of aggression, covert CIA operations toppling sovereign foreign governments everywhere, support for brutal dictatorships (Musharraf, Pinochet, the Shah, et al.), the illegal and brutal use of torture, Drone warfare crisscrossing the airspace of any country in need of a good bombing, the use of weapons of mass destruction (Little Boy, Fat Man, Agent Orange, depleted uranium, et al.), and the use of economic rape and militarized plunder.

Summers has always struck me as a legendary gangster with a high IQ.

—Cornel West

A particular moment in the career of economist Lawrence Summers perfectly showcases the Empire's penchant for economic rape. Summers has been a much celebrated economist in the Empire's employ, receiving rave reviews from one of his recent bosses, Barack Obama, who said, "I will always be grateful that at a time of great peril for our country, a man of Larry's brilliance, experience and judgment was willing to answer the call and lead our economic team." When he's not claiming that men make better science and math teachers than women,[87] Larry has a sterling resume in service to America's wealthy elite. He was Secretary of the Treasury under Bill Clinton, where he was instrumental in abolishing the Glass-Steagall Act that separated commercial and investment banking—the abolition of which clearly led to the 2008 financial crisis with his Wall Street pigs perched at the trough. When he was President of Harvard University, Summers questioned the intellectual and academic legitimacy of African American studies and then tried desperately to screw over Dr. Cornel West. In fact, Harvard's Faculty of Arts and Sciences gave Summers a vote of no confidence for his infamous foot in mouth disease. Summers was also once the Chief Economist of the World Bank—the institution famous for strategically racking up huge debt in poor countries.

A real mensch...

In 1991, when Summers was riding high at the World Bank, he lobbied for "the dirty industries" (companies dumping waste in third world countries) to transition themselves into poorer countries where the inherent and expected damage to people's health as well as third world ecosystems would be less visible—and who really gives a shit about these expendable organisms anyway. He also pointed out the economic boom that would manifest itself in a world of cheap labor. Larry wrote, "I think the economic logic behind dumping a load of toxic waste in the lowest-wage country is impeccable and we should face up to that."[88]

Again, a cursory glance at Washington's real-life behavior, and not a warm embrace of rhetoric, defines America not only as an obvious empire but also as an equally dangerous rogue state.

Empire as Terrorist?

When defining terrorism, or what actually constitutes terrorism, or even who qualifies as a terrorist, governments and organizations have had a very difficult time reaching a consensus—primarily because, similar to defining a "rogue state," these determining bodies are juggling the literal-neutral-straightforward approach with the "propagandistic" approach. There's also a more obvious reason: they see themselves in the mirror and that can't be easy. State University of New York Professor Mark Selden writes:

> American politicians and most social scientists *definitionally exclude* actions and policies of the United States and its allies as terrorism.[89] [Emphasis added]

Noam Chomsky is not surprised. "It comes as no surprise," he writes, "that the propagandistic approach is adopted by governments generally, and by their instruments in totalitarian states." But governments need salesmanship and the mainstream media is more than willing to oblige. Chomsky concludes, "More interesting is the fact that the same is largely true of the media and scholarship in the Western industrial democracies, as has been documented in extensive detail."[90]

There is no universally accepted definition of terrorism but there are numerous variations on the theme, and they all point in the same ugly direction.

The UN General Assembly Resolution 49/60, adopted on 9 December 1994:

> *Criminal acts intended or calculated to provoke a state of terror in the general public, a group of persons or particular persons for political purposes.*

The U.S. Army Manual:

> *...calculated use of unlawful violence or threat of unlawful violence to inculcate fear. It is intended to coerce or intimidate governments or societies... [to attain] political, religious, or ideological goals.*

The FBI has their own definition of terrorism:

> *The unlawful use of force or violence against persons or property to intimidate or coerce a Government, the civilian population, or any segment thereof, in furtherance of political or social objectives.*

In fact, there are countless "unofficial" definitions but they generally agree on four basic characteristics:

1. the threat or use of violence
2. motivated by a political objective and the desire to change the status quo
3. the intention to spread fear by committing spectacular public acts of violence
4. the targeting of civilians

In a nutshell: "shock and awe."

Donna Jo Napoli is a linguistics professor at Swarthmore College. We embrace her definition because she cuts through all the bullshit and gets to the heart of the matter... frankly the heart of darkness.

> When you say terrorism you do mean "trafficking in terror." Anything that could terrorize people.[91]

Clean. Unmistakable. Obvious.

Once again, just a cursory glance at American history and the imperial behavior of the American Empire will—by definition—illustrate this ill-fated reality. We asked John Perkins the question: *Do specific or general actions by the U.S. qualify as terrorism?*

> The United States government can be a terrorist organization—and has been many times, especially since World War II. We've implemented this fear. We use this fear and violence as a way to get what we want in terms of exploitation of resources in other countries. It's always there in the background. So, for instance, when economic hit men go into work, if they fail, the jackals come in. If the jackals fail, everybody knows that the military lurks in the background.[92]

The double standard and contradiction is palpable as well as flagrant. When Washington orders U.S. forces to indiscriminately slaughter civilians in a foreign land it's categorized by the State Department, the White House, and the compliant media as "targeted airstrikes." Sometimes there's the unfortunate "collateral damage" stipulation because, as we all know, war is hell. So when Give 'em Hell Harry, Camelot Jack, Bull(shit) Johnson, Tricky Dick, Jerry Ford, Dutch Reagan, Pappy Bush, Slick Willie, Baby Bush, Barry Obama, or Drumph orders airstrikes that wipe out a neighborhood of living and breathing human beings—it's okay, it's justified, it's within the boundaries of engagement, or choose any other masturbatory euphemism that's regularly offered up. They all seem to apply.

But when some Fu Manchu character meanders down out of Toro Bora with a "towel" wrapped around his head and starts whacking people, it automatically qualifies as terrorism—which it is. But when the suits and ties do the same thing, and usually much worse, it's diplomatic foreign policy. It's the state protecting their valuable assets. Case closed—without any condemnation by the U.S. corporate press, which oftentimes doubles as a U.S. government apologist. And the spin that follows is clichéd and trite: "a just war," "a humanitarian war," or the all-pervasive "self-defense," as so aptly twisted by the moniker "the Department of Defense."

We interviewed journalist, historian, and filmmaker Tariq Ali on the campus of UCLA. His poignant response accurately deconstructs the issue:

> Modern imperial states utilize terror against their enemies. If you compare the casualties that result from individual terror—the anarchists of the 20th century or say Al-Qaeda today—against the deaths resulting from state terrorism, there's not even a conversation. All states, not just the United States—the Germans during the Second World War, the Soviet Union, the U.S. in Vietnam, I mean there's no comparison to the carnage. So the notion that individual terror threatens such a powerful country as the United States is bogus.[93]

The British Pakistani writer who authored the fiery polemic on U.S. neoliberalism, *Pirates of the Caribbean,* turns some of that fire on his conclusion:

> The real terror that is exercised against the peoples of the world, as we've seen in Hiroshima and Nagasaki, as we see in Iraq today, as we see with Israeli attacks against the Palestinians in Gaza and the occupied territories—no one even comments about that. The Palestinians are casually referred to as terrorists. The daily suffering they undergo is never shown, and when the Israelis attack it's always described as a response to the terror inflicted on Israel, which is a joke. It's a complete joke. Just do the figures and you can see who is killing more people.[94]

Ultimately, like all endeavors in life, perception is the editor of reality. If a being from another world beamed into our reality and observed the gruesome murder of 9/11 from an adjacent New York City rooftop and then stood atop a mountain outside of Baghdad or Fallujah and witnessed the mass murder spree known as "Shock and Awe"—regardless of context because context for carnage is in the eye of the beholder—they would see the same thing: *terrorism.*

Parting Shot: The Perils of Empire

When the United States launched its invasion of Iraq, predicated on the events of 9/11, it was the very quintessence of hubris. Neoconservatives dreamed of re-making the Middle East in their own image. It was in truth, a mad dream—a nightmare born from the drug of sole super power. It's been more than a decade since and none of their "dreams" have come true. Indeed, it's quite the reverse. The Middle East is a tinderbox enclosed in a powder keg. It's more unstable today than it's ever been, perhaps since decolonization. Its people are frustrated and paralyzed—manipulated by powerful princes and predatory armies. In most cases these are forces armed against and killing their own people.

The fruits of empire are foul indeed, and the worst is yet to come.

❖ ❖ ❖

3 There is a Plague Loose Upon the Land

Drift back in time, more than five hundred years to a tropical land mass. A gentle breeze envelops every inch of your naked body as you stand on an unspoiled beach. You drop softly to your knees.

Now, bend forward and get very close to the sand. Close enough you can't glimpse anything else. Cup some of the powder-white sand in your hand... catch the sun ricocheting off the granular matter now slipping through your fingers. In this area now known as the Caribbean, the sand is usually a mix of two distinct types of rock and minerals—the broken down skeletal remains of dead corals and a darker variety, black or brown detrital sand, which is the natural result of the island's rock eroding through the ages. It feels perfect between your fingers because it is.

Close your eyes and focus on the sound of the tide quietly brushing up against the coastline just a few yards away. This ebb and flow is also perfection—perfection that has been washing over this coast for millennia. This sea, the Caribbean Sea, is one of the largest saltwater seas on the planet, but you know that because you can taste the sodium and chloride ions as you jump in... and that's when you realize that the water is unusually warm for ocean water, rendered that way by its tropical location and the influence of the Gulf Stream.

Look down. The water is incredibly clear because there's very little plankton or suspended particles in the tropics. And, as you can notice, the color varies. Some of the sea appears dark and deep blue and that's because the sunlight is scattered by the water molecules. Other sections of the sea are lighter in color; the predominant aqua color you see indicates shallow water because that's where the sunlight reflects off the sand and reefs that are close to the surface. Now, if you're lucky enough to have a MODIS (Moderate Resolution Imaging Spectroradiometer), the image taken from space will make the Caribbean Sea look like a giant watercolor.

Moments flash by and you find yourself back on land. You face the beachhead that leads to a gray and weathered rock formation (a small cliff) that appears to be the foundation for the abundantly green and flourishing subtropical landscape thriving with royal and coconut palms, mahogany, cedar, wild olive, muskwood, and a smattering of red, white, and button mangroves. It might dawn on you that you're glimpsing harmony, maybe paradise.

Now you're flying—because in this world you can—and you're flying fast over the treetops toward the island's highland regions where you encounter a mountain forest dense with palms, Creolean pines, lush ferns, and probably a thousand different species of orchid. Glide to your left where, in stark contrast, you're heading toward an arid landscape dotted with cacti bending every which way but loose.

As you descend over a dry rocky basin you spot a rhinoceros iguana sunning herself between a small cactus and some thorny bushes. Birds indigenous to this Caribbean island dart and glide around you—a parakeet, a rare trogon, a woodpecker, a white-necked crow, and then finally a green-tailed warbler.

Now you bank to the right and ascend slightly over a line of coconut palm trees that reveal a village here in the middle of what you thought was an uninhabited Shangri-La. You see small circular structures that you recognize as homes, where the construction is simple but strong—long poles support woven straw and palm leaves ("green construction" before it was chic to care). Some people leave their homes and you notice that, like you, these men, women, and children are naked or close to naked.

You notice that some of these people are adorned with paint and shells... and the colors, even from up here, are extraordinary. More people gather in the center of the village where you gently hover above a lively festival of these Taino people, historic relatives of the Arawak people, who hail from Central and South America. Your first instinct is correct: these are peaceful people, living in accord with their natural world... and with each other.

And if you could spend one day in their community you would quickly realize that this is a population that lacks guile. Just ask Bartolome de las Casas when you see him—one of the great historic whistleblowers, the Ellsberg of his day. And maybe, just maybe the spirit of this 16th century Spanish historian, social reformer, and slavery abolitionist was coursing through the veins of 20th century English musician John Lennon when he wrote his anthem of hope.

Imagine no possessions
I wonder if you can
No need for greed or hunger
A brotherhood of man
Imagine all the people sharing all the world

It's the perfect soundtrack to transition you back to the beach, back to the sparkling sand, possibly the exact spot where the invaders would plant their poisonous flag. And when they planted this flag, they planted it with great hubris, claiming possession of the so-called "New World"—two massive continents inhabited far and near by countless millions for more than 20,000 years.

By now you've realized where you are. The island of Hispaniola in the last days of 1492. You've spent your entire life listening to and reading safe and guild historians concoct a mythical cover story for this so-called "New World," one that depicts the Americas as virgin land, basically uninhabited except for pockets of savages who were quickly demonized as sub-human, obviously inferior, and marked for removal (instinctually, you know all too well this means extermination and it sickens you). Like most cover stories throughout human political history, the lie is much more effective if it's a GIGANTIC lie and this lie was a GOLIATH. And once the lie is securely in place, you recognize that the rest is easy because the inferior savage has no rights to life, liberty, or the land they've inhabited for thousands and thousands of years.

Now turn around toward the water. Look closely on the horizon. You'll see a dark cloud rising. At first you might surmise that it's a storm front gathering to the east with its distant rolling thunder shaking the earth. But it's not. It's rising too fast and rumbling too hard for any weather pattern this planet has ever seen. Hell, this thing dwarfs the sweeping and surging power of a tsunami. It's clear that this beast even chases the sun.

So here you stand on this pristine beach in the waning days of the 15th century, witnessing the beginning of the end for a civilization that stretches from what is now the northern shores of Alaska and Canada to the southern tip of South America. It was a remarkable civilization with bustling population centers, teeming with merchants, artists, musicians, farmers, men, women, and children. The reality of the Aztec civilization in Mexico is the perfect antidote to the convenient lie generated by Western conquerors and their mythmakers that the Americas, this "New World," was a vast uninhabited landmass, barely populated by nomadic savages in need of taming or eradication.

Behold—paradise found.

That's what Hernan Cortés thought when he and his Spanish army brazenly ambled into Central Mexico where an estimated population of 25,000,000 inhabitants lived in and around the Valley of Mexico and its centerpiece—the Lake of the Moon. The people built their cities and towns on and around this interconnected waterway. They built dams and dikes. They built up a central metropolis on the lake as vast as Manhattan. This Aztec capital boasted a population many times that of London and other European cities of the day.[1] Cortés stood on the edge of a thriving archipelago. His companion and chronicler, Bernal Diaz del Castillo, gazed out over the same iridescent beauty and later remembered:

> I stood looking at it and thought that never in the world would there be discovered lands such as these.[2]

In fact, that's what you're thinking as you stand naked on this pristine beach, where a massive beating is about to be unleashed on these unsuspecting and guileless people—one that starts in the Caribbean as slaughter, butchery, and carnage, and then expands throughout the Americas as genocide. Holocaust.

A final solution.

Ladies and gentlemen, please put your hands together and give a big warm welcome to the fury zeroing in on the idyllic Caribbean—the imminent dawn of *The American Empire.*

In the prologue to his remarkable work, *American Holocaust*, professor and author David Stannard draws the historical thread from 1492 right into the heart of the American Century.

> *In the darkness of an early July morning in 1945, on a desolate spot in the New Mexico desert named after a John Donne sonnet celebrating the Holy Trinity, the first atomic bomb was exploded. J. Robert Oppenheimer later remembered that the immense flash of light, followed by the thunderous roar, caused a few observers to laugh and others to cry. But most, he said, were silent. Oppenheimer himself recalled at that instant a line from the Bhagavad-Gita: "I am become death, the shatterer of worlds."*
>
> *There is no reason to think that anyone onboard the Nina, the Pinta, or the Santa Maria, on an equally dark early morning four and a half centuries earlier, thought of those ominous lines from the ancient Sanskrit poem when the crews of the Spanish ships spied a flicker of light on the windward side of the island they would name after the Holy Saviour. But the intuition, had it occurred, would have been as appropriate then as it was when that first nuclear blast rocked the New Mexico desert sands.*
>
> *In both instances—at the Trinity test site in 1945 and at San Salvador in 1492—those moments of achievement crowned years of intense personal struggle and adventure for their protagonists and were culminating points of ingenious technological achievement for their countries. But both instances also were prelude to orgies of human destructiveness that, each in its own way, attained a scale of devastation not previously witnessed in the entire history of the world.*
>
> *Just twenty-one days after the first atomic test in the desert, the Japanese industrial city of Hiroshima was leveled by nuclear blast; never before had so many people—at least 130,000, probably many more—died from a single explosion. Just twenty-one years after Columbus's first landing in the Caribbean, the vastly populous island that the explorer had re-named Hispaniola was effectively desolate; nearly 8,000,000 people—those Columbus chose to call Indians—had been killed by violence, disease, and despair. It took a little longer, about the span of a single human generation, but what happened on Hispaniola was the equivalent of more than fifty Hiroshimas.*
>
> *And Hispaniola was only the beginning.*

❖ ❖ ❖

4 The Murderers of the World Arrive in the Americas

There is no more glaring distortion in the history learned by generations of Americans—in textbooks, in schools, in the popular culture—than in the story of Christopher Columbus.

—Howard Zinn

They came, from feverish, fetid cities and sewers of a repressive Spain, driven by dreams of avarice. Poor, young, maddened as hatters they were—for their homes, their villages, and the rapidly vacated prison cells, held no promise. Their cohorts to the west would later leave the crowded, loud, vaporous and unjust realm of British princes, with mirages of money, gold, land, and wealth swimming in their diseased retinas. They left the cold, clammy, rainy shores of home to enter what must have seemed paradise—the balmy, sunlit shores of Turtle Island.

They each and all met beings of a rare and unblemished beauty: sun-kissed men, women, and children, living in virtual gardens of a kind of Eden, resplendent with health, vitality, and love of their lands, their gods, their cities—and even those storm-tossed, haggard, smelly, fish-colored strangers. For though they spoke in strange tongues, and wore rough, ragged, stinking tunics, and had metals they had never seen before, were they not people? Were they not also human?

What does one do when one sees people in hunger, in distress, ill, and perhaps a bit mad? What's the worst that could happen? People help people; yes, even strangers with thick tongues speaking gibberish. This, the Peoples of the lands that would one day be called the Americas, did.

They tended wounds. They fed the hungry. They taught the stupid fellow-beings how to farm, and how to listen to the land that is the Mother of us all.

How could they know that this *was* the worst thing they could do? How could they know that this sick, feverish people would repay their kindness with genocide? How could they know that these blue-eyed god-men, greedy people, would turn on the hands that fed them, and not just bite them, but slice them from their attached sinews and bone, bind them in chains, rape their daughters and mothers, corrupt their sons, burn their villages to ash, and wipe them from the face of their Mother, wipe them from existence?

From these sailors, these shipmates, these "explorers," would come a holocaust of epic and ungodly proportions. For the Peoples of Turtle Island, the Aztec, the Maya, and a million other clans, bands, and tribes, had nurtured a ravenous beast, which would leap at their throats, destroy their lives and dreams, and wreak unholy havoc and terror on the world under the guise of "liberty."

The world would be transformed by the loving-kindness of the people we have come to call Indians. For, in welcoming these foreign peoples into their homes, they opened the door to almost-total destruction.

This story, the end of their world, marked the emergence, in the brief span of five centuries, of one of the most ruthless and voracious empires this earth has ever seen.

"Why should you destroy us?"

It would be nice to think that things could have evolved differently in the Americas. Some historians blissfully write a kind of hope-history, as in "what if?" Columbus did this or "what if" De Gama did that?

These are mere mind games; word plays of wasted time, for things happened as they did, because, regrettably, the forces launching those ships across the surging seas, were powerful and deep. For, truth be told, neither Spain, England, France, nor Holland were nice places, for the simple fact that much of Europe was a cesspool of disease, of class and religious conflict, of social and official violence. That is to say, it was a place ripe for leaving.

When written accounts were published about a land of honey, of endless spring, of sweet flowing waters, imagine the psychological forces drawing on such people, to this "new," fresh, clean land. Oppressed at home under rapacious nobility, threatened with the sulfurous fires of hell by a venal sacerdotal class hungry for indulgences, the seaward route to this New Eden must have seemed like a great escape. Millions of Europeans would be drawn to this New Europe; a place where every dream could be made reality—if only those pesky "Indians" weren't in the way.

This is not to suggest that the Southern Europeans had an identical view as their western colleagues, for the Spanish saw these teeming lands as a place rich in slaves, while their brethren of England wanted the land—with the natives preferably gone.

Where they united in view and action was the ruthless extermination of "Indians" by hook or starvation, and if all else failed, by Christianity.

When the Spanish hit the Indies, they burned through those societies like a hurricane of fire, while villages perished by the lethality of the disease they imported. Cities once vibrant with life, commerce, and culture, became charnel houses of bone. When the Spanish encountered indigenous people, they chained them, recited the cruel "*requerimiento*" to people who hadn't the faintest notion of what they were saying, or even its intent, and enslaving them, sent them into the mines for gold or silver. The document read to them had the following message:

> I certify to you that, with the help of God, we shall powerfully enter into your country and shall make war against you in all ways and manners that we can, and shall subject you to the yoke and obedience of the Church and of Their Highnesses. We shall take you and your wives and your children, and shall make slaves of them, and as such shall sell and dispose of them as Their Highnesses may command. And we shall take your goods, and shall do all the mischief and damage that we can, as to vassals who do not obey and refuse to receive their lord and resist and contradict him.[1]

On Sunday, 14 October 1492, Cristóbal Colón (aka Christopher Columbus) wrote in his diaries, *El Diario de Cristóbal Colón,* the following passage that clearly underscores the burgeoning European motives of hegemony and conquest. From the outset, slavery was also in the air; Columbus' observance is an obvious harbinger of the transatlantic slave trade lurking on the horizon. After the obligatory salutation, "In the Name of Our Lord Jesus Christ," Cristóbal Colón speaks from the heart:

> ...[T]he people here are simple in war-like matters, as your Highnesses will see by those seven which I have ordered to be taken and carried to Spain in order to learn our language and return, unless your Highnesses should choose to have them all transported to Castile, or held captive in the island. I could conquer the whole of them with fifty men, and govern them as I pleased.[2]

The Spaniards wanted the natives alive, if only to work for them as gold slaves. The English wanted their land—period. They had little use for living natives. And yet, even this is a bit of an exaggeration, for as historian David Stannard informs us, the numbers of people left dead in the wake of the Spanish gold-hunger is, to say the least, staggering. This brief paragraph should more than suffice:

> By the time the sixteenth century had ended perhaps 200,000 Spaniards have moved their lives to the Indies, to Mexico, to Central America and points further to the south. In contrast, by that time, somewhere between 60,000,000 and 80,000,000 natives from those lands were dead. Even then, the carnage was not over.[3]

Somewhere between sixty million and eighty million natives. Dead.

Extinguished. Slaughtered. Liquidated.

That's how these Americas came to be. They are the bones upon which this beast was fed and raised. This was the Europeans' response to those who succored their sick and starving, wet and cold, voyagers from the sea.

Many Americans are aware of the name "Pocahontas," recognizable if only because the name was used in a popular Disney film which tells the story of a beautiful Indian maiden who saves the life of a white guy. There is, in fact, a basis to this tale, but as in most American "Disney-fied history," much is left out.

There was a maiden named Pocahontas—and she did save the life of John Smith. What American history books usually exclude is the reply given by her father Wahunsonacock (circa 1547-1619, known to the whites as Powhatan), when Smith threatened him, about a year after his life was spared. The father of Pocahontas, responded to Smith's threat thus:

> [W]hy should you take by force that from us which you can have by love? Why should you destroy us, who have provided you with food? What

> can you get by war? We can hide our provisions, and fly into the woods; and then you must consequently famish by wronging your friends. What is that cause of your jealousy? You see us unarmed, and willing to supply your wants, if you come in a friendly manner, and not with swords and guns, as to invade an enemy. I am not so simple, as not to know it is better to eat good meat, lie well, and sleep quietly with my women and children; to laugh and be merry with the English; and, being their friend, to have copper, hatchets, and whatever else I want, then fly from all, to lie cold in the woods, feed upon acorns, roots, and such trash, and to be so hunted, that I cannot rest, eat, or sleep. In such circumstances, my men must watch, and if a twig should but break, all would cry out, *"Here Comes Capt. Smith;"* and so, in this miserable manner, to end my miserable life; therefore, exhort you to peaceable councils; and, above all, I insist that the guns and swords, the cause of all our jealousy and uneasiness, be removed and sent away.[4]

And what, instead, was "sent away?" The dozens of clans-tribes-and-nations of the Powhatan Confederacy, a united force of more than 30 such peoples, covering hundreds of miles in area. "We fed you!" the tribes exclaimed in a thousand, or a half million tongues. "We broke bread with you (or smoked the pipe), how could you be so evil toward us?"

By the time comprehension dawned on them, it was too late. So many of the People had perished, and too many Europeans were flooding these shores, north and south.

Creation of "the Other"

We are all tempted to make assumptions based on our own experiences, biases, and worldviews. History degrees do not wipe these factors from consciousness. We look at the vast, almost incomprehensible carnage, and ask—how can this be? How can human beings do these kinds of things to other human beings?

The uncomfortable answer is that humans learn by rote, by observations, and by doing. Before the deed is the thought, and in the realm of the mind, the "Other" (as in other than human) is created, embellished, and ostracized from the notion of normality. In the Spain that launched this monstrous *requerimiento,* is it coincidence that the very year marking the transatlantic voyage of the Niña, Pinta, and Santa Maria, marks also the culmination of the Reconquista ("Reconquest") and the expulsion of both Jews and Muslims from the Iberian Peninsula?

Jews posed a particular problem in the European Christian communities, for they are intrinsically the seed stock from which Christ, and thus, Christianity, was born. But their stubborn refusal to adopt the central tenet of the divinity of Christ marked them as enemies of the faith. And although Jews were expelled from several European nations in the Middle Ages (France, England, etc.), royal, church, and communal pressure (i.e., social terrorism) against Jewish communities in Spain forced many Jews to convert to Christianity. Even these people—called *conversos*—were ever suspect, deemed false converts and thus subject to intense scrutiny and, when appropriate, public violence.

After forcing them (and Muslims) to wear designations on their clothes identifying their faith, Christians embarked on public attacks that burned, flayed, and slaughtered them—"the Others." Stannard recounts their final expulsion on a date of particular renown:

> On the very day that Columbus finally set forth on his journey that would shake the world, the port of the city he sailed from was filled with ships that were deporting Jews from Spain. By the time the expulsion was complete between 120,000 and 150,000 Jews had been driven from their homes (their valuables, often meager, having first been confiscated) and then they were cast out to sea. As one contemporary described the scene:
>
> > "It was pitiful to see their sufferings. Many were consumed by hunger, especially nursing mothers and their babies. Half-dead mothers held dying children in their arms... I can hardly say how cruelly and greedily they were treated by those who transported them. Many were drowned by the avarice of the sailors, and those who were unable to pay their passage sold their children."[5]

These events dovetailed with the voyage of Columbus. That is to say, the tormentors of the expelled Jews were the same kind of men who would inflict immense and unimaginable cruelties on the Mayans, Aztecs, and millions of other peoples.

They learned it at home.

In the minds of the Spaniards, were these people not like the Jews, Others? Were they not anathema to the Mother Church? Among the English, a similar historical legacy was being made, for the British antipathy to the Jews was perhaps equal to the Spanish, but another group became the proving ground for their colonist, expansionist, and imperialist practices.

In England, the Irish served the function of exampling the Other. Stannard explains:

> Britain's people considered themselves the most civilized on earth, and before long they would nod approvingly as Oliver Cromwell declared God to be an Englishman. It is not surprising, then, that English tracts and official minutes during this time described the "wild Irish" as "naked rogues in woods and bogs [whose] ordinary food is a kind of grass." Less ordinary food for the Irish, some reported, was the flesh of other people, sometimes their own mothers—which, perhaps, was only fair, since still other tall tales had it that Irish mothers ate their children. The Irish were, in sum, "unreasonable beasts," said William Thomas, beasts that "lived without any knowledge of God or good manners, in common of their goods, cattle, women, children and every other thing."
>
> Such brutishness was beyond the English capacity for tolerance. Especially when the vulgarians in question occupied such lovely lands. So, as they had for centuries, the English waged wars to pacify and civilize the Irish.[6]

This demonization of the Irish (as the Jews and Muslims of Spain) allowed the British aristocracy to justify conquest, exploitation, and finally, state terror against them—for they were England's "Other" (the first of many, as history would prove).

These internal Others were the primers for graduate-level repression abroad, as practiced against "Indians," and shortly thereafter, Africans for centuries. Driven by a malevolent church and the ravenous royal houses of their lands, how can anything—anything at all—surprise us when we witness the sheer madness they visited upon the (relatively) dark-skinned peoples they met in this world they called new? They were, to the invaders, "new," even though these societies had existed for 40,000 years, and they were "vulgarians" even though these natives' lives, spent in cities of splendor and delight, had no peer in the dark, dank, cold places of the invaders' origin. They, in all their various manifestations, lived life in ways unimaginably different (and better!) than these explorers. Their only deficit was in the arts of war and death, and against these, they could not compete.

The "Indians" (especially in what would later be called Hispaniola, Cuba, Central America, and Mexico) lived lives that would have been the burning envy of all Europe. When Spanish invader Hernán Cortés reached the island city of Tenochtitlan, he called it the most beautiful city on earth. Roughly the size of modern-day Manhattan, it was home to some 350,000 Aztecs. Cortés' chronicler, Bernal Diaz del Castillo, wrote that the cities of the Aztecs were spacious, sweet smelling, and "wonderful to behold." Its buildings were made of stone, with framing and furnishings of fragrant cedar wood, and the inhabitants used canoes to travel to and from this splendid, beautiful island.[7]

The Spanish were so dazed by what they saw that they imagined they were in a dream. But before they left, they transformed it into a living hell—a nightmare that may have begun in 1492, but one that did not end there. Truth be told, the lives of the aboriginal peoples of the Americas remained hellish for centuries.

It has been some 500 years of hell.

Were they "jealous" of the lives lived by these peoples, as Wahunsonacock (aka Powhatan) had claimed? Were they driven mad by irrational hatred and fear, inculcated with the demented narrow-mindedness of a repressive religious teaching? Or were they simply driven by whips of greed?

As human beings are complex creatures, every one of these descriptions may have been impetus for their response to being strangers in paradise. Upon first contact with these peoples, the Spaniards extolled them as exemplars of beauty, gentleness, and generosity. Before long, these beings of virtue and peace would be transformed into "red devils," for the green toxin had permanently changed the game.

Like the outsiders within the tribes of Europe (Jews, Muslims, Irish, et al.) they were beyond the pale of considerations. They would serve as slaves, miners, and whores—or not be allowed to live at all.

Paradise Lost

It is both painful and difficult to recite the horrific happenings to the indigenous peoples of the Americas at the hands of the invaders. Yet, this is a story that must be told—and retold—if only to wash away the sweet lies that Americans tell themselves, and then brutally instill in their children. There is virtually nothing that the Europeans didn't do to those they held in thrall.

They killed with a fury that would have made the Nazis blush. They enslaved, they slew, they massacred, they raped, they burned, they starved, and they broke the Indians on the wheels of hatred like old glass. They killed and killed... and then killed some more. They made the good old American saying, "The only good Indian..." into a motto that yet lives in the American soul, a motto of internalized massacre.

They made these people pray to their sleeping, drugged gods, for the blessing of death.

Indeed, the gold lusting invaders were so dazzled by their success, they spoke openly of their monstrous exploits in correspondence to their homes and colleagues, words not necessarily intended for posterity. And even so, what was there to worry? Those who would read their words centuries hence would be their descendants, their progeny, and as such, they would be the benefactors of their crimes and massacres. How could they protest, if they would inherit the riches and ill-gotten wealth of this luxurious new earth?

When the first Portuguese governor of Brazil arrived on its well-watered coasts, so great was the indigenous population that he declared it virtually inexhaustible. But more important is how he framed this idea, in a turn of phrase that can only be called savagely interesting. It would be impossible to have a lack of these people, he says (and one supposes he was thinking of slaves), "even if we were to cut them up in slaughterhouses."[8]

What a thought... and this is not a Portuguese peculiarity. The great chronicler, Bartolomé de Las Casas, the Christian missionary, played the role of spot reporter in his coverage of how his fellow Spaniards treated those they met upon arrival in the Indies and the island of Hispaniola:

> Once the Indians were in the woods [fleeing the violence and oppression of the Spanish—ed.], the next step was to form squadrons and pursue them, and whenever the Spaniards found them, they piteously slaughtered everyone like sheep in a corral. It was a general rule among Spaniards to be cruel, but extraordinarily cruel so that harsh and bitter treatment would prevent Indians from daring to think of themselves as human beings or having a minute to think at all. So they would cut an Indian's hands and leave them dangling by a shred of skin and they would send him on saying "Go now, spread the news to your chiefs."

> They would test their swords and their manly strength on captured Indians and place bets on the slicing off of heads or the cutting of bodies in half with one blow. They burned and hanged captured chiefs.[9]

They spared no one: babies, the aged, the pregnant, the sick. And they did this to send a message? A short and effective commercial?

What was it but terrorism?

If it was terrorism, it was terrorism of a kind the world has rarely, if ever seen. This is not to say that the world was without experiences of great terror, for Europe, for centuries, suffered attacks on its cities and cathedrals from the ravages of the Berserkers (known to us as the Vikings). They slew and ravaged and destroyed with a kind of sadism that was remarkable for its ferocity. But they rarely settled, for their object was riches. They struck, they plagued, and before long, they were gone.

When the Europeans came to the Americas, they remained, and the original peoples were pushed out of existence. They sought to get the maximum exertions out of them (in the south), or the maximum space away from them (in the north). In any event, the central objective was to take all that could be taken, whether slaves, land, gold, silver, or jewels—whatever. The Peoples were superfluous, for was not the supply inexhaustible?

Stannard, again citing the reports of Las Casas, describes a world so rife with murder that numbers were unnecessary. What was important was gold, and slaves to mine the gold. Like parasites feeding on the remains of whatever was left alive once the winds of epidemic fever had passed over the native populations they encountered, the Spanish adventurers invaded, conquered, and enslaved the peoples living in the rest of Mexico and in what today is Guatemala, Belize, Honduras, El Salvador, Nicaragua, Costa Rica, and Panama. No one knows how many they killed, or how many died of imported disease before the conquistadors arrived, but Las Casas wrote that Pedro de Alvarado and his troops by themselves "advanced killing, ravaging, burning, robbing and destroying all the country whenever he came." In all, he said:

> By other massacres and murders besides the above, they have destroyed and devastated a kingdom more than a hundred leagues square, one of the happiest in the way of fertility and population in the world. This same

> tyrant [Alvarado] wrote that it was more populous than the kingdom of Mexico; and he told the truth. He and his brothers, together with the others, have killed more than four or five million people in fifteen or sixteen years, from the year 1525 until 1540, and they continue to kill and destroy those who are still left and so they will kill the remainder.[10]

If such estimates are stable over time, Las Casas described an area of 300 square miles, as a league is equal to 3 miles in area on land. It might be enough to say that they slew the Indians without mercy or care, but that could never be the entire story, for there was a method to their madness.

The invaders sought gold, so many Indians were assigned to "white lords" to serve as human tools of labor and gain. Under the Columbus-authorized system of *encomiendas*, the indigenous peoples were allotted to Spanish masters who could work them, exploit them, or abuse them, as was their pleasure. In too many cases to count, they simply worked them to death. A modern-era historian has written:

> Some of the *Indians* even as late as the 1580s were being broken physically, their insides literally bursting in some instances from the heavy loads they had to carry. Unable to endure more, some of them committed suicide by hanging, starving themselves, or by eating poisonous herbs. Encomenderos forced them to work in open fields where they tried to care for their children. They slept outside and there gave birth to and reared their babies, who were often bitten by poisonous insects. Mothers occasionally killed their offspring at birth to spare them future agonies... [Other] working mothers present a poignant image when we hear of them returning home after weeks or months of separation from their children, only to find that they had died or had been taken away.[11]

Invader pressures and oppressions such as these led to precipitous population declines across vast areas of the region. Stannard estimates that the central Mexican population dropped from more than 25,000,000 upon Spanish arrival to less than 1,300,000 only seventy-five years later!

In almost every country they reached, populations declined by at least 90% of their pre-1492 levels, and some considerably more than that. In the tens of thousands of years of their long and varied existence, never had a scourge like this blighted their lives, and populated their living nightmares. For many, death was a blessing; and for some, acquiescing to the horrors of slavery—or soul death—was preferable to the continuation of terror visited upon them by the Christians.

We get some sense of how the aboriginal Peoples saw these Christians through the voice of a cacique named Hatuey, who, in a final bid for freedom away from the Spanish monsters, took his people and fled to Cuba. Once there, in a place called Punaa Maisi, he assembled his fellow clansmen and explained to them that the whites were crazed for gold. He bade his people to throw all of their golden trinkets into the river nearby, so as not to attract the greed of these invaders. But it mattered naught, for the Spanish followed them, and when they were found, they slew most of them, enslaving the rest. As for Hatuey, he was condemned to death by being burned at the stake. In his final moments, as he was being tied to the stake, a Franciscan friar offered to convert him, so that his soul might ascend to heaven with Jesus. Hatuey replied that if heaven was the abode of Christians, he preferred hell.[12]

For millions of peoples whom we insist on calling "Indians," Christ was a marker for disease, torture, pestilence, devastation, and massacre. There is little wonder that few would choose to adopt such an option. Not freely, anyway. For most of this horror came in the name of this mysterious Christ—this god of death. Some priests blessed the devastations carried on in the name of Christ, for they saw the hand of God in this continental extinction of this new world of unbelievers.

Moreover, didn't Mother Church condone and bless this savagery? Didn't the Church and the Highnesses at home profit from this unparalleled transfer of indigenous wealth to their coffers?

The indigenous of the southern continental regions certainly had reasons for a major beef, to be sure. But one could hardly limit it to that region. Many miles northward would find different ethnic groups, linguistic groupings, clans and tribes, but with similar experiences of world-threatening invaders. Similarly, they nurtured those who would later strangle their peoples, steal their lands, and grind their lives into the dust.

Stannard's account of the attack upon the Pequot village by the Connecticut militia is an example of how the English, under commander John Mason, brought war to their hosts and neighbors:

> The British swarmed into the Indian encampment, slashing and shooting at anything that moved. Caught off guard, and with apparently

few warriors in the village at the time, some of the Pequots fled, "others crept under their beds," while still others fought back "most courageously," but this only drove Mason and his men to greater heights of fury. *"We must burn them,"* Mason later recalled himself shouting, whereupon he "brought out a Fire Brand, and putting it into the Matts with which they were covered, set the Wigwams on fire." At this, Mason says, "the Indians ran as Men most dreadfully Amazed":

> "And indeed such a dreadful Terror did the Almighty let fall upon their Spirits, that they would fly from us and run into the very Flames, where many of them perished... [And] God was above them, who laughed his enemies and the Enemies of his people to Scorn, making him as a fiery Oven: Thus were the Stout Hearted spoiled, having slept their last Sleep, and none of their Men could find their Hands: Thus did the Lord judge among the Heathen, filling the Place with dead Bodies!"[13]

The British-born governor, William Bradford, reacted to the massacre with typical English delight:

> It was a fearful sight to see them thus frying in the fire and the streams of blood quenching the same, and horrible was the stink and scent thereof; but the victory seemed a sweet sacrifice, and they gave the praise thereof to God, who had wrought so wonderfully for them, thus to enclose their enemies in their hands and give them so speedy a victory over so proud and insulting an enemy.[14]

If we are to take the governor's report seriously, then we can only assume that the pride or insult of Pequot "War" (perhaps Massacre would be more honest) was prosecuted on a false claim, based on pretext rather than a true *casus belli.*

In that respect, this trait continues to resonate within American statecraft and warfare.

As for the Pequots, their days were numbered. Few escaped the slaughters of their English tormentors. Those that survived did so in chains in the West Indies, where they were shipped as a consequence of their survival. Banished from the lands of their fathers, they were sent to dwell among African captives in the slavery factories of the Bahamas and Jamaica. The real tragedy is that they, for living, could be called the lucky ones.

The fate of the Pequots would soon be visited upon their brethren, the Narragansets and the Wampanoags. Interestingly, when the Pequots were first attacked by the English, their rivals, the Narragansets, acted as scouts for the British. But when they saw the kind of tactics their white allies were using, the Narragansets backed out of the "war," and took the rear—shocked by the English way of battle. Their "allies," finished with the Pequots, would soon turn their enmity at them, and wipe them off their lands as well, for it was the wars against the Narragansets and Wampanoags that constitute what English historians have called "King Phillip's War." In fact, it was the English version of total war, in which all were combatants—whether suckling babe, the infirm, or aged. It was, as Stannard writes, "a seventeenth century My Lai,"[15] a reference to the infamous American massacre of men, women, children, and even animals during the Vietnam War. In one early attack, the English invaders slew six hundred Wampanoags, which prompted the Puritan Christian cleric, Cotton Mather, to delightfully describe the mass murder as a "barbeque."[16]

These "tawny pagans" (a term of the Rev. Mather), as formally "allies" of the English, knew something about their warfare, and as such, mustered, as best they could, something of a defense. But English weapons, soldered with English armor, proved too great an advantage, and before long, the Narragansets were broken, and those few who survived were shipped off to Spain, or the West Indies, to live their lives as slaves of Europeans.

Although some remained in their former territory, they too were brought under English subjection, and reduced to slavery in the lands of their fathers. This near-total eradication of indigenous peoples in New England was the impetus for the rape of the Indians all across the breadth of the constantly expanding colonial territory. American politicians ran on their Indian hatred, and won big votes with their pledges to "exterminate" them all—literally.

Some two centuries later, a Pequot survivor, William Apes, English-speaking and educated, would give voice to a people vanishing from memory. In a eulogy to King Phillip (aka Metacom), Apes, a Methodist minister, author, and veteran of the U.S. Army, would remind those listening in Boston's Odeon Theatre that the so-called pagans of his people were better Christians than the whites:

> How inhuman it was in those wretches to come into a country where nature shone in beauty, spreading her wings over the vast continent,

> sheltering beneath her shades those natural sons of an Almighty Being, that shone in grandeur and luster like stars in the first magnitude in the heavenly world; whose virtues far surpassed their more enlightened foes, notwithstanding their pretended zeal for religion and virtue. How they could go to work to enslave a free people, and call it religion, is beyond the power of my imagination, and out-strips the revelation of God's word. Oh, thou pretended hypocritical Christian, whoever thou art, to say it was the design of God, that we should murder and slay one another, because we have the power. Power was not given to us to abuse each other, but as a mere power delegated to us by the King of heaven, a weapon of defense against error and evil; and when abused, it will turn to our destruction.[17]

It might be said that Rev. William Apes, by the early 1800s, had been Americanized (or perhaps Anglicized), but he, an ardent opponent of slavery, saw how precisely unchristian the Americans were, and condemned it in the strongest possible terms, publicly. But, as the old adage related, prophets are seldom heard in their own country, and Rev. Apes (ca. 1798-1837) would not live the additional generation required to see the dawn of the U.S. Civil War, that would split this country asunder over the central issues of slavery. Raised in Western ways on land once teeming with Apes' ancestors, the Connecticut of this modern era has an official population estimate for Native Americans standing at <0.05%![18]

George Washington may be known fondly as the "father of his country" among Americans, but among native peoples, Washington was regarded as a terrifying bogeyman. In 1792, a survivor of the great Iroquois Confederacy told Washington to his face: "... [T]o this day, when the name is heard, our women look behind them and turn pale, and our children cling close to the necks of their mothers."[19]

Father of *whose* country?

The same might be easily said of most other so-called "Founding Fathers" (with the possible exception of Tom Paine), for Adams, Jackson, Monroe, and others were well known for their antipathy to the native peoples. Jefferson the "founding father" of slaves, openly advanced the notion of using "the hatchet" against any Indian that opposed American expansion, and further stated:

> If ever we are constrained to lift the hatchet against any tribe, we will never lay it down till that tribe is exterminated, or is driven beyond the Mississippi...[20]

In truth, time and expansion meant the Mississippi wasn't far enough. They would be pushed from the Atlantic coast to the Pacific in the American lust for *lebensraum*. Jefferson's policy was simple and frighteningly clear: "extermination" or "removal."[21]

Indeed, the relative ease with which the English drove ancient peoples out of New England helped drive the passionate push westward that grew in lockstep with the growth of the colonies, and thereafter, the United States itself. The English way or the Spanish way was but a quibble of methodology. All of the invaders to Turtle Island (north and south) sought to extinguish the original peoples, and exploit them, when seen as profitable. This is but one page of the American holocaust, which may aptly be termed the American genocide. For, by whatever method they could devise—by craft, by stealth, by misdirection or legalized lies—the objective was to take the lands of the redskins.

And that they did.

"Go West, Young Man"

> *As a society we are so ashamed of our own history that we cannot give it an honest rendering in our schools and in our history books. We tremble to face it.*
>
> –Charles Sullivan, writer & cabinetmaker

As these words were being written into printed memory, a commercial came on boasting a miniseries entitled, "Into the West." Beautiful actors and actresses graced the screen, and before long, the promo promised, the story would be told of how—well, how the West was "won." Perhaps, for once, the advertising promises what it will deliver, but, if so, it will be a rare feat. For, as the African American axiom relates, "The greater story ain't never been told."

The actual history of how the West was stolen is a tale seldom taught to Americans, especially its children. For schools are political institutions, presided over by political institutions (as in school boards), and as in recent enactments in Arizona's legislature, certain histories are not deemed "American" enough to be dispensed to children—especially nonwhite kids, like Latinos.[22] These politicians doubtless know history's power, or else there would be no bars placed around the library, locking out all but pre-approved accounts of "how the West was won." We think in terms imposed by the invaders and the victors: "Indians." "Settlers." "Pioneers."

According to the Declaration of Independence, when the Americans drew up their writ against the repressive English king, the indigenous peoples were described in a way that supports the call for rebellion against such an unjust sovereign:

> He has excited domestic insurrections against us, and has endeavored to bring on the inhabitants of our Frontiers, the merciless Indian Savages, whose known Rule of Warfare, is an undistinguished Destruction, of all Ages, Sexes and Conditions.[23]

Merciless Indian Savages?

This description is particularly ironic given its author, Thomas Jefferson, a Shadwell, Virginia lawyer who would later call for the "extermination" of those who dared stand in the way of American progress westward. Jefferson knew, as did his recent English forebears, that the Indian way of war was profoundly different from the Anglo-American way. The Indians, as did many indigenous peoples, considered war a kind of sport among men, where the object (or even intention) was rarely death—and the killing of noncombatants was virtually unheard of. There was no honor in a warrior slaying a woman or a child. Many Indian tribes developed a kind of warfare called counting coup, where a brave would ride or run up his opponent, and strike him, or some other minor interplay. This demonstration of his braveness was considered a way of proving his honor, and though men left such wars with wounded pride, they often left it alive. If wounded, this was considered a badge of honor, for it brought luster to the warrior's legend.

Historian and author James Loewen has described the remaining stereotypes ascribed to Indians:

> Our textbooks do not teach against the archetypes of the savage Indian that pervades popular culture. On the contrary, textbooks give very little attention of any kind to Indian wars. As a result, my college students still come up with *savage* when I ask them for five adjectives that apply to Indians. Like much of our "knowledge" about Native Americans, the "savage" stereotype comes particularly from Western movies and novels, such as the popular "Wagons West" series by Dana Fuller Ross. These paperbacks, which have sold hundreds of thousands of copies, claim boldly, "The general outlines of history have been faithfully followed." Titled with state names—*Idaho!, Utah!,* etc—the novel's covers warn that "marauding Indian bands are spreading murder and mayhem among the

> terror-stricken settlers." In the Hollywood Old West, wagon trains were invariably encircled by savage Indian hordes. In the real West, among 200,000 whites and blacks who journeyed across the Plains between 1840 and 1860, only 362 pioneers (and 426 Native Americans) died in all the recorded battles between the two groups. Much more commonly, Indians gave the new settlers directions, showed them water holes, sold them food and horses, bought cloth and guns, and served as guides and interpreters. These activities are rarely depicted in movies, novels, or our textbooks. Inhaling the misinformation of the popular culture, students have no idea that natives considered European warfare far more savage than their own.[24]

As for the reputed "savagery" of the Indians, we would be well to remember that of virtually all the cases of whites being brought to Indian land, few, if any, wished to return to the whites. Meanwhile, most Indians fled life among the whites (primarily because they were most unwelcome in their midst). Ben Franklin, the oldest man at the Constitutional Convention, remarked, "No European who has tasted Savage Life can afterwards bear to live in our society."[25] If Franklin was correct in his assessment, then which society was truly more savage?

What qualities of life among the Indians were so magnetic to whites who fled their lives or were kidnapped and stayed? Franklin explained, "all their government is by Counsel of the Sages. There is no Force; there are no Prisons; no officers to compel Obedience, or inflict Punishment."[26]

Yeah, pretty savage, huh?

Among the Pilgrims, any white person caught living in Indian lands was subject to harsh punishments: including the death penalty.

Like the zephyr (the west wind), the lessons learned back east traveled across the land with vigor and speed. Indians were to be tricked, trapped, and barely tolerated; their lands were to be transferred to white hands, by any means necessary. In fact, in this great land grab, nothing—not morality, not religion, not pity, certainly not the law—nothing was to stand in the way of this great, central purpose.

Nothing.

We have written earlier that Indian lands were often stolen by lies and law. That is the truth. Nowhere is it clearer than in the case of the land theft of the Cherokees of Georgia. What is particularly ironic is that the Cherokees were widely regarded at the time as the "civilized tribe," as by this time they were largely Christians (having adopted the Moravian practice), they were literate (one of their number, Sequoyah, developed an alphabet to represent their spoken language), they published a local newspaper, and they lived in western-style brick homes. Of course, none of this really meant anything to the whites: other than their lands looked quite splendid.

A flood of whites invaded Cherokee territory, and the leaders of the People went to court to fight this illegal intrusion and trespass on their lands. The Cherokees literally took their case to the U.S. Supreme Court—and won! But it was all to no avail, for an American president had no intention to let a little thing like a judicial opinion block white settlers from red lands. When Andrew Jackson heard about the court ruling, he all but ignored it, saying, "[Chief Justice] John Marshall has made his decision, now let him enforce it."[27]

The Cherokees, their homes and offices burned to the ground, their fields and game destroyed, at the brink of mass starvation, under threat of death by the national army, marched away from the homes of their ancestors to Indian Territory (modern-day Oklahoma), and, with most on foot, began what historians have called the "Trail of Tears." They marched through cold, wind, rain and snow; and they dropped like flies from the sheer injustice of it. One American soldier who witnessed the scene recorded his observations for a later day:

> The long, painful journey to the west ended March 26th, 1839, with four-thousand silent graves reaching from the foothills of the Smoky Mountains to what is known as Indian territory in the West. And covetousness on the part of the white race was the cause of all that the Cherokees had to suffer. Ever since Ferdinand de Soto made his journey through the Indian country in the year 1540, there has been a tradition of a rich gold mine somewhere in the Smoky Mountain country, and I think the tradition was true. At a festival at Echota on Christmas night 1829, I danced and played with Indian girls who were wearing ornaments around their neck that looked like gold.
>
> In the year 1828, a little Indian boy living on Ward creek had sold a gold nugget to a white trader, and that nugget sealed the doom of the Cherokees. In a short time the country was overrun with armed brigands claiming to be government agents, who paid no attention to the rights of the Indians who were legal possessors of the country. Crimes were committed that were a disgrace to civilization. Men

were shot to death in cold blood, lands were confiscated. Homes were burned and the inhabitants driven out by the gold-hungry brigands.

Chief Junaluska was personally acquainted with President Andrew Jackson. Junaluska had taken 500 of the flower of his Cherokee scouts and helped Jackson win the battle of the Horse Shoe, leaving 33 of them dead on the field. And in that battle Junaluska had drove his Tomahawk through the skull of a Creek warrior, when the Creek had Jackson at his mercy.

Chief John Ross sent Junaluska as an envoy to plead with President Jackson for protection for his people, but Jackson's manner was cold and indifferent toward the rugged son of the forest who had saved his life. He met Junaluska, heard his plea but curtly said, "Sir, your audience is ended." The doom of the Cherokee was sealed. Washington, D.C. had decreed that they must be driven West and their lands given to the white men, and in May 1838, an army of 4000 regulars, and 3000 volunteer soldiers under command of General Winfield Scot, marched into the Indian country and wrote the blackest chapter on the pages of American history.[28]

Junaluska, his face wet with tears, would lament, "Oh my God, if I had known at the battle of the Horse Shoe what I know now, American history would have been differently written."[29]

U.S. Private John G. Burnett published this account in 1890. When the cross-country trek was over, some 8,000 Cherokees had perished, with hundreds of their Black slaves (they were, after all, "civilized").

No one bothered to count the dead Blacks.

The Trail of Tears, the government expulsion of Indians from their homelands for the sake of white settlement, was the beginning of the push westward that would spell disaster and devastation for many, many Indian clans, tribes, bands, and nations.

It is common for people of later generations to look upon the days before their birth as a kind of, if not ancient, then, irrelevant history, for those who lived then, are not alive now. It is an echo of the 21st century that was surely echoed in the 20th: "Why should we care about stuff that happened before we were born? It has nothing to do with me!" How many millions of youth have drudged their way through history classes, with such ideas bubbling in their heads?

But the story of the Trail of Tears is as real as America, and perhaps history was so boring because it was taught with an objective to comfort children with lullabies of sweetness and light; to speak of "good Indians" and "bad Indians"—and, worse still, "The Indians *gave* us..."

Gave us?

An American president, one whose name still resonates in the American mind, directly benefited from the carnage and chicanery of stolen Indian territories of the displaced Cherokee Nation—and that president was Theodore Roosevelt. James Bradley's recent work, *The Imperial Cruise,* doesn't directly explore the theft of Indian land and the subjugation of Indian communities into wards of the state, which marked the passing of the 19th century into the 20th, but he views it as a stepping stone toward America's rapacious leap into becoming an empire, empowered by the vast disposition of the world's lands and peoples—especially its yellow, brown, and black peoples. On the background of Teddy Roosevelt, America's 26th president, the highlights of the life of his mother are here recounted to show how the boy (to paraphrase Freud) became the father of the man:

> Teddy's MOTHER, MARTHA BULLOCH ROOSEVELT, a Southern belle whose family owned an enormous plantation, further defined the future president's worldview. Roswell, Georgia, from where she hailed, was founded in 1839 on land that had been seized from the Cherokee nation, which was uprooted by U.S. Army troops and marched forcibly to Oklahoma in the brutal journey now infamous as the "Trail of Tears." Unable to adjust to chilly northern climes, her stern husband's ways, and New York Society, Martha was usually ill and required constant care. From her sickbed she captured young Teddy's imagination by telling him stories of the thickheaded Bulloch slaves and the military exploits of her Bulloch relatives.
>
> In story after story, the young boy heard Martha's forebears and their courage under fire, their fearlessness, and their willingness to kill if need be. In Martha's accounts, two things became clear: first, that Teddy was part of a superior race; and second, that the most masculine men didn't need barbells to prove their manliness—they had rifles.[30]

"T.R." was the very epitome of a racist imperialist, and one should hardly be surprised by this fact, given his upbringing. This worldview never left him, and it formed the substructure from which he viewed all of human history, as well as in his interactions with foreign nations throughout his presidential terms (1901-1909).

France's great researcher and observer of 19th century American life, Alexis de Tocqueville, in a sarcastic aside to the contrast between the Spanish and Anglo-American methods of land-theft, opined, "the conduct of the United States American toward the natives was inspired by the most chaste affection for legal formalities.... It is impossible to destroy men with more respect to the laws of humanity."[31]

Americans had indeed perfected the peculiar technique of using law, whilst ignoring justice. The American predilection for legal niceties was seen, more often than not, in the untold number of treaties signed by the Americans with often non-representative Indians, ceding valuable lands to them. American political and military leaders were infamous for promising virtually anything, and then promptly violating every sworn tenet thereof. The great Hunkpapa Sioux leader Tatanka Yotanka (called "Sitting Bull" by whites) spoke openly and forcefully about the white inability to speak truth to Indian people, and their determination to violate treaties at will, or simply lie. Yotanka (ca. 1830-1890) asks simply:

> What treaty that the whites have kept has the red man broken? Not one. What treaty that the whites ever made with us red men have they kept? Not one. When I was a boy the Sioux owned the world. The sun rose and set on their lands. They sent ten thousand horsemen to battle. Where are the warriors today? Who slew them? Where are our lands? Who owns them? What white man can say that I ever stole his lands or a penny of his money? Yet they say I am a thief. What white woman, however lonely, was ever captive or insulted by me? Yet they say I am a bad Indian. What white man has ever seen me drunk? Who has ever come to me hungry and gone unfed? Who has ever seen me beat my wives or abuse my children? What law have I broken? Is it wrong for me to love my own? Is it wicked in me because my skin in red; because I am a Sioux; because I was born where my fathers lived; because I would die for my people and my country?[32]

When nations enter into treaties, of course differences arise, for often they are conducted across remarkable distances of language and culture. That said, one presumes that treaties are made in relative good faith. This could rarely (if ever) be said when Americans convened with American Indians. In August of 1873, the Crow leader, Blackfoot (ca.1795-1877), spoke at a U.S.-Crow Treaty Council. His remarks boiled down to the question, "What's the use of us making a treaty with you guys?" Such a question arose because, in Blackfoot's understanding, the Americans had no intention of keeping them!

> I have said before that we are friends, and that we like each other; yet we have different thoughts in our heads. The first time I went to Fort Laramie and met the peace commissioners, what each said to the other, we said "Yes, yes." The second time we went, we signed the treaty; but neither of us, my white friends nor the Indian chiefs, said, "Yes, yes," to what is in that treaty. What we said to them, and what they said to us, was "Good." We said, "Yes, yes," to it, but it is not in the treaty. Shane was there the first time, and what he interpreted to us are not the words that are in the treaty. The first time we went, we did not sign the treaty; we only said "Yes, yes," to each other. The Indian way of making a treaty is to light a pipe, and the Indians and their white friends smoke it.
>
> When we were in council at Laramie, we asked whether we might eat the buffalo for a long time. They said yes. That is not in the treaty. We told them we wanted a big country. They said we should have it; and that is not in the treaty. They promised us plenty of goods, and food for forty years—plenty for all the Crows to eat; but that is not in the treaty. Listen to what I say. We asked, "Shall we and our children get food for forty years?" They said "Yes"; but it is not that way in the treaty. The land that we used to own we do not think of taking pay for. We used to own the land of the Mud River Valley. These old Crows you see here were born there. We owned Horse Creek, the Stinking Water, and Heart's Mountains. Many of these Indians were born there. So we owned the country about Powder River and Tongue River, and many of our young men were born there. So we owned the mouth of Muscle-shell, and Crazy Mountain, and Judith Basin; many of our children were born there. So we told the commissioners. They said "Yes, yes"; but there is nothing about it in the treaty. We told them there were many bad Indians, but that we would hold on to the hands of the white man, and would love each other. We told them the Piegans, the Sioux, and other tribes have killed the white men. We told them the whites were afraid of them. I asked them to look at us; that we had no arms, and they should not be afraid of

> the Crows. They said "Yes, yes"; but it is not so written in the treaty.[33]

A generation before the signing of the Laramie "treaty," one of the biggest-selling books of the era, considered a bible of science by some, was *Types of Mankind,* which gave a scientific gloss to white, Aryan supremacy over the original peoples of the Americans, and further, that their "extinction" was inevitable. The book, used as a standard textbook well into the 20th century, made the following remarks about Native Americans:

> His race is run, and probably he has performed his earthly mission. He is now gradually disappearing, to give place to a higher order of beings. The order of nature must have its course... Some are born to rule, and others are born to be ruled. No two distinctly marked races can dwell together on equal terms. Some races, moreover, appear destined to live and prosper for a time, until the destroying race comes, which is to exterminate and supplant them.[34]

A generation after the signing of the Laramie treaty, the nation would be awash in massacres: Sand Creek, Wounded Knee, and others that have become epithets of a vile history. What was Sand Creek? The massacre of Sand Creek, in eastern Colorado (1864) wasn't the worst, nor even the most costly in human lives lost, but rather it is distinguished by the way the white press openly drove the affair, with headlines and writing that was virtually dripping with bloodlust.

As with any community with both whites and Indian inhabitants, the smallest conflict would get magnified, but the Rocky Mountain News took it to another level. As with other such sites, Indian land was often the place where white settlers claimed squatter's rights—in this case rights to Arapahoe and Cheyenne lands. The settlers joined the local newspaper for an especially ugly and vociferous campaign that focused on Indian hatred and talk of extermination. In the paper's March 1863 edition, the editor wrote (of the Indians): "They are a dissolute, vagabondish, brutal and ungrateful race, and *ought to be wiped from the face of the earth.*" [Emphasis added]. Of the several dozen stories published that year in the Rocky Mountain News, over a third of the ones involving Indians openly called for the extermination of the Sand Creek villagers.[35] The next year was marked by the campaign for statehood, and, to support that cause, the paper went into overdrive, pushing the "threat" of the Sand Creek Indians—all of whom were unarmed!

When a white settler got into any conflict, and especially if a death was involved, the Rocky Mountain News leapt to the fore, using such instances to heap blame on the Sand Creek villagers. When a family of settlers was killed, the die was cast, even though the Sand Creek people (again, unarmed) had nothing to do with it.

But as in many areas of war, pretexts are as good as reasons, and this was a perfect pretext for a massacre. The paper, backed by the territory's governor, made it plain, urging all readers to join in the "extermination against the red devils."[36] The governor bolstered the call by issuing a proclamation naming the Sand Creek villagers "hostile," which not only opened them to attack, but gave the right to citizens and militia to "pursue, kill and destroy" all of them.

When 700 heavily armed U.S. soldiers assembled, under the command of Colonel John Chivington, people knew this would end in bloodshed. That's because Chivington was well-known for saying it was his policy to "kill and scalp all, little and big."[37] When they entered the village on November 29, snow was underfoot. The creek was still and icy. Dawn had not yet broken as the cavalry counted more than 100 lodges—a village of mostly women and children, with most of the men away on a buffalo hunt. One guide reported that there were nearly 600 people in the camp, with 35 braves, and a few dozen old men.

It mattered not.

Even the village's 111 men of warrior age—armed only for the hunt, having turned in their other weapons to the U.S. commander at nearby Fort Lyons, and considered non-hostiles by the U.S. Government—could not have stopped the maniacal desires of Colonel Chivington who said, "Well, I long to be wading in gore."[38]

His wish would soon be granted. When Chivington's troops entered the village, they saw various signs of non-hostility, including the rather remarkable scene of Cheyenne leader, Black Kettle, who tied two signs to his lodge pole: a white flag and an American flag. Black Kettle urged his people to, literally, rally around the flag of the Americans. When they did so, it became a banner of massacre, for the U.S. troops opened up on those in the flag's vicinity. Then, as women and children ran, they were chased, shot, scalped, and mutilated. Women running from Black Kettle's lodge ran to the riverbank, and frantically tried to cover themselves in clay and sand, to better hide from their pursuers. It was not to be. Robert Bent, a scout for the Americans, described the chilling vista before him:

> After the firing the warriors put the squaws and children together, and surrounded them to protect them. I saw five squaws under a bank for shelter. When the troops came up to them they ran out and showed their persons, to let the soldiers know they were squaws and beg for mercy, but the soldiers shot them all… There were some thirty or forty squaws collected in a hole for protection; they sent out a little girl about six years old with a white flag on a stick; she had not proceeded but a few steps when she was shot and killed. All the squaws in that hole were afterwards killed, and four or five bucks outside. The squaws offered no resistance. Everyone was scalped. I saw one squaw cut open with an unborn child, as I thought, lying by her side. Captain Soulé afterwards told me that such was the fact… I saw quite a number of infants in arms killed with their mothers.
>
> I went over to the ground soon after the battle [reported Asbury Bird, a soldier with Company D of the First Colorado Cavalry]. I should judge there were between 400 and 500 Indians killed… nearly all men, women and children were scalped. I saw one woman whose privates had been mutilated… Next morning after the battle [said Corporal Amos. C. Miksch, also of Company C], I saw a little boy covered up among the Indians in a trench, still alive. I saw a major in the 3rd regiment take out his pistol and blow off the top of his head. I saw some men unjoining fingers to get rings off, and cutting off ears to get silver ornaments…[39]

It is difficult to recount these reports, made in a Congressional Hearing in Denver's Opera House. Some of the reports are so gruesome we've omitted them from these pages. Suffice it to say that the carnage knew no bounds.

Shortly thereafter, Colonel Chivington proudly sent messages to the press bragging that he and his boys ended "one of the most bloody Indian battles ever fought" against "one of the most powerful villages in the Cheyenne nation," which was utterly destroyed.[40] When those outside of Colorado heard of the Sand Creek massacre, they were outraged, for despite Chivington's account, one senator, surveying the field, found a litter of skulls, so small-toothed that it obviously bore the proof of the infancy of the Cheyenne "warriors."But, politicians are, after all, politicians. When the question was put to the [white] Coloradans about the role of the Indians in the newly born state's future, the answer blew the roof off the joint: "EXTERMINATE THEM! EXTERMINATE THEM!"[41] The visiting congressmen quietly packed their gear and left the region, and nothing else was either said nor done. Chivington, meanwhile, rose to fame and fortune, and was sought out as a speaker on the "Indian Wars."

And why not? America's frontier president, Teddy Roosevelt praised the massacre as "righteous and beneficial a deed as ever took place on the frontier."

If you, the reader, were to check out the massacre today, even in that great tavern-betting final arbiter—*The World Almanac*—you will find a mention that states some "150 killed" at Sand Creek.[42] But the contemporaries, who saw the bodies and smelled the flood of blood, knew better. They knew the American Way of Massacre.

Wounded Knee

Wounded Knee has a resonance far exceeding that of Sand Creek, perhaps because it has found its way into (at least some) of the nation's literature, and thus, albeit grudgingly, into some part of our consciousness. Perhaps Wounded Knee survives because it occurred a generation after Sand Creek, and its grim aftermath was captured in the harsh black and white reality of Warren K. Moorehead's bulky camera. (Although Moorehead was escorted off the Pine Ridge reservation in South Dakota by the U.S. Army the day before all hell broke loose on 29 December 1890, his camera stayed behind, and was used to capture the aftermath of the massacre.)

The lifeless figures of scores of men, women, and children have a perverse similarity, with all its horror, to the photos of the infamous My Lai massacre in Quảng Ngãi Province, South Vietnam, where American soldiers from Company C, 1st Battalion, 20th Infantry Regiment, murdered hundreds of unarmed civilians. It was a different era and on the opposite end of the planet, but the images are always the same: bodies, still as cord wool, tossed into silent ditches. Wounded Knee. Manila. My Lai. It's all the same. They are place-names of U.S. carnage incarnate.

L. Frank Baum, perhaps one of the nation's most renowned fiction writers, wowed American readers with his book, *The Wizard of Oz* (which of course later thrilled audiences as a film classic). But he was also a working journalist and editor of South Dakota's *Aberdeen Saturday Pioneer,* a kind of South Dakotan version of Colorado's *Rocky Mountain News.* Just a week and a half before the bloodlust of Wounded Knee burst forth into destiny, Baum issued the following call for the eradication of the Lakota Sioux:

> The nobility of the Redskin is extinguished, and what few are left are a pack of whining curs who lick the hand that smites them. The Whites, by law of conquest, by justice of civilization, are masters of the American continent, and the best safety of the frontier settlements will be secured by the total annihilation of the few remaining Indians. Why not annihilation? Their glory has fled, their spirit broken, their manhood effaced; better that they should die than live the miserable wretches that they are.[43]

One wonders if Baum was trying to convince the Lakota or himself about the rightness of this act of "annihilation."

In the space of days, hundreds of Lakota would be set upon by U.S. Army Hotchkiss guns (more cannon than gun) and their "miserable" existences were soon ended. When the smoke cleared, over two-thirds of the dead were Lakota women and children. Wounded Knee would mark the bookend of the last chapter of the so-called Indian wars. It would be the harbinger of a century of such bloodletting that the world would regard it as an era of nightmare.

But long before Verdun, before Dachau, Treblinka, Manchuria, Nagasaki, or Hiroshima, there were massacres like Wounded Knee for five centuries, blessed by priests and promoted by politicians. The tormentors, genocidaires, rapists, and torturers were Spanish, English, Portuguese, and Danish. They were Europeans sent by a crucified Jew to vanquish paradise and bring Hell to this green earth. They purified this new space with fire, blood, dung, and bones, and called it holy before the Lord. Of the people they met, who once radiated beauty and health like demigods in a terrestrial heaven, they left a bare remnant, less than one-half of one percent. Their job done, they celebrated the death of an estimated 100,000,000 people by pronouncing them savages, and praising Christopher Columbus—the "discoverer."[44]

An indigenous writer from the Maya would preserve the following words into the text, *Chilam Balam*, regarding the "white lords" who invaded Mayan life:

> They taught fear and they withered the flowers. So that their flower should live, they maimed and destroyed the flowers of others... Marauders by day, offenders by night, *murderers of the world.*[45]

❖ ❖ ❖

5 African Captivity
One Thousand Years of Hell on Earth

It is easy for us to assume that we've just read a typo: *1,000 years?* That can't be right. And in truth, it isn't. It is *too conservative.*

For over a millennium ago, more than ten centuries before this present era, thousands upon thousands that became millions upon millions of people, were sold into the captivity of foreigners, and marched or were driven to the coasts of Africa's eastern shores, to be transported to what we today call the Middle East, to serve wealthy Arab families for the rest of their lives—as trendy doormen, sexual slaves, and toilers in the dreaded salt mines (yes, salt mines!) of southern Iraq.

Those who marched inland walked across hundreds and then thousands of miles —an African "Trail of Tears"—to service the fleshpots of Cairo, Baghdad, or Kufa; or to be despoiled of their labor at the whim of the wealthy city-dwellers.

It must be said that these captives were sold into bondage by African tribal chiefs, for many of them were indeed prisoners of tribal wars, and slavery was often the high cost of losing a battle with a stronger adversary. The island site once known as Zanzibar was often the coastal launch point for ships sailing to the Middle East; or, given the widespread traffic on the seas by Arab sailors and merchants, some passages were bound for ports of call as distant as China. According to scholars, the era of the arrival of African captives in the Middle East is indeterminate.[1] However, some suggest it predates the rise of the Islamic era, and this is supported by the contemporary report of the faith's foundation with the life and liberty of the Black slave, Bilal Ibn Rabah, who, having adopted the new faith, is ransomed by the prophet Muhammad from captivity, for his refusal to renounce under torture.

Bilal, according to Islamic tradition, had a voice so beautiful and captivating that he was chosen as the first *muezzin*—or one who calls people to the daily prayers. But his very existence at the dawn of this new age is a testament to the existence of the reality of African captivity in the North African and West Asian regions. While this is indeed an extended historical period, and thus far too complex to summarize in this work, it is noteworthy to tell a segment which gives us some flavor of the period and the environment.

To this very day, in the southern Iraqi city of Basra lives a dark-skinned people who are the remnants of the captives brought to the salt mines from East Africa, principally Zanzibar (today a part of the United Republic of Tanzania). They are also the descendants of one of the greatest slave revolts in world history, known by Arab historians as "The Revolt of the Zanj." The term "Zanj" was a reference to their place of origin (Zanzibar, East Africa), but, as one might expect, after years and centuries of such use, it came to have a distinctly racial connotation, applicable to any black-skinned Iraqis regardless of their lineage. Historian Alexandre Popovic expressed the psychosocial power of the term this way: "... if there are no Zanj who are not black, there are many blacks who are not Zanj."[2]

It is also true that where there are slaves, there is antipathy, derision, and hatred of them, of which Arab society was no exception. It is further true that Arab society featured a religiously-approved (or sanctioned) practice of slavery that was employed in the subjugation of many peoples, from many lands and climes, whether European, Zanj, Asian, and others. However, this does not challenge the fact that the East Africans formed an important and growing slave resource for Arab societies, and both preceded and succeeded the more notorious Atlantic slave trade that largely peopled the plantations, farms, fields, and factories of the West.

Sometimes a world dwells in a proverb, which may be seen in the Arab axiom, "As if one spoke Arabic to a Zendj."[3] This suggests a socially accepted stigma against the Zanj ('Zendj'), which denotes their stupidity, linguistic limitations, and perhaps their presumed inability to assimilate into Arab societies.

But, as ever, where there is oppression, there is too, resistance.

The Revolt of the Zanj

People resort to revolt when their lives or their life options become intolerable. They prefer death to the horrific, albeit living alternatives. In ancient Rome, slave revolts rocked the empire, the most famous of which was led by the ex-gladiator,

Spartacus (ca. 71 B.C.). He and his forces dominated southern Italy until Marcus Licinius Crassus led the battle to defeat and suppress the revolt, by instilling state terror, and crucifying some six thousand resistors.

Lesser known is the revolt that shook the very foundations of southern Iraq, and the caliphate of the era. Alexandre Popovic recited the history of the revolt's onset, and their early efforts to expand it:

> The revolt was probably declared on Wednesday, 26 Ramadan 255/ September 7, 869. Rebels intercepted a group of fifty slaves who were on their way to work. After binding the leader hand and foot, they went on to another work site where they did the same thing. Five hundred slaves, including a captain Abu Hudayd, are reported to have joined them, then another 150 slaves, among whom were Zurayq and Abu I-Hanjar, and yet another 80 slaves, among whom were Rashid al-Magribi (Mughabi) and Rashid al-Qurmati. Such occurrences were constantly repeated, and the ranks of the insurgents continued to grow.
>
> In due time, Ali b. Muhammad called together and addressed all of the men who had joined his cause. After promising the improvement in their conditions with much wealth, he solemnly swore that he would never deceive them or fail to support them.
>
> Turning towards the slaveholders, he reminded them that they deserved death for the way they had behaved toward their slaves and for doing things forbidden by God. They replied that the slaves would leave them before long and offered him money to return them. Ali b. Muhammad ordered the slaves to beat their masters and overseers, and when each had received 500 blows, he released them after making them take a solemn oath not to reveal to anyone his whereabouts or the number of his troops. One of the slave owners crossed the Dujayi and went to warn the overseers of the large camps where 15,000 slaves were working.[4]

This army of slaves and the dispossessed swept through southern Iraq like a wave, growing by the day. They were slaves no more—they were rebels. They were revolutionaries. They took city by city, especially in Iraq's canal regions. These black rebels set up a state, printed their own coin, and established a capital city in al-Mukhtara. Ali b. Muhammad took the title al-Mahdi (Arabic for messiah). His armies took the cities of Khuzestan, Ramhormoz, An Numaniyah, and Jaranaya. His troops even advanced on Baghdad, and fought in Mecca.[5]

For fifteen years the rebellion raged, at so hot a fever pitch that the caliph was forced to withdraw from his seat in Baghdad; however, as historically has been the case with revolts, rebel turncoats in the pay of Abbassids turned on the rebellions, Ali's generals were captured, and shortly thereafter Ali b. Muhammad was captured and beheaded (ca. 270/883).

With the execution of Ali bin Muhammad, Al-Mahdi of al-Muktara and Emir of the Zanj Rebel Revolutionary State, the long "Revolt of the Zanj" was brought to its conclusion. This is but one expression of the outcome of the Eastern slave trade among the peoples of East Africa who were taken into bondage.

Nor is this an ancient story that only has resonance in the distant past. Although no one knows the number, there are an estimated 500,000 black Iraqis today, in a nation of some twenty-seven million people. After the post-9/11 Iraq war, and the election of the first African-American president of the United States, black Iraqis looked to the Americans as a possible source of their social relief from inequalities there. Said Jalal Chijeel, secretary of the Free Iraq Movement, "We heard Obama's message of change. Iraq needs change in how they see their own black-skinned people. We need out brothers to accept us."[6]

While they may or may not be descendants of the Zanj ("while all Zanj are black, not all blacks are Zanj"), they are the great-great grandsons and granddaughters of Africans, and thousands of years later, in the lands of their birth, they experience the lack of jobs, repression, and anti-Black hatred that afflicts African peoples around the world.

Khalid Majid, a 36-year-old black Iraqi father, took his 6-year-old daughter to school, but had to withdraw her when her classmates addressed her by the term "*abd*"—the Arabic word meaning slave. "It is my wish that she will read and write," said Majid, "but I cannot let her have these... problems."[7]

Into the West

At least five centuries after the start of the Eastern slave trade, Europe's elites began licking their chops at the lure of "free" labor. This became the case especially after the erroneous discovery of what we continue to call "the Indies," Columbus's landing on the islands of the Caribbean.

As we have seen, the first slaves in the Americas were the indigenous peoples of this land, those we now term "Indians." But, so great was the greed, and so voracious the violence, that, in a relatively short period of time, the slave stocks of Indians were depleted. And although historians, archeologists, epidemiologists, and others attribute this spectacular die-off to the pestilential pathogens brought over by the Europeans (and their horrific violence unleashed against the Indians, once Europeans were secure in their domination), one cannot ignore the deep and perhaps unfathomable sense of loss occasioned by this devilish invasion and the broken hearts of the people who saw their world destroyed before their eyes.

But just because the aboriginal peoples of the Americas died off in great numbers, did not mean that the greed that launched their killers across the Atlantic died with them. For the Spanish, English, and other invaders knew too well, that this "new" earth held riches beyond their wildest dreams of avarice. They knew they wouldn't do the work, so they needed new laborers. New slaves.

Enter, the Africans.

Most of us think of Christopher Columbus as the explorer, captain and Admiral of the trek to the Americas, but few know that he had an earlier career as a kidnapper and African slave trader.[8] This first-hand expertise gave him a leg up on the exploration gamble, as he decided to kidnap Indians for shipment to Spain, to show off his exotic treasures to the royal court (and the trade investors). One of his lessons from this infernal enterprise was when one kidnaps a man, to also kidnap a woman, for this would have a calming effect on the male captive.

At the time of the American explorations, southern Europe was awash in slaves, but these people were, more often than not, prisoners of war, and included such various tribes as Turks, Bulgarians, Tatars, Armenians, and Africans. A brisk business developed on the Mediterranean. Many of these people were Africans described as Moors, captured in wars, who began to swell the burgeoning slave economy. For Muslims (and Jews) dwelling in post-1492 Europe, slavery often befell them, or their children, for they were nonbelievers, and, as such, subject to the pains of captivity. Most of these Muslims were Moors (Africans) and were subject to not just slavery, but deportation abroad.

The vast majority of these people were put in chains aboard slave ships and transported to the Indies, or Brazil, and forced to build the infrastructure of the societies that would one-day blossom forth. Shackled in what some have termed "floating tombs,"[9] some 30% of the human cargo didn't survive the trip from the Mediterranean to the Americas. By 1502, historians Mary Frances Berry and John Blassingame report, the slave trade that began as a business swelled into a boom.

> The first Americans arrived in the New World in 1502; by the time the slave trade ended in the 1860s, more than 100 million blacks had either been killed or transplanted from their homeland. Although statistics on the trade are imprecise, it appears that from 400,000 to 1 million of the 10 to 50 million Africans forcibly transplanted to the Americas came to North America between 1619 and 1808. Eventually, the raids of such groups as the Ashanti, and Dahomey so disrupted and depopulated West African states that rulers began to protest against the trade. In the sixteenth century, for example, the King of the Congo, Nzenga Meremba, sent word to the Portuguese, "it is our will that in these kingdoms of Congo there should not be any trade in slaves nor any markets for slaves." African rulers, unfortunately, were powerless to stop the trades.[10]

We must occasionally stop, if only to marvel at the sheer scope of these enterprises. Hundreds of millions of people, pushed into the living death of slavery. Indians. Then Africans. Utilized as things—chattel—to enrich others, and to build the lives of others, while denied the most fundamental attributes of life itself.

It teaches us that the world we behold today was built on bondage and bones. Mega-torture. Death. Devastation.

Holocausts.

This was not an event. It was the daily work of centuries, to build white wealth, and desecrate the lives, dreams, and souls of hundreds of millions. It wasn't, strictly speaking, just slavery, for many Africans came from societies where slavery was as rain. This was something new in the world: *racialized* slavery; slavery as a marker for not only social degradation, but as an equation of blackness itself. Africans, many of whom came directly from their West African homelands, had never seen such a thing. Few could comprehend it.

And what was this new form of slavery? The great American writer and thinker W.E.B. Du Bois would describe it in its essential, economic, and social terms, as "slave-based capitalism":

> [T]he iron curtain was not invented by Russia; it hung between Europe and Africa half a thousand years. When producer is so separated from the consumer in time and space that a mutual knowledge and understanding is impossible, then to regard the industrial process as "individual enterprise" or the result of "private initiative" is stupid. It is a social process, and if not socially controlled sinks to anarchy with every

> possible crime of irresponsible greed. Such was the African slave trade, and such is the capitalistic system it brought to full flower. Men made cotton cloth and sold sugar; but between the two they stole, killed, and raped human beings, forced them to toil for a bare subsistence, made rum and synthetic gas, herded white labor into unsanitary factories, bought the results to their work under threat of hunger which forced down their wage, and sold the sugar at monopoly prices to consumers who must pay or go without. A process of incredible ingenuity for supplying human wants because in its realization is a series of brutal crimes.[11]

The erudite Du Bois, a Harvard-trained scholar, surely gives us a nuanced, intellectually laden view of what Americans once termed "the peculiar institution." Nevertheless, his argument seems lacking when we discuss something so vital to American economic, social, cultural, and psychosocial development.

It's one thing to intellectually understand the brutality of slave-based capitalism, but it takes the specificity of human experience to feel the true horrors of slavery.

The greatest freedom fighter in American history, Harriet Tubman, who was known as "General Moses" during her lifetime for freeing so many African captives, and who lived her first decades of life in "the peculiar institution," gives us a down-to-earth, more experiential view. Slavery was described by Tubman as "the next thing to hell." Indeed, Thomas Jefferson, the nation's third president, (his slaveholding we detailed in Chapter 1), said that one hour of American slavery was "fraught with more misery than ages of that," which the white American colonists "rose in rebellion to oppose."[12]

Slavery, as practiced in the last five hundred years against hundreds of millions of Africans, was, in a manner of speaking, life devoid of life, for in law, practice, custom, and tradition, the lives of Africans were of value only to the extent it served capitalist purposes. One could neither marry, nor parent, nor own property, nor protect either, for in this profound racialized slavery—slavery equated with blackness—one's essential worth, as human, was diminished, denied, and destroyed. That was one of the most prevalent features of Western slavery—an endless assault on the very personhood of a people.

Stannard states that this Western branch of the global slave trade took the lives and/or freedoms of 60,000,000 Africans, and by so doing transformed Africa and Europe in ways that we are just now beginning to understand.[13] The numbers alone are dizzying, but to offer some perspective, it is important to seize them and grasp their meaning.

When we speak of the eradication of the lives and/or freedom of sixty million people, we are talking roughly (in contemporary comparative terms) about the almost total destruction of France; the destruction of Canada (twice!); the liquidation of the United Kingdom; or the erasure of South Africa. What this meant, moreover, was the depletion of young people from vast tracts of African societies—the young, the strong, and the new blood with which to replenish societal structures, clans, families, and nations. For slavery was the forced extraction of labor power: those who could do work which could be exploited. This meant young people. To be more precise, the vast majority of people who were brought into captivity in the Americas were young African males. Most African females who were captives were sold into intertribal slavery, where their sexual and reproductive facilities could be exploited.

We must remind ourselves that the slavery system was a labor system, and it was the very foundation of the building of much of what we today call the West. The great Black historian, J.A. Rogers, made that point decades ago:

> Indeed the rise of America from a wilderness over which roamed Indians and buffaloes to world power; from a people once so pressed by hunger that some were driven to cannibalism to a nation with enormous surpluses of food is nothing short of the miraculous. Britain took 1,920 years to become the world's foremost power—1,643 years from Julius Caesar's invasion, 55 B.C., to the defeat of the Spanish Armada in 1588; and another 277 years to Waterloo 1815. The United States took only 353 years, that is from the founding of St. Augustine, Florida to the end of World War I... why did America take the lead so early in the New World? The answer is trade... it was trade in molasses... why molasses? Molasses meant rum. Why rum? Rum was for exchange of Africans on the African west coast. In short, it was the sale of Africans in the New World—the slave trade—that laid the financial foundation of the United States.[14]

It is a measure of the depths of our own Eurocentric thinking that, in many ways, our minds and very perceptions have been so racialized and colonized that our language reflects a worldview vastly at odds with reality. That is to say, how we look at huge swaths of people is an outdated artifact of how Europe projected the entire world upon its lens, and the afterimages still resonate within us. For, do we not still refer to Indians as Indians—even when we know full well that this relic is based on a great mistake of geography and space, made by Columbus and his fellow navigators? Before the Columbian era, neither the word, nor the notion existed, for inasmuch as people defined themselves, they did so as clans, tribes, or mostly matrilineal orders of identity.

In a strikingly similar fashion, we may see the projection of Africans as an artifact of the European world, of division, categorization, and differentiation. For, in Africa (called by many names throughout human time), when all are Africans, who is not? Akan, Peul, Fulani, Ashanti, Madinke, Zulu or the like. Stannard expands on that view, illustrating how this form of cultural blindness spelled doom for the vast millions of people held under this ethnic umbrella:

> A list of distinctions marking the uniqueness of one or another group that has suffered from genocidal mass destruction or near (or total) extermination could go on at length. Additional problems emerge because of a looseness in the terminology commonly used to describe categories and communities of genocidal victims. A traditional, Eurocentric bias that lumps undifferentiated masses of "Africans" into one single category and undifferentiated masses of "Indians" into another, while making the fine distinctions among the different populations of Europe, permits the ignoring of cases in which genocide against Africans and American Indians has resulted in the *total* exterminations—purposefully carried out—of entire cultural, social, religious, and ethnic groups.[15]

This worldview opened up the possibilities of the vast genocides that made America possible. For, it eased the way for the toxin of racism to take root, which in turn justified the unnamed, unmentioned holocausts of which we speak. For, what does it matter what happens to niggers or redskins? They're just Indians—and, as we all know, "the only good Indian is a dead Indian." And it did not take long for "Indian" to become "African." As Europeans sought to de-Indianize Indians, they similarly sought to de-Africanize Africans, by outlawing African languages, drafting laws to make drums illegal, and forcibly changing names of African people. Indeed, the term African became, well—negroized. And that which could be thought of as Africanic was forbidden, criminalized, demonized in public consciousness and then in social practice. Africa became the psychosocial repository for all that was deemed negative, a kind of American alter ego hidden in its repressed nation-self. And by so doing, it gave a perverted sense of inflated value to whiteness that it did not heretofore possess. It gave life to this psychosis, energizing it into a core constituent of the American personality.

For, what was American citizenship initially, if not whiteness? Shortly after the U.S. Revolutionary War, the virgin Congress began its first session with a passion: who could be a citizen? Historian James Bradley answers this question:

> [T]he laws of the new nation followed the path of White supremacy. The legislation defining who could become an American citizen, the naturalization Act of 1790, begins: "All free white persons..." While Congress debated whether Jews or Catholics could become citizens, no member publicly questioned the idea of limited citizenship to only "free white persons."[16]

That rule of naturalization, i.e., who may become a citizen, was the essential law of the land until the early-20th century. We are therefore not discussing colonial-era, or post-revolutionary history; we are discussing the present. Indeed, as if that wasn't enough, nearly a century after the passage of the Naturalization Act, Congress sweetened the pot by the 1882 Chinese Exclusion Act, which specifically barred resident aliens from becoming naturalized (this act, which established a ten year block to such naturalizations, was later made permanent in law).

This is significant in that it follows the amendment of the U.S. Constitution, and its commonly called "Reconstruction Amendments" (i.e., the 13th, 14th and 15th Amendments), which granted rights of citizenship to "All persons born or naturalized in the United States (14th Amendment). In the eyes of Congress, at least, perhaps Chinese folks were not yet "persons."

As for Africans, the 14th Amendment became much more of a dead letter on arrival, allowing terrorist armies of the south, and political repression of the north, to ride rampant over the so-called "rights" of Black people for more than a century after the constitution was amended. In every sense that mattered, slavery continued under the peonage of the sharecropping system and under the rubric of state power, whereby people were penalized and forced to do free labor under the notorious convict-lease system. Here, because that laborer had no individual monetary value, bosses would, quite literally, work a man (or woman!) to death, for such an event could be remedied by simply going out and arresting someone else.

Again, it is important to note that we are not discussing ancient history, for peonage was a very real phenomenon lasting well into that latter part of the 20th century. The scholar-historians Berry and Blassingame relate:

> Slavery is just as much an "institution" now as it was before the war. The Georgia Baptist Convention agreed with this view in 1939: "There are more negroes by these debt slavers than we actually owned as slaves before the War Between the States."[17]

Thousands of people wrote to the U.S. Justice Department seeking support in their struggles against peonage, or protesting their treatment by landowners. The government filed their letters, but did little else. Members of the U.S. Communist Party turned up the heat and began a mass campaign against the practice of peonage. Otto Huiswoud, a Black member of the American Communist Party, spoke out forcefully against peonage in 1930, saying it brought to mind the system of slavery that was supposedly abolished in 1865, and adding:

> [T]he Southern Negro was practically completely re-enslaved on the plantations. The courts enacted innumerable laws which served to keep the Negro under the complete domination of the landowners. Every instrument at its disposal was used by the ruling class to shackle the Negro workers and bind them to the plantations... The Negro tenant farmer, sharecropper, and farm workers are virtual slaves on the land. The poor farmer and sharecropper can never hope to own the land he tills, due to a credit and mortgage system which chains him to the land, but even the implements, crops—everything is mortgaged, placing them under complete domination of the white ruling class... Peonage, debt and convict slavery, vagrancy laws, disfranchisements, segregation, lynching and mob violence are the methods used to mercilessly exploit and oppress the Negroes in the South. These are the methods used by the capitalist class in order to extract super profits from their labor.[18]

Thus we see how even slavery survived slavery—albeit under another name.

You may have noted that we've shifted between slavery and legalized post-slavery in an attempt to dispel a persistent illusion of separation. The only real separation between slavery pre-1865 and the de facto continuation of slavery thereafter, was the illusion of legality, for the law was virtually always the tool of the wealthy and the powerful, and as such, arrayed against the weak and the powerless. It mattered little that the "law"—as represented by what we are taught—is "the Supreme Law of the Land" (as claimed by Article VI; Clause 2 of the U.S. Constitution), for between such lofty statements and what people experience in the real world, was another experience entirely.

Are we suggesting that the Constitution was meaningless? No, we are not. But what we are suggesting is that the Constitution was conveniently ignored, forgotten, and expressively violated—*for centuries!*—when it was convenient for economic, political, and judicial elites to do so. Thus, it is not we who are shifting, but life itself, as lived in the web of politics, economics, and the quicksand of the law.

The Law of the Outlaw: Slave Law

We have suggested that law dwelled at the intersection between the slave and post-slave era. It is thus worthwhile for us to examine what law meant during the long night of legal slavery, and how it survived in another incarnation into this post-slavery period.

It is difficult to locate the laws and decisions of this past era, including their context, even though there are massive digitized legal databases. Unfortunately, much of the flavor and spirit of the old days does not survive—and in some cases is simply irretrievable, as not all legal documents are included in these databases. Luckily for us (and you!), we've been able to locate, via the ancient artifact of books—on paper—statutes and cases that illustrate the cruelty, coldness, and veiled malice of the law, especially respecting those who sought its protection: the poor, the captive, the oppressed—the Africans. To be sure, American legislators didn't have to look far for inspiration for American law sought to implement ideas from the Roman imperial and civil law, with certain peculiarities—as a template upon which to protect the slave owners and the wealthy from legal challenge. They did so by a simple expediency: *Black people could not sue or be heard in U.S. Courts.*

George M. Stroud, a Philadelphia lawyer, compiled *Stroud's Slave Laws* shortly before the explosion of the Civil War. In the following passage, Stroud illustrates that most American lawyers and jurists looked to Rome for guidance:

> The civil law—except where modified by statute or by usages which have acquired the force of law—is generally referred to in the slave-holding states, as containing the true principles of this institution. It will be

> proper, therefore, to give an abstract of its leading doctrines; for which purpose, I use *Dr. Taylor's Elements of the Civil Law,* page 429: "Slaves," says he, "were held *pro nullis; pro mortius; pro quadrupedibus.* They had not head in the state, no name, title or register; they were not capable of being injured: nor could they take by purchase or descent: they had no heirs, and therefore could make no will: exclusive of what was called their *peculiam,* whatever they acquired was their master's; they could not plead nor be pleaded for, but were excluded from all civil concerns whatever; they could not claim the indulgence of absence *respublica causa;* they were not entitled to the rights and considerations of matrimony, and therefore, had no relief in case of adultery: nor were they proper objects of cognation or affinity, but of *quasi-cognation* only: they could be sold, transferred, or pawned as goods or personal estate; for goods they were, and as such they were esteemed: they might be tortured for evidence, punished at the discretion of their lord, or even put to death by his authority." This description is to be taken as applicable to the condition of slaves at an early period of the Roman history [before the fall of the Roman empire]...[19]

If one forgives the Latin references, the meaning can be gleaned simply enough. Slaves were, in essence, non-persons. Things. "Goods." Of no name, nor any human relation worthy of legal respect (that's what the term "cognation" means). But let us see what the actual law was, rather than the dry, Latin-heavy description offered in a tome on civil law.

Two generations before the Civil War, North Carolina's Supreme Court had occasion to recite the precise meaning of slavery in American life. The court's words are instructive:

> The end (of slavery) is the profit of the master, his security, and the public safety. The subject is one doomed in their own person and his posterity to live without knowledge and without the capacity to make any thing of his own, and to toil that another may reap the fruits. Such services can only be expected from one who has no will of his own [or] who surrenders his will in implicit obedience to that of another. The power of the master must be absolute to render the submission of the slave perfect. In the actual condition of things it must be so. There is no remedy. This discipline belongs to the state of slavery. They cannot be disunited without abrogating at once the rights of the master and absolving the slave from his subjection. It constitutes the curse of slavery to both the bond and free portions of

> our population; but it is inherent in the relation of master and slave.
> *The State (N.C.) vs. Mann,* 2 Devereux Rep. 263, 266 (1829).[20]

That was the law of the "republic of liberty." Consider, then, the worth of the life, or well being, of a captive in such a republic. Stroud from Philadelphia writes:

> Where the *life* of the slave is thus feebly protected, his *limbs,* as might be expected, share no better fare. I quote again from the act of 1746, of South Carolina, "In case any person shall willfully cut out the tongue, put out the eye, castrate, or *cruelly* scald, burn, or deprive any slave of any limb or member, or shall inflict *any other cruel punishment, other than by whipping or beating* with a *horsewhip,* cowskin, switch, or small stick, or *by putting irons on, or confirming or imprisoning such slave,* every person shall, for every such offense, forfeit the sum of one hundred pounds current money." [2 Brevard's Dig. 241]
>
> This section has, so far as I have been able to learn, been suffered to disgrace the statute-book from the year 1746 to the present hour. Amidst all the mutations which Christianity has effected within the last century, she has not been able to conquer the spirit which dictated this abominable law to say nothing of the trifling penalty for *mutilation,* what idea of humanity must a people entertain, who, by *direct legislation,* sanction the beating, *without limit,* of a fellow-creature with a *horsewhip or cowskin*— and the infliction of any torture which the ingenuity and malignity of man may invent, in the application of irons to the human body, and the perpetual incarceration, if the master so will, of the unfortunate slave, in a "dungeon-keep," however loathsome? Such, nevertheless, is the just interpretation of this law—a law too, which at that same time denominates these very acts, WHICH IT AUTHORIZES, *cruel* punishments.[21]

It should be noted that the law critiqued here by Stroud was a statute drafted to *protect* the slave. If this be law, then what could be illegal?

Many states in the region had similar laws, and to further isolate and dehumanize the African captives, laws forbade such persons from testifying—against whites. Virginia's statute read as follows: "Any negro or mulatto, bond or free, shall be a good witness in pleas of the commonwealth for or against negroes or mulattoes, bond or free, or in civil pleas where free negroes or mulattoes shall alone be parties, *and in no other cases whatever.*" Similar statutes could be found in Missouri, Mississippi, Alabama, Kentucky, Maryland, North Carolina, and Tennessee.[22]

What this meant in real life was that *all* Africans, ("bond or free"!), had no legal recourse for any injury done to them, when whites were the witnesses or perpetrators. What boundless crimes did laws such as these not protect? For, law it was—in name. Did it protect the defenseless? Did it prove justice for those who suffered from most rank injustice? Did it protect life? Yet, just as we continue to call "Indians" *Indians,* we also call the process of the most profound injustices "law," as if we are creatures more of habit than reason.

We are also taught that courts are places where injustices are redressed, despite a history that, quite frankly reflects the exact opposite. This may be seen in many ways, but let us examine slavery from the perspective of the highest court in the land, that "Court Supreme."

In the infamous Supreme Court case, *Dred Scott v. Sanford* (1857), Chief Justice Roger B. Taney wrote for the court majority, that Africans, *even if later free from bondage,* could never become citizens of the United States. The court's words have echoed through time, and time has turned those words into a source of shame for the institution. Taney wrote, in part:

> [The language, meaning and customs of the Declaration of Independence, reflected] [t]hat neither the class of persons who had been imported as slaves, nor their descendants, whether they had become free or not, were then acknowledged as a part of the people, nor intended to be included in the general words used in that instrument, [for] they had, for more than a century before been regarded as beings of an inferior race, and altogether unfit to associate with the white race, either in social or political relations, and so far inferior that they had no rights which the white man was bound to respect, and that the negro might justly and lawfully be reduced to slavery *for their benefit.*[23] [Emphasis added]

This is the law of white supremacy, one enshrined in the opinion of the highest court in the land. Opinions such as these, and the executive branch's fierce embrace of the Fugitive Slave Law, caused national consternation. These opinions, and others like them, inflamed people, especially in the free Black communities of the North.

Boston became a hotbed of abolitionist resistance to slavery, and the warped laws passed, with the courts and legislatures in support thereof. One such local abolitionist leader, Reverend Theodore Parker, a Unitarian minister, brought his oratory of fire and righteousness to the city's famed Faneuil Hall, speaking to a mass protest of the Fugitive Slave Law that made Bostonians accomplices in the crimes of slavery:

> Now, brethren, —you are brothers at any rate, whether citizens of Massachusetts or subjects of Virginia, - (I am a minister), and, fellow-citizens of Boston, there are two great laws in this country; one of them is the LAW OF SLAVERY; that law is declared to be a "finality." Once the Constitution was formed "to establish justice, promote tranquility, and secure the blessings of liberty to ourselves and our posterity." Now, the Constitution is not to secure liberty; it is to extend slavery into Nebraska; and, when slavery is established there, in order to show what it is, there comes a sheriff from Alexandria to kidnap a man in the city of Boston, and he gets a Judge of Probate, in the county of Suffolk, to issue a writ, and a Boston man to execute that writ! [cries of "shame, shame"].
>
> Slavery tramples on the Constitution; it treads down State rights. Where are the rights of Massachusetts? A Fugitive Slave Law Commissioner has got them all in his pocket. Where is the trial by jury? Watson Freeman has it under his Marshals staff. Where is the great right of personal replevin [a legal remedy in which a court requires the return of specific goods], which our fathers wrested, several hundred years ago, from the tyrants who once lorded it over Great Britain? Judge [Peleg] Sprague trod it under his feet! Where is the sacred right of habeas corpus? Deputy Marshal Riley can crush it in his hands, and Boston does not say anything against it. Where are the laws of Massachusetts forbidding state edifices to be used as prisons for the incarceration of fugitives? They, too, are trampled under foot. "Slavery is a finality."
>
> I say, there are two great laws in this country. One is the slave law: that is the law of the President of the United States; it is Senator [Stephen A.] Douglas's law; it is the law of the Supreme Court of the United States; it is the law of the Commissioner; it is the law of every Marshal, and of every meanest ruffian whom the Marshal hires to execute his behests. There is another law, which my friend, Mr. [Wendell] Phillips has described in language such as I cannot equal, and therefore shall not try; I only state it in its plainest terms. It is the law of the people, when they are sure they are right and determined to go ahead [cheers].[24]

This gives us some hint of the tenor and tone of the burgeoning resistance to the Slave Power (or "Slavocracy"—the powerful coalition of southern slave and plantation owners), and the government officials who turned a blind eye to it. Rev. Parker had his equal in many an American city (especially in the North), which looked with extreme disfavor to the southern stranglehold on the U.S. government, and the national laws in support of slavery. But, of course, resistance to the Slave Power—and slave law—did not end in the pulpit. It came from many in the community, Black and white alike—abolitionists in the foremost ranks of the opposition.

Few spoke with the fire and conviction of Frederick Douglass, an escaped captive from the Tidewater basin of Maryland. By stealth and cleverness he learned how to read, and he used his hard-earned knowledge to become the nation's foremost anti-slavery figure, and a voice that struck like lightning in the Slave South, sending his adversaries into conniption fits of fury. One of his most oft-quoted and best-remembered speeches was given in commemoration of the Fourth of July, the day celebrated throughout the country as a national holiday of liberty. Douglass spoke, but it was hardly what those who invited him wished to hear, for he came, not to praise American liberty, but to expose its innate spirit of *un*freedom. Douglass roared into American history:

> Fellow citizens, pardon me, allow me to ask, why am I called upon to speak here today? What have I, or those I represent, to do with your national independence? Are the great principles of political freedom and of natural justice, embodied in that Declaration of Independence, extended to us? And am I, therefore, called upon to bring out humble offering to the national alter, and to confess the benefits and express devout gratitude for the blessings resulting from your independence to us?
>
> Would to God, both for your sakes and ours, that an affirmative answer could be truthfully returned to these questions! Then would my task be light, and my burden easy and delightful. For who is there so cold, that a nation's sympathy could not warm him? Who so obdurate and dead to the claims of gratitude, that would not thankfully acknowledge such priceless benefits? We as stolid and selfish, that would not give his voice to swell the hallelujahs of a nation's jubilee, when the chains of servitude had been torn from his limbs? I am not that man...

> I say it with a sad sense of the disparity between us. I am not included within the pale of this glorious anniversary! Your high independence only reveals the immeasurable distance between us. The blessings in which you, this day, rejoice, are not enjoyed in common. The rich inheritance of justice, liberty, prosperity and independence, bequeathed by your fathers, is shared by you, not by me. The sunlight that brought lights and healing to you, has brought stripes and death to me. This Fourth of July is yours, not mine. You may rejoice, I must mourn. To drag a man in fetters into the grand illuminated temple of liberty, and call upon him to join you in joyous anthems, were inhuman mockery and sacrilegious irony. Do you mean, citizens, to mock me, by asking me to speak today? If so, there is a parallel to your conduct. And let me warn you that it is dangerous to copy the example of a nation whose crimes, towering up to heaven, were thrown down by the breath of the Almighty, burying that nation in irrevocable ruin! I can today take up the plaintive lament of a peeled and woe-smitten people![25]

In Douglass, the slavocracy had an implacable foe that knew them and opposed them more deeply than any of their white abolitionist foes in the North. For Douglass was driven, not by religious devotion, nor by simple moral opprobrium to "the peculiar institution" of slavery, but by the experiences of his very life—the feelings that tore at his very soul, and the horrors that seared him. He was, moreover, a brilliant orator, a skilled journalist and editor, and an abolitionist who could speak from a knowledge base that was virtually unassailable. For this, those forces of the Slave Power both hated and feared his noble voice.

He was not done. As he ended his historic speech of 5 July 1852, he hurled lightning bolts at his audience of patriotic worshipers of the flag, like the Yoruba god Ogun, by speaking with a truth that thundered down through centuries:

> At a time like this, scorching irony, not convincing argument, is needed. O! Had I the ability, and could reach the nation's ear, I would, today, pour out a fiery stream of biting ridicule, blasting reproach, withering sarcasm, and stern rebuke. For it is not light that is needed, but fire; it is not the gentle shower, but thunder. We need the storm, the whirlwind, and the earthquake. The feeling of the nation must be quickened: the conscience of the nation must be roused; and its crimes against God and man must be proclaimed and denounced.
>
> What, to the American slave, is your 4th of July? I answer; a day that reveals to him, more than all other days of the year, the gross

> injustice and cruelty to which he is the constant victim. To him, your celebration is a sham; your boasted liberty, an unholy license; your national greatness, swelling vanity; your sounds of rejoicing are empty and heartless; your mockery; your prayers and hymns, your sermons and thanksgivings, with all your religious parade and solemnity, are, to him, mere bombast, fraud, deception, impiety, and hypocrisy—a thin veil to cover up crimes which would disgrace a nation of savages. There is not a nation on the earth guilty of practices more shocking and bloody than are the people of the United States, at this very hour.
>
> Go, where you may, search where you will, roam through all the monarchies and despotisms of the Old World, travel through South America, search out every abuse, and when you have found at last, lay your facts by the side of the everyday practices of this nation, and you will say with me, that, for revolting barbarity and shameless hypocrisy, America reigns without a rival.[26]

Douglass gave voice to the muffled mouths of millions.

Douglass, born Frederick Augustus Bailey, upon his escape from captivity, took the name Douglass, and to distinguish himself, added the additional "s." Although he is now regarded as one of the greatest Black national leaders produced by Black America, his worth was recognized soon after his escape, and he ascended to the top ranks of the nascent abolitionist movement.

In what must be a remarkable document of the era, the *Rochester Democrat and Chronicle* (N.Y.) of 18 June 1879, named him as "among the greatest men, not only of this city, but of the nation as well—great in gifts, greater in utilizing them, great in his purpose that inspired it."[27]

Douglass, despite the tortuous conditions of his birth, life, and challenges of American captivity, was a man of extraordinary breadth and largeness of heart. He stood for freedom against slavery, to be sure. But he also stood on behalf of all oppressed: women, struggling workers in England, Scotland, Ireland and beyond. In an 1846 letter to *The Liberator* newspaper, Douglass noted:

> [T]hough I am more closely connected and identified with one class of outraged, oppressed and enslaved people, I cannot allow myself to be insensible to the wrongs and suffering of any part of the great family of men. I am not only an American Slave, but a man, and as

such, am bound to use my powers for the welfare of the whole human brotherhood... I believe that the sooner the wrongs of the whole human family are made known, the sooner those wrongs will be reached.[28]

While this escaped American captive had a deep and broad heart for suffering humanity, he spared no effort to attack and criticize the blatant hypocrisy and sheer will of the Slave Power. He did so for decades, using pen, book, newspaper, and tongue. In 1850, giving a speech in upstate New York, Douglass unleashed his brilliant and burning tongue—an oration more sermon on the mount than political speech:

> You hurl your anathemas at the crowned headed tyrants of Russia and Austria and pride yourselves on your Democratic institutions, while you yourselves consent to be the mere *tools and body-guards* of the tyrants of Virginia and Carolina. You invite to your shores fugitives of oppression from abroad, honor them with banquets, great with ovations, cheer them, toast them, salute them, protect them, and pour out your money to them like water; but the fugitives from your own land you advertise, hunt, arrest, shoot, and kill. You glory in your refinement and your universal education; yet you maintain a system as barbarous and dreadful as ever stained the character of a nation—a system begun in avarice, supported in pride, and perpetuated in cruelty. You shed tears over fallen Hungary, and make the sad story of her wrongs the theme of your poets, statesmen and orators, till your gallant sons are ready to fly to arms to vindicate her cause against the oppressor; but, in regard to the ten thousand wrongs of the American slave, you would enforce the strictest silence, and would hail him as an enemy of this nation who dares to make those wrongs the subject of public discourse!
>
> You are all on fire at the mention of liberty for the enslaved in America. You discourse eloquently on the dignity of labor; yet you sustain a system which, in its very essence, casts a stigma upon labor. You can bare your bosom to the storm of British artillery to throw off a three-penny tax on tea; and yet wring the last hard-earned farthing from the grasp of the black laborers of your country. You profess to believe 'that, of one blood, God made all nations of men to dwell upon the face of the earth,' and hath commanded all men, everywhere, to love one another; yet you notoriously hate (and glory in your hatred) all men whose skins are not colored like your own. You declare before the world, and are understood by the world to declare that you *"hold these truths to be self-evident, that all*

> *men are created equal; and are endowed by their Creator with certain inalienable rights; and that among these are, life, liberty, and the pursuit of happiness"* and yet you hold securely, in a bondage which, according to your own Thomas Jefferson, "*is worse than ages of that which your fathers rose in rebellion to oppose,"* a seventh part of the inhabitants of your country.
>
> Fellow-citizens, I will not enlarge further on your national inconsistencies. The existence of slavery in this country brands your republicanism as a sham, your humanity as a base pretense, and your Christianity as a lie. It destroys your moral power abroad; it corrupts your politicians at home. It saps the foundation of religion; it makes your name a hissing and a bye-word to a mocking earth. It is the antagonistic force in your government, the only thing that seriously disturbs and endangers your *union.* It fetters your progress; it is the enemy of improvement; the deadly foe of education; it fosters pride; it breeds insolence; it promotes vice; it shelters crime; it is a curse to the earth that supports it; and yet you cling to it as if it were the sheet anchor of all your hopes.
>
> Oh! Be warned! A horrible reptile is coiled up in your nation's bosom; the venomous creature is nursing at the breast of your youthful republic; *for the love of God, tear away* and fling from you the hideous monster, and *let the weight of twenty millions crush and destroy it forever!*[29]

Douglass used his eloquent opposition not only to lash out at slavery, but in his fierce criticism of what he saw as Lincoln's diffidence about using African troops in the Civil War. He likened it to Lincoln fighting a war with one arm tied behind his back. When Lincoln relented and ordered the formation of the U.S. Colored Troops, it marked a turning point in the War, and a break in American history. Yet, still Douglass did not relent.

Ever the radical, ever in support of a social and political revolution, Douglass criticized Lincoln's behavior as a Commander-in-Chief of the Armies, when it came to the shameful treatment of Black soldiers. As Black historian-scholar, Lerone Bennett has noted, in his own work of criticism, *Forced into Glory*:

> Since Lincoln didn't seem to be serious about these matters, Douglass came out against his re-nomination, saying that the so-called emancipation was a fraud and that Lincoln was neither an emancipator nor a great leader. In a letter to an English supporter, dated June 1864, he denounced Lincoln's betrayal of the spirit of emancipation

and charged that Lincoln and his hand-picked military commanders were 'practically re-establishing' the slave system in Louisiana.

> Douglass's bill of indictment against Lincoln was long, and personal: 'The treatment of our poor black soldiers—the refusal to pay them anything like equal compensation though it was promised them when they enlisted; the refusal to insist upon the exchange of colored prisoners when colored prisoners have been slaughtered in cold blood, although the President has repeatedly promised this to protect the lives of his colored soldiers—have worn my patience threadbare. The President has virtually laid down this as the rule of his statesmen: Do evil by choice, right by necessity."[30]

When anti-Lincoln General George McClellan was nominated by the Democrats on a pro-slavery platform, Douglass, albeit reluctantly, came over to Lincoln's side. Douglass was in his ear, remaining a distinctive and powerful voice of the voiceless; and use his voice, he did. Yet, while he gave all he could to support the fight for freedom, he was not alone. The passions unleashed by the horrors, terrors, and mass violence of slavery moved many people beyond their fears, and into the warm sunlight of resistance. Many, many people found ways to revolt with their feet, by simply fleeing the slavocracy.

As we have seen, Douglass was a prominent member of the tribe. There were, of course, others who had different voices, reflecting similar viewpoints. One voice was that of Jourdan Anderson, a former captive who rose from the very nexus between freedom and slavery. Anderson, with whimsy and a touch of tongue-in-cheek, crafted a letter in reply to that from his former owner, Colonel P. H. Anderson of Big Spring, Tennessee. Jourdan Anderson wrote the following:

> Dayton, Ohio
> August 7, 1865
>
> To My Old Master, Colonel P. H. Anderson, Big Spring, Tennessee
>
> Sir: I got your letter, and was glad to find that you had not forgotten Jourdan, and that you wanted me to come back and live with you again, promising to do better for me than anybody else can. I have often felt uneasy about you. I thought the Yankees would have hung you long before this, for harboring Rebs they found at your house. I supposed they never heard about you going to Colonel Martin's to kill the Union soldier that was left by his company in their stable. Although you shot me twice

before I left you, I did not want to hear of your being hurt, and am glad you are still living. It would do me good to go back to the dear old home again, and see Miss Mary and Miss Martha and Allison, Ester, Green, and Lee. Give my love to them all, and tell them I hope we will meet in the better world, if not in this. I would have gone back to see you all when I was working in the Nashville Hospital, but one of the neighbors told me that Henry had intended to shoot me if he ever got the chance.

I want to know particularly what the good chance is you propose to give me. I am doing tolerably well here. I get twenty-five dollars a month, and victuals and clothing, have a comfortable home for Mandy—the folks call her Mrs. Anderson,—and the children—Hilly, Jane and Grundy—go to school and are learning well. The teacher says Grundy has a head for a preacher. They go to Sunday school, and Mandy and me attend Church regularly. We are kindly treated. Sometimes we overhear others saying, 'Them colored folks were slaves' down in Tennessee. The children feel hurt when they hear such remarks; but I tell them it was no disgrace in Tennessee to belong to Colonel Anderson. Many darkeys would have been proud, as I used to be, to call you master. Now if you will write me and say what wages you will give me, I will be better able to decide whether it would be to my advantage to move back again.

As to my freedom, which you say I can have, there is nothing to be gained on that score, as I got my free papers in 1864 from the Provost-Marshal-General of the Department of Nashville. Mandy says she would be afraid to come back without some proof that you were disposed to treat us justly and kindly; and we have concluded to test your sincerity by asking you to send us our wages from the time we served you. This will make us forget and forgive old scores, and rely on your justice and friendship in the future. I served you faithfully for thirty-two years, and Mandy twenty years. At twenty-five dollars a month for me, and two dollars a week for Mandy, our earning would amount to eleven thousand six hundred and eighty dollars. Add to this the interest for the time our wages have been kept back, and deduct what you paid for our clothing, and three doctor's visits to me, and pulling a tooth from Mandy, and the balance will show what we are in justice entitled to. Please send the money by Adam's Express, in care of V. Winters, Esq., Dayton, Ohio. If you fail to pay us for the faithful labors in the past, we can have little faith in your promise in the future. We trust the good Maker has opened your eyes to the wrongs which you and your fathers have done to me and my fathers, in making us toil for you for generations without recompense. Here I draw my wages every Saturday night, but in Tennessee there was never any pay-day for the negroes any more than for the horses and cows. Surely there will be a day of reckoning for those who defraud the laborer of his hire.

In answering this letter, please state if there would be any safety for my Jill and Jane, who now grown up, and both good-looking girls. You know how it was with poor Matilda and Catherine. I would rather stay here and starve—and die, if it come to that—than have my girls brought to shame by the violence and wickedness of their young masters. You will also please state if there has been any schools opened for the colored children in your neighborhood. The great desire of my life now is to give my children an education, and have them form virtuous habits.

Say howdy to George Carter, and thank him for taking the pistol from you when you were shooting at me.

From your old servant,
Jourdan Anderson[31]

Anderson was writing at the dramatic, earth-shattering dénouement of the Civil War, when the nation, through its Constitution, and its feat of arms (Black arms, in significant measures, we might add) spelled an end to the Slave Power. He thus felt confident that the horrid old days were over, forever. He did not foresee, that within a relatively short period of years, North and South would reconcile over the bones of white supremacy. In fact, both North and South put Anderson and his fellow abolitionists, who were departing the field with the fife and drum of victory resounding, on notice regarding their presumed victory—a victory history proved Potemkin. Douglass hurled his own omen to history as well:

> Slavery has been fruitful in giving itself names. It has been called "the peculiar institution," "the social system," and the "impediment." It has been called by a great many names, and it will call itself by yet another name: and you and I and all of us had better wait and see what new form this old monster will assume, in what new skin this old snake will come forth next.[32]

What new skin, indeed?

❖❖❖

6 The American Revolution:
Who Won? Who Lost?

Who doesn't know the story of the American Revolution?

When we were children in elementary school the lesson was repeatedly and deeply imbedded in the mind. The lessons of our childhood teaching continue to resonate within us, like peals of a bell rung long ago:

- George Washington is the father of our country.
- The American Revolution was fought to break the ties of English tyranny and to secure the freedom of all men.
- The Constitution created by our founders was written to protect, extend, and be the guarantor of those freedoms.

That is not just the stuff of our distant childhood. We continue to make such proclamations today that fill the sails of our national rhetoric in Washington, D.C., or in state capitals, in our professional press—and beyond.

But like children's dreams of Santa Claus, these dancing sugarplums cannot sustain us when we learn the truth. For centuries, teachers have stood before classes (of both children and adults) regurgitating these national myths, cramming it into the minds of millions. If that is your inclination, and you wish to remain in slumber, kindly pass over this chapter, for that is not our view.

A People's Almanac?

We are both students of history, to be sure, but we look at it from a completely different perspective, one learned and deepened under the influence of Howard

Zinn, perhaps the preeminent historian of the last quarter of the 20th century, who was an advocate (and avatar) of the idea now known as "history from below."

Zinn, who came to teaching history late, had the advantage of seeing and learning how the world really works, not from the front of a classroom, stuffed with dusty texts, but as a shipyard worker, as a bombardier during the close of World War II, and later, at Spelman College, in Atlanta, Georgia, amid the fire and chaos of the Civil Rights Movement. Born into a poor, Jewish immigrant family in New York, he lived his pre-college life as a member of that broad swath of humanity known as underdogs, and he never lost that perspective.

After he left the Air Force, armed with the GI Bill, he went to Columbia and earned his Ph.D., but the grit of Brooklyn remained in his voice, under his fingernails, and in his great, capacious heart. His masterwork, *A People's History of the United States: 1492-Present,* was a runaway best-seller, and continues to be the balm of young folks unlearned in true American history, as well as the bane of American nationalists and imperialists, for it breaks dangerous new ground.

Because of Zinn's upbringing, his class-consciousness, and the horrors he beheld in the war, he never lost sight of the average, everyday people of the world. His take on the initial drama of the American experience is therefore founded on the dual groundings of humanism and truth, the latter of which could be characterized in part as the rejection of rhetoric. So, who waged the American Revolution—in fact, not in rhetoric? We might invoke the spirit of Zinn's pursuit of historical truth by asking the age-old question: who built the pyramids of Egypt? For immediately, the most learned amongst us might reply, and with some authority, that they were built by the Pharaoh Khufu (perhaps more commonly known by his Hellenized named, Cheops), of the IVth Dynasty (ca. 2680 BCE). Yet, Zinn would ask, "Did he lay the bricks?"

Seen from this light, Zinn never loses focus on the many people—men, women, indigenous, immigrant, Angolan, poor, working class, soldier, radical—who did the scut-work, the real work, that made America possible—and, moreover, tried to forge a newer, better, more just America. That focus, we freely confess, has not been the majority mode of discourse, nor near enough central to the telling of the story of what America was and is.

We endeavor to do so here.

That said, let us make a thumbnail sketch of the revolution as it is commonly and broadly understood, to at least orient ourselves on the subject. To do this we cite the widely read *World Almanac* to give their short version of this momentous conflict:

> **American Revolution.** The British colonies in North America attracted a mass immigration of religious dissenters and poor people throughout the 17th and 18th cent., coming from the British Isles, Germany, the Netherlands, and other countries. The population reached 3 million non-natives by the 1770s. The indigenous population was greatly reduced by European diseases and by wars with the various colonies. British attempts to control colonial trade and to tax the colonists to pay for the costs of colonial administration and defense clashed with local self-government and eventually provoked the colonies to a successful rebellion.[1]

As far as it goes, we are forced to admit, that the writers, editors, and fact checkers of the Almanac did a pretty good job here. Notice their reference to "poor people." This is a fact.

As far as it goes.

Few (if any) schools provide students with the *World Almanac* (even though millions of people read items from it annually), yet we must remember that it does not depart from the traditional view. In short, it does not—unlike those millions of people from Britain and Germany—dissent.

One more point in its favor, is its reference to taxes—the trigger of the revolution, so to speak. Yet it does not tell us of the many, many mini-revolutions that tore throughout the colonies, a point that Zinn tells with force and feeling.

For revolutions never just spring into being, like dew on a spring meadow. Revolutions have roots, deep wells of discontent, and conflict. People resort to the revolutionary option when there are no more doors open to them.

In pre-revolutionary America, life was hard, traumatic, and frightfully unequal. Howard Zinn, speaking to a legion of students at Portland, Oregon's Reed College in 1995, gives us some taste of the forces brewing in the colonies: not against the British, so much, as against the rich Americans who dwelled amongst them:

> I remember going to school my impression was that those people who came from England all dressed in the same simple way. It was a very

> egalitarian society, and they signed the Mayflower Compact, which proved it. But no. In fact, there were people who came here as Black slaves, and other people who came here as indentured servants, large numbers of women came as you might say servants and sex slaves to serve the men who were already here, the labor force that had to be satisfied in some way. Others came here with enormous grants of land given by the king or Parliament. So from the beginning there were very rich and very poor. That pattern continued all through American history. The poor resisted and rebelled. There were slave rebellions and servant rebellions, and the poor of the colonies rioted. The flour riots, the bread riots. The people attacked the warehouses where the flour was stored, flour that was not being made available to them because they couldn't afford the prices that were being charged for the flour. They stormed and opened up the warehouses and took the flour so they would make bread and feed their families. Riots against impressment, because they were being impressed to fight the wars of the British in the last seventeenth and eighteenth centuries. This was all before the American Revolution. Tenant Insurrections against landlords. Crowds marching to jails and freeing the prisoners who had been imprisoned because of failure to pay their debts.[2]

Riots? Food riots? Bread riots? Before the revolution? Who knew? Who taught this? (Besides Howard, that is.)

Before the Tea Party

The answer, of course, is that few history teachers have taught this—certainly not at the primary education level where children learn the fundamentals of their nation's history. Doubtless, some of those children were taught to memorize The Stamp Act, but few of them (or us) can really recall its significance.

The Stamp Act was one of many taxes imposed on the colonies to recoup the serious economic losses of the so-called French and Indian War (1763), which was actually a war between the French and the British (the French lost). With the war over, the British passed the Stamp Act, which required all publications and legal documents to bear such a stamp, the cost of which constituted a tax, which of course riled the increasingly individualist American colonists. Thomas Hutchinson, lieutenant governor of Massachusetts, saw first-hand the rage the stamp lit among colonial populations. He wrote a contemporary account of the upheaval that illustrates how hated and resisted it was:

The distributor of stamps for the colony of Connecticut (Jared Ingersoll) arrived in Boston from London; and, having been agent for that colony, and in other respects of a very reputable character, received from many gentlemen of the town such civilities as were due to him. When he set out for Connecticut, Mr. (Andrew) Oliver, the distributor for Massachusetts Bay, accompanied him out of town. This occasioned murmuring among the people, and an inflammatory piece in the next Boston Gazette. A few days after, early in the morning, a stuffed image was hung upon a tree, called the great tree of the south part of Boston (subsequently called the Liberty Tree)...

Before night, the image was taken down, and carried through the townhouse, in the chamber whereof the governor and council were sitting. Forty or fifty tradesmen, decently dressed, preceded; and some thousands of the mob down King Street to Oliver's dock, near which Mr. Oliver had lately erected a building, which, it was conjectured, he designed for a stamp office. This was laid flat to the ground in a few minutes. From thence the mob proceeded for Fort Hills, but Mr. Oliver's house being in the way, they endeavored to force themselves into it, and being opposed, broke the windows, beat down the doors, entered, and destroyed part of his furniture, and continued in riot until midnight, before they separated...

Several of the council gave it as their opinion, Mr. Oliver being present, that the people, not only of the town of Boston, but of the country in general, would never submit to the execution of the stamp act, that the people of Connecticut had threatened to hang their distributor on the first tree after he entered the colony; and that, to avoid it, he had turned aside to Rhode-Island. Despairing of protection, and finding his family in terror and great distress, Mr. Oliver came to a sudden resolution to resign his office before another night...

The next evening, the mob surrounded the house of the lieutenant-governor and chief justice (Hutchinson's own home). He was at Mr. Oliver's house when it was assaulted, and had excited the sheriff, and the colonel of the regiment, to attempt to suppress the mob. A report was soon spread, that he was a favourer of the stamp act, and had encouraged it by letters to the ministry. Upon notice of the approach of the people, he caused the doors and windows to be barred; and remained in the house...

> Certain depositions had been taken, many months before these transactions by order of the governor, concerning the illicit trade carrying on; and one of them, made by the judge of the admiralty, at the special desire of the governor, had been sworn to before the lieutenant-governor, as their chief justice. They had been shown, at one of the offices in England, to a person who arrived in Boston just at this time, and he had acquainted several merchants, whose names were in some of the depositions as smugglers, with the contents. This brought, though without reason, the resentments of the merchants against the persons who, by their office, were obliged to administer the oaths, as well against the officers of the customs and admiralty, who had made the depositions; and the leaders of the mob contrived a riot, which, after some small efforts against such officers, was to spend its principal force upon the lieutenant-governor. And, in the evening of the 26th of August, such a mob was collected in King Street, drawn there by the bonfire, and well supplied with strong drink. After some annoyance to the house of the registrar of the admiralty, and somewhat greater to that of the comptroller of the customs, whose cellars they plundered of the wine and spirits in them, they came, with intoxicated rage upon the house of the lieutenant-governor. The doors were immediately split to pieces with broad axes, and a way made there, and at the windows, for the entry of the mob; which poured in, and filled, in an instant, every room in the house.[3]

Hutchinson here speaks of himself, in the style of the day. His house wasn't just trashed: he ordered his family to evacuate the home and resolved to stand against the mob, but his daughter talked him out of the dangerous notion by swearing to stay with him unless he joined the rest of the family. His house was stripped, and the articles with which it was furnished were ripped off the walls, hurled into the streets, burned, or stolen.

These Stamp Act protests took place eight years before the better-remembered Boston Tea Party. *Eight years.* This should give us some sense of how fervent the ferment was against not merely the Brits, but their agents and abettors among the colonists who supported taxes levied by the crown and parliament.

In a Frequent State of Rage

The Stamp Act was ugly, it was angry, and it reflected the antipathy of the colonists against the British on the one hand, and the Tories among them who wanted to continue their colonial relationship with the so-called mother country, England. Those many of us who were marred by the traditional histories taught to American schoolchildren were taught that Americans were united in their resistance to the British.

Nothing could be further from the truth. Again, we turn to Zinn to give us a deeper, and broader view:

> From the very beginning this country has not been a country of common interests. We have been a country driven by class conflict. It was not *we the people* who created the Constitution of the United States. It was fifty-five rich white men in Philadelphia who did. They did not do so for the benefit of the majority of the people in the colonies, they did it for the benefit of the elite who were going to replace the British elite in running the new independent government. They did it for the benefit of the bondholders, the slaveowners, the merchants, and the land expansionists.[4]

Zinn reminds us that things were seldom as presented in our safe, childlike history, painted in soft pastel colors. Pre-revolutionary America was a land deeply divided, along many lines:

> Before the Revolution there were food riots and slave rebellions and tenant uprisings. From 150 years before the Revolution this country has been filled with these conflicts between the rich and poor. During the Revolution, which is presented in schools as unified colonists fighting heroically for independence against England, the country was divided.[5]

Zinn, in his distinctive, conversational tone, provides us some valuable insight into the times that were, when the poor were in a frequent state of rage against the moneyed interests that took more and more in taxes for a government that served to alienate them from their very lands. This helps to explain the antipathy revealed in the anti-tax protests in the north. Let us recall Mr. Hutchinson's observation that:

> [T]he people, not only of the town of Boston, but of the country in general, would never submit to the execution of the stamp act...

These people didn't hate the taxes because they came from "Mother England"—they hated the taxes because they were often desperately poor and could ill afford to pay them. They looked with loathing and contempt at those who were wealthy, and that deep-seated anger and hatred was known, felt, and understood, by all who had eyes.

As we shall see, those feelings would effect not only the pre-revolutionary period, but also the composition and tenor of the Revolution itself. Popular rebellions weren't so much against Britain as they were against the wealthy and well-to-do. And the people also looked askance at their local and regional officials, and demanded that they take their side—the people's side. This can be seen clearly in the actions written about by Joseph Clarke of Massachusetts, who, in an August 1774 letter to a friend, revealed the power and will of the Crowd over their judicial and local government officials:

> We arrived in town about noon this day and found all the people gathered before us. A committee from the body of the county had just waited upon the court to demand a satisfactory answer, that is, whether they meant to hold their commissions and exercise their authority according to the new act of parliament for altering the constitution of the province, which being answered in the negative, it was put to a vote after the Sd [said] message and answer were read to the people assembled before the meeting house, whether they were willing the Court should sit; it passed in the negative.
>
> Then the people paraded before Mr. Parson's (Landlord Parsons), from thence marched back again to the meeting-house and demanded the appearance of the judges. The judges came according to their desire, and amidst the Crowd in a sandy, sultry place exposed to the sun as far as they were able in such circumstances gave a reasonable, and, to the major part, a satisfactory answer to such questions as were asked.
>
> It was also demanded of them that they should make a declaration, in writing, signed by all the justices and lawyers of the County, renouncing in the most express terms any commission which should be given out to them or either of them under the new arrangement, which was immediately complied with and executed accordingly.
>
> The People then reassembled before Mr. Parson's house...(Major) Catlin falling into a personal quarrel, at length gained the attention of the people. They considered him as an object worthy of their malice, as he was an officer of the court. He was treated with candor and too mildly to make any complaint. His boasted heroism failed him in the day of trial, and vanished like a puf(f) of smo(ke). He and O(liver) Warner, who came to his assistance in the quarrel, made such declarations as were requested of them, and then were dismissed, unhurt, and in

peace. Your uncle may say what he pleases with regard to their abuse of him, but I was an eye witness to the whole, and you I believe will be satisfied that no abuse was intended when I tell you what easy terms they requested and were satisfied with, namely, only a declaration that he would not hold any office under the new act of parliament.

Col. (John) Worthington was next brought upon the board. The sight of him flashed lightening from their eyes. Their spirits were already raised and the sight of this object gave them additional force. He had not refused his new office of counselor. For that reason especially he was very obnoxious. But the people kept their tempers. He attempted to harangue them in mitigation of his conduct, but he was soon obliged to desist. The people were not to be dallied with. Nothing would satisfy them but a renunciation in writing of this office as Counselor and a recantation of his address to Gov. (Thomas) Gage, which last was likewise signed by Jona(than) Bliss and Caleb Strong....

Jonathan Bliss next came upon the floor, he was very humble and the people were very credulous. He asked their pardon for all he had said or done which was contrary to their opinions; and as he depended for his support upon the people, he begged to stand well in their favor.

Mr. Moses Bliss was brought into the ring, but the accusation against his was not well supported and he passed off in silence. The Sheriff was the next who was demanded; he accordingly appeared. He was charged with saying some imprudent things, but none of them were proved, and he departed. But he was humbled. Col (Israel) Williams took the next turn. He went around the ring and vindicated himself from some accusations thrown upon him and denied some things that were laid to his charge.

He declared in my hearing that "altho he had heretofore differed from the people in opinion with regard to the mode of obtaining redress, he would, hereafter, heartily acquiesce in any measures, that they should take for that purpose, and join with them in the common cause. He considered his interest as embarked in the same bottom with theirs, and hoped to leave it in peace to his Children."

Capt. (James) Merrick of Munson was next treated with for uttering imprudent expressions. I thought they would have tarred and feathered him, and I thought he almost deserved it. He was very stubborn,

> as long as he dare be, but at length he made some concessions. But not till after they had carted him. No man received the least injury, but the strictest order of justice was observed. The people to their honor behaved with the greatest order and regularity, a few individuals excepted, and avoided, as much as possible, confusion.
>
> The people of each town being drawn into separate companies marched with staves and musick. The trumpets sounding, drums beating, fifes playing and colours flying, struck the passions of the soul into a proper tone, and inspired martial courage into each.[6]

This is, to our minds, a remarkable passage. For it shows us not just the people in a state of rage at their leaders, but a people united in opposition to them.

But it does more.

It shows a kind of direct democracy at work to control and censure the works of their "betters." It shows the People working to make sure that those who claim to rule, serve *their* interests—not those of the Crown—or Parliament.

What "new act of parliament" was the Crowd resisting? It may be that the People were incensed by an act signed into English law in March-May of that year, called the "Intolerable Acts," designed to punish Boston after the Boston Tea Party (December 1773), in which three shiploads of tea were thrown overboard into the Boston Harbor in protest of taxes on the beverage. According to Parliament's new decree, the Boston Harbor was blocked to all outgoing international transit, those charged with involvement in the "tea party" were to be tried in England, and the charter of Massachusetts was repealed.[7]

Joseph Clarke's letter to a friend gives us some important insight into how some segments of the colonial population viewed their—we hesitate to use the term—"political leaders" during the pre-revolutionary period, and to say it was quite unflattering is understatement. It shows us that for many, many generations, people have viewed their governments with distaste, and perhaps more importantly, with distrust.

All of the significant indications are there in language and action. Demands to explain their positions, and written, signed documents stating their opposition to the taxes and laws of Mother Country England's Parliament. One can only with great difficulty see similar interactions with politicians of the present era, although the enmity and distrust of government has been growing by leaps and bounds since the quiescent '50s (*nineteen*-50s, that is).

During Clarke's generation, it might be safe to say that no local or regional politician (almost all of whom, we should be reminded, were either appointed by, or sworn to, the Crown) was really trusted by the common, working people.

That is certainly the flavor of his document.

Reunion with the Parent State?

If the common, working people had little trust for their leadership, how did the higher-ups view the people? As they were, more often than not, the literate, moneyed, and propertied classes, their narratives and accounts have survived from the period in remarkable abundance. Even so, they are largely searched by scholars, who, depending on their bent, censor, or shall we say, "underreport" the tone of many of their private writings.

Again, we must turn to Zinn, whose works highlight some of these private communications, and provide us with an insight that casts a far different light upon the pre-revolutionary, revolutionary, and post-revolutionary years in America.

We shall here cite briefly from a lengthy letter written by a U.S. artillery commander to George Washington, about the dangerous uprisings happening around the country, post-Revolution (1786):

> (T)hey [i.e. the rebel colonists] see the weakness of Government(,) they feel at once their own poverty compared with the opulent, and their own force, and they are determined to make use of the latter in order to remedy the former. Their creed is that the property of the United States has been protected from the confiscations of Britain by the full exertions of all, and therefore ought to be the common property of all.[8]

This letter, from General Henry Knox, writing to this former commander, General Washington, was a quiet alarm at the heart of the new government. It was a whisper that was meant to move the wealthy classes to discipline the poor. Think of his saying in a more recent example and contemporary parlance: "Hey, George! We're threatened by pre-communism! These scumbags think they've got a right to our stuff!"

That's certainly the spirit of the message.

But Knox was far from alone, for in the highest levels of government, there was considerable trembling and lack of sleep. Let us consider the words and views of the revered Founding Fathers of the American Revolution as they met in secret (with windows boarded up, so that the "rabble" wouldn't see them) in Philadelphia, writing the Constitution. One of those present left no doubt of his views. Alexander Hamilton famously said, when someone referred to "the people": "The people, sir, are a great beast."[9] Do you really think he cared about "the people?" Of Hamilton, the Columbia Encyclopedia notes in part:

> As secretary of the treasury (1789-95) under Pres. Washington, Hamilton sponsored legislation to pay off the debt of the Continental Congress and to charter the Bank Of The United States. To raise revenue he advocated a tariff on imported manufactures and excise taxes. By these measures he hoped to strengthen the federal government and tie it to persons of wealth.[10]

Hamilton was hardly alone in his preference for the propertied, for quite a few of these wealthy lawyers who sat down in 1787 Philadelphia to pen a constitution, even wanted to shop around for some royal blood to rule these unruly Americans.

Delaware's delegate to the Philadelphia convention, James Dickinson, who signed the Constitution, simply refused to sign the Declaration of Independence. Why? Because he was a monarchist. Nathaniel Gorham, of Massachusetts, wanted to seat a royal on the American throne so much that he secretly conducted a correspondence with people in Europe to find someone to take the scepter of power. Hamilton, of New York, admired monarchy. William Samuel Johnson, sitting for Connecticut, was described as "the nearest thing to an aristocrat in mind and manner." This lawyer never supported the War of Independence simply because he couldn't "conscientiously" come to battle against England. George Read, a wealthy lawyer who represented Delaware was described as one who "lived in the style of colonial gentry." Delegate Read wanted all states abolished, and the presidency would be for life, with absolute veto power over any other government authority.[11]

These are some of the venerable Founders.

Gouverneur Morris (1752-1816), although born in Morrisania, New York, represented Pennsylvania at the convention, and had a hand in the writing of the Constitution. Of the tolling masses outside the shrouded walls of the convention, Morris pondered with dread: "The mob begins to think and to reason... I see and see with fear and trembling, that if the disputes with Britain continue, we shall be under the domination of a riotous mob. It is to the interest of all men therefore, to seek reunion with the parent state."[12]

Wait. Did you read that? "Reunion." "The mob." Who do you think this guy was siding with? The foreign dictator, King George III; or the People?

These are revolutionaries? Or were they politicians, riding the tiger of popular discontent, and trying to wedge a bit in its mouth—the better to control it and direct it? For, how can you represent someone, if you fear them?

These are some of the venerable Founders.

Their interests and arguments could not be further from those expressed in the country at large, which groaned under the avarice of the tax collectors and privileged classes. At one of the scores of illegal conventions held around the colonies, where men (mostly men, anyway) gave voice to their material anguish, and their enmity at the non-representative legislatures, one Plough Jogger said the following:

> I've labored hard all my days and fared hard. I have been greatly abused, have been obliged to do more than my part in the war; been loaded with class rates, town rates, province rates, Continental rates, and all rates... been pulled and hauled by sheriffs, constables and collectors, and had my cattle sold for less than they were worth. I have been obliged to pay and nobody will pay me. I have lost a great deal by this man and that man and t'other man, and the great men are going to get all we have, and I think it is time for us to rise up and put a stop to it, and have no more courts, nor sheriffs, nor collectors, nor lawyers, and I know that we are the biggest party, let them say what they will... We've come to relieve the distresses of the people. There will be no court until they have redress of our grievances.[13]

Revolutions are funny things. When they begin, no one really knows where they will end, for the forces unleashed thereby can run in many and sundry directions, often far afield from those who claim to have started them. The propaganda crafted by pro-Revolutionary journalist and pamphleteer, Thomas Paine, brought such ridicule to the English Crown, that many, many people had lost their former reverence for the very notion of kings. But the voices like those of Plough Jogger, a poor farmer, were being echoed in other colonies, provinces, and states, in public conventions and gatherings that drew hundreds and thousands of people. And people like him, in agreement with his antipathy against the government, literally closed down courts, and called judges before them to explain themselves.

Now this was revolutionary.

Elsewhere, in another context, we have noted the treatment of American soldiers of the Revolutionary War. But after hearing the voices of the opulent leaders of the revolutionary (that is to say, its political leaders), perhaps a brief portion of the written recollections of an actual soldier might be in order. Joseph Plumb Martin was such a man, and his comments, though more than 200 years old, have a tone and ring that, with updates to linguistic style, would fit neatly in today's post-war discussions about the inevitable betrayal of the young by their elders—especially the wealthy, connected, politicians who work so feverishly to declare wars. Joseph Plumb Martin wrote:

> When those who engaged to serve during the war enlisted, they were promised a hundred acres of land, each, which was to be in their or the adjoining states. When the country had drained the last drop of service it could screw out of the poor soldiers, they were turned adrift like old worn-out horses, and nothing said about land to pasture them upon. Congress did, indeed, appropriate lands under the designation of "Soldier's Lands," in Ohio state, or some state, or a future state, but no care was taken that the soldiers should get them. No agents were appointed to see that the poor fellows ever got possession of their lands; no one ever took the least care about it, except a pack of speculators, who were driving about the country like so many evil spirits, endeavoring to pluck the last feather from the soldiers. The soldiers were ignorant of the ways and means to obtain their bounty lands, and there was no one appointed to inform them. The truth was, none cared for them; the country was served, and faithfully served, and that was all that was deemed necessary. It was, soldiers, look to yourselves; we want no more of you. I hope I shall one day find land enough to lay my bones in. If I chance to die in a civilized country, none will deny me that. A dead body never begs a grave—thanks for that.[14]

Martin goes on to describe mind-numbing hunger, cold, and fatigue. He writes that the Army promised food, but rarely, if ever, lived up to that promise. They promised changes of clothing to last the years of soldiering, but he saw a fourth of the troops "had not a scrap of anything but their ragged shirt flaps to cover their nakedness." The beef, flour, and other rations promised were barely edible, and never at the weights promised. He wrote that he had gone up to five days with nary a morsel of food to nibble at. While we have considerably condensed Martin's remarks, in order to provide the reader with a glimpse of the breadth and scope of colonial discontent with the leaders among them (both British and American), we could not dispense with his withering observations of the well-to-do classes who, with the revolution over, had no use for his services. In truth, every major (and some minor) American war has had this outcome: 1) mobilization, which calls for the sacrifices of true patriots; 2) battle, which demands the performance of the highest (and lowest) martial spirit to achieve military and political objectives; and, 3) demobilization, where the soldiers are tossed into the dustbin of history, polished on high holy days of political grandstanding, but otherwise, gone with the wind.

Martin's bitterness, is almost infectious:

> Many murmur now at the apparent good fortune of the poor soldiers. Many I have myself seen, vile enough to say that they never deserved such favor from the country. The only wish I would bestow upon such hardhearted wretches is that they might be compelled to go through just such suffering and privations as that army did, and then if they did not sing a different tune, I should miss my guess.
>
> But I really hope those people will not go beside themselves. Those men whom they wish to die on a dunghill, men, who, if they had not ventured their lives in battle and faced poverty, disease, and death for their country to gain and maintain that independence and Liberty, in the sunny beams of which, they, like reptiles, are basking, they would many or the most of them, be this minute in as much need of help and succor as ever the most indigent soldier was before he experienced his country's beneficence.
>
> The soldiers consider it cruel to be thus vilified, and it is cruel as the grave to any man, when he knows his own rectitude of conduct, to have his hard services not only debased and underrated, but scandalized and vilified. But the Revolutionary soldiers are not the only people that

endure obloquy; others, as meritorious and perhaps more deserving than they, are forced to submit to ungenerous treatment.[15]

Joseph Plumb Martin spoke for many, many other veterans of the war, who found the country that they returned to independent, to be sure, of Britain, but not of the wealthy classes who had replaced them in rule. They may have detested the taxes levied from London's Parliament, but they found a new, native, taxing authority that virtually bled them dry.

It was a recipe for disaster, which was not long in coming.

The post-revolutionary period set the stage for a heightened level of conflict: that of poor farmers (many of whom were vets of the just-concluded war), and the urban classes, which taxed everything except breath. Here, as Zinn highlights, two great social forces collided, and it would have dire consequences for the future of America:

> [A] rebellion of farmers had taken place in western Massachusetts. You probably know about that: Shays' Rebellion. You know it from those multiple-choice tests. But you will not learn of the connection between Shays' Rebellion of 1786 and the Constitutional Convention of 1787. You will not learn about that in your classes in school or in orthodox histories. But the fact is that when Shays' Rebellion took place, thousands of farmers gathering around the courthouses, many of them veterans of the Revolutionary War, because their farms were being taken away from them, their livestock, their land being taken away from them because they couldn't afford to pay the taxes levied on them by the rich who controlled the legislature of Massachusetts. So they surrounded the courthouses and wouldn't let the proceedings go on, the auctioning off of their farms.[16]

Due to our upbringing, and our teaching, we are wont to view Captain Daniel Shays as a rebel. But whom did he rebel against? What did he rebel against? Surely he did not rebel against the Revolution. Indeed, as a captain in the Revolutionary Army, he fought against the British, thereby contributing to the American victory. Shays rebelled against the poverty and outrageous taxation that he and thousands of other ex-revolutionary soldier-farmers faced when they came back. They learned that the Revolution to which they were loyal wasn't loyal to them. They were taxed to the point of insurrection, and joining together with other like minds, thousands of soldier-farmers organized, and laid siege to western

Massachusetts. They attacked the Springfield arsenal, for this was but another battle to make the Revolution real to them and to men like them.

The bigwigs in the capital city (Philadelphia) were going bonkers at this revolt, and resolved to ensure such threats to their property and power would not raise their heads again (remember General Knox's private correspondence to Washington?).

The wealthy leaders in power decided they needed a strong central government—not for the British, they were beaten—but for people like Captain Shays and others who wanted to use the freedoms gained by the Revolution to better their lives, and those of the People. Their struggles were just beginning. Like soldiers of the recent Revolutionary War (and generations of soldiers to come) they learned that what they thought they fought for, and what they actually fought for, were quite different.

"Hell itself, could not have vomited anything more black than his design of emancipating our slaves..."

While the American Revolution was boiling between the colonies and the Mother Country, there was a vast and growing population in cities and rural districts throughout the colonial territories that were initially on the periphery. That's because their deeply felt causes—for freedom—did not concern the two European powers engaged in international battle. In a struggle for freedom and independence, those most in need of freedom were not on the agenda. Indeed, quite the reverse.

For, on the eve of the Revolution, those white men of the 13 colonies in America who owned substantial property, who filled the air with yells for "liberty" from the British tyrant, held in thrall tens of thousands of shackled others, and denied even the peace of personhood. Historian Herbert Aptheker, a groundbreaking scholar of the 20th century, noted the glaring contradiction:

> A letter written July 31, 1776, by Henry Wynkoop, a resident of Bucks County, Pennsylvania, to the local Committee of Safety requested the dispatching of ammunition in order to quiet "the people in my neighborhood (who) have been somewhat alarmed with fears about negroes and disaffected people injuring their families when they are in the service."[17]

What do you think they were more concerned about—fighting the British, or keeping their "negroes" in line? When the newly established government began trying to recruit soldiers for the upcoming war, a lot of people simply weren't interested. Howard Zinn continues:

> Many working people and farmers enlisted, but many others did not. In the South they were very disgruntled, not patriotic, and unenthusiastic about the rebellion. General Washington had to send General Greene to coerce and threaten people in order to get them into the military.[18]

Why do you think it was so hard, especially for Southerners with perhaps the deepest military tradition of any sector in the nation? Because they had to choose between keeping their slaves or getting "Independence" from England. Which cause do you think was more important to them?

In truth and fact, there was another reason why the white, armed South was reluctant to rumble against the British. And it had everything to do with self-interest, and little to do with independence. Consider this: Do you know how many Blacks fought for the Revolution (against the inclinations of General Washington, we might add)?

Five thousand men.

How many fought on behalf of the Crown?

An estimated sixty-five thousand. *65,000.*

Those tens of thousands of Black soldiers didn't serve in British regiments because of love of "Queen and country." They too, pursued their own self-interest. For they heard, through the ever-present grapevine, that the British would grant freedom to any Black man who joined their side. The numbers tell that story with eloquence greater than poetry. The British even equipped them with uniforms emblazoned with the motto, "Liberty to Slaves" on their tunics.

Lord John Murray Dunmore, Virginia's colonial Governor, organized what he termed the "Ethiopian Regiment" for Black soldiers. The very idea sent Virginians into conniption fits. This Black regiment helped the British capture and put to the torch Norfolk, VA, on New Year's Day, 1776. And when the war was irrevocably done for the British, some 20,000 Africans sailed with them when they sailed away from their former colonies. They were resettled in the West Indies, in parts of Canada, and in other far-flung lands under British dominion. They lost the Revolutionary War, sure. But they too, were no longer slaves.

Seen from that context, who lost?

But there are at least two sides to every battle, and the Americans, who lost some crucial clashes with the British, reconsidered their initial reluctance to embrace Black manpower. So, like their British cousins, Americans began making promises to their Black inhabitants, the better to spur them into the fight.

In their work on Albert Einstein and his little recognized efforts to counter racism in America, authors Fred Jerome and Rodger Taylor offer some useful historical perspective on the Princeton, New Jersey, area during the revolutionary period:

> A part of the story most people haven't heard is that black colonial Americans in the community of Princeton and beyond played a significant role in this critical victory. Several colonial African Americans, including many from the elite all-black First Rhode Island Regiment [*see endnote] fought in the battle. Black Revolutionary War veteran Oliver Cromwell recalled in the spring of 1852, at the age of one hundred, how Washington's army "knocked the British about lively." Some of the fighting took place in Princeton's African American community. "Nineteen Hessian soldiers were killed on Witherspoon Street. For years after the battle residents spoke of being terrorized by a ghost of a Hessian soldier who was killed in the fight."
>
> In these times, many enslaved African Americans ran from bondage, spurred by principles of democracy, equality and liberty. A Princetonian who went by the name of Prime was one such individual. His owner, Absalom Bainbridge, supported the British. Bainbridge enlisted and served as a physician to the Loyalist troops stationed in Long Island. Prime, forced to travel with his owner, bolted and returned to Princeton. There he was advised to join the Continental Army, which he did with the hope that this service would earn him freedom.
>
> However, after the war, Prime was not legally released. He lived a quasi-free existence until 1784, when he was captured by slave hunters. At that time his legal representatives filed a petition for manumission. Prime's lawyer argued that Absalom Bainbridge had lost all property rights when he became an enemy of the state and joined the British Army. The court ruled in Prime's favor, and he was finally freed.[19]

In Howard Zinn's plain-spoken way, he states openly what Blacks knew in their hearts:

> There were people in this country who were not going to benefit from the Revolution and they knew it. As the Revolutionary War progressed it became clear that Blacks were not going to gain anything. It was not the Americans who welcomed Blacks into the armed forces and promised them freedom. It was the British. Indians had nothing to gain from the Revolution, and as soon as the English left, the line they had drawn along the western border prohibiting colonists from going westward into Indian territory was obliterated. American colonists were free to move into Indian territory.[20]

The American Revolution is dated from 1775 to 1783; or, from the beginning of armed conflict (at the Battles of Lexington and Concord, in Massachusetts, in April 1775) to the cessation of hostilities and the signing of the Treaty of Paris between the two combatants (Britain and the US) in 1783. Yet, for more than half a million African captives, the years after the Revolution meant more of the same, with liberation nowhere in sight. It brought them the same miseries, the same oppression, the same shackles, the same ships, the same assaults on the self and the soul, the same rapes, beatings, and terrors.

It brought the same *un*freedom.

Should they have celebrated such a revolution? Should they have sung the songs of liberty, whilst manacled and shackled, whipped and scarred?

We have seen earlier a letter from a worried white Pennsylvanian on the Revolution's eve. Nearly a decade after its end, Henry Wynkoop raises his voice again, this time, not in a private letter to a correspondent, but in a published correspondence appearing in the *Boston Gazette* of 3 September 1792. It reads:

> The negroes in this town and neighborhood, have stirred a rumor of their having in contemplation to rise against their masters and to procure themselves their liberty; the inhabitants have been alarmed and keep a strict watch to prevent their procuring arms; should it become serious, which I don't think, the worst that could befal (sic) us, would be their setting the town on fire. It is very absurd of the blacks, to suppose they could accomplish their views, and from the precautions that were taken to guard against surprise, little danger is to be apprehended.[21]

Yes. Absurd. It *was* absurd for Africans (or should we say, "negroes"?) to expect liberty after a revolution was fought for just such a thing. For, truth be told, the revolution was but for *white liberty,* not for the freedom of either Africans or Indians.

Quite the reverse.

To the southern gentry, one thing mattered above everything else: property. For, in that era, property meant slaves—and slaves meant wealth. The southern sectors of the colonies were late and reluctant to join the rumbles of resistance boiling up in Boston and New York. Indeed, to the British, the South represented, for a time, safe territory, for its Loyalist, Tory population was more numerous than in the North. Lord Dunmore, almost singlehandedly, changed that equation by touching a raw nerve that stimulated a response he did not anticipate.

When the rumblings of resistance in Virginia did begin, the royal governor Dunmore moved to seize gunpowder and shot from the local armory. This enraged other Southern slaveholders, deathly afraid of slave revolts, who saw it as an attempt at disarmament. Agitated by reports of militias marching on Virginia's then-capital, Williamsburg, Dunmore took the next step, hoping to cow the frightened population. He let it be known that he was considering assembling African troops to defend the Loyalist cause, and in support, he would free those who flocked to this standard.

Indeed, Dunmore's edict of 7 November 1775 became the first Emancipation Proclamation of a government in America calling for the freedom of African slaves. The document announced: "I do hereby further declare all indented servants, Negroes, or others (appertaining to Rebels) free, that are able and willing to bear arms, they joining His Majesty's Troops as soon as may be, for the more speedily reducing the Colony to a proper sense of their duty, to His Majesty's crown and dignity."[22] Dunmore's Proclamation, although drafted on the 7th, was not released publicly until a week thereafter, for he sought the proper timing to use this powerful weapon.

After a British regiment, supported by escaped African captives, bested a Virginia militia unit at Kemp's Landing, south of Norfolk, Dunmore sensed the time was ripe. For the victory was affected, in part, by the capture of one of the militia's colonels, by two of his turned slaves. With two colonels captured, several militiamen slain, and the rest of the American forces put to flight, Dunmore dropped his trump card: his proclamation.

The November 14th announcement had effects that even he could not foresee.

Among the captive Africans, this was the greatest news imaginable, and Blacks began slipping away from plantations and homes with increasing numbers. At Mount Vernon, the stately mansion and plantation house of perhaps the most prominent American in the colonies, the property's manager, Lund Washington, wrote to his distinguished cousin, George, what the proclamation meant, warning "there is not a man of them but would leave us, if they could make their escape." The reasoning was simple: "Liberty is sweet."[23]

For white Anglo colonists, however, the proclamation worked a reverse magic. It bound north and south in allegiance against the crown, and in the words of Edward Rutledge, a signer of the Declaration of Independence, the edict of Lord Dunmore worked "an eternal separation between Great Britain and the Colonies." Indeed, according to Rutledge, a South Carolinian, it worked better "than any other expedient."[24] A white Philadelphian wrote of the Dunmore Proclamation, "Hell itself, could not have vomited anything more black than his design of emancipating our slaves... The flame runs like wild fire through the slaves."[25]

"More black?" Hmmmmm. The City of Brotherly Love has spoken. Again.

And even as the Dunmore declaration sped throughout the Anglo-American population up and down the eastern coastline, it spread throughout the captive African community as well. John Adams noted to his southern colleagues at the 1775 Continental Congress that "the Negroes have a wonderful art of communicating intelligence among themselves; it will run several hundreds of miles in a week or fortnight."[26]

The news of potential freedom spread like quicksilver (but accuracy may have suffered in the telling and re-telling). Historian Woody Holton writes how many Africans in America heard and interpreted the news whispered along the grapevine:

> Many enslaved Americans carried the rumors about British aid for black insurrection one step further: they believed that the whole purpose of the expected British invasion of the South was to liberate them. In South Carolina, a slave reported that Thomas Jeremiah, a free black fisherman

> and harbor pilot that hoped to link the British army with rebel slaves, told enslaved workers "the War has come to help the poor Negroes." Further south in St. Bartholomew Parish at about the same time, a black preacher named George told gatherings of slaves "That the Young King, meaning our Present One, came up with the Book, and was about to alter the World, and set the Negroes Free." George was executed. The widespread belief among black southerners that the British intended to free them was known to whites. John Drayton reported many years after the revolution that Arthur Lee's assertion that the London government meant to incite an insurrection was "the more alarming; because it was already known, [slaves] entertained ideas, that the present contest was for obliging us to give them their liberty." The rumor that freeing the slaves was one of Great Britain's principal aims—perhaps even the primary one—might have been fabricated by black leaders in the hope that it would serve as a self-fulfilling prophecy. If a real slave revolt crystallized around the apocryphal story of a British army of liberation, British statesmen might indeed be drawn into an alliance with the slave rebels.[27]

Hope, as the old adage goes, may spring eternal, but they are not necessarily sufficient to transform unfortunate facts on the ground, for Dunmore's declaration fell short of what Africans hoped for (total emancipation), and that which propertied, landed whites feared (the same). It also deeply mobilized white rebels against the Crown, formed the gist of the breach between kingdom and colonist.

It should be noted what Lord Dunmore's declaration was, and what it wasn't. It was an official British governmental order of potential freedom for those who fought on their side against the colony's militias. It was not an edict of total emancipation freeing all of the enslaved, which would have crippled southern economies by essentially seizing their most valuable property: human chattel. It was, moreover (much like Lincoln's Emancipation Proclamation of roughly a century later) an act born in military necessity, to bolster the forces of the Empire against the restless colonies. That said, it drew tens of thousands of captive Africans from out of their shacks, hovels, and chains, for a taste, even a hope, of freedom.

One may question many things, but never their motivation.

The victory at Kemp's Landing, on the Elizabeth River (near Norfolk) became the occasion for Dunmore to publish his edict. But there are ebbs and flows of military fortune, of which few men can predict. For it would be on the Elizabeth River where the Ethiopian Regiment would meet its firmest resistance, and in many ways, its denouement.

On December 9, 1775, six hundred Loyalists (with half of these composed of the Ethiopian Regiment) met their opponents at Virginia's Great Bridge over the Elizabeth. The American rebels vanquished Dunmore's forces, and compelled him to flee Norfolk, for safety aboard British ships in the Chesapeake Bay.[28] This turn of affairs had two immediate effects. It made it far more difficult for African captives to contact the British forces (as they were no longer on land). And perhaps more troubling, it showed that Dunmore was in retreat—not on offense. But there was more that would conspire to doom the Regiment's deepest hopes. Disease.

As Dunmore's retreating forces took to the seas for safety, the Regiment (followed by an enormous train of camp followers, women, children, lovers, and friends) was struck by smallpox. At the Great Bridge, even the Americans had to admit that the Ethiopian troops fought "with the intrepidity of lions."[29] But a year later, in June 1776, Dunmore would have to admit that smallpox "carried off an incredible number of our people, especially blacks."[30]

Governments can ill govern from sea. They must be seen as governing where most men dwell: on land. From the Chesapeake Bay, Dunmore sailed north to New York City since the major trading port and banker for the slave states was, amongst its moneyed elites at least, a Tory city, almost to the last. Lord Dunmore's gamble, by first hinting, then threatening, then proclaiming, and finally fielding Black troops against the rebels ricocheted back on him, for it became a tool of coherence amid the rebels, who fumed, north and south, against the temerity of the British, using "their" Blacks against them.

Virginians called his edict "Damned, infernal, diabolical."[31] Philip Fithian, a tutor in Virginia's northern region, would write in his diary, "The Inhabitants of this Colony are deeply alarmed at this infernal scheme," adding, "it seems to quicken all in Revolution to overpower him however at every risk."[32]

To whites in the colonies, Lord Dunmore had gone too far. To captive Africans, he had not gone far enough. But wars, like revolutions, have unintended consequences.

It is true that barely 1% of captive Africans drew to the standard of King George III, yet that doesn't make the number negligible. For Africans formed at least 25% of the population in many parts of the South. Indeed, in some counties, for instance in South Carolina, African captives formed the majority of the population base. No doubt some feared leaving their known environs for the unknown. Others had issues of whether to trust either side (for both were white). Still, tens of thousands of people made their way to the British lines. When we consider that on the American side, there was little appetite to employ Black troops, and that the Loyalists offered the promise of freedom to those who signed up, we should not be surprised that Dunmore's forces received so much support.

As the war heated up (in considerable part due to Dunmore's declaration), Africans, especially those who had some skill as seamen or pilots, found few barriers to touching base with the British—who represented freedom to them. For promises of liberty were sweeter than the certainty of perpetual captivity.

Black Pioneer

Despite the victories and losses of war, such events can sometimes push certain individuals into action and furthermore their lives give insight into the shared experiences of the many. Nearly lost in the shifting sands of history was one-such man, Thomas Peters. Born in the Yoruba regions of Nigeria to an Ibo clan, Peters was captured in 1760 in the trans-Atlantic slave industry. It was onboard a French slaving vessel that he was brought to port in New Orleans. He was made captive, but he was never mentally enslaved, for his thirst for freedom spurred him ever onward to his natural right of liberty. For Peters this didn't mean those rights boasted of by the European tribes, whose treaties and constitutions promise one thing but deliver quite another. He meant liberty. True liberty. Freedom.

Three times he escaped while in Louisiana; and three times he was recaptured. He suffered greatly for such prison breaks. He was whipped severely, thereafter branded, and finally had ankle shackles fitted about him. His continued resistance wore out his French slaveholder, who sold him to another in a land north of Louisiana.

Peters, now living in bondage in Wilmington, North Carolina, on the Cape Fear River, continued his efforts to be free. Here, he is thought to have acquired his skills as a millwright (one who plans or builds mills, or works on the machinery of such a structure), for Wilmington was a port city, and more than three-fifths of the African captive population in Cape Fear worked in the timber industry or naval stores.[33] As stevedores, sawyers, carpenters, tar burners, or carters, these people kept Cape Fear's economy thriving.

Peters' life was revealed to us through the work of noted historian Gary Nash, who writes in light of his study of the economy of the region. Perhaps not surprisingly, Peters' life is not well documented in extant texts. Yet this man would distinguish himself in his long struggle for Black freedom. As one who now worked on the docks, rather than a plantation, Peters and his contemporaries had a degree of mobility and skill that others inland never experienced. Many people learned how to navigate skiffs, ferryboats and other such craft as used in hauling pine timber to the mills. The man who claimed ownership of him, an immigrant Scotsman named William Campbell, was a leading member of the Sons of Liberty in Wilmington, and later functioned in the Committee Safety there. As such Peters could not help but hear a good amount of rhetoric about "liberty," "freedom," and "independence." Imagine the impact of such terms on a man who truly knew their worth—a worth far greater than Colonial rhetoric. As such, he surely also heard the dread in the whispering of the area's whites, who feared slave uprisings more than they feared the British. There is more than a touch of irony that, in a region called Cape Fear, emotion suffused public consciousness, in anticipation of not just the British, but the uprising of the Africans.

Janet Schaw, visiting the region, wrote that the whites there feared the Crown made secret promises that "every Negro that would murder his master and family" [would] "have his master's plantation." Moreover, "The Negroes have got it amongst them and believe it to be true. Tis ten to one they may try the experiment..."[34]

We must understand that it was in the very nature of slave societies for fear and paranoia to be the situational norm. For while slaveholding society instilled in law that slaves were but mere things (i.e., chattel), and said so in their social discourse, and expressed this regard in their interaction with the enslaved, nevertheless they were not foolish enough to believe it, internally. They knew that, at any moment, those seething unblushing masses could rise up and end their existences. Hence the fact that of all of the thirteen colonies, the southern ones were the most martial, the heaviest armed, and the most alert. They learned, over centuries, that such attention was necessary.

That said, the slightest words, especially those born in human resentment, could result in wildly exaggerated fears of uprisings, further resulting in truly draconian white communal responses of violence to stifle the tremors within.

In a brief case in point, a fellow named Jeremiah was said to have been spreading the word around Charleston's harbor that "there is a great war coming soon" and that the British would "come to help the poor negroes."[35] For this message, Jeremiah, a fisherman and boat pilot (and a "free" Black man to boot!), was seized, arrested, undoubtedly tortured, and charged with plotting a slave insurrection, as well as planning to guide British vessels around the dangerous sandbar blocking the port to Charleston's harbor. Despite the efforts of the newly arrived English royal governor to spare him, white Charlestonians hanged him and burned him at the stake. Governor William Campbell (not Thomas Peters' owner), hearing the evidence arrayed against Jeremiah, would write to a fellow English correspondent, "my blood ran cold when I read what ground they had doomed a fellow creature to death." His efforts to try to save the fisherman elicited such white anger in Charleston that they threatened to hang the man on his doorstep if he granted the man a pardon.[36]

It was in this climate of slender hope and engorged fear that Peters likely learned of Lord Dunmore's Emancipation Proclamation. Nash writes:

> When Dunmore's Proclamation reached the ears of Thomas Peters and other slaves in Wilmington in November 1775, a buzz of excitement must surely have washed over them. But the time for self-liberation was not yet ripe, because hundreds of miles of pine barrens, swamps, and inland waterways separated Wilmington from Norfolk, where Lord Dunmore's British forces were concentrated, and slaves knew that white patrols were on watch throughout the tidewater area from Cape Fear to the Chesapeake Bay. The opportune moment for Peters arrived four months later. On February 9, 1776, white Wilmingtonians evacuated the town as word arrived that the British sloop *Cruizar* was tacking up the Cape Fear River to bombard the town. A month later, four British ships arrived from Boston, including several troop transports under Sir Henry Clinton. For the next two months, the British controlled the river, plundered the countryside, and set off a wave of slave desertions. Seizing the moment, Peters and his family made their escape. Captain George Martin, an officer under Sir Henry Clinton, organized the escaped slaves from the Cape Fear region into the company of Black Pioneers, as Peters testified seven years later at the end of the war. Now, in the spring

of 1776, the days of an uncertain freedom began for Peters' family.[37]

Peters made the most of this opportunity. As a member of the Black Pioneers, he was with the Brits when they took Philadelphia in August of 1776. The city, under British occupation, became a magnet for Blacks fleeing the south. A white legislator would write in deep lamentation about the "invasion of this state, and the possession the enemy obtain of this city and neighborhood, [a] great part of the slaves hereabout were enticed away by the British army."[38]

For those wearing the British uniform, and many of their family members, the British offered land, tools, and rations for three years. When the war ended, thousands of Africans boarded British boats and vessels for points North (Canada), South (the British holdings in the Caribbean Sea), and other Black possessions.

Peters, his wife, Meg, and their two children, sailing away from the land of their captivity, were blown off course, and had to winter in Bermuda, a British Island off the Coast of Cape Hatteras of North Carolina. And when better sailing weather arrived, the family left for Nova Scotia in southeastern Canada, finally living a life of freedom that millions would not know for more than a century after enduring American slavery and later U.S. apartheid.

But Peters was not one to sit idle. He was a rolling stone who couldn't be stopped short of death itself. When, after several years in the cold climate, denied fundamentally fair treatment among all dwelling there, Peters canvassed the local Black refugees and embarked on another voyage: this time to London.

Peters arrived in London virtually penniless, but he was armed with a petition signed by some 200 Black families of Nova Scotia, praying for a place where they could truly be free under British dominion. Peters—if ever a former slave could be called a lucky man—had the gift of great timing, for upon arrival in England, he found himself amidst a fervent abolition campaign that was moving Parliament. When he returned to Canada, he came with a final trek for the refugees out of Nova Scotia.

By late 1791, fifteen ships set sail for Sierra Leone, the British-made African colony on Africa's great west coast. The vessels held hundreds of Black Canadian souls, striving to touch their ancient homeland. They met the worst storms and gales in memory, and lost dozens of people to ship sickness, but Thomas Peters, according to Sierra Leonean legend, led those disembarking from the ships singing (although sick from shipboard fever), "The day of jubilee is come; return, ye ransomed sinners home."[39]

Peters, and his family, and hundreds of his friends and neighbors, many of them his former fellow soldiers of the old Black Pioneers, had returned to the land of their ancestors. Millions of Black people in America would never have the chance to breathe free air. Peters lived several months of such freedom, before succumbing to the fever. His bones were laid to rest in Freetown, where several of his descendants still dwell. He was born in Africa, stolen to French-American territory, sold to the Carolinas, stole away to the British, fought the Americans, lived in Canada, returned to Africa, and left his loved ones in freedom.

Truly, the British had lost one of their prized possessions to a war in which they could not prevail: the colonies. Yet, for thousands of Blacks, they won something more precious: liberty.

"Indians"—Between a Rock and a Hard Place

For the First People, the coming of the whites to Turtle Island was bad enough, but it was about to get progressively worse. That's because the indigenous people on the east coast witnessed, for centuries, the unremitting land hunger of the whites and their growing propensity for a kind of war of extermination of which they could hardly conceive.

Let us not suggest that they were all pacifists. They were not. But war was between warriors, not women. Certainly not children. But these English, these people from across the sea fought to destroy everything: crops, dwellings, cattle, and—amazingly—children.

After years of war, the western tribes (that is, those to the west of the colonial borders), were too numerous and too strong to be disposed of as their coastal cousins. The colonists and the British had to bargain, and to treat, by swearing on pieces of paper that they were indeed, men of truth and trust. The Great King from across the Great Sea sent his captains and lieutenants to swear not to encroach on their sacred lands, and, for a time, the indigenous people believed them.

The First People learned that the Great King was growing tired from his recent war with the Franks, another European tribe that had a long and hateful relationship with the English. They thought long and hard about these things, and learned how to play the English and French against each other—to divide these tribes, keep them off balance and thus weaker.

However, fine diplomatic speech and civilized manners didn't keep the English from encroachments on Indian lands. Giving battle did. In what came to be called Pontiac's Rebellion, indigenous nations united to teach the British a lesson by raiding twelve British forts and attacking settlements in Virginia. According to a Virginian, Peter Fontaine, writing in August 1763, warriors from various nations in and around the Great Lakes region "entered into a combination against us, resolved, it seems to prevent our settling any farther than we have, viz., much about the Blue Ridge of mountains."[40]

Britain emerged from the war with the French for domination of Canada as the victor, but strength has its limits. They emerged economically spent, and if you recall the colonial conflicts surrounding the Stamp Act, you recall that the purposes for the added taxes was to recoup the costs of the war that came to be called the French-Indian War. It formally ended in 1763, and the British wanted to go easy with the Indians to avoid riling them up with incursions on their lands. So, the King instructed his governors to refuse to grant land leases on such territory, which essentially kept the western borders of Americana at the Appalachians.

But the whites were chomping at the bit to get more and more of that rich, fertile land—and by this we don't mean merely the yeomanry (the small landholders, considered beneath the gentry, and a kind of middle class of the colonial era), nor the multitudes of poor, landless tenants.

Among the landed gentry—the wealthiest men in the colonies, many of whom have sent their names down to us to the present age—was a land-thirst more ravenous than those situated beneath them on the colonial ladder of rank. For these men (among them, George Washington and Thomas Jefferson) were, literally, the richest men in the colonies. And what do rich men want?

More riches. And among all classes of people in the colonial era, land held the best promise for entry into the temple of wealth. (If there was anything more coveted than land, it was perhaps slaves—to work the land, to produce more wealth.)

The indigenous people used war, guile, threats, and sweet words to try to hold on to that which they too, considered the most valuable of things (land), but Europe bled immigrants in an explosion of numbers that pushed more and more against the borders erected by Britain, and that land-hunger would transform into hatred for those impeding their westward aims and yearnings: the British for blocking their ambitions, and the Indians for being there.

As historian Gary Nash has written in his earlier works, this era of American life had the germ of the potential for being quite different than what came to be, for this land-space, being so capacious, could have developed into a tri-racial nation-state (or confederacy) where all dreams could've been given room to flourish. Red, white, and black, as Nash envisioned. But that was not to be, because the matrix upon which the American story was written, was Eurocentricity, white supremacy, Indian hatred, and Black subordination—slavery and exploitation.

The wealthy elites in power at the inception sought mightily to pit others against others, the better to obscure their common interests and prevent their focused anger and energy against their oppressors. The greatest fear of the wealthy elites was that the poor and dispossessed would see the commonalty between them, to craft a larger notion of "us." For such an insight could have upset the precarious apple cart of imperial expansion.

That said, there was considerable mixing of Indians and whites, which brought forth some interesting personages who stayed true to their native roots and fought with vigor against white expansionism and land-hunger while maintaining a foothold in the white world. The military and political careers of some, like Joseph Brant and Cornplanter, give us some insight into the woes of war and politics between peoples—even those of dual communities.

A child is born in an Iroquois village in the region now called Ohio, and named Thayendanegea, but Brant is the name he would be better remembered by. His 1742 birth to a family of English and Iroquois would result in a youth and life of bilingualism and biculturalism. Brant was the brother of Degonwadonti (aka Molly Brant), the Mohawk wife of Sir William Johnson, and the king's emissary to the Six Nations—the Iroquois-led confederacy of major nations in the colonial regions that would one day become America.

Sir William Johnson was a man deeply committed to his mission, which was to secure the allegiance of the Iroquois to the British imperial project in North America. To that end, Johnson spoke the language of the Iroquois, wore the garb, married a native maiden, and even took an Iroquois name: Warraghiyagey—"man who does much business"—to show his oneness with them. But he didn't do these things because he desired to do so. He was the Northern Superintendent of Indian Affairs for His Majesty, King George III. He was doing his duty to his prince.

Johnson's brother-in-law, Joseph Brant, began his martial life as a 13-year-old, when he fought alongside British and Americans against the French at Crown Point during the Seven Year's War. And when Pontiac's wars swept through the Ohio country (as it was known then), he aided the colonists by battling against Pontiac's armed insurgency.[41] But the Iroquois were in a ticklish position, both among other tribal allies, and also with their white allies, for as time went on, and conflicts arose between allies, which side would this powerful nation take?

The war-fever sweeping the colonies and the native territories was so powerful that private armies began to arise, among the Americans and the indigenous, bodies of armed men unsanctioned by the authorities on either side. Led by brash, young, hotheaded men, they were open to great acts of boldness, as well as unplanned acts of foolishness. For the Americans, Ethan Allen and Benedict Arnold vied for supremacy in who could garner the greater glory. A surprise dawn attack on Fort Ticonderoga and Crown Point resulted in its ignoble surrender by the British officer, with no shots being fired. The taking allowed both Allen and Arnold to crow. Yet the capture of the two forts, situated in northern New York not far from the Canadian border, ended up placing Iroquois headmen on the horns of a dilemma: for the Iroquois had a long and (for them) good relationship with the British, who (after some compelling) restrained the Americans from seizing or venturing on their lands. They had signed treaties with the English, and more importantly, the British were the main source of their goods—especially their war material. With the Ticonderoga taken, that flow of arms vanished.

Changed situations brought changed alliances, and Joseph Brant became one who called for battle against the Americans, for Iroquois and British security. At a Grand Iroquois council meeting in July of 1775 (three months after the taking of Fort Ticonderoga), Brant staged a mock feast, at which he boasted of devouring "a Bostonian" and "drink[ing] his blood" (really an ox and a measure of red wine). Meanwhile, Allen, emboldened by his seizure of Ticonderoga, attacked Montreal with his own sparse forces (refusing to wait for reinforcements by American General Richard Montgomery). The capture of Montreal, a city of some 9,000 souls by 110 men would place Allen at the very pantheon of military geniuses.

Well, Montrealers apparently had other ideas: they surrounded and outnumbered

Allen's party, and sent them fleeing for their lives. With only 38 men left, Allen decided that discretion was the better part of valor, and tendered his sword to Peter Johnson, the mixed-race son of Sir William Johnson. For his recklessness, Allen would be clapped in irons, pending transport to England to stand trial for treason.[42]

As fate would have it, Joseph Brant would also be en route to England but for an entirely different purpose. Brant was acting as an emissary of the Mohawk nation, to seek military aid from the British. Brant and his loyalist partner, Guy Johnson (the late Sir William's son-in-law), were seeking his father-in-law's position, the Northern Superintendent of Indian Affairs in the colonies. As they sailed for London aboard the *Adament*, Ethan Allen and thirty-three of his fellow soldiers were shackled below deck.

Brant spent several months in England, taking in the sights, as well as conducting meetings with George III's colonial secretary, Lord George Germain, who was as determined as his sovereign to bring the hardheaded Americans to heel. Brant explained to Lord Germain, "It is very hard, when we have let the King's subjects have so much of our lands for so little value, they should want to cheat us in this manner of the small spots we have left for our women and children to live on. We are tired out in making complaints and getting no redress."[43] As with much Native American and indigenous oration, his words were powerful and moving regarding the concerns of his people. But, given the forces at play during the revolution, it was like fighting fire on two sides of a burning building. For, in truth, neither side cared much for the Indians. Each cared only about who could utilize them for their purposes and for their tactical and special advantage.

Brant was out of the colonies for eight months, and in that period, some significant changes occurred. For one thing, the colonies had issued a rather cheeky Declaration of Independence; in response, the British increased its forces, with General Howe in command of 15,000 troops (as well as naval power along the coast able to quiet any city). The English had bested the Americans in Montreal, inflicting tremendous casualties, and forcing their retreat. (During Brant's absence, the Americans captured both Montreal and Quebec, only to fall prey to pestilence—that ancient warrior, smallpox—which cut through the Americans along with the help of the biting Canadian cold and British reinforcements.)

Britain was determined to hold fast to its rich and fertile American colonies. It was a gold mine of raw materials and its markets had a yen for goods shipped back from the Mother Country. If it took war to bring them back in line, so be it.

As for Brant, like his American counterpart, Ethan Allen, he had a penchant for going his own way, and ignoring, or disobeying his elders and his headmen. Also like Allen, once back in his homeland, he built his own unsanctioned, unapproved armed forces—an amalgam of Mohawks, Oneidas, and a mix of white frontiersmen, as well as immigrants from Scotland, Ireland, and England. They went from clan to clan, nation to nation, trying to convince them to unite and fight against the American threat. But, although some things had changed in Brant's eight-month absence, other things remained the same—principally the indecision of the Iroquois.

The cooler heads among them prevailed that the Iroquois Confederacy should have no truck with the British nor the Americans in their internecine war between white brothers and cousins. Historian Gary Nash hits the proverbial nail on the head when he characterizes the forces facing the Iroquois nation and their numerous Indian confederates, clans, and sub-clans:

> For some 200,000 Native Americans composing eighty-five nations east of the Mississippi River, the onset of full-scale war between the American colonists and the British in 1776 greatly complicated goals of political independence and territorial preservation—their guiding principles since the first encounters with the intruding Europeans. African Americans who had neither liberty nor land fought for the former in order to someday gain the latter. But Native Americans, who had both, reached a critical point in struggling to preserve them. Like most African Americans, the majority of Native Americans painfully reached the conclusion that preserving political and territorial integrity could best be achieved by fighting the side that proclaimed the equality of all men and with the side that the Americans accused of trampling their God-given, natural, irreducible rights. The logic of nearly two hundred years of abrasive contact with colonizing Europeans compelled the choice. After all, it was the settler-subjects of the English king who most threatened Indian autonomy, just as it was royal power before the Revolution that had attempted to protect Indian land from colonizer encroachment.[44]

Brant, with his irregular, unsanctioned, and unauthorized army, set out to do what Allen could not—succeed. Unlike his rash contemporary, where Brant was bold in military tactics, he was wiser in strategy, and used what later generations would call guerrilla guile to achieve his objectives. He avoided set battles, and wagered on traps, ambushes, and skirmishes that bled his better-supplied and armed enemy.

Brant's Volunteers, with some Iroquois support, laid siege to Fort Stanwix (today a national memorial standing on 16 acres in upstate NY), at that time America's westernmost post. While one part of the Volunteers hit the fort, another part lay in wait for American reinforcements. Brant's men and boys ambushed some 800 American men and boys rushing to relieve Fort Stanwix. Under command of General Nicholas Herkimer, the regiment fell, six miles from the fort, right into a trap near Oriskany. But it is one thing to trap prey, as the old adage goes: "Sometimes you get the bear; and sometime the bear gets you." The losses there were horrendous.

The Seneca Chief, Blacksnake, beheld the scene, and later remarked, "There I have seen the most dead bodies all... over that I never did see, and never will again. I thought at the time the blood shed [was] a stream running down on the descending ground during the afternoon, and yet some living were crying for help."[45]

Americans sustained deep losses here, but for the pro-British side, the Mohawk and Seneca warriors took the deepest cuts. When the British lifted the siege, without accomplishing their goal, perhaps this was a harbinger of things to come... and not good things.

Brant's Volunteers, the closest configuration of a pan-Indian army since Pontiac's Rebellion of 1763, had its setbacks (as does every army, certainly), but it also had days of brilliance. For, as a guerrilla fighter (contemporaries would call him an "Indian fighter") his objective was to harry, harass, and destabilize American homesteads on Mohawk and Iroquoian lands. This he did with discipline and focus.

The popular press of the day, which engaged in Indian-hating as if it were a national sport, referred to him as "monster Brant," although, from his perspective, he gave as good as he got.[46] The practice may have infuriated Americans, but, truth be told, the Americans adopted some pretty similar tactics in their battles with the British. Furthermore, guerrilla warfare has always been the tactic of the weak against the strong. As long as one lives to resist another day, the field is open for conflict.

As the long, hard war slogged to its end, Brant felt that his people would get a good settlement, as they had fought so long and vigorously. But, as has been witnessed over centuries of European statecraft, wealthy white interests prevailed over any others at the table of negotiation and deal making. In fact, when the First Nations learned that the peace treaty signed between the Americans and the British bore no mention of their nations, they were, understandably, quite thunderstruck. The King's representatives fought fiercely for the rights of American (read: white) Loyalists, but the interests of the Indian allies were not worthy of mere mention. In what Nash has termed "the lamest rationalizations in the history of treaty-making," he quotes Lord Shelburne, George III's representative, saying, "the Indian nations were not abandoned to their enemies; they were remitted to the care of neighbors, whose interest it was as much as ours to cultivate friendship with them, and who were certainly the best qualified for softening and humanizing their hearts."[47]

What the indigenous peoples and nations won on the field of blood, they lost at the stroke of the pen. For the British, masters of a global empire, it was a frustrating loss, but, all things considered, they were still the imperial presence of which it was said: "The sun will never set on the British Empire!" For perhaps a third of Asia, half of North America, Ireland, Wales, and Scotland were theirs to command. They didn't like it, surely, but they were large enough to sustain the loss.

For the indigenous people and nations of what would come to be called America, one war had ended; and another was about to commence. For them, surely, the American Revolution was the beginning of their end. They had been betrayed, crossed and double-crossed—again. As ever, treaties were but pre-cursors of very bad news to come.

Revolutions Under the Revolution

We have seen (have we not?) some of the struggles, battles, and conflicts that tore at the fabric of early American colonial society, long before, after, and indeed during the Revolution. At the deep bottom of American society festered an inchoate rage that rarely bled through the straightjacket of history, for it did not serve the national and, indeed, global project of Americanization. It was not seen as patriotic, the leitmotif by which much, nay, most history has been both taught and written.

American patriots, with tri-cornered hats, knee breeches, and silk stockings manfully manned this American Revolution against tyranny, injustice—and (why not?) "the American Way." Let us be clear: it may be that children cannot bear to be taught the ugly viscera of U.S. history. Perhaps. But we are not children, and given the intolerably poor state of much primary and secondary American education, and the relatively tiny number of Americans who can afford the obscene prices of college and university, when (or how) will the broad masses of Americans learn their own history?

We believe that even with the efforts of those such as Zinn, Nash, and others—including our contributions here—the usual parade of platitudes will likely continue, leaving most Americans underserved. Such a state of affairs is not only dangerous to our collective self-image, it poisons the well of the future, for it is precisely that hubris and blindness that gave birth to 9/11, and yes—the 9/11s to come.

But we must also state that history—the full scope of history—is itself dangerous. Howard Zinn, who inspires both of us, said as much in his 2007 book, *A Power Governments Cannot Suppress,* in the essay "Mississippi Freedom Summer": "Education can, and should, be dangerous to the existing social structure." Howard, a dedicated history teacher for much of his adult, post-military life, was speaking about the power of history to transform consciousness. But it's a measure of the palliative, drug-like effect of today's smothering media (and by this we mean virtually all forms—movies, entertainment, TV shows, and the like) that many of us still do not know the whole story.

We know some of what riled up American colonists, but, when the chances presented themselves, they were more rebellious, more radical, than most of us were ever taught. *And this was years before the Revolution.*

Consider this. When we think of New Jersey, the image emerges of a relatively quiet state, nudged between two bigger, more boisterous neighbors: New York and Pennsylvania. (OK, perhaps some of us think of *The Sopranos,* right?) Did you know that thirty years before the Revolution, farmers seized local jails, to break their friends out? Repeatedly? For years? Early in *The Unknown American Revolution,* Nash recounts those days of rage in the Garden State:

> In mid-September 1745, about 150 New Jersey farmers armed with "clubs, axes, and crow bars" descended on the jail in Newark, the capital of the royal colony of New Jersey. They demanded that the sheriff release Samuel

Baldwin, who had been arrested for cutting down trees on lands claimed by Governor Lewis Morris, a man of great wealth and the owner of scores of slaves. When the sheriff refused, the crowd mobbed him. They tore the jail door off its hinges and set Baldwin free. Triumphantly making their way out of town, they vowed to mobilize again and bring "fighting Indians" with them on the next occasion that one of their own was imprisoned.

Fourteen weeks later, when the sheriff followed orders from the royal governor to arrest three of the farmers involved in the September jailbreak, the defiant yeomen assembled again. Armed with clubs, they freed one of the prisoners as he was being transferred from one jail to another. Trying to uphold royal authority, the sheriff called out thirty militiamen to surround the Newark jail and prevent further breaks. Undaunted, three hundred determined farmers, marching under a pennant, confronted the militia. "Those who are under my list, follow me," shouted Amos Roberts, a yeoman leader. With that, the farmers overpowered the militiamen, thrashed the sheriff, freed their friends and marched out of town...

Other similar events followed. In July 1747, two hundred men marched into Perth Amboy in East New Jersey and vowed that if they were challenged "there should not have been a man left alive, or a house standing." Springing open the town jail, they freed one of their imprisoned leaders."[48]

Imagine that—over a generation before the Revolution.

Think of the racial strife that continues to plague American society today; the injustices amidst the vast silences. We act, frankly, as if we do not see what we see, and so it gets progressively worse because we have internalized and normalized what would be unspeakable injustices if it happened to us (or anyone we knew and loved). Moreover, think how often you've read histories where someone is overtly racist or cruel, and we are told to see things as they were then—and to not project our present understandings on them. That sounds reasonable, doesn't it?

And then we espy a figure, situated in his own time and circumstance, who speaks words of such power that it radiates as timeless truths. That's the case of a man named Benjamin Lay, born in England to a poor Quaker family. As if that were not enough, he was a dwarf, who was described as homely. He took to the sea, and worked in that realm for seven years before he and his wife, after spending some time in the West Indies, decided to settle in Philadelphia.

During their time in the Islands, they saw first-hand the naked brutality and violence of slavery. Imagine his surprise when he disembarks in Philadelphia, and sees slavery openly practiced—by other Quakers! Lay may have had a certain exterior visage, but inside dwelled the soul of a prince. He went straight to the Quaker meeting, and began to, well, raise hell about the practice of slavery. His Quaker brothers and sisters were shocked by his outspokenness.

Nearly half a century before the Revolution, Lay, by his "crazed zealotry" (according to his detractors) and "uncompromising... conscience," set the stage for the abolition movement that would strike America to its core over a century later. As you read Nash's account, you might think you're reading about someone in the 21st century who goes to great lengths to abstain from and avoid the moral and ethical abuses of the modern world:

> Lay was a strict vegetarian, refusing to eat anything provided through the death of an animal. He sometimes lived in a cave on his small farm outside Philadelphia. He and his wife made homespun clothes to avoid materials made by enslaved Africans. He publicly smashed his wife's teacups to discourage the use of slave-produced sugar. Taking his cause to the quiet Quaker meetings, Lay made himself impossible to ignore. On one occasion, he stood outside a meeting with one bare foot buried in deep snow to dramatize how badly slaves were clothed in winter. He also kidnapped a Quaker child to bring home to Friends the grief suffered by African families when their children were snatched by slave traders separated from their parents by sale at the owners' hands.[49]

Was this guy an activist or what? And this was in the 1730s!

But Benjamin Lay wasn't finished. He wrote and published in 1737, a book: *All Slave-keepers, That Keep the Innocent in Bondage, Apostates.* The responsible, reasonable Quaker leaders (some of whom owned slaves) repudiated Lay's tract, so, Nash reports:

> [H]e upped the ante. Bursting into the annual gathering of Quaker leaders, he plunged a sword into a hollowed-out book resembling a Bible that he had filled with a bladder of red pokeberry juice. By splattering Quaker leaders with "blood," he showed them that they committed spiritual and physical violence by trading and holding slaves, whether or not they treated them well and taught them Christian principles.

> Invading the churches of other denominations, Lay carried his case to the public that slavery was 'the mother of all sins' until he died in 1759.[50]

Lay was a giant of a man: a pre-revolutionary abolitionist. Many of us tend to think that the radical days are isolated to the 1960s, but, clearly, that is not so.

Americans, of every stripe and fashion, were always a pretty radical bunch. When you really consider it, only a radical bunch of folks could even think that the widely accepted idea, "the divine right of kings," was bogus. Indeed, the poor and working people of the country, before there was a United States of America, were far more radical than those we today hail as revolutionaries and "founding fathers." They were radical because they had to be. They were oppressed by an obscenely rich oligarchy, which thought of them as "the unthinking multitude," and the "dregs of society."[51]

Those were the thoughts of the patriots too, wealthy men like Washington, Jefferson, Adams, Robert Morris, and Alexander Hamilton.

Adams, too, looked down upon women, even if he looked up to his Abigail. But more importantly, he had personal thoughts of the Revolution that no schoolchild in America has ever heard: "The history of our Revolution, will be one continued lie from one end to the other."[52]

For it was not a revolution in support of freedom, not for those most in need of freedom: captives seized in Africa.

It was not a revolution to give liberty to the millions of masses who had no wealth: it took hundreds of years before they could even vote.

It was not a revolution for nearly half of the country: women. Only in the first quarter of the 20th century could one seriously discuss their right to vote.

It was not a revolution to do anything for Indians—except exterminate them.

It was not a revolution for those immigrants who swarmed this land to escape the class and religious wars that raged against them.

Indeed, it wasn't really a revolution at all. It was a baron's revolt—a change of management from the British lords and ladies of empire.

It was a fight about who would rule this land. Who would be Master, George III? Or George Washington?

Who would profit?

❖ ❖ ❖

7 The Monroe Doctrine
Dreaming of Eminent Domain Forever

The devil is right at home. The devil, the devil himself is right in the house... and the devil came here yesterday. Yesterday the devil came here. Right here... and it smells of sulfur still today.

—Hugo Chavez, holding a copy of Noam Chomsky's *Hegemony or Survival,* addresses the UN General Assembly, New York City, October 20, 2006

One day after Japanese planes bombed Pearl Harbor, U.S. President Franklin Delano Roosevelt addressed a joint session of Congress and famously defined December the seventh, nineteen hundred and forty-one as "a date which will live in infamy." In fact, there are many dates "which will live in infamy" and one of those dates is December the second, eighteen hundred and twenty-three when another American president, James Monroe, also addressed a joint session of Congress. It was Monroe's seventh annual State of the Union Address... and the words he spoke that day not only cemented the foundation of the American Empire but also unleashed the modus operandi of U.S. foreign policy that rages hard to this day. With history as our witness, the "Monroe Doctrine" codified the forceful expansion of the Empire and later, through its official corollary[1] disgorged by "Big Stick" Teddy Roosevelt, the U.S. would assume "the exercise of an international police power"[2] to this day.

The doctrine was primarily composed by then Secretary of State and future U.S. president John Quincy Adams (along with cabinet members John C. Calhoun and William Wirt). In his book *Imperial America,* Gore Vidal sardonically defines the "all-purpose" Monroe Doctrine as "the invention of John Quincy Adams,"[3] an imperial tool that has functioned and evolved for almost 200 years as a declaration of hegemony as well as a trigger for unilateral intervention throughout the Americas and, by extension, the world. Initially, the primary objective of the Monroe Doctrine was to ensure and solidify an American sphere of influence over the Western Hemisphere as Latin American colonies were breaking the stranglehold of Spanish and Portuguese colonial occupation. For the U.S. government it was the moment in time to draw a hard line in the sand between the anticipated interference throughout the Americas by "Old World" European empires versus Washington's own designs on "New World" dominance. Prior to making a final decision to "go public" with the principles set forth in his inaugural address, Monroe sought the advice of ex-President Thomas Jefferson, whose answer as historian John A. Crow writes, "is almost as famous as the doctrine itself."[4] From his slave compound and plantation at Monticello, Jefferson wrote:

> Our first and fundamental maxim should be never to entangle ourselves in the broils of Europe. Our second, never to suffer Europe to intermeddle with cis-Atlantic affairs. America, North and South, has a set of interests distinct from those of Europe and peculiarly her own. She should therefore have a system of her own, separate and apart from that of Europe. While the last is laboring to become the domicile of despotism, our endeavor should surely be to make our hemisphere that of freedom.[5]

Clearly, this presidential warning on inaugural day 1823 was the origin of the notion "America for Americans" and along with Jefferson and Adams, Monroe told Europe to stay grounded on their side of the big pond—just like Eddie Murphy told some rednecks in *48 Hours*: *"And I want the rest of you cowboys to know something, there's a new sheriff in town... and his name is Reggie Hammond. So y'all be cool. Right on."* And that new sheriff was the budding American Empire. In his address, Monroe made his point abundantly clear. But without a hint of comedic self-awareness, nor even the slightest nod to the absurdity of announcing control over a place you can't really command, Sheriff Monroe proclaims:

> In the discussions to which this interest has given rise and in the arrangements by which they may terminate the occasion has been judged proper for asserting, as a principle in which the rights and interests of the United States are involved, that the American continents, by the free and independent condition which they have assumed and maintain, are henceforth not to be considered as subjects for future colonization by any European powers.[6]

Leading up to 1823, two diplomatic issues prompted Secretary of State Adams and President Monroe to openly declare America's sphere of influence over the Americas. The first was a fairly minor controversy with Russia, which still had colonial claims on the northwest coast of the American continent (Russian settlements stretched as far south as current-day Bodega Bay in California). Adams and Monroe made it clear in the presidential address that the American continents were now off limits for colonization as well as any imperial intentions by European powers.[7] The second, more pressing issue, centered on the Americans' fear that the Holy Alliance—a union between the reactionary governments and emperors of Russia, Austria, Prussia, and France—would re-energize their colonial efforts in the growing Latin American states that just gained their independence from Spain and Portugal. History has proved that the fear of the Holy Alliance's desire to meddle in Latin America was an imaginary danger, but the die was cast in America's founding doctrine on international relations.[8] What began as a quasi-defensive policy statement in a presidential address would over time evolve, morph, and expand into an imperial battering ram of monumental proportions.

As we will detail, American presidents and policy makers have used the foundation and basic tenets of the Monroe Doctrine, as well as its general braggadocio, to justify almost every act of U.S. aggression across the planet—from James K. Polk's belligerent reassertion of the Doctrine to validate his war against, and massive land-theft of, Mexico in 1846, to George W. Bush's perverse precept regarding preemptive attack used to rationalize America's so-called war on terror and the subsequent murder spree in the Middle East. No longer just the province of the Western Hemisphere, America's use of this imperial canon became all pervading and global.

Writing in his detailed study, *The Monroe Doctrine: Empire and Nation in Nineteenth-Century America,* Jay Sexton argues, "Generations of Americans would proclaim that Monroe's message embodied fundamental principles of American statecraft. But they would disagree with one another over its meaning, purpose, and application. There would be as many Monroe Doctrines as foreign policy perspectives."[9]

Political analyst William Blum summed up the amorphous and shape-shifting doctrine in straightforward fashion, writing that, "the U.S. government conferred upon the U.S. government the remarkable and enviable right to intervene militarily" wherever and whenever it deemed appropriate.[10] As history marched on, the use of the Monroe Doctrine (and its subsequent corollaries) was embraced and exploited by Washington at any given moment. Ultimately, the Monroe Doctrine was a lot like "Grandma's nightshirt"—*it covered everything.*

In many respects, the late Venezuelan President Hugo Chavez standing at the rostrum before the United Nations General Assembly, playfully waving Noam Chomsky's searing indictment of U.S. foreign policy as a portal into the ages—a gift to all the victims who were turned to dust by American thirst for power. It was a remarkable moment as if—in the personification of Chavez—the victims raised their voices to say, "We see through your façade, we reject the myth, we acknowledge the genocide, the slavery, the massacres, the predatory capitalism on robber baron steroids, the lies of liberty and democracy—all of it—we see through all of it—and this man Chomsky, one of your own, also sees through all of it. He nails the current and past mandarins to the cross. Hegemony or survival!" (Too bad Chavez's checkered legacy in Venezuela doesn't live up to the lofty sentiments espoused above.)

> *The past is never dead. It's not even past.*
>
> –William Faulkner, *Requiem for a Nun*

America's Deoxyribonucleic Acid

As we've discussed in previous chapters, American exceptionalism is like a main circuit cable that runs through the heart of the American Empire. In fact, the very idea of elite "exceptionalism," especially as endowed by Providence, has been the foundation of every empire since humans crawled out of the proverbial muck. In this regard, the American Empire is no exception. And the Monroe Doctrine—that protectorate manifesto of hemispheric rule—has been the perfect protean tool for politicians and rulers to use as their flexible "legal" and "moral" rationale for America's colonial and imperial adventures. This doctrine, along with the spurious state of mind known as American exceptionalism, re-imagines the necessary historical concepts to reflect the current political and cultural environments.[11] Author Gretchen Murphy, in her book *Hemispheric Imaginings: The Monroe Doctrine and Narratives of U.S. Empire,* identifies the arc of the Monroe Doctrine in the pantheon of American credentials:

> After 1895 the Doctrine for the first time assumed its status as a sacred national tradition and cherished document, akin to the Declaration of Independence and Washington's Farewell Address.[12]

Murphy notes the slow evolution of the Monroe Doctrine in America's foreign policy, a policy that nevertheless remained expansionist:

> After 1823, no one made formal mention of Monroe's words as a precedent until 1845, when Polk cited Monroe's principles to defend the rights of the United States to the Oregon territory.[13]

Interestingly enough, the U.S. Department of State's own Office of the Historian illustrates a direct reference to America's religious-like fervor to expand:

> For their part, the British also had a strong interest in ensuring the demise of Spanish colonialism, with all the trade restrictions mercantilism imposed. Earlier in 1823 British Foreign Minister George Canning suggested to Americans that [the] two nations issue a joint declaration to deter any other power from intervening in Central and South America. Secretary of State John Quincy Adams, however, vigorously opposed cooperation with Great Britain, *contending that a statement of bilateral nature could limit United States expansion in the future.* He also argued that the British were not committed to recognizing the Latin American republics and must have had imperial motivations themselves.[14] [Emphasis added]

John Quincy Adams, like all the other American founders before him, knew a good imperial playground when he saw one. It just took some time to marshal the forces necessary to make the move. Years passed into decades before Monroe's words coalesced into an official term that would define American policy even though the policy was being loaded and holstered, ready to use. Murphy writes:

> Even the phrase "Monroe Doctrine" sits uncertainly between politics and culture. It was coined in 1853, when Congress debated a joint resolution to declare as law what had hitherto been referred to as "the principles of Mr. Monroe" or "the Monroe declaration." But exactly who coined the term is also uncertain.[15]

As is the case with most historical cornerstones at their moment of conception, the Monroe Doctrine was not the rock-solid sanctified foreign policy gospel it later grew to be.[16] Ironically, as popular as the accepted spirit of the doctrine was throughout the 19th century, Murphy declares that the haziness of its directive was palpable:

> Popular sentiment of the era overwhelmingly affirmed that the Monroe Doctrine was still relevant, although, as a few skeptics pointed out, no one seemed to agree on exactly what it stated, how it should be applied, or where its jurisdiction should be in the twentieth century.[17]

In the years immediately following Monroe's articulation, the doctrine offered little relevancy to the U.S. government. At the time, the "Old World" European powers, who inspired the spirit (and the fear) of Monroe's admonition, were entwined in their own century of turbulence—a century that was ushered in by the revolutionary movements that shook France to its core both before and after the reign and subsequent wars of Napoleon. The Industrial Revolution swept across Europe, propelling mass modernization as well as urbanization, and then for almost half a century, British manufactured goods dominated world trade. Industry and growth were so alive in Great Britain, many referred to it as "the workshop of the world."[18]

So as Europe roared through the 19th century, it was redefining itself through revolution as well as tectonic shifts in power as evidenced by Germany's rise during the latter half of the century in the persona of Prussian statesman, Otto Von Bismarck, who dominated European affairs until the eve of the 20th century. The "Old World" was handling its own massive growth. Clearly, Europe was busy with commerce as its colonial endeavors waned. The initial fear of Europe pursuing foreign entanglements in the Western Hemisphere, in reality, was much ado about nothing. The original intent of the Monroe Doctrine as written and stated by Adams and Monroe was a practical non-issue at the time and was essentially ineffectual and without teeth since the U.S. didn't have credible armed forces to back up their tough words. In fact, the U.S. didn't have much of a chance to invoke and implement the inherent threat of the doctrine to would-be aggressors because guess who came to dinner? *Nobody.* Truth be told, the doctrine had little if any impact on U.S. foreign policy for at least thirty years after Monroe pulled the trigger.[19]

In 1836 there was a ripple of tension between the U.S. and Great Britain when the former objected to latter's alliance with the emerging Republic of Texas and its ties to the Spanish Empire. The objection was rooted in the principles set forth by Monroe and Adams more than a decade before. The great irony is that, as stated above, the U.S. could not back-up their bold words with formidable action. In reality, the U.S. relied on Great Britain's unspoken and implied support of Monroe's warning in order to oppose the Spanish Empire's drive to restore its colonies. By proxy, the Royal Navy actually enforced America's hemispheric muscle as part of their wider 19th century "Pax Britannica" made possible by Great Britain's unchallenged sea power.[20]

The American Revolution dispensed with one empire and gave birth to another. The 19th century unfolded with the new nation—this new embryonic American Empire—growing and evolving at breakneck speed. The American leadership had their sights set on the western horizon, well beyond the boundaries of the original 13 states hugging the Atlantic coastline. With an economy bolstered by free slave labor coupled with a hostile and belligerent expansion plan driven by holy genocide, the country grew in leaps and bounds. The leaders of this blossoming juggernaut, all deeply inspired by the 18th century European Enlightenment, had visions of grandeur, visions of this new Israel—this new promised land—following Jesus Christ and the sun right to the shores of the Pacific. In fact, the rolling-thunder march across the continent was the first real expression of U.S aggression against sovereign nations and sovereign peoples. U.S. imperial designs had become obvious and were strutting center stage.

The United States, this up-and-coming world power, measured success using the yardstick of expansion. The framers of the new nation envisioned expansion as the means to "greatness and the foundation of its democracy."[21] In her extraordinary tome, *Masters of War: Latin America and U.S. Aggression,* Clara Nieto frames U.S. expansion in no uncertain terms:

> Vigorous expansion—manifest in the Monroe Doctrine—was the expression of the "Founding Fathers'" belief that their mission lay in extending the territorial, economic, and political dominion of the great North American nation and thus "extend[ing] the area of freedom."[22]

Nieto then explains the expansion of the mission as time rumbled forward. The Monroe Doctrine was gaining traction:

> Monroe's successors added other principles, doctrines, and policies that strengthened this expansionist and redemptive vocation. "Manifest destiny" was an expression of their self-professed "ideological and moral superiority" over the rest of the globe. Andrew Jackson (1829-1837) saw the extension of the United States' authority over "semi-barbarous peoples" to bring them civilization and "teaching inferiors

to appreciate the blessings they already enjoyed but were inclined to overlook" as the "inevitable historical mission" of the United States.[23]

> *"Monroeism" carries a deeply negative meaning in Latin America and the Caribbean. Throughout the region, the mere mention of the Monroe Doctrine hints at impending U.S. aggression.*
> – Saul Landau, Philip Brenner, *Killing the Monroe Doctrine*

We cannot discuss the sledgehammer-like impact of the Monroe Doctrine (and its many historic transmutations) on the unfortunate victims of the world without revisiting the overarching drive of venomous Anglo-Saxon supremacism, "what public figures in the United States would later call 'Manifest Destiny'—and Adolf Hitler," Ward Churchill writes, "would subsequently term *Lebensraumpolitik.*"[24] Wild forest activist, writer, and cabinetmaker Charles Sullivan distills down the march of empire this way:

> The history of the US has been an unbroken chain of events that is carrying us into a future of unspeakable violence and misery. The doctrine of manifest destiny was then, as now, essentially racist and bigoted in its worldview. Let's not forget that it was this paradigm of superiority in the eyes of a god made in their own image that not only permitted, it provided the spurious moral authority for the genocide of the American Indian, the plunder of the land for its resource value, the theft of the land from its original inhabitants, the enslavement of the Negro, subjugation of women and endless war on the poor. What manifest destiny has done to America it will, if left to its own devices, do for the entire world.[25]

Racist indeed. It is the ugly thread in American history that runs from the very moment Columbus stepped foot on the remote Bahamian island of Samana Cay, through Indian removal (read: ethnic cleansing), the terrorism of slavery, the Moro Massacre of "Pacific negroes" or "niggers,"[26] the detonation of Little Boy and Fat Man over Hiroshima and Nagasaki, and finally the delivery of daisy cutters and cluster bombs to tame some "sand niggers"[27] at the dawn of the 21st century.

Appetite for Destruction

The text of James Monroe's seventh inaugural address that would later solidify into the "Monroe Doctrine" was based on the founders' thirst for expansion—an expansion they knew full well would rely heavily on a "removal policy" otherwise known as extirpation—a sterile academic word for butchery, slaughter, and massacre. Take your pick—it all adds up to extermination... and no founding father was better at advocating and laying out the plan for extermination than Thomas Jefferson.

Though, the "Father of the Country," George Washington, was probably a close second. The Iroquois, Mohawk, and Onondaga nations knew full well that his middle name was probably "Extirpation." Really, they did. In fact, they called him "Town Destroyer"[28] because the first George W. was well known for ordering scorched earth murder sprees throughout the colonies. In *American Holocaust,* Professor David Stannard writes:

> As one of the Iroquois told Washington to his face in 1792: "to this day, when that name is heard, our women look behind them and turn pale, and our children cling close to the necks of their mothers." They might have clung close to the necks of their mothers when other names were mentioned as well—such as Adams or Monroe or Jackson.[29]

Or Monticello Tom.

As a child, Jefferson envisioned adventures and exploration deep into the American west. The Library of Congress' exhibition on Jefferson states that, "His father Peter was a surveyor, mapmaker, and land speculator on the Virginia frontier. Jefferson spent his childhood in the Blue Ridge Mountains on the western edge of the Virginia Piedmont. Though he never physically ventured beyond the Virginia Blue Ridge, Jefferson had a life-long commitment to supporting western exploration and asserting American claims to western lands."[30]

Well, Tom got his wish.

As president in 1807, Jefferson directed his Secretary of War (so much more to the point than Secretary of Defense) to use "the hatchet" on any Indians that had the temerity to defy U.S. expansion.[31] Stannard continues Jefferson's historical tirade:

> "If ever we are constrained to lift the hatchet against any tribe, we will never lay it down till that tribe is exterminated, or is driven beyond the Mississippi," continuing, "in war, they will kill some of us; we shall destroy all of them." These were not offhand remarks, for five years later, in 1812, Jefferson again concluded that white Americans were "obliged" to drive the "backward Indians with the beasts of the forests into the

> Stony Mountains"; and one year later still, he added that the American government had no other choice before it than "to pursue [the Indians] to extermination, or drive them to new seats beyond our reach." Indeed, Jefferson's writing on Indians are filled with the straightforward assertion that the natives are to be given a simple choice—to be "extirpate[d] from the earth" or to remove themselves out of the Americans' way. Had those same words been enunciated by a German leader in 1939, and directed at European Jews, they would be engraved in modern memory.[32]

Stannard is not finished because here's a classic example of how the lie replaces the truth, how the myth gains fame and fortune and the reality is buried in books like this one. Here's the grim practice of safe and guild historians shoveling shit:

> Since [these words] were uttered by one of America's founding fathers, however, the most widely admired of the South's slaveholding philosophers of freedom, they conveniently have become lost to most historians in their insistent celebration of Jefferson's wisdom and humanity.[33]

Safe and guild historians also minimized and downplayed the reality that America's founders ferociously cried "havoc" and then let slip the dogs of war in their unabated appetite for empire. In an interview for this book with American dissident Noam Chomsky, he spoke to this point:

> We don't think of the United States as being an empire in the way we think of say, Britain, as being an empire, but that's what some historians of empire call the "Salt Water Fallacy." Britain's empire happened to be disconnected through salt water; the American empire happens to be contiguous, but the conquests were, in many respects, similar, and in the American case, much worse because they actually eliminated a large part of the native population.[34]

For centuries, British colonialists engaged in the language of Social Darwinism to promote and justify Anglo-Saxon expansion and domination of other peoples around the globe. The new American imperialists also employed this language and spirit as their justification for pillage, enslavement, and ethnic cleansing. Three hundred and twenty years before Monroe's words emboldened the American founders' epic plans for expansion, Christopher Columbus wrote a letter to King Ferdinand and Queen Isabella that was bold if not shocking in its brutal honesty. Columbus brags about his easy conquest of these guileless people (sometimes by force and violence), who believe that his ships and men come from the heavens. Columbus makes it abundantly clear that the natives cannot match their force and weapons, nor do they want to, and that the Spaniards can take any item or person that they deem necessary, such as "slaves, as many as they shall order, and who will be from the idolaters." Of course, all of this is accomplished with the help of "Our Redeemer" and with "solemn thanks to the Holy Trinity... because not only Spain but all Christendom will have hence refreshment and gain."[35]

Again, this appetite for destruction and conquest was planted in America's DNA long before the republic was a twinkle in the founders' eyes. Expansion through murder and genocide became acceptable—mantle in the Empire's foundational bedrock.

Political scientist and long time critic of empire, Michael Parenti, told us, "That's what's so refreshing about Columbus' letter to Ferdinand. He's talking like one gangster to another, 'we can enslave, we can rip them off, we can enslave.' But most of the time, in imperialism, that isn't the way it works. Most of the time you cloak your plunder, you cloak your murder always in the highest terms. And so you listen to Governor Winthrop [in the Massachusetts colony, circa 1630] and he talks about 'clearing God's land of these savage devils, getting rid of them, and turning it into the garden that it should be.'" Parenti concludes, "It's amazing how frequently doing God's work entails stealing property and murdering people."[36]

It's the Money, Stupid

As we've seen, the holy grail of destiny—America's manifest and holy exception—has fueled the rabid and fanatical thirst for expansion. It is a thirst that still thrives for control and expansion during the first decades of the 21st century. It is a thirst that has yet to be quenched by time or deed because the idea of Empire's expansion cannot cease or slow down until the insatiable engine of capitalism itself ceases. Or implodes. Or is exchanged for a more humane model. Simply put, the American Empire and capitalism are joined at the hip. Charles Sullivan frames it this way:

> This is what is really meant by the New World Order extolled by George H. Bush at the onslaught of the first Persian Gulf War. Thus, the terms "manifest destiny" and "capitalism" are interchangeable. They mean essentially the same thing.[37]

Follow the money. Always follow the money. Sullivan continues:

> So deeply imbedded in the American psyche is the precept of capitalism and its twin—manifest destiny that few of us even bother to question it. But the more we buy into these lies the harder it will be to extricate ourselves from them.[38]

As the character Gordon Gekko so confidently affirmed in Oliver Stone's *Wall Street*, "GREED IS GOOD." But the idea of bold-faced greed (read: capitalism) as a feel-good motive doesn't go down well with the masses. Res publica needs a story or a myth that acts as a rationale for the theft and the depravity committed in their name, financed by their tax dollars, and ultimately carried out with their approval—either tacit or overt. It's the lie that will help the medicine go down.

The choices for the lie are usually the same. They include:

1. The Myth of the Dangerous Demon Savage *(who needs to be removed because they're wasting some really good land and resources and therefore have no God-given right to it)*
2. The Myth of the Inferior Beings *(who need to be used but marginalized and god forbid one of them marries your daughter)*
3. The Myth of Our God Is Bigger, Better, and Mightier Than Your God *('nuff said, although this religious choice has many subsets)*
4. The Myth of Ridding the World of Tyranny, Dictatorship, and Despotism *(and then replacing it with democracy—unless, of course the tyrant, dictator, or despot is good for business, then fuggedaboutit)*

Now, these lies work well solo, in tandem, you can mix and match, or in some cases it's "all of the above"—especially when the aggression and slaughter ain't goin' real well.

Clearly, the "racialized" hymn to U.S. expansion and imperialism has included "all of the above." It's been an ode to capitalist white Christian authority, once proclaimed by Max Weber as the "protestant ethic and the spirit of capitalism." Charles Sullivan writes, "Christian fundamentalism has too often provided the bogus moral authority behind the precepts of manifest destiny and capitalism."[39]

Appetite for Destruction (Part Deux: The Expansion of Slavery)
—or—
Who Said Dat?

Since James Monroe's words—and the actions unleashed by the subsequent Monroe Doctrine—are so steeped in the founders' righteous desires and motivations, it demands that we look closely at the *raison d'être* for their actions over the first one hundred years of the Republic. Think of it as a "character study," for if we are to base the march of America's destiny on the foundation set forth by the founders and framers of the nation, we ought to be well-versed in the reality of their behavior and not the ensuing and accepted myths. And if you look at the facts, those first one hundred years of the American nation can only be defined and characterized by the continuation of native genocide and the expansion of slavery.

The accepted myth that was well crafted and signed into the nation's history books—or as James Loewen describes them, "Lies My Teacher Told Me"—is a tale that begins with a battle against British tyranny, a battle that magically evolved into a glorious expansion across virgin lands by independent rugged pioneers who built their new country—their "New Jerusalem"—from sea to shining sea. Nothing could be further from the truth.

> *Whoever debases others is debasing himself.*
>
> —James Baldwin, *The Fire Next Time*

Color has always played a major and dominant role in the machinations of Euro-American expansion as well as its bastard stepchild: U.S. imperialism. Messrs. Red, Black, Yellow, and Brown have been on the receiving end of empire, while Mr. White has been the ultimate taskmaster. So would a book about empire, genocide, and manifest destiny be complete without a parlor game? Probably not, so let's play *"Who said dat?"*

> In general, their existence appears to participate more of sensation than reflection. To this must be ascribed their disposition to sleep when abstracted from their diversions, and unemployed in labour. An animal whose body is at rest, and who does not reflect, must be disposed to sleep of course. Comparing them by their faculties of memory, reason, and imagination, it appears to me that in memory they are equal to the whites; in reason much inferior, as I think one could scarcely be

> found capable of tracing and comprehending the investigations of Euclid; and that in imagination they are dull, tasteless, and anomalous. It would be unfair to follow them to Africa for this investigation.[40]

Okay, was it:

> A) Nathan Bedford Forrest (original Grand Wizard of the Ku Klux Klan)
> B) Jefferson Davis (President of the Confederate States of America)
> C) Simon Legree (slave master extraordinaire from *Uncle Tom's Cabin*)
> D) Thomas Jefferson (enlightened American icon and founding father)

Well, if you said Thomas Jefferson then you win two tickets to tour his slave plantation hidden deep in the Virginia countryside, on a hill, overlooking the lie of history. In the same book of writings, *Notes on the State of Virginia,* Jefferson rolled out this beauty:

> The first difference which strikes us is that of colour. Whether the black of the negro resides in the reticular membrane between the skin and scarf-skin, or in the scarf-skin itself; whether it proceeds from the colour of the blood, the colour of the bile, or from that of some other secretion, the difference is fixed in nature, and is as real as if its seat and cause were better known to us. And is this difference of no importance? Is it not the foundation of a greater or less share of beauty in the two races? Are not the fine mixtures of red and white, the expressions of every passion by greater or less suffusions of colour in the one, preferable to that eternal monotony, which reigns in the countenances, that immovable veil of black which covers all the emotions of the other race? Add to these, flowing hair, a more elegant symmetry of form, their own judgment in favour of the whites, declared by their preference of them, as uniformly as is the preference of the Oranootan [orangutan] for the black women over those of his own species. The circumstance of Superior beauty, is thought worthy attention in the propagation of our horses, dogs, and other domestic animals; why not in that of man? Besides those of colour, figure, and hair, there are other physical distinctions proving a difference of race. They have less hair on the face and body. They secrete less by the kidneys, and more by the glands of the skin, which gives them a very strong and disagreeable odour.[41]

Now, how offended will you be if we characterize Monticello Tom as a rapist? You may want to toss this book aside before it bursts into flames.

But you can't put it down if you want an honest rendering of your own history because, quite simply: history defines the future... and if America continues the lie, the future is doomed—or as Orwell wrote in *1984*: "Everything faded into mist. The past was erased, the erasure forgotten, the lie became the truth."

This is why Jefferson is under the magnifying glass. His impact on the soul of America is immeasurable. The legacy of not only the Monroe Doctrine, but also much of the legacy of the entire nation, can be traced back to this one man. Here's the case outlined by journalism professor Robert Jensen from his book *The Heart of Whiteness: Confronting Race, Racism and White Privilege*—and you know what? It's completely logical and totally on target. Jensen asks, "Wait just a minute—Jefferson raped a slave? The author of the Declaration of Independence was not only a slave-owner but a rapist? That description is not heresy but simple logic."[42] Jensen continues:

> The historical consensus is that Jefferson had sex with Sally Hemings, one of the 150 slaves at Monticello, the Jefferson plantation. Even the official guardian of the Jefferson legacy acknowledges this: "The DNA study, combined with multiple strands of currently available documentary and statistical evidence, indicates a high probability that Thomas Jefferson fathered Eston Hemings, and that he most likely was the father of all six of Sally Hemings's children appearing in Jefferson's records."[43]

Rape is universally defined as sex that is forced upon a person without his or her consent. Jensen continues this line of reasoning:

> Slaves do not consent to their enslavement. To ask whether a slave consents to any particular order given by a master under such conditions is a meaningless question. Sally Hemings was a slave. Thomas Jefferson owned her. Jefferson had sex with Hemings. Therefore, Jefferson raped Hemings, who under conditions of enslavement could not give meaningful consent. That he raped her at least once we know with "high probability." That he raped her five other times is "most likely." That he raped her numerous other times is certainly plausible.
>
> This is hardly surprising; white slave owners routinely raped their slaves. When stated generically—"white masters sometimes raped their African slaves"—the statement doesn't spark controversy. What reason is there to assume Jefferson was different? Since he was willing to own other human

> beings and force them to work, why would we expect him to be unwilling to force at least one of them to have sex? Why should the same term applied to other slave owners not be used to describe Jefferson's conduct?[44]

But American leaders, American historians, and the vast majority of the American people have a religious-like zeal to embrace the lie and perpetuate a much different story about their history in general and a figure like Jefferson in particular. This is how the masses justify and then go along with the reprehensible actions of their government. Ultimately, the lie gives them cover. Jensen quotes distinguished liberal journalist Bill Moyers from his 2004 PBS television show *NOW* when he discussed Jefferson's relationship with Hemings:

> The hands of Thomas Jefferson that wrote, "life, liberty, and the pursuit of happiness," also stroked the breasts and caressed the thighs of a slave woman named Sally Hemings, who bore him six children and whom he never acknowledged.[45]

Stroked? Caressed? Even a compassionate and intelligent journalist like Moyers uses easy and soft language to gently frame the forced physical relationship between slave master and slave. To reference George Carlin once again—"Language always gives you away." And here, "stroked" and "caressed" turns rape into lovemaking. Add to this relationship formula the fact that Jefferson was forty-seven and Hemings sixteen. *Sixteen.* That brings up an entirely different crime but how much can you take?

Jensen then underscores how important it is to understand this connection when attempting to grasp and acknowledge the reality of American history:

> Americans seem to have a strong need to tell a different story about Jefferson, even when acknowledging these unpleasant realities about his life. I know of no history textbook in which there is an acknowledgement that Jefferson raped at least one of his slaves. Why? Because to acknowledge such things that bluntly is to take a step on the road to coming to terms with the three racist holocausts that have formed the United States of America. It's to acknowledge that the story we tell ourselves about this country is as much myth as fact. It's to face the ugly, brutal, violent racist history of the country; understand that our affluent society is the product of that history; and then recognize that such violence continues to protect our affluence and perpetuate racialized disparities in the worldwide distribution of wealth.[46]

The Greek philosopher Aristotle suggested, "From the hour of their birth, some men are marked out for subjection, others for rule." Almost twenty-one hundred years later and with the strokes of a quill pen and five words, Thomas Jefferson obliterated Aristotle's hierarchy when he wrote: "all men are created equal." Journalist and historian Henry Wiencek writes that, "In his original draft of the Declaration, in soaring, damning, fiery prose, Jefferson denounced the slave trade as an 'execrable commerce... this assemblage of horrors, a 'cruel war against human nature itself, violating its most sacred rights of life & liberties.'"[47] Many historians agree that had these words been included in the Declaration of Independence, the new American nation would have been dedicated to the eradication of "this assemblage of horrors" from its very birth. But Jefferson and others caved in to the political and economic pressures of the day and this crucial language disappeared, setting the stage for this "cruel war against human nature itself" to continue for another eighty-plus years, followed by Jim Crow, separate but equal, and the familiar ugly strain of American racism that inflicts this country to this very second. By 1790, Jefferson's silence on slavery was deafening. Wiencek continues:

> The very existence of slavery in the era of the American Revolution presents a paradox, and we have largely been content to leave it at that, since a paradox can offer a comforting state of moral suspended animation. Jefferson animates the paradox. And by looking closely at Monticello, we can see the process by which he rationalized an abomination to the point where an absolute moral reversal was reached and he made slavery fit into America's national enterprise.[48]

Indeed, an enterprise growing large just a few years before the Monroe Doctrine triumphantly rode off into history. This is the foundation from which American expansion, imperialism, and empire sprang forth—all bolstered by America's ongoing wars of dispossession.

"Our Peculiar Institution"

As President, Jefferson's actions cultivated what would soon evolve into this aggressive American policy on expansion and destiny—a position that greatly influenced James Monroe and John Quincy Adams and the actions they set in motion on 2 December 1823. In the 1790s and into the early 1800s, Jefferson—the so-called architect of American liberty—had a glorious chance to turn the tide on slavery in North America as the Haitian Revolution unfolded on the

French island colony of Saint-Domingue, where African slaves were tirelessly revolting against white European colonial rule. When the revolution began, the American government—led by George Washington as well as numerous American merchants—helped to finance the white French planters, advancing them cash, food, arms, and ammunition. Clearly, the Americans believed that a successful slave revolt in the "pearl of the Antilles" would ignite similar rebellions throughout the colonies. By 1798, the planter regime was crumbling and, at the request of the Haitian revolutionary leader Toussaint L'Ouverture, the U.S. Congress authorized President John Adams to reopen trade with Haiti. This successful slave revolt—a defining moment for African freedom in the Americas—was on the precipice of glory until Thomas Jefferson reached the White House in 1801.[49] "Jefferson was terrified that the creation, and flourishing, of a black republic in the New World would serve as a model for the rebellion of America's own slaves," writes Harvard professor Henry Louis Gates, "and that, at all costs, would be unacceptable."[50] Gates continues:

> As early as 1793, Jefferson wrote to James Monroe that, "Never was so deep a tragedy presented to the feelings of man... I become daily more and more convinced that all the West India Island will remain in the hands of the people of colour, and a total expulsion of the whites sooner or later take place. It is high time we should foresee the bloody scenes which our children certainly, and possibly ourselves (south of the Potomac), have to wade through and try to avert them." Two years later, in a letter to Aaron Burr, Jefferson compared the Haitians to assassins and referred to them as "Cannibals of the terrible republic."[51]

Jefferson clearly laid the groundwork for aggressive western expansion that included the overt expansion of slavery. When he acquired the Louisiana Territory from France in 1803, some 828,000 square miles, the new nation almost doubled in size. "No one points out," stresses James Loewen in *Lies My Teacher Told Me*, "that it was not France's land to sell—it was Indian land. The French never consulted with the Native owners before selling."[52] What Jefferson actually did was preside over the wholesale increase of the South's plantation system. Supporters of Jefferson, probably better described as apologists for Jefferson, usually defend and re-write his dark side with the idea that he was simply a product of his times and/or that he was wedged between a political rock and a hard place trying valiantly to hold together the new precious republic. Bullshit. It was about money. Jefferson was enamored with the money he was making on his slave holdings. All these bastards were. Yale University professor and historian David Brion Davis describes slavery as an economic juggernaut this way:

> American slaves represented more capital than any other asset in the nation, with the exception of land. In 1860 the value of Southern slaves was about three times the value of the capital stock in manufacturing and railroads nationwide.[53]

No wonder the Monroe Doctrine grew in popularity and interpretations—the expanding Empire needed to protect its turf from intervention by the old world powers, whether or not the threat of intervention was real or imagined. The skittish new country needed to protect its newly stolen treasure—and not just from old world empires looking to reenergize their colonial tendencies but from a growing worldwide abolition movement that had its sights on ridding America of slavery, its "peculiar institution."

(This phrase belongs to John C. Calhoun, the pro-slavery leader in the U.S. Senate from South Carolina, who vehemently opposed the abolition of slavery as well as attempts to limit the expansion of slavery into the newly minted western territories. He was also a key advocate of the 1850 Fugitive Slave Law. We would characterize this southern gentleman as a "douchebag" (probably worse), but in 1957 a Senate Committee selected John Caldwell Calhoun as one of the greatest United States Senators of all time. Do you really need to know anything else about the bullshit Americans tell themselves?)

But it was Jefferson's economically-inspired expansion of slavery that cut a gruesome path through the 19th century, one that helped to fuel the brutal march of American destiny through the killing fields of expansion. Plain and simple, Monticello Tom fell in love with his profits. In the *Smithsonian* magazine (that bastion of radical thought), Henry Wiencek elaborates on Jefferson's economic designs:

> He was making a 4 percent profit every year on the birth of black children. The enslaved were yielding him a bonanza, a perpetual human dividend at compound interest. Jefferson wrote, "I allow nothing for losses by death, but, on the contrary, shall presently take credit four per cent. per annum, for their increase over and above keeping up their own numbers." His plantation was producing inexhaustible human assets.[54]

Wiencek continues as Jefferson kisses the cheek of liberty and then collects his thirty pieces of gold.

> In another communication from the early 1790s, Jefferson takes the 4 percent formula further and quite bluntly advances the notion that slavery presented an investment strategy for the future. He writes that an acquaintance who had suffered financial reverses "should have been invested in negroes." He advises that if the friend's family had any cash left, "every farthing of it [should be] laid out in land and negroes, which besides a present support bring a silent profit of from 5. to 10. per cent in this country by the increase in their value."[55]

The article goes on to describe whipping slave children at Jefferson's blacksmith shop and nailery on the plantation's famed Mulberry Row:

> This world was crueler than we have been led to believe. A letter has recently come to light describing how Monticello's young black boys, "the small ones," age 10, 11 or 12, were whipped to get them to work in Jefferson's nail factory, whose profits paid the mansion's grocery bills. This passage about children being lashed had been suppressed—deliberately deleted from the published record in the 1953 edition of Jefferson's Farm Book, containing 500 pages of plantation papers.[56]

In his in-depth look at Jefferson and slavery, historian Robert McColley writes, "The years of slavery's supposed decline were in fact the years of its greatest expansion... a social and economic institution of such power that it sustained and extended an economic system whose demands went far to determine the domestic and foreign policy of the 'agrarian' party in our early history."[57] David Brion Davis holds no punches as he underscores Jefferson's impact on the expansion of empire and slavery when he writes, "When the chips were down, as in the Missouri crisis, he threw his weight behind slavery's expansion, and bequeathed to the South the image of anti-slavery as a Federalist mask for economic exploitation."[58]

In fact, this compulsive and cumulative fixation on American exceptionalism is the foundation and dark legacy that led to the articulation and growth of the Monroe Doctrine. Once again, American myths about national character constantly overshadow the historical realities. From the mid-19th century on, bolstered by the zealotry of Manifest Destiny and American exceptionalism, expansion across the North American continent was a "Yellowbrick Road" of lies, deceit, and destruction. In a city and a house built by slaves, President Monroe and Secretary of State Adams were the first generation of leaders to re-interpret and expand the mission after America's founders set the grand illusion in motion.

America is false to the past, false to the present, and solemnly binds herself to be false to the future.

—Frederick Douglass (July 5, 1852)

As the 19th century roared into the 1850s, rising local and regional tensions engulfed the nation with the expansion of slavery at the core of a ticking time bomb. What an economic boom it would be if the entire country could be built on the backs of slave labor! And, at the same time Indian "removal" was also going very well. "As pronouncements of Angloamerica's 'Manifest Destiny' to enjoy limitless expansion intensified," explains Ward Churchill, "so too did calls for the outright eradication of Indians."[59] In fact, "By 1840, with the exception of a handful of tiny Iroquois reservations in upstate New York and the remaining Seminoles in the Florida Everglades," writes Churchill, "the eastern third of what would become the continental United States had been cleared of its indigenous population."[60]

The new nation needed a neighborhood to expand from and dominate. Jefferson's Louisiana Purchase was the first practical step. The Monroe Doctrine was the all-important second step. The third key step was the Mexican-American War; and this massive land-grab was instrumental in adding a geographic stranglehold for U.S. security and prosperity in the western hemisphere. It was also the major mid-century cornerstone of the aforementioned imperial crusade. In his book, *So Far from God: The U.S. War With Mexico, 1846-1848,* military historian (and son of the former U.S. president) John S.D. Eisenhower frames then President James Polk's 1845 State of the Union address as a harbinger of war with Mexico. "Polk's message," Eisenhower writes, "had been heralded as a reaffirmation of the Monroe Doctrine, second only in importance to the first. Hyperbole aside, it left no doubt where he stood. The text reviewed the many wrongs that Mexico had perpetrated against a patient United States."[61] Of course, since then American presidents have been citing "the many wrongs" of many foreign countries as justification to launch another war to protect American interests. Dylan was wrong. The times, they are not changing.

With the illegitimate "moral" sanctions of Social Darwinism already wiping out the native population as well as enslaving the African population, the flag-waving, feel-good Americans turned their racially-charged expansionist dreams toward the so-called mongrel Mexicans to the west—a move that solidified what University of Wisconsin history professor Reginald Horsman termed "romantic racial nationalism."[62] As the sun continues to travel west, the Anglo-Saxons continue to prove that civilization indeed follows earth's nearest star. Horsman concludes:

> By 1850 American expansion was viewed in the United States less as a victory for the principles of free democratic republicanism than as evidence of the innate superiority of the American Anglo-Saxon branch of the Caucasian race. In the middle of the nineteenth century a sense of racial destiny permeated discussions of American progress and of future American world destiny. Many think of rampant doctrines of Caucasian, Aryan, or Anglo-Saxon destiny as typical of the late years of the nineteenth century, but they flourished in the United States in the era of the Mexican War.[63]

In the wake of the 1845 Annexation of Texas, the Mexican-American War raged from 1846 to 1848. Most historians agree that this U.S. invasion of Mexico was a clear-cut act of aggression on the part of Washington. "In 1846, we produced our first conquistador, President James K. Polk," writes Gore Vidal. "Polk deliberately started a war with Mexico because, as he later told historian George Bancroft, we had to acquire California."[64] And "acquire" they did—more than 500,000 square miles in the lopsided Treaty of Guadalupe Hidalgo. The land mass pilfered during the invasion includes what today would be all of California, Nevada, Texas, Utah, New Mexico, Arizona, and parts of Wyoming, Colorado, Kansas, and Oklahoma.

Not bad.

In fact, this land-theft by the United States government equaled nearly half of Mexico's national territory. In his memoir, published in 1885, ex-President Ulysses Grant, who was a young army lieutenant in the U.S. invasion of Mexico, recalled:

> Generally, the officers of the army were indifferent whether the annexation was consummated or not; but not so all of them. For myself, I was bitterly opposed to the measure, and to this day regard the war, which resulted, as one of the most unjust ever waged by a stronger against a weaker nation. It was an instance of a

republic following the bad example of European monarchies, in not considering justice in their desire to acquire additional territory.[65]

As well, Grant expressed the belief that this "unjust" war (read: invasion and slaughter) against a significantly weaker nation (sound familiar?) invited a karmic boomerang of immense proportions:

> The Southern rebellion [Civil War] was largely the outgrowth of the Mexican war. Nations, like individuals, are punished for their transgressions. We got our punishment in the most sanguinary and expensive war of modern times.[66]

But not all Americans view this slice of murder and plunder as a bad thing—far from it. The Tennessee State Library and Archives, along with the Secretary of State's office, recently published this piece of saccharin-sweet, sugarcoated "history," the headline of which boasts:

> "Gloriously Fighting a Glorious Cause"

The first paragraph rewrites a bloodthirsty history into feel-good myth: "Fueled by patriotism and faith in Manifest Destiny, the American public was in an expansionist mood in the early 19th century. Tennessean James K. Polk, elected president in 1844 on a campaign pledge to annex Texas and Oregon, moved promptly to fulfill that promise. Both territories soon won statehood in the 'Glorious Constellation' known as the United States of America."[67] There's bullshit and then there's major league bullshit.

Frederick Douglass—the former slave, abolitionist, and editor of the abolitionist newspaper "The North Star"—framed the Annexation of Texas and the impending war on Mexico to an audience in Belfast, Ireland as a "conspiracy from beginning to end—a most deep and skillfully devised conspiracy—for the purpose of upholding and sustaining one of the darkest and foulest crimes ever committed by man."[68]

This so-called "Mexican-American War" was steeped in deep and ugly racial hatred as perpetrated by the American government. From the safe confines of Washington and New York, the architects of this massive land grab and attempted expansion of slave-holding territories were charging hard on the galloping stallion of white supremacism (in duty to capital). For them, it was a great two-for-one deal: continue building "their" new nation on the backs of African slave labor while simultaneously sending the dirty Mexicans running for the hills far south as America expanded its conquest to the Pacific. American newspapers and prominent scribes helped to sell the polluted set-up. Walt Whitman thought it was a terrific idea, suggesting, "backward Mexico had to be annexed as part of bringing civilization to the world."[69] The famous transcendentalist, Ralph Waldo Emerson, was also a fan of America's destiny at any cost: "[I]t really doesn't matter by what means Mexico is taken, as it contributes to the mission of 'civilizing the world.'" Emerson also predicted that as the years passed into history, the entire episode "will be forgotten."[70]

If Emerson came back from the dead and walked the current border between the U.S. and Mexico, we wonder if the famous "Sage of Concord" would realize how misbegotten his support for this international crime proved to be. "In the darkest hour of the longest night," ol' Waldo would be frozen in his tracks with "them transcendental blues."[71]

Despite strong resistance against the war from many Americans, including Henry David Thoreau ("Civil Disobedience," 1849), the war on Mexico was incredibly popular and the U.S. victory over the much weaker Mexican nation catapulted American patriotism into the stratosphere. The incursion and successful occupation also secured the country's fervent belief in Manifest Destiny, with the Monroe Doctrine as the perfect table-pounding pronouncement.

Teddy Roosevelt's Big ~~DICK~~ Stick Foreign Policy

> *To me, war is nothing but a whole lot of prick waving... a lot of men standing around in a field waving their pricks at one another. Men are insecure about the size of their dicks and so they have to go to war over it. That's what all that asshole jock bullshit is all about. That's what all that adolescent macho male posturing and strutting in bars and locker rooms is all about. It's called "dick fear." Men are terrified that their pricks are inadequate, and so they have to "compete" to feel better. And because war is the ultimate competition, basically men are killing one another in order to improve their self-esteem. You don't have to be a history major or a political scientist to see the Bigger Dick Foreign Policy Theory. It sounds like this: "What? They have bigger dicks? Bomb them!" And of course, the bombs, and the rockets, and the bullets are all shaped like dicks. It's a subconscious need to project the penis into other people's affairs. It's called "fucking with people."*
>
> —George Carlin, "Jammin' in New York," (1992)

Eighty-one years after James Monroe rattled the imperial saber, another U.S. President, Theodore Roosevelt, began swinging the imperial saber with reckless abandon. "He was a lover of war,"[72] writes Howard Zinn, regarding TR's record of supporting imperial violence and murder. In a talk at M.I.T., Noam Chomsky added the underlying motive fueling Teddy's love for war: "Roosevelt was a shocking racist. I don't use the analogy lightly, but it's a fact that you have to go to the Nazi archive to find anything similar."[73] And then with his usual nuanced contempt, Gore Vidal framed Roosevelt's entire war-like oeuvre when he characterized TR's macho man behavior this way: "Give a sissy a gun and he will kill everything in sight."[74]

Warmonger. Raging racist. American sissy. And the man who ordered and wore Brooks Brothers suits into battle is also carved into a granite mountain the Lakota Sioux called "Six Grandfathers," adding insult to injury for the native spirits as his Injun-hating visage stares out over an area (*HeSapa*—"Black Mountains") inhabited since approximately 7000 BC by the Arikara, Cheyenne, Crow, Kiowa, Pawnee, and Lakota people. In 1886, Teddy gave a speech in New York that should be performed and recorded by one of Hollywood's finest and then broadcast from giant speakers on Mount Rushmore for the simpletons who stand in awe at the base of that geological monstrosity in South Dakota. Here's what one of America's great heroes (Teddy Bear himself) had to say about the race of human beings his beloved brethren wiped off the face of the earth:

> I don't go so far as to think that the only good Indians are dead Indians, but I believe nine out of every ten are, and I shouldn't like to inquire too closely into the case of the tenth. The most vicious cowboy has more moral principle than the average Indian.[75]

At first light over the 20th century, America was indeed a global power and its leaders repeatedly—even habitually—summoned the Monroe Doctrine as authorization for various acts of aggression. In many instances, including U.S. dealings with the Far East, American leaders greatly expanded its boundaries.

"When he became president," writes historian James Bradley in The Imperial Cruise, "Roosevelt embraced the Monroe Doctrine as justification to wield the Big Stick, dispatching the U.S. Navy to quell a 'revolution' in Colombia, an action that allowed him to tear Panama away from that country. Then he extracted canal rights from Panama 'in perpetuity.' Roosevelt later admitted that he 'took the Canal and let Congress debate.'" Teddy was never short on tabloid-like threats bouncing around inside his head. Bradley continues: "He boasted 'that if any South American country misbehaves,' it should be 'spanked,' and once wrote, 'I am so angry with that infernal little Cuban republic that I would like to wipe its people off the face of the earth.' Big stick, indeed."[76]

As Bradley correctly points out, Roosevelt "embraced" Monroe's early vision with vigor. In fact, throughout the evolution and growth of the Monroe Doctrine no addendum was more dramatic than the professed "Roosevelt Corollary"—the 1904 articulation by TR in his State of the Union address that offered a more overt imperialist threat, one that began to encompass the reality of American military muscle paving the way for—and the protection of—American corporate business interests. Here is Roosevelt's imperial forewarning:

> All that this country desires is to see the neighboring countries stable, orderly, and prosperous. Any country whose people conduct themselves well can count upon our hearty friendship. If a nation shows that it knows how to act with reasonable efficiency and decency in social and political matters, if it keeps order and pays its obligations, it need fear no interference from the United States. Chronic wrongdoing, or an impotence which results in a general loosening of the ties of civilized society, may in America, as elsewhere, ultimately require intervention by some civilized nation, and in the Western Hemisphere the adherence of the United States to the Monroe Doctrine may force the United States, however reluctantly, in flagrant cases of such wrongdoing or impotence, to the exercise of an international police power.[77]

Progressive?

Echoing the old adage, "the more things change, the more they stay the same," a *Washington Post* headline in 2011 linked at the hip two war-happy U.S. executives: Teddy Roosevelt and Barack Obama. "OBAMA INVOKES TEDDY ROOSEVELT IN SPEECH ATTACKING GOP POLICIES" roars the headline. The writer, David Nakamura, reminds us that, "The president chose this town of 4,600 in eastern Kansas as a historical echo of a speech delivered a century earlier by Theodore Roosevelt... That speech, which became known as 'the New Nationalism' speech, was one of the early cornerstones of 20th-century progressivism."[78] Progressivism? This is an all-too-typical characterization of an unreflective historical perspective. As is the case with Mr. Obama, there is a laughable Orwellian chasm between what Roosevelt is remembered for and what he actually did. In fact, the similarities between Teddy and Barry are strikingly similar when it comes to the spectacular differences between perception and reality. Sam Bradley, writing on the website "1984 Recurring" states:

> The evidence is overwhelming that Roosevelt's intentions were not particularly progressive. Be it the lack of fundamental reforms for workers, or attitude towards large corporations; Roosevelt's domestic policy seems to lack any progressive sincerity and radicalism, especially compared to socialist thinkers such as Eugene Debs.[79]

In *A People's History of the United States,* Howard Zinn discusses the purported "Progressive Era" in U.S. history—a legend that lionized TR. "True, this was the 'Progressive Period,' the start of the Age of Reform," writes Zinn, "but it was a reluctant reform, aimed at quieting the popular risings, not making fundamental changes. What gave it the name 'Progressive' was that new laws were passed."[80]

Zinn could just as easily be writing about the administrations of Barack Obama. As the 20th century unfolded, activists—populated by committed socialists, communists, and anarchists—generated a groundswell of political activism aimed at overturning the harsh conditions and oppressive reality brought on by the robber barons of the Gilded Age. Professor Zinn frames the "progressivism" of Roosevelt (and later Woodrow Wilson and others) as an effective strategy to co-opt the true radical spirit of this growing revolution. Once again, eerily similar to the Obama White House attempting to co-opt the radical free spirit of the Occupy Movement for political gain as well as governmental and corporate control. Also eerily similar to the co-opting of the original American Revolution by the colonial elite—"a Baron's Revolt... fought for the 'liberty' of deciding who would hold Africans in bondage—the Americans or the British? Who would receive the fruits of this stolen land that African labor produced?"[81]

Set aside the safe and guild historians, those sentinels of the status quo, and you will find critics who consider Teddy's progressive era to be a myth of legendary proportions. Howard Zinn is one of those nonconformists. His dissent included these sharp historic observations regarding TR's empire-driven progressive exploits:

> It was a time of public investigations aimed at soothing protest... Undoubtedly, ordinary people benefited to some extent from these changes. The system was rich, productive, complex; it could give

> enough of a share of its riches to enough of the working class to create a protective shield between the bottom and the top of the society... Fundamental conditions did not change, however, for the vast majority of tenant farmers, factory workers, slum dwellers, miners, farm laborers, working men and women, black and white.[82]

Many historians concur that the progressive movement, with a new emphasis on strong government designed to stabilize the capitalist system, was a "Trojan Horse" maneuver to protect and benefit the upper class. In his book *Triumph of Conservatism*, historian Gabriel Kolko digs beneath the surface of spin. "Progressivism was initially a movement for the political rationalization of business and industrial conditions," he writes, "a movement that operated on the assumption that the general welfare of the community could be best served by satisfying the concrete needs of business." Kolko then gets to the heart of the matter: "But the regulation itself was invariably controlled by leaders of the regulated industry, and directed toward ends they deemed acceptable and desirable." Kolko defines "political capitalism" as "the utilization of political outlets to attain conditions of stability, predictability, and security—to attain rationalization—in the economy."[83]

Zinn concurs:

> For instance, Theodore Roosevelt made a reputation for himself as a "trust-buster" (although his successor, Taft, a "conservative," while Roosevelt was a "Progressive," launched more antitrust suits than did Roosevelt). In fact, as Wiebe points out, two of J. P. Morgan's men—Elbert Gary, chairman of U.S. Steel, and George Perkins, who would later become a campaigner for Roosevelt—"arranged a general understanding with Roosevelt by which... they would cooperate in any investigation by the Bureau of Corporations in return for a guarantee of their companies' legality." They would do this through private negotiations with the President. "A gentleman's agreement between reasonable people," Wiebe says, with a bit of sarcasm...
>
> Richard Hofstadter, in his biting chapter on the man the public saw as the great lover of nature and physical fitness, the war hero, the Boy Scout in the White House, says: "The advisers to whom Roosevelt listened were almost exclusively representatives of industrial and finance capital-men like Hanna, Robert Bacon, and George W. Perkins of the House of Morgan, Elihu Root, Senator Nelson W. Aldrich... and James Stillman of the Rockefeller interests." Responding

> to his worried brother-in-law writing from Wall Street, Roosevelt replied: "I intend to be most conservative, but in the interests of the corporations themselves and above all in the interests of the country."
>
> Roosevelt supported the regulatory Hepburn Act because he feared something worse. He wrote to Henry Cabot Lodge that the railroad lobbyists who opposed the bill "are very short-sighted not to understand that to beat it means to increase the movement for government ownership of the railroads..."
>
> The Progressive movement, whether led by honest reformers such as Senator Robert LaFollette of Wisconsin or disguised conservatives like Roosevelt... seemed to understand it was fending off socialism.
>
> It seems quite clear that much of this intense activity for Progressive reform was intended to head off socialism.[84]

There it is, the crux of the matter: socialism.

Alleged "progressivism" at home with gunboat diplomacy abroad. Barack and TR—two rough riders a century apart. Drone attacks wiping out families in the Middle East coupled with presidential kill lists. Massacres in the Philippines or the scheme to "steal Panama from Colombia to build the canal."[85] But of course both men are awarded Nobel Peace Prizes (along with another hot shot—mass murderer, Henry Kissinger).

So once again we are faced with the duality of American history: how can the textbooks and other works of fiction portray this granite-chiseled man on Rushmore as a progressive (he was in fact the Progressive Party candidate for president in 1912) when Roosevelt's murderous and imperial actions abroad speak volumes to the Empire's hegemonic guilt? It's clear that TR's legacy as a "progressive" is American history drunk on a concoction of Monroe Doctrine infused with Manifest Destiny.

Mainstream historians have celebrated the professed "Progressive Era" as a watershed moment for the human condition in the United States as well as other industrialized nations through government regulation of corporate-owned industry. That's true when you compare the introduction of even minor regulatory measures to the hell, misery, and anguish of the Gilded Age, robber barons, and the long shadow of American slavery that infects American society to this very day. Stand in the batter's box and get hit by ninety-five mile an hour fastballs—it's brutal and vicious. Stand in the same batter's box and get hit by sixty-eight mile an hour curveballs—it's a little less brutal and vicious, but you're still being pummeled. The same holds true for the oppression of workers and poor people in any society. If the 1% shits on the masses a little less, does it really matter? Can immoral acts be a little less immoral?

The Gospel of America

Driven by visions of divine stewardship over the planet and fueled by the sanctified spirit of the Monroe Doctrine (and later by Manifest Destiny), the 19th century was surely a baptism by fire for the American Empire—a blast-off through the killing fields of those less civilized. It is this same pious spirit that extends the long arm of capitalist conquest to every corner of this celestial rock

There were many plots and schemes carried out by the emerging American Empire during the 19th century. One of their greatest hits was the Philippine War, championed at the time by historian Henry Brooks Adams—the grandson of Monroe Doctrine architect John Quincy Adams and well-known anti-Semite. Gore Vidal reminds us that the acorn didn't fall far from the tree. Regarding the younger Adams' embrace of "Big Stick" violent diplomacy, Vidal writes, "This is why, quite seriously, he wanted to extend the Monroe Doctrine to the Pacific Ocean. For him 'War (was) the ultimate form of economic competition.'"[86] In fact, the budding empire had a great front man in Brooks Adams, waxing poetic about the glories of American expansion and conquest on all fronts:

> The West Indies drift toward us, the Republic of Mexico hardly longer has an independent life... With the completion of the Panama Canal all Central America will become a part of our system. We have expanded into Asia, we have attracted the fragments of the Spanish dominions, and reaching out into China we have checked the advance of Russia and Germany... The United States will outweigh any single empire, if not all empires combined. The whole world will pay her tribute.[87]

War is too nice a word to use for what the new empire—in the hands of William McKinley, William Howard Taft, and of course Teddy Roosevelt—rained down on the people of the Pacific, beginning in the Philippines. The butchering for dollars was not lost on Mark Twain when he wrote this passage following the Moro Massacre in 1906:

> We have pacified some thousands of the islanders and buried them; destroyed their fields; burned their villages, and turned their widows and orphans out-of-doors; furnished heartbreak by exile to some dozens of disagreeable patriots; subjugated the remaining ten millions by Benevolent Assimilation, which is the pious new name of the musket; we have acquired property in the three hundred concubines and other slaves of our business partner, the Sultan of Sulu, and hoisted our protecting flag over that swag. And so, by these Providences of God—and the phrase is the government's, not mine—we are a World Power.[88]

It was also not lost some sixty years later on Soviet Premier Nikita Khrushchev who pronounced the Monroe Doctrine dead when the bellicose Russian proclaimed that it "should best be buried as every dead body is so that it does not poison the air by its decay."[89] If the Monroe Doctrine died in the ice fields of the Cold War, then its reanimated corpse has returned to saunter through the spirit and policy of American foreign policy to this very moment. Writer Charles Sullivan projects the consequences of this historical reality:

> If we allow this unjust and inhumane conquest to move across the world, we can expect the continuation of the mass murders that America has always purveyed, the continued theft of land from sovereign nations, destruction of biological and cultural diversity, slavery, and the wholesale conversion of other religious sects to one world religion–that of manifest destiny, Christian fundamentalism, and capitalism.[90]

"Troublemaking in the Hemisphere"

"Monroe's words outlived the parochial concerns of that era to provide the philosophical underpinning for U.S. foreign policy for decades to come," writes academic Daniel Erikson in his essay "Requiem for the Monroe Doctrine."[91] A close study of U.S. foreign policy over the past two centuries clearly reveals that the ever-changing storyline out of Washington is almost embarrassing in its obvious transparency, especially when it comes to the public rationales for aggression. In her remarkable examination of U.S. belligerence in Latin America, Clara Nieto concludes in *Masters of War* that since the articulation of the Monroe Doctrine, "These policies have formed a coherent interventionist policy—whether open or covert—designed to impede changes that might affect the political or economic interests of the United States."[92]

With reference to the idea of "protecting our turf" as a pretext for global economic expansion, Noam Chomsky states that, "World War II was a real watershed."[93] World War II either destroyed completely or seriously smashed the economies and manufacturing infrastructure of American allies and enemies alike. Chomsky explains that, "Our national territory was never under attack and American production tripled." According to Chomsky in *How the World Works,* the United States owned "50% of the world's wealth and controlled both sides of both oceans. There'd never been a time in history when one power had such overwhelming control of the world, or such overwhelming security."[94] And with that unprecedented control and security in their back pocket, U.S. policy makers switched into high gear. These were resolute strategists working for the State Department and for the Council on Foreign Relations, ("one major channel by which business leaders influence foreign policy") who "agreed that the dominance of the United States had to be maintained."[95] Amazingly enough, these detailed and capacious plans are all on the public record in this "open society," documents like "National Security Council Memorandum 68" (NSC 68—1950). Chomsky pushes the story forward:

> There policies were, in fact, already being implemented. In 1949, US espionage in Eastern Europe had been turned over to a network run by Reinhard Gehlen, who had headed Nazi military intelligence on the Eastern Front. This network was one part of the US-Nazi alliance that quickly absorbed many of the worst criminals, extending to operations in Latin America and elsewhere.[96]

Perfect bedfellows.

The historic State Department planner-advisor-and-diplomat George Kennan (also known as "The Father of Soviet Containment"), made a significant impact on determining the geo-political Cold War landscape in the post World War II world. In fact, Kennan's writing greatly inspired the so-called "Truman Doctrine," another tributary of the Monroe Doctrine aimed at curtailing Soviet expansion. In "Policy Planning Study 23" (written by Kennan), the ghoulish specter of American exceptionalism roars loudly. Here in black and white is an excerpt of what was once a top-secret document:

> We have about 50% of the world's wealth but only 6.3% of its population... In this situation, we cannot fail to be the object of envy and resentment.

> Our real task in the coming period is to devise a pattern of relationships which will permit us to maintain this position of disparity... To do so, we will have to dispense with sentimentality and daydreaming... We should cease to talk about vague and unreal objectives such as human rights, the raising of the living standard, and democratization.[97]

Chomsky zeroes in on Kennan's primary interest and concern when he cites Kennan during a briefing for U.S. ambassadors in Latin America:

> US foreign policy must be "the protection of our [i.e. Latin America's] raw materials." We must therefore combat a dangerous heresy which, US intelligence reported, was spreading through Latin America: "the idea that the government has direct responsibility for the welfare of the people." US planners call that idea *Communism,* whatever the actual views of the people advocating it. They can be church-based self-help groups or whatever, but if they support this heresy, they're Communists.[98]

During a 1955 "high-level study group," which was actually part of the public record, Kennan suggests the end game for those populations who may rightfully deviate from Washington's wishes:

> The final answer might be an unpleasant one, but... we should not hesitate before police repression by the local government. This is not shameful since the Communists are essentially traitors... It is better to have a strong regime in power than a liberal government if it is indulgent and relaxed and penetrated by Communists.[99]

Woodrow Wilson is often viewed as a great bastion of American liberalism, but a closer read of history rather than the agreed-upon myth suggests another pseudo-progressive. Noam Chomsky circles back and connects the dots between the ever-evolving Monroe Doctrine and Wilson's use of its imperial blank check:

> Policies like these didn't begin with postwar liberals like Kennan. As Woodrow Wilson's Secretary of State [Robert Lansing] had already pointed out 30 years earlier, the operative meaning of the Monroe Doctrine is that "[In its advocacy of the Monroe Doctrine] the United States considers its own interests. The integrity of other American nations is an incident, not an end." Wilson, the great apostle of self-determination, agreed that the argument was

> "unanswerable," though it would be "impolitic" to present it publicly.
>
> Wilson also acted on this thinking by, among other things, invading Haiti and the Dominican Republic, where his warriors murdered and destroyed, demolished the political system, left US corporations firmly in control, and set the stage for brutal and corrupt dictatorships.[100]

The evolution of the Doctrine has continued unabated in the arsenal employed by Washington and Wall Street. Overt land-grabs, as evidenced in the fiasco conquest of Mexican territory as well as the extermination and removal of indigenous populations, were replaced by a broader, more complex and strategic siphoning of foreign wealth, resources, and control of external populations. Bureaucrats, diplomats, and corporate strategists became more sophisticated with their various heists and ongoing larceny. Throughout the history of the Cold War—from the death and destruction of Hiroshima and Nagasaki to the final proxy wars with the Soviets in Latin America—U.S. policy makers have whipped out the Doctrine at the drop of a hat to inhibit Soviet influence and not just in obvious places like Cuba, and of course Central and South America. The "spirit" of the Doctrine traveled far from the western hemisphere and inspired U.S. aggression throughout Europe and Asia. Nieto digs deeper into Washington's escalation of the Monroe Doctrine's spiritual journey through the latter half of the 20th century:

> In a famous 1946 speech Churchill alerted the world to the danger of Soviet expansion, articulating the concept of an Iron Curtain going up between Eastern and Western Europe. The world was divided in two, the great powers confronting one another and their interests in conflict; capitalism vs. communism, democracy vs. totalitarianism.
>
> The following year Truman declared that the United States would defend the "free world"—another new concept—against Communist expansion. "The free countries of the world expect us to maintain their freedom. If we fail we could endanger world peace, and we would surely put the welfare of this nation in danger." [Truman's speech to Congress, 1947] The Truman Doctrine rationalized Cold War policies and globalized the Monroe Doctrine.[101]

At the height of the Vietnam War, American dissident and antiwar activist Chomsky was witnessing the insanity of American policy in Southeast Asia and couldn't help but see the fingerprints of destiny—*exceptionalism*—and of course the galloping ghosts of Adams and Monroe. In his seminal work, *American Power and the New Mandarins,* Chomsky writes:

> To prove that we are menaced is of course unnecessary, and the matter receives no attention; it is enough that we feel menaced. Our policy must be based on our national heritage and our national interests. Our national heritage is briefly outlined in the following terms: "Throughout the nineteenth century, in good conscience Americans could devote themselves to the extension of both their principles and their power on this continent," making use of "the somewhat elastic concept of the Monroe Doctrine" and, of course, extending "the American interest to Alaska and the mid-Pacific islands."[102]

Chomsky is shining a bright light on the immense impact that the Monroe Doctrine had on American foreign policy as well as its dramatic evolution through the heart of the 19th century. It was an evolution that encrypted the core essence of ultimate American destiny deep into the DNA of the country, transforming its citizens, government leaders, institutions, and corporate masters into the self-proclaimed rulers of the world. Michael Parenti outlines the march of this repressive apparatus as re-defined by the Eisenhower administration:

> In 1957, the U.S. Congress approved a presidential resolution known as the "Eisenhower Doctrine," which designated the Middle East as an area vital to the national interest of the United States. As with the Monroe Doctrine and Truman Doctrine, "the U.S. government conferred upon the U.S. government the remarkable and enviable right to intervene militarily" in yet another region of the world, notes political analyst William Blum. Soon after, the CIA began operations to overthrow the democratically elected Syrian government and embarked upon a series of plots to eradicate Nasser (of Egypt) and his irksome nationalism. If anyone was acting like a Hitlerite destabilizer in the Middle East, it was not President Nasser.[103]

Citing the Monroe Doctrine (or its related manifestations) as rationale for almost any U.S. action in a sovereign land has been commonplace over the last two centuries. In fact when an American president or leader invokes the Doctrine as the basis for aggression, intervention, or even for saber-rattling "diplomatic" threats, it's as if Moses has drifted down from the mount with his tablets: Commandment

11—the Monroe Doctrine. (But that's unfair to Moses… maybe it's more like Tony "Scarface" Montana's garish statue that read: *"The World Is Yours."*)

"In September 1962," writes Clara Nieto, "the United States administration and Congress, citing the Monroe Doctrine, unleashed a tenacious and belligerent campaign against Cuba."[104] Some one hundred and forty years after the enunciation of the Monroe Doctrine, John Kennedy's use of the age-old canon as the "legitimate" rationale for his administration's actions against Cuba was nothing new. What was new was the undeniable fact that invoking this "line in the sand" dogma in the nuclear age pushed the world to the brink of annihilation. It was a choice (as Chomsky suggests) between hegemony and survival. With James Monroe's words in his back pocket, Kennedy went to work—by land, by sea, by air—to combat what Washington of course viewed as Soviet aggression in the western hemisphere. The common paraphrase was catchy: "a mere 90 miles from U.S. soil." Cuban president Fidel Castro saw the relationship differently: "Cuba needs to account to no one for the measures it takes in its defense."[105]

When writing about the American Empire's phobic and neurotic expansion into Latin America, and specifically into Cuba, Chomsky underscores the American government's—and their corporate partner's—mindset with regard to self-rule and economic fairness:

> The case of Cuba is again instructive. Arthur Schlesinger, reporting the conclusions of a Latin American study group to President Kennedy in early 1961, described the Cuban threat as "the spread of the Castro idea of taking matters into one's own hands;" a serious problem, he elaborated, when "[t]he distribution of land and other forms of national wealth [in Latin America] greatly favors the propertied classes… [and]… The poor and underprivileged, stimulated by the example of the Cuban revolution, are now demanding opportunities for a decent living… Meanwhile, the Soviet Union hovers in the wings, flourishing large development loans and presenting itself as the model for achieving modernization in a single generation." In public Schlesinger describes the problem faced by Kennedy as Castro's "troublemaking in the hemisphere."[106]

Imagine for a moment any foreign nation attempting to disarm U.S. nukes, stating that the weapons of murder, terror, and death pose a threat to the people and interests of their country. Imagine any foreign nation attempting a blockade of New London, Connecticut, and the nuclear submarine hub that lives there, stating that the vessels of murder, terror, and death pose a threat to the people and interests of their country. Imagine any foreign nation moving on Wall Street and co-opting control of a U.S. bank, stating that their predatory practices pose a threat to the people and interests of their country. Well, you can't because the possibility of that action would be considered absurd, illegal, and by some—immoral. Unfortunately, that's the exact behavior and real-life march of U.S. power across the planet—and now even aimed at us from space. It's just as Teddy Roosevelt envisioned: "the exercise of an international police power."

Neighborhood Bully

Ronald Reagan was the last U.S. cowboy whose policies in the western hemisphere, and specifically in Latin America, so sharply echoed the core principles of the Monroe Doctrine. This was clearly demonstrated by the Reagan administration's undying support for the rebels fighting against the Sandinistas in Nicaragua—an obvious proxy war against the Soviet Union. In fact Reagan pulled out all the stops, spinning his administration's support of the rebel forces seeking to overthrow the Nicaraguan government by calling them the "moral equal of our Founding Fathers and the brave men and women of the French resistance."[107]

The idea of the "neighborhood bully" is clearly evident in all recent U.S. operations around the world. It is political theater with dire consequences for the so-called antagonists in this perverse and ongoing passion play. It's not so complicated, say it like it is: "Let's kick the shit out of defenseless peons." A classic example of America's neighborhood bully concept in practice was the U.S. invasion of the malevolent and treacherous superpower known as Grenada—another Reagan administration incursion, this one in 1983. In *Masters of War,* Clara Nieto calls the world's reaction to the Empire's bully behavior as "international disgust" and then frames the historical context:

> The invasion of Grenada left the world community indignant, stupefied, and disgusted. Governments, institutions, organizations, churches, prominent personalities, and parliaments of many countries condemned the United States government. Even Reagan's loyal ally, British Prime Minister Margaret Thatcher, complained that the United States had the nerve to invade an island of the British Commonwealth and violate its sovereignty without informing Her Majesty... Castro called it a "Pyrrhic victory and a disastrous moral defeat." For Latin America it was the renaissance of the worst moments of the Monroe Doctrine and the Big Stick.[108]

We now turn to Max Boot for support. Mr. Boot is a self-proclaimed *über*-conservative who describes the core essence of his ideas as "American might to promote American ideals."[109] Mr. Boot embraces American imperialism and American exceptionalism with gusto. A devotee of both Teddy Roosevelt and Ronald Reagan, Mr. Boot believes the U.S. must act as a world police agency since "there is nobody else out there."[110] Once again we visit Gretchen Murphy's book *Hemispheric Imaginings: The Monroe Doctrine and Narratives of U.S. Empire.* Ms. Murphy captures the honest essence of American power as she frames the imperial "stylings" of Max Boot:

> In a February 18, 2003, editorial titled "America's Destiny is to Police the World," journalist Max Boot argued that the imminent war with Iraq was not a break with traditional American foreign policy, but rather its logical extension. The 2002 Bush Doctrine of preemption, Boot explained, merely expanded the Monroe Doctrine to a global scale. In the late nineteenth and early twentieth centuries, the Monroe Doctrine provided the most common terms through which Americans in the United States imagined and articulated their nation's diplomatic and military place in the world.
>
> Then as now, Boot writes, the world needs a police power, and while in the early twentieth century "the western hemisphere was the only place where the U.S. exercised military hegemony," today the United States exercises "almost as much power everywhere around the world as it once had only in the Caribbean. Spatial division of the world into hemispheres was only incidental, he implies; what really matters about the Monroe Doctrine is that it articulates a unilateral responsibility to promote peace and democracy abroad."[111]

Sure, the history of the Monroe Doctrine and all its subsequent corollaries speaks volumes about promoting peace and democracy abroad. We guess that's accurate if you completely dismiss the actual mountain of evidence to the contrary. After Murphy sets aside Mr. Boot's mythical (delusional would be more accurate) take on America's imperial history, she frames her response in a measured but poignant fashion:

> Here we can observe one of the most striking features of the Monroe Doctrine: its extraordinary flexibility. A statement of protection slips into one of control, and a statement of hemispheric separation evolves into one of global responsibility.[112]

Reign of Terror

As Michael Parenti is fond of articulating: the American Empire is "so good at imperialism," but not so good at their supposed mission from God. We're told that Monroe's "Yellowbrick Road" America leads to a freer, more civilized world, where in fact history continues to demonstrate that it leads ruin. It's the poison in the well.

In many respects, the Monroe Doctrine was the single spark that ignited a firestorm, one that rages to this day—a firestorm initiated by many imperial, colonial, religious, and economic factors, and the baseless moral license for the terror was codified by Messrs. Jefferson, Adams, and Monroe. Author Glen Ford encapsulates this reign of terror since the dawn of the 20th century:

> U.S. foreign policy reflects the nation's origins and ghastly evolution into a globe-strutting mob, that empowers itself to kill at will. A million dead Filipinos at the turn of the 20th century; aerial bombing of Haitian villages less than a generation later; the totally unwarranted nuclear annihilation of two cities at the very end of World War Two; two million dead Koreans shortly thereafter; three million dead Vietnamese in the next decade; and, since 1996, six million Congolese—all, and many, many more, slaughtered in the name of U.S. civilizational superiority—the ghastly opiate of the white American masses.[113]

And then, of course, the killing fields of empire leads right to the doorstep of America's client state Israel and its bombardment and murder in neighboring states—the most obvious of course raining down death and destruction on the open air apartheid prison of Palestine.

Whether it's the American Empire, their client states, or friendly states, the vision of the Monroe Doctrine has yielded the reality of war and murder everywhere. Teddy Roosevelt would be proud, for "the exercise of (his) international police power" has been at the center of this freak show. So as we look back at the lasting legacy of the Monroe Doctrine from our perch here in the first decades of the 21st century, we see what can only be called a reign of terror.

❖ ❖ ❖

8 La Otra America
The United States Invades Mexico

In nearly all the Americas, few indigenous cultures were more developed, more cosmopolitan, and more urbane than the Aztecs living in the lands now known as Mexico, which featured cities of tremendous beauty, vibrant economies, and a rich cultural-spiritual lifestyle.

The first Spaniard who beheld these vistas of central Mexico, called Tenochtitlan, the Aztec capital, home of some 350,000 souls, "the most beautiful city on earth."[1] Although Hernán Cortes could not have seen all the cities of the earth, as one of the most traveled men of his era, he could not have been far off. But his was the view not only of some earthly Shangri-La, it was the end of an ancient era, and the beginning of a Spanish Empire that would embark on a campaign of destruction seldom seen on earth.

The central rivers of blood that fed the post-conquest re-creation of Mexico were of Indian, European, and African origins, and they produced a state that, while it did not create the marvels of its predecessor, did manage to establish a nation of relative stability—albeit atop the skulls and bones of untold numbers of indigenous people. But, as it was, like its northern neighbor, born of conquest, imperial greed, and slavery, it was also a land ripe for revolution, as contesting forces within society would fight for political and economic hegemony.

From Cortes to Polk

Jumping forward in time, we want to address—from the Mexican perspective—this fledgling nation's central external threat: that of the United States of America, which early on viewed Mexico's northern lands as acreage for the American crop of slavery. Although this is mostly forgotten lore of another age for most Americans, for the post-Revolutionary generation of Abraham Lincoln and his contemporaries, this was their Vietnam, their Gulf War, their Afghanistan.

In 1846, few U.S. politicians were more outspoken about Mexico's upcoming war than a U.S. Representative from Illinois named Lincoln. He used "spot resolutions" to ask where "on American soil" have Mexicans harmed Americans? His challenge opposed President James Polk's claim, that "Mexico... has invaded our territory and shed American blood upon the American soil."[2] But while American soldiers were indeed killed by Mexican cavalry, it was not on American but Mexican soil, for the internationally recognized border between the two countries was the Nueces River, some 150 miles south of the present Rio Grande border. Moreover, it was not Mexico who had invaded America, but President Polk who sent General Zachary Taylor and some 7,000 U.S. soldiers into the northern range of Mexico, embarking on an invasion of rape and savagery.

It is not for naught that what Americans call the Mexican-American War, the Mexicans call The American Invasion.[3] The American pundits of the Mexican War generation praised the violence, with one wag for the *New York Herald* writing, when reports returned of civilian casualties and rape perpetrated by U.S. soldiers on Mexican women, that nevertheless the nation of Mexico would, "Like the Sabine virgins... will soon learn to love her ravisher."[4]

Polk may have been a good liar, but he was a poor planner, for what at first seemed a cakewalk soon required some 100,000 troops, and lasted for several years. And, despite the repellant language of "lovers," Americans cared little for Mexicans, and one congressmen, Senator Lewis Cass of Michigan, made it plain by stating baldly, "We do not want the people of Mexico, either as citizens or subjects. All we want is a portion of territory."[5]

One could hardly be plainer than that.

A Colonel Dissents

It's relatively easy for us, in this age, to discuss the events of the Mexican-American War—or, if you prefer, the American Invasion—and pick a side based on which facts or events we want to embrace as truth. More important are the actors embedded in the amber of time, who are in the moment—thinking, feeling, reacting.

Thanks to the work of Howard Zinn (and his colleague Anthony Arnove) many of these actors are accessible, and through their voices offer us tremendous insights of the actual viewers and participants of the great and terrible dramas that swept through Mexico both before and during the Invasion. One man uniquely placed to call the shots as he saw them was U.S. Colonel Ethan Allen Hitchcock, whose diary reflects his initial and visceral impressions regarding the impending American military venture, and the ambitions (or mendacity) of its military and political leaders. Colonel Hitchcock's first entry begins on the eve of the war, and proceeds apace with building passion and a sense of indignation:

> Fort Jessup, La., June 30, 1845. Orders came last evening by express from Washington City directing General [Zachary] Taylor to move without any delay to some point on the coast near the Sabine or elsewhere, and as soon as he shall hear of the acceptance by the Texans convention of the annexation resolutions of our Congress he is immediately to proceed with his whole command to the extreme western boarder of Texas and take up a position on the banks of or near the Rio Grande, and he is to expel any armed force of Mexicans who may cross that river. [William W.S.] Bliss read the orders to me last evening hastily at tattoo. I have scarcely slept a wink, thinking of the needful preparations. I am now noting [writing] at reveille by candlelight and waiting the signal for muster... Violence leads to violence, and if this movement of ours does not lead to others and to bloodshed, I am much mistaken.
>
> 29th Aug. Received last evening... a letter from Captain Casey and a map of Texas from the Quarter-master-General's office, the latter being the one prepared by Lieutenant Emory; but it has added to it a distinct boundary mark to the Rio Grande. Our people ought to be damned for their impudent arrogance and domineering presumption! It is enough to make atheists of us all to see such wickedness in the world, whether punished or unpunished...
>
> 8th Sept... General Taylor talks, whether sincerely or not, of going to the Rio Grande. This is singular language from one who originally and till very lately denounced annexation as both injudicious in policy and wicked in fact! The 'claim,' so-called, of the Texans to the Rio Grande, is without foundation. The argument of Mr. [Robert J.] Walker passes by the treaty of 1819, by which the United States gave up all west and south of the Sabine, either saying nothing about it or presuming that it was not valid. Yet we took possession of Florida under that treaty... [W]e have no right whatever to go beyond the treaty.

As for Texas, her original limit was the Nueces and the hills ranging north from its sources, and she has never conquered, possessed, or exercised dominion west of the Nueces, except that a small smuggling company as this place, living here by Mexican sufferance, if not under Mexican protection, has chosen to call itself Texan, and some of the inhabitants have chosen to call themselves Texans...

C.C. [Corpus Christi], Sept. 20... He [Taylor] seems quite to have lost all respect for Mexican's rights and willing to be an instrument of Mr. Polk [the President] for pushing our boundary as far west as possible. When I told him that, if he suggested a movement (which he told me he intended), Mr. Polk would seize upon it and throw the responsibility on him, he at once said he would take it, and added that if the President instructed him to use his discretion, he would ask no orders, but would go upon the Rio Grande as soon as he could get transportation. I think the General wants an additional brevet [medal], and would strain a point to get it...

2nd Nov. Newspapers all seem to indicate that Mexico will make no movement, and the government is magnanimously bent on taking advantage of it to insist upon "our claim" as far as the Rio Grande. I hold this to be monstrous and abominable. But now, the United States of America, as a people, are undergoing changes in character, and the real status and principles for which our forefathers fought are fast being lost sight of. If I could by any decent means get a living in retirement, I would abandon a government which I think corrupted by both ambition and avarice to the last degree...

March 23rd. As to the right of this movement, I have said from the first that the United States are the aggressors. *We have outraged the Mexican government and people by an arrogance and presumption that deserve to be punished. For ten years we have been encroaching on Mexico and insulting her...* Her people I consider a simple, well-disposed, pastoral race, no way inclined to savage usages... [Emphasis added]

26th March... We have not one particle of right to be here. Our force is altogether too small for the accomplishment of its errand. It looks as if the government sent a small force on purpose to bring on a war, so as to have a pretext for taking California and as much of this country as it chooses; for, whatever becomes of this army, there is no doubt of a war between the United States and Mexico.[6]

That this was an American soldier, a Colonel no less, writing such honest and insightful dialogue can only be termed remarkable, even if it was his private journal. But, throughout the U.S., antiwar ferment was bubbling. People felt the injustice of the war, despite the patriotic blathering of the political and journalistic elites. In fact, these strong antiwar feelings would return time and time again over the next hundred and fifty years plus to rock those in power who sought to use war to secure raw materials and to prop up U.S. corporate hegemony. And, despite the claims of democracy, time and time again, the corporate view prevails, for the political class served them then, as now. 19th century American business wanted expansion of slavery, expansion of territory, and therefore expansion of wealth. War was and remains the heartbeat of big business.

Soldiers Dissent

The Mexican-American War, again like so many other wars, was sold as a cakewalk, but became a conflagration, for Mexico (as would any country) fought fiercely for its lands against the American invaders. What's more, this trumped-up war delivered an extraordinary event, one of truly historic proportions: American soldiers, led by Irish Americans, defected from the imperial forces and joined the Mexican defenders!

Under the name of San Patricio Battalion (in honor of the Irish patron saint, St. Patrick), men of various nationalities took up arms against the American expansionists. To urge men to join, a San Patricista, Juan Mata, penned the following leaflet on June 6, 1847:

> CATHOLIC Irish, Frenchmen and German of the invading army!
>
> The american nation makes a most unjust war to the mexicans, and has taken all of you as an instrument of their iniquity. You must not fight against a religious people, nor should you be seen in the ranks of those who proclaim slavery of mankind as constitutive principle. The religious man, he who possesses greatness of mind, must always fight for liberty and liberty is not on the side of those who establish differences in mankind, making an unhappy and innocent people, earn the bread of slavery. Liberty is not on the part of those who desire to be the lords of the worlds, robbing properties and territories which do not belong to them and shedding as much blood in order to accomplish their views, views in open war with the principles of our holy religion... The mexican people raises every where in order to wage an insurrectionary

> war, and that american army however large it may become, shall find here a grave. The mexican people wishes not to shed the blood of those who profess their own religion, and I, in the name on the inhabitants of the state of Vera Cruz invite you to abandon those ranks to which you must not belong. I have given the necessary orders, so that, should you abandon them, you may be respected in all the towns and places of the states where you happen to go, and all the requisite assistance shall be given to all, till brought before me. Many of your former companions fight now content in our ranks. After this war is over, the magnanimous and generous mexican nation will duly appreciate the services rendered, and you shall remain with us, cultivating our fertile lands. Catholic Irish, French and German! Long Live Liberty! Long Live our holy Religion!![7]

While the soldiers of San Patricio Battalion fought against the American expansionists, they did not prevail. And in the annals of (American) history they have all but vanished. But this has not been the case in Mexico, where the San Patricio Battalion is considered heroes of the nation.

What San Patricio's champions do in fact give us is a glimpse of what might have been; what the world might have looked like if this impressive anti-imperialist impulse had prevailed. For one thing, it was multinational (albeit composed only of European nationalities). It was also anti-slavery, a profound development of the time, especially poised against the Slave Colossus of the North. The history of such a social force could have transformed what came to be world history, given the immense impact of the United States on regional and world events.

Mexico's "Maroon Experience"

As has been witnessed earlier, America cared little for the people; land was what they wanted—just as they wanted Spain's lands in Florida, Cuba, and beyond. They dreamed of an awe-inspiring slave power, from which yet more wealth could be super-exploited. On that score, Mexico was on the right side of history as they outlawed slavery by 1829, more than 30 years before the U.S. would be forced to do so by exigencies of a horrible civil war.

It is not coincidence that 1829 was the year the country abolished slavery. This was also the year that Mexico elected a Black (and Indian!) man to hold their highest civil office of President: 179 years before the U.S. manages to elect a bi-racial man of African ancestry! This man, Vicente Guerrero, lived an extraordinary and remarkable life, as written by historian William Loren Katz:

Not only did Mexico's maroon experience prepare its dark people and mixed races to march to independence, but it cast up a leader in Vicente Guerrero, a Black Indian. Born in Ixtla in 1782, Guerrero's parents were of mixed European, Indian, and African stock. As a young man, Guerrero became a mule driver, and in 1810, he was one of the first to enlist in the war for independence.

> In his first battle, he was commissioned a captain. As the conflict dragged on for years, the leading revolutionaries died or were captured. But with two thousand ragged men carrying guns and ammunition taken from fallen Spanish soldiers, Guerrero kept the spark of rebellion alive in the Sierra Madre Mountains. Repeatedly Spanish officials tried to persuade the charismatic young man to surrender and return home. They even sent his father to ask him to accept a pardon. Guerrero fought on.
>
> By 1821 the independence movement was headed toward success. Guerrero's incorruptibility gave it strength and drew peasant support. "His swarthy face, resonant voice, and flashing eyes made him an object of profound respect even among his enemies," reported U.S. historian H. H. Bancroft.
>
> This Black man, who only recently became literate, had helped shape Mexico's Constitution. It was he who wrote the clause: "All inhabitants whether White, African, or Indian, are qualified to hold office."[8]

During his tenure as President, Guerrero ended slavery, abolished the death penalty, constructed schools, and opened libraries for poor people. Although this was years before the American Invasion, it colored Mexican society, and sent it on a trajectory that was doomed to collide with the growing Slave Power in the North.

We cannot speak of these events in isolation, for, in truth, both societies were born on the shredded backs of African slaves, which was the lamentable, yet undeniable, engine of immense wealth. Nevertheless, it was in the context of Guerrero's presidency and Mexico's abolition of slavery that threatened America's freedom to exploit slaves. It would be difficult to overstate the antipathy held by many Americans for their neighbors south of the border. Frederick Douglass, himself an escaped captive, minced no words as an antiwar figure who condemned the Mexican War. Douglass possessed the discernment and brilliance of speech to show how the two horrific endeavors of slavery and expansionist wars were joined with bonds of iron:

You know as well as I do, that Faneuil Hall has resounded with echoing applause of a denunciation of the Mexican war, as a murderous war—as a war against the free States—as a war against freedom, against the negro, and against the interests of the workingman of this country—and as a means of extending that great evil and damning curse, negro slavery. (Immense applause.) Why may not the oppressed say, when an oppressor is dead, either by disease or by the hand of the foeman on the battlefield, that there is one the less of his oppressors left on earth? For my part, I would not care if, tomorrow, I should hear of the death of every man who engaged in that bloody war in Mexico, and that every man had met the fate he went there to perpetrate upon unoffending Mexicans. (Applause and hisses.)

A word more. There are three millions of slaves on this land, held by the U.S. government, under the sanction of the American Constitution, with all the compromises and guaranties contained in that instrument of favor of the slave system. Among those guaranties and compromises is one in which you, the citizens of Boston, have sworn, before God, that three millions of slaves shall be slaves or die—that your swords and bayonets and arms shall, at any time at the bidding of the slaveholder, through the legal magistrate or governor of a slave Stave, be at his service in putting down the slaves. With eighteen millions of freemen standing upon the quivering hearts of three millions of slaves, my sympathies, of course, must be with the oppressed. I am among them, and you are treading them beneath your feet. The weight of your influence, numbers, political combinations and religious organizations, and the power of your arms, rest heavily upon them, and serve at this moment to keep them in their chains. When I consider their condition—to the history of the American people—how they bared their bosoms to the storm of British artillery, in order to resist simply a three-penny tea tax, and to assert their independence of the mother country—I say, in view of these things, I should welcome the intelligence tomorrow, should it come, that the slaves had risen in the South, and that the sable arms which had been engaged in beautifying and adorning the South, were engaged in spreading death and devastation there. (Marked sensation.)

There is a state of war at the South, at this moment. The slaveholder is waging a war of aggression on the oppressed. The slaves are now under his feet. Why, you welcomed the intelligence from France, that Louis Phillippe had been barricaded in Paris—you threw up your caps in honor of the victory achieved by Republicans over Royalty—you shouted

> aloud—'Long Live the Republic!'—and joined heartily in the watchword of 'Liberty, Equality, Fraternity'—and should you not hail, with equal pleasure, the tidings from the South, that the republicans of France achieved against the royalists of France? (Great applause, and some hissing.)[9]

Douglass's voice, while certainly distinctive, was one among many at the dawn and the height of the war, for people could sense that this was a war based on vast untruths, for expansionist purposes. As we quoted more extensively in Chapter 7, Ulysses S. Grant—who fought in Mexico as a young officer—later termed the war as "one of the most unjust ever waged by a stronger against a weaker nation."[10] While the statement, in and of itself was not especially extraordinary, that the writer here was a former U.S. president (Grant made the comment in his memoirs)—and a general of the national army, is remarkable. If only he witnessed the America that America would become, he could never have written such a line.

But to become the America that would morph into the greatest empire since Rome, America had to expand its horizons—and expand it did, with a ruthlessness that was breathtaking.

Casus Belli

We have written of Polk's attempt to sell the Mexican-American War as a just retort to the claim that "Mexico... has invaded our territory." In fact, on the very day he was inaugurated into office, Polk told his secretary of the Navy, George Bancroft, that one of his main objectives was to acquire the precious Pacific coastline of California—the American Invasion became the methodology toward that end. And what did it matter that there were some thirteen thousand American casualties? Or that countless numbers of Mexicans perished in this war for land? The American border thickened and western territories were opened to American exploitation.

As in most imperial and expansionist wars, people are superfluous. They are obstacles to geo-political objectives. If the occupation and colonization of Ireland opened up the world to British imperialism, then Mexico (and Cuba, and Puerto Rico, and Haiti, etc.) opened the door to the American Empire. For here we see imperialism in embryo: the machinations that undergirded the why's of war. Historian Anders Stephanson, in his work *Manifest Destiny,* provides an interior perspective to this era of empire building that resonates in the present era. Stephanson writes of the counsels of the powerful, where rhetoric may be born, but deeper truths are spoken:

> Polk could intensify his moves against Mexico. His eye all along had been on the territory between Texas and the Pacific, especially Alta California (the present day state of California) with the prized harbor of San Francisco Bay. This immediate issue concerned the disputed southwestern, formally Texas, border with Mexico. Nothing essential was really at stake, but the dispute was useful to Polk in making the situation acute. Earlier, he had made clear to Mexico that a settlement should ideally also include the American purchase of San Francisco Bay with surroundings, possibly the huge New Mexico territory as well. A Mexican coup, however, had thwarted all hope for such an easy solution. There remained military action. Yet Polk and his advisers were not keen on any grand war effort. Senator Thomas Hart Benton's retrospective view was to the point: 'They wanted a small war, just large enough to require a treaty of peace, and not large enough to make military reputations, dangerous for the presidency. Never were men at the head of government less imbued with military spirit, or more addicted to intrigue.'
>
> The chief intrigue concerned the exiled Mexican general Santa Ana, whom Polk planned secretly to ferry back from exile and assist in resuming power, after which, in return, he would gratefully sell the desired territory to the United States. On the assumption that this would mean a short, little war, that indeed the United States would even be greeted as liberators, Polk confidently advanced American troops to the Rio Grande. When the Mexican Army retaliated, Polk declared that the United States had been invaded and so war began. With an American army apparently already in battle, the Whig opposition chose to support funding for the war. Meanwhile, the navy and western irregular troops attacked California in accordance with long-standing secret orders.[11]

"...the United States would... be greeted as liberators?" Does this not ring a bell? It tells us in our times, at the opening of the 21st century, we are still using the imperial playbook of the 19th century. Our political parties have flipped into new incarnations, and some (like the Whigs) no longer exist as political entities. Yet, there is a fatal continuity that continues to this day. It is embodied in the way the U.S. looks upon the world as something to be conquered, exploited, assimilated, and digested.

As prey.

Mexico was easy pickings for the U.S., and as his successors would do two centuries thereafter, Polk accused and defined the aggressed nation as the aggressor, and enough of the American public "bought it" to be feasible. Like Rome, the American Empire saw threats everywhere, and when there were none they manufactured them. At the time of the Mexican-American War, Mexico's population was about seven million souls. The United States, by contrast, was home to some twenty-two million.[12]

As we have seen above when an American officer is quoted, he describes the nation and people in distinctively non-aggressive terms: "pastoral race," "no way inclined to savage usages," and the like.[13] When Rome was the terror of the world, one of its victims described the Roman attitude. American thinker, Michael Parenti, in his *The Assassination of Julius Caesar*, cites Anatolia's exiled ruler, King Mithridates, for this poignant observation: "The Romans have constantly had the same cause, a cause of the greatest antiquity, for making war against all nations, peoples, and kings, the insatiable desire for empire and wealth."[14] Parenti further draws from the Roman historian Tacitus's *Agricola* to give voice to a chief of the Caledonians, Calgacus, of the first century, who describes his Roman enemies with as trenchant a critique as history has accorded us:

> [Y]ou find in [the Romans] an arrogance which no reasonable submission can elude. Brigands of the world, they have exhausted the land by their indiscriminate plunder, and now they ransack the sea. The wealth of an enemy excites their cupidity, his poverty their lust of power... Robbery, butchery, rapine, the liars call Empire; they create a desolation and call it peace...
>
> [Our loved ones] are now being torn from us by conscription to slave in other lands. Our wives and sisters, even if they are not raped by enemy soldiers, are seduced by men who are supposed to be our friends and guests. Our goods and money are consumed by taxation; our land is stripped of its harvest to fill their granaries; our hands and limbs are crippled by building roads through forests and swamps under the lash of our oppressors... We Britons are sold into slavery anew every day; we have to pay the purchase-price ourselves and feed our masters in addition.[15]

This, Roman historians and expansionists called Pax Romana (the Roman Peace). Similarly, the wake of the American Invasion of Mexico, predicated on weak, insupportable pretexts, American boosters have called Pax Americana.

The American Invasion, which stirred up intense and spirited debate, also found its ambivalent supporters among American's intellectual and cultural elites. Men we regard today as bright and shining lights of their age gave their measure of blessings to this imperial adventure. For, although they may have opposed the way the United States stole Mexican lands, they approved the result if not the methodology. And among this elite also existed the aura of destinarianism:[16] the deeply felt view that America was part of a divine mission to bring forth liberty to the dark "savages," of the natives, of the Mexicans, and to all non-whites the world over. In reality this divinity was more like an incubus, drawing forth nightmarish visions of global power and ultimate domination over the Other.

The Mexicans, some argued, may have done the U.S. no wrong, but they had to understand that, as celebrated American author Ralph Waldo Emerson put it, "it is very much certain that the strong British race, which has now overrun so much of this continent, must also overrun that tract [Texas], and Mexico and Oregon also, and it will in the course of the ages be of small import by what particular occasions and methods it was done. It is a secular question."[17] It is odd that Emerson would choose this particular formulation to make his pro-imperial point, for in addition to being an author and transcendentalist, he was, for a time, a Unitarian minister. Perhaps history could re-characterize Emerson as a "Machiavellian transcendentalist."

For some, it would seem, empire conquers all.

Emerson's colleague (and also a fellow New England clergyman), Theodore Parker, considered the Mexican War "mean and wicked." But, though the method of acquisition may have been wrong, the end gave the affair a different light. Parker concluded:

> But this may be had fairly; with no injustice to any one; by the steady advance of a superior race, with superior ideas and a better civilization; by commerce, trade, arts; by being better than Mexico, wiser, humaner, more free and manly.[18]

Of the Mexicans themselves, he considered them "a wretched people," even though they "abolished slavery", and did not "covet" their neighbors lands, as did the "superior race" of Anglo-Americans.

To vary our portrait of the times and the men (and women) who inhabited it, it would do well to note the observations of John Quincy Adams, the ultimate New Englander, who, alone, among his colleagues who inhabited the White House, left it to sit in congress. There Adams stood as an abolitionist wall, and, unlike Lincoln, not only opposed the Mexican-American War, but used his powers to vote against appropriations for it.

That said (as we have discussed in more detail in Chapter 7), he was also the principle author of the Monroe Doctrine, or the notion that the hemisphere was for Americans only—forbidding "foreign" interference. Or, as put by scholar/diplomat Clara Nieto, the western hemisphere was "The Americas for the United States."[19] Adams was, by any measure, a continentalist, and as principle architect of the Monroe Doctrine, it should not surprise us that the words "destiny" and "manifestation" appear therein. Perhaps Adams, as an ardent abolitionist, saw the new lands as extensions of Slave Territory, and thus objectionable. Perhaps the post-president Adams of 1846 saw things differently than the man of thirty years before, who co-created the Monroe Doctrine, and was compelled to that rare action of voting against appropriation for the war. For, in this distinction, he went farther than Lincoln, the "Great Emancipator."

War is the mother of many ills and many opportunities.

It was, upon U.S. victory over the Mexicans, possible, if not probable, that the Americans could have claimed the entire country. Empires often have appetites larger than their abilities to consume nations. Yet, it did not. While congress was then the plantation of both Lincoln and Adams, there were other voices raised that also viewed total annexation as not favorable—albeit for very different reasons. One significant example was South Carolina's Senator, John Calhoun (oddly enough, Adam's vice-president from 1825 to 1832), who strongly dissented against the total acquisition of Mexican territory. Quoth the Senator, "We have never dreamt of incorporating into our Union any but the Caucasian race... Ours, sir, is that Government of a white race."[20]

For this, at least, the Mexicans should consider themselves lucky in their remaining nationality and sovereignty. Their fate could have resembled that of Cuba, or Haiti, or Puerto Rico. That is to say, it could have been occupied for years by U.S. troops who, once empowered by bayonets, wrote special privileges and property into foreign constitutions, or suppressed native dissidents or national minorities (as they did in Haiti and Cuba, respectively). Think of it—ever wonder how Guantanamo Bay came to become U.S. "territory"?

Perhaps Mexico was simply too large to swallow whole—nonetheless, after the "war," at least 8 current U.S. states were gobbled and carved up: California, Texas, Nevada, Wyoming, Utah, New Mexico, Colorado, and most of what is now Arizona—all of it once Mexican land, part of Mexican territory.[21] Today, in all of these non-U.S. states, there exists a palpable antipathy toward Mexicans, and attempts to disfranchise, if not remove Mexican history, Mexican culture, and above all—Mexicans.

Of lies, of bullying

We have seen how the great Black orator, Frederick Douglass, has held forth against the American Invasion. While Douglass himself spoke forcefully against the military adventure, he did not end his attack there. He used his primary organ, *The North Star,* to damn the invasion, and Douglass did not bite his tongue, nor did the paper he edited curb its pen. In a lengthy editorial entitled, "The War with Mexico," the Rochester, New York, journal thundered against the prevailing national mood that called for war:

> Whig as well as Democratic governors stand stoutly up for the war: experienced and hoary-headed statesmen tax their declining strength and ingenuity in devising ways and means for advancing the infernal work: recruiting sergeants and corporals perambulate the land in search of victims for the sword and food for powder. Wherever there is a sink of iniquity, or a den of pollution, these buzzards may be found in search of their filthy prey. They dive into the rum shop, and gambling house, and other sinks too infamous to name, with a swine-like avidity, in pursuit of degraded men to vindicate the insulted honor of our Christian country.
>
> Military chieftains and heroes multiply, and towering high above the level of common men, are glorified, if not deified, by the people. The whole nation seems to "wonder after these bloody beasts." Grasping ambition, tyrannic usurpation, atrocious aggression, cruel and haughty pride, spread, and pervade the land. The curse is upon us. The plague is abroad. No part of the country can claim entire exemption from its evils. They may be seen as well in the State of New York, as in South Carolina; on the Penobscot, as on the Sabine. The people appear to be completely in the hands of office seekers, demagogues, and political gamblers.

> Within the bewildering meshes of their political nets, they are worried, confused, and confounded, so that a general outcry is heard—"vigorous prosecution of the war!"—"Mexico must be humbled!"— "Conquer a peace!"—"Indemnity!"—"War forced upon us!"—"National honor!"—"The whole of Mexico"—"Our destiny!"—"This continent!"—"Anglo Saxon blood!"—"More territory!"—"Free institutions!"—"Our country!"—till it seems indeed "that justice has fled to brutish beasts, and men have lost their reason." The taste of human blood and the smell of powder seem to have extinguished the senses, seared the conscience, and subverted the reason of the people to a degree that may well induce the gloomy apprehension that our nation has fully entered on her downward career, and yielded herself up to this revolting idea of thousands of her own men, and the slaughter of tens of thousands of the sons and daughters of Mexico, have rather given edge than dullness to our appetite for fiery conflict and plunder.
>
> The civilization of our age, the voice of the world, the sacredness of human life, the tremendous expense, the dangers, hardships, and the deep disgrace which must forever attach to our inhuman course, seem to oppose no availing check to the mad spirit of proud ambition, blood, and carnage, let loose in the land.[22]

Those were the roots and fruits of the Mexican War. The lessons learned, of lies, of bullying, of cloaking conquest in Honor, Freedom, Manifest Destiny, and Anglo Saxon Blood, would launch America's imperial project out into the world, the results of which we are just beginning to reckon.

Mexico today—tomorrow the world!

❖ ❖ ❖

9 Life & Death in the Empire's Backyard

Imperial Hubris South of the Border

For more than 150 years, the United States, as the Big Boy on the American block, has lorded over its Latin American neighbors to the South, under the aegis of what it has named and defended as the Monroe Doctrine of 1823.

First declared at the 2 December 1823 State of the Union address to Congress by President James Monroe, the speech set forth U.S. power and primacy over the Caribbean as well as the Latin American continent, and served as a warning to any (other) European power to butt out.

Most of us who were awake during history class can recall the phrase "The Monroe Doctrine," but we would wager few of us were actually exposed to the words stated by James Monroe when he put the ideas before Congress justifying American primacy. That's probably because, by our lights today, we see them as repellant, false and, well, frankly racist. Let us, for the sake of clarity for those of us that missed or misremember, share some of the words uttered by Monroe that would go on to become loosely codified as The Monroe Doctrine:

> The American continents... are henceforth not to be considered as subjects for future colonization by any European powers...
>
> In the wars of the European powers in matters relating to themselves we have never taken any part, nor does it comport with our policy to do so...

> We owe it, therefore, to candor, and to the amicable relations existing between the United States and those powers to declare that we should consider any attempt on their part to extend their system to any portion of this hemisphere as dangerous to our peace and safety. With the existing colonies or dependencies of any European power we... shall not interfere. But with the governments... whose independence we have... acknowledged, we could not view any interposition for the purpose of oppressing them, or controlling, in any other manner, their destiny, by any European power, in any other light than as a manifestation of an unfriendly disposition of the United States.[1]

Wow.

Essentially, it says, (if interpreted through, say, a Mafioso argot): "Lookit our boy Joey Clams. He don't seem to understand that this here is our spot, our corner. Ya wanna come in? Ya gonna get whacked. It's that simple."

Now, *that's* gangsta.

From 1823 to this very day, this has been the operative policy governing U.S.-Latin American (and Caribbean!) interactions and, for virtually that entire time, it has worked to the dire detriment of millions of people south of the border. The Monroe Doctrine has exposed them to U.S. aggression, U.S. intervention, U.S. paranoia, as well as the subsequent widespread death and destruction that these phenomena entail.

The hypocrisy of such a doctrine is self-evident, for in addition to staking claims to sovereign lands, it further purports to protect Latin Americans by defending them from continued European oppression. But who is there to protect them from the avaricious, intrusive, belligerent *norteamericanos*? And how does one come to dominate an entire continent? Apparently, according to U.S. policy, by declaring it a "doctrine."

What that meant in the real world was described in a confidential memo from U.S. Undersecretary of State Robert Olds in this 1927 message to his colleagues at State: "We do control the destinies of Central America. Until now Central America has always understood that governments which we recognize and support stay in power, while those which we do not recognize and support fail."[2] (Much the same could be said of all of Latin America, as this continent's tortured history has shown.)

The Olds memo, if written in Latin, could have been scripted by a Senator of Rome. This is the language of Empire. *We* control who runs, who wins, who loses. *We* decide who lives—and who dies. How has this oppressive reality made the people of Latin America feel for well more than a century? How do you think they feel now? Once again, we turn to Howard Zinn to help encapsulate the decades of domination and control:

> [The U.S.]... had insisted... on a Closed Door in Latin America—that is, closed to everyone but the United States. It had engineered a revolution against Colombia and created the "Independent" state of Panama in order to build and control the Canal. It sent five thousand marines to Nicaragua in 1926 to counter a revolution, and kept a force there for seven years. It intervened in the Dominican Republic for the fourth time in 1916 and kept troops there for eight years. It intervened for the second time in Haiti in 1915 and kept troops there for nineteen years. Between 1900 and 1933, the United States intervened in Cuba four times, in Nicaragua twice, in Panama six times, in Guatemala once, in Honduras seven times. By 1924 the finances of half the twenty Latin America states were being directed to some extent by the United States. By 1935, over half of U.S. steel and cotton exports were being sold in Latin America.[3]

Andrew Jackson, the 7th U.S. President (1829-1837), gave voice to the yearning of North Americans for expansionism of the American idea, without respect to the wishes of those on the receiving end of such an aggressive process. The basis of this expansionism was America's purported "ideological and moral superiority" over the rest of the earth. (It's interesting that advocates of this expansionism never said what the application of this supposed superiority was quite obviously predicated on—"military superiority".) Jackson was in lockstep with this notion, and supported the extension of U.S. authority over "semi-barbarous peoples," so that they could bring the light of "civilization" to the great unwashed masses.[4]

What the Monroe Doctrine was, under its frothy promises of protection, was a sad truth: that the U.S., after all was said and done, was an empire. American journalist, author, and social critic, Walter Lippman, writing in 1927, defines this with a directness that was quite rare for the period:

> All the world thinks of the United States today as an empire, except the people of the United States... We shrink from the word "empire," and

> insist that it should not be used to describe the dominion we exercise from Alaska to the Philippines, from Cuba to Panama, and beyond...
>
> [W]e control the foreign relations of all the Caribbean countries; not one of them could enter into serious relations abroad without our consent. We control their relations with each other. We exercise the power of life and death over their governments in that no government can survive if we refuse it recognition. We help in many of these countries to decide what they call their elections, and we do not hesitate, as we have done recently in Mexico, to tell them what kind of constitution we think they ought to have. Whatever we may choose to call it, this is what the world at large calls an empire, or at least an empire in the making. Admitting that the word has an unpleasant connotation, nevertheless it does seem as if the time has come for us to look the whole thing squarely in the face and to stop trying to deceive ourselves.[5]

It was precisely this pathology of imperialism that has infected the southern hemisphere since Monroe and continues today in furtherance of American objectives (that is, corporate wealth and expanding bottom lines).

Guatemala

For our purposes in discussing American intervention in, and paternal domineering over, Latin America, we begin in 1950s Guatemala because it precedes our main stage—Cuba—and because it sets the stage for the dramas and tragedies to come.

The year is 1954, and Guatemala's legally elected government faces an invasion by paid mercenaries, armed and trained by the American CIA in military bases in both Nicaragua and Honduras. The invasion is accompanied by American air power: four fighter planes manned by U.S. pilots. The U.S.-trained and equipped mercs are used to transform Guatemala from the site of the most democratic government in its history, to one of the most barbaric. Installed as the locus of power in the country is Colonel Carlos Castillo Armas, a man also trained in military school at Fort Leavenworth, Kansas. Armas replaced the elected President, Jacobo Arbenz, a Socialist, who incurred the wrath of the Americans by his government's expropriation of 234,000 acres of land owned by United Fruit Company, which rejected compensation from the government as "unacceptable."

Armas repaid the favor to his masters by returning the land to the American company, abolishing taxes on capital investments (of foreigners), erasing the secret ballot, and sending thousands of political opponents to prison. But Guatemala had other, more interesting payoffs for the Yankees. It became the model by which agents and operatives of the CIA would practice their peculiar brand of statecraft with the overthrow of governments. They would utilize such tactics across the continent—and globally.

According to some reports, the CIA accomplished their Guatemalan victory by deep deceit. They ran fake radio reports in the capital, which described huge armies taking cities and villages on the periphery. Arbenz, listening to the broadcasts, apparently believed no resistance was possible. As a direct result of the CIA operation, Guatemala became a land of arch repression and its U.S.-trained death squads brought misery, pain, and torture to countless people for decades.

And that was just the beginning.

Cuba

Even though we tend to view Cuba from a mid-20th century lens, it's interesting how history at least tries to repeat itself. For more than a century before the modern era, at the time of the 19th century, Cuban rebels were on the brink of sending their Spanish overlords back to Barcelona. Cuban rebels and nationalists opposed Spain's grip on the island, and fought the empire to a virtual standstill.

In marched the U.S., loudly proclaiming that they had come to "help," "defend," and "protect" those fighting for liberty. In point of fact the Americans, despite their noble promises, wanted Cuba for the most vile of reasons: to extend slave labor to the Caribbean Sea's largest island. And Spain, seen as "old Europe," was regarded as a spent force (which, in fact, it was).

For 10 long years, Cubans held an uprising against Spain (1868-1878), forcing Spain to make a number of concessions (which it then proceeded to ignore). In 1895, poet, patriot, and revolutionary, Jose Marti staged the Cuban Independence movement to break Spain's hold on the island. Americans, vowing support for Cuban liberty, entered the conflict (uninvited) several years thereafter. There was a good reason the Cubans didn't invite or seek U.S. aid.

They didn't need it.

James Bradley writes in his book, *The Imperial Cruise:*

> In contrast to the American Revolutionary War, Cuban freedom fighters would have beaten the Spanish without foreign aid. (Indeed, impartial observers noted that U.S. troops could not have landed if the Cubans had not fought the Spanish back.) But Teddy [Roosevelt] saw things differently:
>
> "The Cuban soldiers were almost all blacks and mulattoes and were clothed in rags and armed with every kind of rifle. They were utterly unable to make a serious fight, or to stand against even a very inferior number of Spanish troops, but we hoped they might be of some use as scouts and skirmishers. For various reasons this proved not to be the case, and so far as the Santiago Campaign was concerned, we should have been better off if there had not been a single Cuban with the army. They accomplished literally nothing, while they were a source of trouble and embarrassment, and consumed much provisions."[6]

Remarkable. TR was shorthand for Teddy Roosevelt, but it could have equally been shorthand for Truly Racist.

(Incidentally, this period also saw Washington's interference and imposition on Cuban Independence, resulting in American policymakers virtually writing Cuba's Constitution and the passage of the Platt Amendment, which ceded Cuban territory to the U.S.—including the future site of the notorious Guantanamo Bay Naval Station, perhaps better known as the U.S. warmongers' favorite brig and torture center.)

> *If I could only live to see it, to be there with you. What I wouldn't give for twenty more years! Here we are, protected, free to make our profits without Kefauver, the goddamn Justice Department and the F.B.I. ninety miles away, in partnership with a friendly government. Ninety miles!... Michael, we're bigger than U.S. Steel.*
>
> —Hyman Roth to Michael Corleone, relaxing at the Capri Hotel, Havana (*The Godfather: Part II*)

Despite victory against the Spanish Empire, the Cuban people were still ruled by a colonial hand from afar—ninety miles north to be exact. The truly brilliant chronicler, Clara Nieto, a former diplomat, in her layered, informed, and insightful *Masters of War*, gives a historical perspective of mid-20th century Cuba, and its struggle against the U.S.-supported dictator, Fulgencia Batista, and the young rebels, led by Fidel Castro, who dared to oppose him:

> There was no organized and cohesive labor or farm workers' movement in Cuba to oppose Batista. Political parties were broken up into factions, with no political directions. The secretary general of the Cuban Workers Federation (CTC), Eugenio Mujal Barniol, was a pawn of the regime, in the service of the employers and foreign business interests. Mujal shattered labor unity; under the pretext of anti-Communism he persecuted labor leaders who refused to obey his dictates, removed honest ones from office, and replaced them with token leaders loyal to him. He prohibited strikes and did not protest against the repression of the working classes, which included armed assaults on union headquarters.
>
> Fidel denounced the repression and corruption of the regime and its cohorts. The continual student demonstrations resulted in confrontations with the police, leaving hundreds wounded and arrested. Legal avenues of resistance did not exist, and justice was bought and sold. The only alternative to bring about change was an armed struggle. Fidel and a small group of rebels began to obtain arms and to train clandestinely. The group, led by university students and comprised of workers, laborers, and campesinos [peasants], grew quickly.
>
> Fidel stepped up his denunciation of corruption, accusing the regime of sharing the spoils and the *vende-patrias* (sell-outs) with converting Cuba into a Yankee semicolony in exchange for millions in bribes. He denounced the press for being bought off by Batista, with swarms of journalists receiving *botellas* (bribes). He also accused the courts of being submissive to the dictator, and he condemned the torture and murder of opposition leaders, students, and unionists and the brutality of the rural police, whose victims were the campesinos.[7]

Moreover, the island became a virtual paradise for the Mafia, which owned hotels, casinos, sparkling nightclubs, banks, and, perhaps more troubling—whorehouses. (Francis Coppola's acclaimed blockbuster film, *The Godfather Part II*, briefly depicts this period of Cuban history with remarkable authenticity.)

The rebels, although badly outnumbered and terribly outgunned, were not lacking in audacity, for they famously attacked the Moncada barracks in Santiago de Cuba, the second most important military installation in the country. On Santa Ana's Day, July 26, 1953, they hit Moncada, a fortified, high-walled installation housed with twice their number. The rebels expected the day's celebrations to lower the fort's security, but the guards were more alert than they supposed, for they hit the alarm, and before the rebels knew it, they were trapped.

The two forces battled it out and, when the smoke cleared, the rebels had clearly lost both the element of surprise and the conflict. But what they lost militarily was more than offset by the excitement they engendered in Cuban society, for though they were badly out numbered, they caused twice the casualties of their adversaries.

The captured rebels were beaten, grotesquely tortured, and killed under the dictator's orders. These acts caused considerable alarm in Cuban society, so the regime mitigated their punishments to soften their sordid public profile. Nonetheless, the electrifying Moncada attack marked the day that the armed struggle had come to Cuba.

The unpopular Batista regime, seen as an instrument of foreign power, seemed on the wane; while the young rebels, bearded, bold, and bodacious, captured the hearts of many Cuban nationalists, who longed to be free of the gringos.

When Fidel Castro and two compañeros were found in a sugarcane field five days after the storming of the fort, widespread public disgust regarding the dictator's brutal torture campaign was probably the decisive factor in the Guardia letting them live.

Castro was given a secret trial to ensure that his words would not reach and perhaps further inflame the people. Batista was no fool, for he knew that Fidel, trained as a lawyer, would conduct his own defense—and put the government on trial. Indeed, Castro condemned the corruption of the Batista regime and their kowtowing to foreigners and set forth the basis for the establishment of a revolutionary government, sovereignty, the reinstatement of the 1940 Cuban constitution (abrogated by Batista), land reform, along with the abolition of the vast land holdings of the *latifundia* (the large landed estates), as well as the nationalization of utilities.

Predictably, Castro's attacks didn't make the morning *periodico.* But his words did see the light of day when two women—fellow rebels of the army that attacked Moncada: Haydee Santamaria and Melba Hernandez—smuggled out the trial records of Fidel's defense and published it under the title, "La historia me absolverá" ("History Will Absolve Me"), perhaps the most famous line of his secret trial.

Fidel would be sentenced to fifteen years in prison; his younger brother Raul would be sentenced to thirteen. Other survivors were given lesser sentences. Here again public opinion would come into play and Batista would grant amnesty to all of the rebels after two years in prison.

Several weeks later, Fidel left for Mexico to clandestinely build an army, all the while under the police surveillances of the Mexican government, the FBI, agents sent by Batista, and even spies from the dictator in the Dominican Republic, Rafael Trujillo. From this nucleus would come the core of the Rebel Army that would return to Cuba (aboard the leaky boat *Granma*) that would again attack Cuban forces, lose some casualties, and gain greater confidence and skills.

Two years after the rebels returned to Cuba, Batista, betrayed by his own army and officers, would flee the island and the rebels would take the state and write a new history for the nation. But the success of Cuban rebellion against the corrupt leaders of their country would make the tiny island nation "Public Enemy Number One" of the Empire.

In any sane situation, one would think that the hardest part was over. But, alas, this was not a sane situation. For generations of Cubans would learn that this victory marked the beginning of a greater war—the real war. The war with the Empire. Because, as in the Roman example, an empire needs total subservience, and the U.S. used all means and methods to try to bring the Cubans to heel—to make them cry, "Tio!" ("Uncle!")

They used spies, internal attacks on land, buildings, livestock; bombs, betrayers, and sabotage—every tool imaginable (including trying to kill Fidel at least nine times!). Indeed, they used terrorism, and the Cubans, stubborn as mules, refused to budge. For the Cubans are proud of their sovereignty, and will not bow, even to the most powerful government the world has seen (since Rome). Why was Washington opposed to the Cuban takeover? Howard Zinn explains:

> The revolution was a direct threat to American business interests. Franklin D. Roosevelt's Good Neighbor Policy had repealed the Platt Amendment (which permitted American Intervention in Cuba), but the United States still kept a naval base in Cuba at Guantanamo, and U.S. business interests still dominated the Cuban economy. American companies controlled 80 to 100 percent of Cuba's utilities, mines, cattle ranches, and oil refineries, 40 percent of the sugar industry, and 50 percent of the public railways.[8]

These were not, of course, the only reasons. Cuba was poised to present to the world a viable alternative: a socialist alternative. This, the Empire could not, and would not, endure.

Nevertheless, Cuba went to work to build its renewed country and give agency to its people. It waged its own internal "war"—against illiteracy—that has no peer in history. It sent teams of children throughout the country to teach peasants (the poor and the rural folk) how to read. This war against illiteracy was an unqualified success—for the peasants, and for Cuba's international standing.

But to the Americans, Cuba's efforts were for naught. They had done the intolerable: they had disobeyed the big boy on the block, the neighborhood bully. Clara Nieto writes that Washington began immediate action to wreck this revolution:

> The United States was not disposed to "tolerate" the fact that this small Caribbean Island would threaten its hegemony and leadership of the hemisphere, break its unity, and demolish its interests. Open and covert aggression began at once. According to documents declassified by the United States government in 1990, in March 1959 [U.S. President Dwight D.] Eisenhower ordered the CIA to set into motion "Operation Pluto," an extensive effort to subvert the Revolution and overthrow Fidel. Immediately CIA agents began to infiltrate, and terrorist actions and sabotage in commercial and public centers ensued. Pirate aircraft took off from Florida to drop napalm on Cuban sugar refineries and important economic targets. And the CIA provided arms, money, and equipment to a counterrevolutionary group that was forming in the mountains of Escambray in central Cuba.[9]

The terrorism and bombings of Cuban land and property was only the softening up before the Big One: an economic embargo that would cripple the island's economy; and then, an invasion. But the U.S., with its public speeches about national sovereignty and democracy, could hardly justify an invasion of the island, so a proxy war would suffice. Howard Zinn gives a concise account of the American proxy war unleashed against the new Cuban state:

> President Eisenhower secretly authorized the Central Intelligence Agency to arm and train anti-Castro Cuban exiles in Guatemala for a future invasion of Cuba. When [John F.] Kennedy took office in the

> spring of 1961 the CIA had 1,400 exiles, armed and trained. He moved ahead with the plans, and on April 17, 1961, the CIA-trained force, with some Americans participating, landed at the Bay of Pigs on the south shore of Cuba, 90 miles from Havana. They expected to stimulate a general rising against Castro. But it was a popular regime. There was no rising. In three days, the CIA forces were crushed by Castro's army.[10]

The U.S. government, embarrassed by the fiasco, tried to duck out of it. Again, Zinn:

> The whole Bay of Pigs affair was accompanied by hypocrisy and lying. The invasion was a violation... of a treaty the U.S. had signed, the Charter of the Organization of the American States, which reads: "No state or group of states has the right to intervene, directly or in-directly, for any reason whatever, in the internal or external affairs of any other state."
>
> Four days before the invasion—because there had been press reports of secret bases and CIA training for invaders—President Kennedy told a press conference: "...there will not be, under any conditions, any intervention in Cuba by the United States armed forces." True, the landing force was Cuban, but it was all organized by the United States, and American war planes, including American pilots were involved; Kennedy had approved the use of unmarked navy jets in the invasion. Four American pilots of those planes were killed, and their families were not told the truth about how those men died.[11]

The Bay of Pigs. In Spanish, Playa Giron. No matter how you spoke of it, it dealt a black eye to U.S. foreign policy and made the Kennedy administration look like amateurs.

Nor did it make the media look like they were actually doing their jobs, for several prominent media outlets—including *The New York Times* and *The New Republic* magazine—completed stories on the imminent invasion ready to print. The Kennedy White House convinced both publications to spike their stories—on the basis of "national security."

Yet, the nation was hardly more secure when the invasion with its foibles and flub-ups became common knowledge. Zinn blames the "liberal–conservative coalition" for this snafu, for they were caught in an anti-communist fever that generated fiasco after fiasco.

The Cuban adventure followed the Guatemalan overthrow by five years, and was designed to replicate the same exercise. It failed primarily because the Cuban leadership, along with its citizenry, were not cowed by threats (and even acts) by Washington. Moreover, they had something to fight for: a revolution against a dictator that had the money, guns, and support of the Americans. They did not want to return to Batista and the reputation as the Mafia whorehouse of the Caribbean.

They did not surrender.

When Batista flew the coop, most of his family went to Jacksonville, Florida, New Orleans, and New York City. He, his wife, and most of his advisors went elsewhere, touching down in Ciudad Trujillo (Trujillo City) in the Dominican Republic. Although the DR's ambassador to Cuba related that there was no notice that the Cuban dictator made known his desire for asylum, the *jefe* there, Rafael Trujillo, accepted their flight, and commenced exploiting the situation to his advantage.

According to Nieto, Trujillo began billing Batista for arms sent to Cuba during his reign, and also began extorting exorbitant fees for his country's services—reaching into the millions. (It should be noted that, as stated by *Bohemia*, a Havana journal, in February 1959, the Batista party fled the island with between $300 to $400 million in jewels and cash.[12] Trujillo was determined to get some of that cream.) When Batista tried to resist these transparent shakedowns, Trujillo gave him the treatment by which dictators are best known: he threw him in prison until he saw the light.

Batista paid the man and then quietly sought escape from such an expensive "asylum." He tried to flee the island on a private plane but Trujillo's forces blocked his exit. Batista found asylum from the revolution in Cuba, but at a very steep price.

Back on the island, in the flush of victory at the Bay of Pigs, the Cubans were triumphant. They had beaten the Colossus of the North at their own game, and they did not hesitate to gloat about it. But the war—the Long War of Empire—had just begun.

Embarrassed, and with copious helpings of omelet on his face, Kennedy had no intentions of laying down the sword. Like many presidents before him, and many after him, losses in war only set the stage for more losses to come. The tools of an ambitious president are almost without limit, for the wealth of the nation is the fund from which the weapons of war, of intrigue, of spy-craft, and subversion are formed.

"Operation Pluto" (interestingly, the name of the Roman god of the underworld and death) had failed, and failed miserably. What does the richest nation in the world do? The answer is obvious: start another operation!

Clara Nieto writes that the U.S. government was so discombobulated by the revolution in Cuba that they made a deal with the devil: they joined forces with La Cosa Nostra—the Mafia—to bring them the head of Fidel Castro. She writes:

> The CIA set up "Operation Mongoose," the most expansive and costly operation at the time, run by Attorney General Robert F. Kennedy and General Maxwell Taylor. No operation had been as carefully tended to, more secretive, of higher priority, or treated with a greater sense of urgency. The Kennedys wanted quick results. The special group created to supervise the operation scheduled Fidel's downfall for October 1962, believing that the operation could count on Cuban popular support. Its planner could not have been more wrong.
>
> The CIA proceeded to recruit agents to infiltrate into Cuba. Most of these were Cuban exiles. It also recruited foreign businessmen and diplomats. The primary objective was to assassinate Fidel. The Senate Commission chaired by Frank Church, which investigated the Watergate scandal in the 1970s, confirmed several of the attempts to assassinate Fidel, some of which were coordinated with the Mafia dons Meyer Lansky, John Roselli, Sam Giancana, and Santo Trafficante, whose businesses in the island were cut off by the Revolution. According to a CIA agent, Robert Kennedy was furious when he learned of such agreements, since they could derail the case he was building against Giancana and Roselli. Several agents testified that the Kennedys were keenly aware of their plans to assassinate the Cuban leader.
>
> The CIA installed an enormous espionage apparatus at the University of Miami, "the biggest base ever created on United States territory," code-named JM WAVE. It had an annual budget of $100 million, 600 employees, and more than 3,000 agents. It was equipped with small boats, mother ships disguised as merchant ships, planes (from the CIA front, Southern Air Transport), a huge arsenal, and safe houses and buildings. Between January

and August 1961 it carried out 5,780 acts of sabotage and terrorism against Cuba, including attempts on Fidel's life with the cooperation of Mafia.[13]

The Mafia and the U.S. Government intelligence agencies: perfect bedfellows.

Fidel Castro would survive ten American presidents, from 1961 to 2008, when he finally stepped down from power due to health problems and advancing age. It seemed he was more "mongoose" than the CIA operation designed to kill him, for he outfought, outfoxed, and outlived his American adversaries to deepen and expand the Revolution, right under the nose of the Empire.

That said, while the American foreign policy establishment could not prevail, it could do untold damage to the economic stability of the Cuban nation. Its embargo, established during the Cuban Missile Crisis of October 1962, cost the country billions of dollars in lost revenues and sales, especially of its premier export, sugar. The U.S. used that embargo for generations to force the Cubans to bend its knee to American power. Despite these epic losses, which ravaged the country (especially after the fall of its primary business partner and benefactor, the Soviet Union in 1991), Cuba has emerged as one of the world leaders in the field of biotechnology.

For its independence from El Norte, it has suffered, and continues to suffer, severe and sustained pain. But it has borne it with pride.

As for United States government making common cause with an overtly criminal organization, one is reminded of the query posed by St. Augustine, one of the Fathers of the Church: "What is a political regime, when devoid of justice, but organized crime?"

Not So Welcome

But what was ailing Cuba was not Cuba's problem alone. All throughout the southern hemisphere we witness the power of America del Norte exercised, in the vast tracts of land owned by U.S. transnationals, in the moneys channeled to "friends," in the training of foreign troops, and in the overt and covert control wielded by Washington over elected and unelected South American governments. Cuba proved the exception, not the rule, in this regard as most Latin nations—inverting a once popular U.S. advertising slogan—would *"rather switch than fight."*

That said, we should not forget a simple truth: governments of countries are not the peoples of countries. We would be wise not to confuse the two, for often, people are bitterly opposed to their governments, especially when they are little more than the puppets of foreign outside interests. For many, perhaps most Latin Americans during the 1960s, this was the case. More often than not, the governments in power, even when elected, represented the privileged elites: the landowners, the wealthy and investor classes. They often displayed crude and shocking contempt for the vast majority of the people, perhaps best shown when that majority were African or Indian populations.

Washington has always looked on Latin America with mild bemusement, as if one were looking at children, or cute animals. Particularly during the 1950s and 60s, U.S. leadership rarely bothered to look beneath the thin veneer they provided to the corporate press, making them quite unprepared for the reality they found when visiting their southern neighbors. When Eisenhower's Vice President, Richard Nixon, was driven through Lima and Caracas on his 1958 tour, he was greeted by insults, stones, and spit. Secretary of State John Foster Dulles was tempted to send in the Marines to rescue the American political leader.

When Eisenhower took his tour, in his last presidential year, February 1960, it was no sweeter. There were so many hostile, anti-American demonstrations, riots, and threats of bombings that the leader of the free world had to be whisked away via helicopter from the Buenos Aires airport to the American embassy. In Argentina, Brazil, Uruguay, and Chile, anti-gringo protests filled the streets to such an extent that the police felt compelled to use water cannons and tear gas.[14]

Clearly, and despite the polite "diplomatese" used by the political leaders and the militaries of these nations, the people held nothing but anger toward the *norteamericanos.* Nor did the Americans' behavior in the Dominican Republic give Latin Americans any reason to think any differently about them.

Santo Domingo

As the seagulls rest on the cold cannon nest
The sea is churning
The marines have landed on the shores
Of Santo Domingo
– Phil Ochs

In 1965, Kennedy's successor, Lyndon Johnson, was sharpening his saber for a war on the Dominican Republic. The Caribbean country was experiencing political conflict following the presidential election of Senor Juan Bosch, which was opposed by the military junta that took power following the CIA assassination of Rafael Leonidas Trujillo.

After the revolution in Cuba, which toppled the U.S.-supported dictatorship, Trujillo, with his ruthlessness against his opponents, his epic greed, and his obnoxious penchant for deflowering (ahem—raping) the various crops of Dominican maidens (and these, often, of his "friends!") was becoming an American embarrassment. At the highest levels in Washington, the message was being sent that Trujillo was getting too big for his britches.

Scholar-activist Eric Thomas Chester, in his work *Rag-Tags, Scum, Riff-Raff, and Commies* recounts the eradication of any ally whom the empire had tired of:

> [T]he conspiratorial network planning the assassination was ready to move, armed with machine guns smuggled by the CIA into the Dominican Republic. On the evening of May 30, 1961, three cars followed the dictator as his chauffeur-driven limousine drove along a coastal highway on the outskirts of Santa Domingo. The pursuing cars hemmed in the limousine and began firing. By 10:00 P.M., three decades of autocratic rule had come to a bloody end. Yet the transition to democratic rule could only begin when Trujillo's death brought with it the end of the Trujillo dynasty.[15]

When young rebels began to stage a coup in favor of Bosch, the senior levels of the Dominican military set the stage for a counter-coup. The U.S., still smarting from its Cuba debacle, unleashed some 400 U.S. Marines and some 40,000 infantry to stifle the rise of another Caribbean revolution.

In order to sell the idea, Johnson did what presidents have been doing for decades. He lied. Citing a diplomatic communiqué from U.S. Ambassador Tapley Bennett, Johnson held several press conferences to state that intervention in Dominican affairs was necessary to protect American lives. Adding some sauce to the concoction, Johnson later announced that some 1,000 innocent people were slain in the streets, some of whom were decapitated. For special effect he reported that half a dozen Latin American embassies were set ablaze. (Contrary to Johnson's account, there were American journalists there who noticed that there were no embassies burning, no decapitations, and no Americans either wounded or killed.)

It didn't matter. Rebels were fighting for Dominican independence, and favored Bosch over any puppets taking orders from Washington. The most eventful battles raged at the Duarte Bridge in Santo Domingo, where, as Chester reports, the side that prevailed would determine the nation's very future. Chester writes:

> For more than three hours, the shock troops of San Isidro inched slowly forward, moving southwest from the bridge into the inner city, capturing the electric power plant a third of a mile south of the bridge along the Ozama River. Yet along the main thrust of the attack, into the downtown area of the Ciudad Nueva, the junta forces were stymied, able to penetrate only five blocks into the rebel zone before pulling back.
>
> During the course of the bloodiest battle of the Dominican revolt, hundreds of people were killed, and hundreds more were injured. When Red Cross officials surveyed the scene soon afterward, they recovered 450 bodies, with an uncounted number having died in hospitals and in nearby homes. The Red Cross placed the death toll for the four days from April 25 to April 29 at 2,500 with most of the fatalities occurring during the battle for the Duarte Bridge. U.S. authorities estimated the toll at close to a thousand for the entire battle, including the preceding days of air raids and the main conflict on April 7; while an observer sympathetic to the rebel cause put the total number of deaths as staggering, considering that the total population of Santo Domingo in 1965 numbered 480,000.[16]

What nation doesn't have the right to revolt? The U.S., born in what was essentially a Baron's Revolt (or a revolt of the rich, for the right to exploit Indian lands and Black slaves), could hardly be heard to say revolts were unacceptable, right?

Well, what the U.S. was, and what it became, were two very different things. For, what was once a small, weak assembly of scattered colonies of an empire, would swell into the most powerful, most militarily potent empire that the world has yet seen. As such, what the Dominicans wanted did not carry the day in Santo Domingo, for the Americans, embarrassed by Cuba, had to send a message to its puppets, satellites, and client states in Latin America that Washington would decide who would prevail in the event of civil conflict.

And they did so.

But why? Was it really about feelings? Even powerful ones? Like fear? We can never ignore the presence of fear, nor its seductive power. But that can hardly be the reason for something so significant as an invasion, right? In fact, it was, sad to say, a reason quite less impressive than fear. It was ambition. Political ambition. Professor Chester explains the reasoning behind the U.S. invasion and occupation of the Dominican Republic:

> President Johnson understood that the United States had made a significant commitment to intervention by deploying more than 500 marines in Santo Domingo. Ever the politician, he prepared to capitalize on this decision for his own political gain by immediately summoning two congressional leaders, Senator Everett Dirkson and Representative Gerald Ford, from a banquet that they were attending that evening. When the two Republican leaders arrived at the White House, they were met by the president, clad in pajamas. Johnson was quick to boast that he had "just taken an action that will prove that Democratic presidents can deal with Communists as strongly as Republicans."[17]

An invasion? An occupation? For domestic political gain? You've read it right here. It was not the first. And assuredly, it will not be the last. But what was the cost of the U.S. invasion to the people of the Dominican Republic? The Americans opposed a popular politician, Juan Bosch, who they feared was a closet communist. It mattered little that they had the right to hold political ideas that the gringos didn't like, or feared. It mattered naught that a good number of Dominicans admired and respected Bosch—or even supported him. What mattered was what the gringos wanted. The gringos wanted someone who would do as he was told, like Trujillo, but wouldn't get too enamored with himself. Thus, the Americans supported Joaquin Balaguer to take over after the stilled staccato of gunfire. Chester writes:

> Balaguer succeeded in holding on to political power for most of the last three decades. Once inaugurated in July 1966, Balaguer acted quickly to decimate the opposition. Death squads killed dozens of left-wing militants, as well as many of those who had led the commando units that had patrolled the rebel zone during the popular uprising. Even those on the moderate left were targeted, with hundreds of activists from Bosch's party, the PRD, brutally executed. During Balaguer's first two terms in office, 1966 to 1974 [after his exile from a short presidency ending in 1962], more than three thousand left-wing activists were assassinated, as the "leadership of leftist parties [was] wiped out." These are staggering figures given the population base of the country, 3.7 million in 1966. In fact, there

> were more assassinations of political dissidents during Balaguer's first years in office than during a comparable period within the Trujillo era.[18]

Political ambition and base domestic political bragging rights sent the peoples of the DR into a living hell for more than a third of a century. The Dominican Republic was but one among many nations that would suffer for the pathologies of the American Empire.

And yet, we must note that the Dominican Republic's neighbors did not take the U.S. invasion lying down. More than half a dozen countries spoke out loudly in both diplomatic and public channels to denounce the actions of the U.S. as violating the many charters and agreements forbidding one state to interfere with the internal affairs of member states.

Throughout Latin America, countries strongly criticized the Johnson administration, and both the U.N. and the Organization of American States (OAS) followed suit, for the American action was a clear violation of the principle of nonintervention, of international law, and the charters of both the United Nations and the OAS. In fact, the OAS and the U.N. Security Council called for an immediate withdrawal of U.S. forces from the country.

But being an empire means never having to say you are sorry, for U.S. diplomats to the OAS turned a critical session into a decision that the U.S. invasion wasn't an invasion, but was instead a "collective action" under a "peace-keeping force."[19] To their eternal credit, Chile, Mexico, Ecuador, Peru, and Uruguay voted against the OAS measure, and Venezuela abstained. The U.S. Ambassador to the United Nations, Adlai Stevenson, tried unsuccessfully to block the U.N. Security Council from even considering the Dominican Republic invasion and occupation, but he failed miserably at this task, for the U.N. devoted some 28 meetings on the subject. The U.N. Secretary General, U Thant (of a nation then known as Burma), actually intervened in the discussion and appointed a Venezuelan diplomat, Jose Mayobre, as his representative to go to Santo Domingo and report back his findings. Señor Mayobre's report delivered a severe critique of the American intervention and occupation, and particularly criticized U.S. troop behavior in Santo Domingo.

But being imperial also means you can dismiss the concerns of your critics (especially Latin ones, it seems). Nieto described the Johnson-era actions that followed the critiques:

> With imperial arrogance Johnson kept the troops and special advisers in place and intervened in the country's affairs at his whim, including placing former president Joaquin Balaguer once again in the presidency; living in exile in New York, Balaguer had served as an adviser to Johnson during the invasion.
>
> The invasion was nothing short of a scandal. Alberto Lieras, the former president of Colombia and one of the mainstays of United States policy regarding Latin America, was afraid that the United States' new acts of aggression would turn the Cold War into a hot one. President Raul Leoni of Venezuela sent Johnson a message condemning the invasion as a "violation of the principle of non-intervention." The Peruvian chancellor maintained that it was the most severe blow of the past few years to the inter-American system of laws. *The New York Times* called the presence of the marines in Santo Domingo unjustifiable. Robert Kennedy thought it was just scandalous.[20]

The Dominican Republic's U.S.-created trauma lasted for decades. We will perhaps never know the full extent of the damage done by this foreign intervention. We do know, however, that it did them little good.

Colombia

During the 1960s, many Latin American countries presented an alternative to conventional political systems by building either a political party or an army of insurgents who felt unrepresented by the usual two political parties. Colombia was such a place.

The Colombians entered the '60s under the influence of Alberto Lieras Camargo, who sought and, for a brief time, succeeded in uniting both the Colombian Liberal Party and the Colombian Conservative Party into a single political entity: the National Front.

This effort was intended to assuage the pain of a profound political gap which left the country embroiled in "The Violence": a wave of political violence aimed at the liberals by the conservative dictatorships which preceded the Liera era, deepened by the subsequent military dictatorship that followed under the command of General Gustavo Rojas Pinilla. The death toll of that era neared some 300,000 souls, most of whom were among the peasants.

National Front president Liera had one problem that plagued his hopes: in politics, where true trust is rare, it takes two sides to make a deal. The liberals (who were absorbing the lion's share of the violence) could strictly agree; but if the conservatives felt it was but a ruse, they would continue to ravage the opposition. This they did.

When General Pinilla ordered an amnesty if guerrillas laid down their weapons and joined the process, it mattered not what they did, for upon disarming, they were frequently hunted by armed forces—and terminated. The National Front was more like a National Fraud, and such actions not only undermined trust in the conservatives of the Front, but also in the liberals and Liera.

That distrust was engendered by a number of events, but perhaps the most destructive was when a popular liberal guerrilla, Guadalupe Salcedo, laid down his weapons only to be riddled by the bullets of his rightist opponents. People learned the hard way that to be armed made a good deal more sense than to acquiesce to a process that was profoundly broken.

With the assassination of Salcedo, once-retired guerrillas, called "bandits" by the press, took to the mountains, and re-armed themselves. The amnesty was broken. New armies were formed, as well as new workers' parties. Often, the army would be the armed branch of a political formation or party. Perhaps the most surprising such allegiance came when Camilo Torres, a Catholic priest, joined the ELN (Ejercito de Liberacion Nacional or Army of National Liberation). As Torres was known as a cultured man, an educated man, and one who came from a prominent family, his enrollment in a guerrilla army sent shockwaves through the nation. For while people quite easily understood why a disaffected worker or an alienated peasant might take the road of war, why a priest? Why a cultured man? Why this man?

It was more than an avocation, a diversion, or an escape for excitement. For Camilo Torres saw the suffering of the poor, and, what is worse, the extreme wealth and waste of the landed classes—the *latifundia.* But the biggest problem for the idealistic young man was the viewpoint of his Mother Church. Nieto writes:

> His drastic step grew out of his frustration with his inability to convince the backward-looking and reactionary hierarchy of the Colombian Catholic Church that the people were suffering great injustices, misery, and poverty, that there had to be a change and that the Church had a responsibility to bring it about. The Church sanctioned him, and he

> submitted to the restrictions it imposed. But he was convinced that his duty as a Christian was not to turn his back on social problems and conflicts, as the high officials of the church did. He recognized that solutions to social conflicts were impossible to attain in Colombia through the limitations of legal avenues. He joined the ELN because its members shared in his goals. He was killed by the army. News of his death had a tremendous impact nationally and throughout Latin America. Camilo became a major figure in the calendar of Latin American revolutionary saints.[21]

Padre Torres may have been the first priest to join the people's army; but he would not be the last. Many religious people, moved by the vast injustice faced in societies more oriented toward Washington than its own citizens, took the revolutionary road to rectify these social imbalances.

Nieto quotes two ELN cadre, who knew and admired Torres. Felipe and Rafael said, "Camilo was our *Commandante* because of what he did, not only as priest, but also as a revolutionary. His investigations, his studies, his leadership of the United Front, his life in struggle go far beyond the priesthood."[22]

Legacy of Ashes

The 1960s was the time where we witnessed an eruption of guerrilla armies opposed to the central state and its oligarchy. As noted earlier, they had little trust for the fusion parties that sounded liberal themes, yet aped the animosity of the right wing against popular armies. Guerilla armies began forming because the central government lacked legitimacy for many, many people. When people like Fidel or Che called the elected leadership "puppets" of the gringos, it had a bite that none could deny.

Various governments took the time to establish a threshold of legitimacy, and they did so, in part, by uniting the two competing streams of political thought, while opposing and targeting those deemed leftist (which meant, among the elites, nothing but Communism).

This deep, unbending anti-communist fervor flowed from two sources: a) the class paranoia of the elites and the *latifundia* class; and b) the American grooming, training, and indoctrination of the higher-ups in the military, usually in American military academies. For the Americans were haunted by the specter of Cuba, and worried incessantly that other countries on the Southern Cone would follow the red road earlier trod by the Castros, Guevara, Juan Almeida and the like.

For home field political advantage in the U.S., this meant that the president who "allowed" another country to fall into the communist/socialist bloc would be blamed for the "loss" and be damningly declared "soft on communism." This political calculation bedeviled every major presidential politician for over half a century, and truth be told, it dogs them still.

For who "loses" a country? Who owns one?

This deep, institutional imperial mindset, exacerbated by the internal interests of the Military Industrial Complex (that is to say, the immense "defense" industries), framed the narrow parameters by which the White House moved and dealt in the realm of foreign policy. It dictated allegiances and determined who were enemies—for the old imperial calculus of Rome inevitably prevailed: "He who is not with me, must be against me."

But, as we have discussed elsewhere, militaristic and ideological concerns are only part of the imperial picture. For, as we have intimated, the CIA coup that drove Guatemala's Arbenz from power was done, in part, at the behest of the United Fruit Company—a powerful multinational, which played a pivotal role in many Latin nations because of its sheer size and wealth. It is not much of an exaggeration to suggest that United Fruit actually controlled several southern governments. Clara Nieto explains the range of their corporate and political powers thusly:

> Given the collaboration, the stupidity, or the venality of the rotating dictators in these countries, United Fruit established dependent economies with semicolonial characteristics. "The Octopus," as the company was known in the region, manipulated governments at will, meddled in their political fights, provided financial assistance to candidates of its choice, and fixed the scales in favor of whoever offered it the most attractive conditions. It was a state within a state. Through pressure, threats, and bribes it obtained concessions and privileges outside the law; tax exemptions, evasion of tariffs and duties, free import and export of earnings, and the payment of a minuscule percentage of its multimillion dollars in profits. Such "services" were repaid with juicy bribes to the countries' leaders, and Washington rewarded their submission by propping up their regimes.[23]

The American company was the major employer in many of these regions, and given their resources, they paid double the average local wage by domestic companies. They also opened up schools and clinics for their employees. But all was not peaches and cream, for they also denied vacation, fired people at will without either grievance or compensation, and bitterly opposed the very notion of unionization. Like their corporate forebears in the U.S., United Fruit and Standard Fruit forbade any worker from collective bargaining. This led to massive protests against the American transnationals.

The multinationals responded as if they were in Chicago during the Roaring Twenties. They unleashed armed paramilitaries to deter the union activists. Union leaders were not only beaten; they were beaten, kidnapped, and shot to death. Nieto informs us that the challenges facing the corporations became, *ipso facto,* the problems of the U.S. State Department, especially as led by John Foster Dulles (the brother of CIA director, Allen Welsh Dulles). Together, the Dulles brothers, who saw the hand of communism in every global conflict, also saw corporate interests as essentially the same as national interests. We can say more: *national security* interests.

Thus, when workers fought to unionize, to better their return on capital (to get raises), to speak out against their venal, repressive governments, for Washington this was big "C" Communism at work. And, as with everything else during the so-called Cold War, it demanded a military response. In fact, Latin American efforts to restrain the excesses of capital were considered wars against the sacred rights of property, and as such, it contravened American prerogatives in their colonial outposts. John Foster Dulles famously said (of General Motors), "We do not have friends; we have interests." Dulles was the architect behind the clumsy coup against Arbenz in Guatemala.[24] When studied closely, these "interests"—more often than not—were indistinguishable from corporate bottom lines.

Zinn, examining this long and "rich" history of bipartisan support for repressions against our so-called neighbors to the south, would call this a "liberal-conservative coalition," and as is usually the case, he would be correct. History clearly reveals that the differences between how U.S. presidential administrations, whether Democratic or Republican, have handled Latin America is often more rhetorical than substantive. (Isn't this the case for much of American foreign policy?) For both supported dictators, both sought to remove leaders with which they disagreed, and both parties interfered with the internal governments of states in which they wanted to play empire. For both were as much directors as captives of the intoxicating power of the CIA.

So, one may recite presidents at will or whim; it matters not. For each and all of them (at least since 1942, when Franklin Roosevelt established the Office of Strategic Services, which later morphed into the Central Intelligence Group and several years later, the Central Intelligence Agency) have fallen under the spell of the invisible army of intelligence, a power answerable only to themselves. That is, at least, its somewhat mythical allure. But in the real world, they have been criminal agents of disorder, destruction, and terror.

The words of former president Dwight Eisenhower (upon leaving office) would be prophetic. Speaking to his CIA chief, Allen Dulles, he remarked, "I leave a legacy of ashes to my successor."[25] (We might add, "Dude. Try a legacy of ashes to ALL your successors.")

The rightist-anti-imperialist writer Chalmers Johnson's assessment of CIA efforts around the world is not promising. In one of his last books, he damns the history of the Agency, and its record of failure:

> The historical record is unequivocal. The United States is ham-handed and brutal in conceiving and executing clandestine operations, and it is simply no good at espionage; its operatives never have enough linguistic and cultural knowledge of target countries to recruit spies effectively. The CIA also appears to be one of the most easily penetrated espionage organizations on the planet. From the beginning, it has repeatedly lost its assets to double agents.[26]

El Salvador: Ripe for Conflict

At first glance, El Salvador seemed like heaven compared to many of its neighbors. For, although it was the smallest country in the region (about the size of New Jersey), it had seemingly been spared the fate of many of its sister states. Despite its small size, it had a dense population, the most industrialized economy, fertile lands producing a premier export crop (coffee), and the highest population growth in the region.

But, apparently, hell is never far from heaven, for it also had the most economically polarized sectors in the region, facing a politically aware peasantry who were not shy to organize fellow workers and to agitate for better pay and better living conditions. Unlike its neighbors, it was not a banana republic, nor had it been invaded by the colossus to the North. In many ways, El Salvador's problems stemmed from the enemy within: it was a nation at the service of the fabled Fourteen Families—a tightly bound and extraordinarily wealthy collective of blood, faith, and greed that considered the peasants clear threats to their class privileges.

El Salvador suffered the greatest gap between rich and poor; and the rich were protected by the armed might of the police as well as state law. The Fourteen Families owned the most fertile lands in the country, as well as the industry, the commerce, and the banking institutions. Clearly, El Salvador was ripe for conflict.

Critic of empire Michael Parenti has illustrated that many countries suffer gravely when they have valuable resources in hand. Parenti calls this a "curse," noting:

> Empires are enormously profitable for the investor interests of the imperial nation but enormously costly to the people of the colonized country. Even today, plundered populations bemoan the *resource curse,* knowing from bitter experience that countries rich in natural resources usually end up as *losers.* Many of the countries of Africa, Asia and Latin America are rich, only the people are poor. The Imperialists search out rich places, not barren ones, to plunder.[27]

The natural resources of El Salvador, the fecundity of its lands, accrued to the owning class—not the laboring class. And the owning class was both ready and willing to utilize the violence of the State to protect their established patrimony. The elites employed its police and military forces to put an end to peasant rebellions against elitist domination over the land and the wealth garnered from production of the land. The state's response to the pleas of their lords led to a bleeding on a scale that the nation hadn't seen since the exterminations of the Indios. Clara Nieto writes:

> In December 1931, a campesino revolt in the coffee-growing zones ended in one of the region's most horrendous massacres, marking one of the darkest pages in Salvadoran history. It lasted three months and resulted in the murders of between 10,000 and 30,000 campesino men, women, and children—the number varied depending on the source. Their blood stained the hands of General Maximiliano Hernandez, who had taken power in a coup the previous month.
>
> The General, when informed that the young Augustin Farabundo Marti—head of the Communist Party he had helped found in 1925—was leading the campesino struggle, ordered him killed. The army

> captured him in the capital, in the company of the students Mario Zapata and Alfonso Luna, and shot them down then and there. Their murders marked the onset of what Salvadoran historians called the Massacre of 1932 and the beginning of General Hernandez's bloody, thirteen-year dictatorship. The oligarchy, the land-owning and coffee-growing bourgeoisie, sectors of the middle class and Washington, all supported Maximiliano because he had eliminated the insurgents and thousands of campesinos accused of "Communist agitation."[28]

In a world where trying to negotiate a raise or the right to a vacation was tantamount to communism, any challenge to the corrupt, controlling, domineering status quo would be seen as a violation subject to deadly state violence. That reality plagued El Salvador throughout this period, even if it was of internal origins. (There are compelling cases that argue even this internal strife was born from decades of Western and European economic influence, cementing the legacy of colonial rule, which established a landed and moneyed aristocracy—one that wanted to maintain its status as "owners" with its oppressive control of workers and peasants.)

Half a century later, Ronald Reagan's disputatious U.N. ambassador, Jeanne Kirkpatrick, would describe Maximiliano as a "hero" to be respected as someone who "made a special contribution to highly valued [public] goods."[29] The voices of capitalism could rarely be heard to be so disrespectful of human life, when "valued" against the sacred right of property. Nieto underscores this point:

> For Salvadorans, however, the Massacre marked a macabre turning point in the nation's history. For the revolutionary poet and writer, Roque Dalton, the carnage of 1932 left a fatal legacy: "Ever since that accursed year, all of us were different people, and I believe that since then, El Salvador is a different country. El Salvador today is, above all, the result of that barbarity. Our rulers may have changed their style, but the basic mode of thought that still beats us down is that of the slaughterers of 1932."[30]

The Massacre of 1932 was, for the most part, a homegrown affair. It was the expression of the propertied classes putting terror into the hearts of the laboring classes. But, fifty years after that event, the United States would enter intimately, fatally, into Salvadoran affairs, usually by way of the classroom.

Classroom? How could a classroom be fatal? Well, it depends on what is being taught. For the Americans, using the institution then-named the School of the Americas (situated in both Panama and Fort Benning, Georgia), U.S. military and intelligence instructors taught generations of Latin American soldiers and officers torture techniques, destabilization techniques, and most importantly: how to serve their elites better by a ruthless and merciless war against the "communists."

The Latins were apt pupils, for they went about their duties with a relish, and waged a war of blood, depravity, and death that permeated Salvadoran society—from its poorest, most distressed strata, to the hallowed halls of the Roman Catholic Church. Anyone—*anyone*!—who dared question the status quo, could be targeted, intimidated—or executed.

Ronald Reagan, in his Grand Crusade against the red devils of communism, launched a campaign of war by proxy, by supporting the Salvadoran government's war against the Salvadoran liberation movements. Of course, to sell to the couch potatoes in the U.S., he had to give it another spin: he was doing it to protect "us"—Americans (or, more precisely, North Americans).

The U.S. supported the government in order "to halt the infiltration into the Americas, by terrorists and by outside interference, and those who aren't just aiming at El Salvador but, I think, are aiming at the whole of Central and possibly later South America and, I'm sure, eventually North America."[31]

Author and anti-imperialist (and, we remind you, former U.S. Foreign Service Officer) William Blum characterized Reagan's remarks as a classic case of "paranoid schizophrenia." It is possible that the administration was no longer able to sell a war program using "democracy," or to "support freedom" (a perennial favorite). It is also possible that Reagan, a B-actor, was simply reading a script handed to him by Warner Bros.—err, we mean the CIA. But it is beyond belief that the man actually believed that the U.S. faced a threat from El Salvador—the tiniest country in the region. That is simply not tenable. It was, at bottom, the selling of fear to the uneducated masses and the old tactic of parading the flag before the mobs.

Nonetheless, the Reagan administration funded a military that created and sustained death squads that were so villainous and blood thirsty that they could make vampires blush. For although American naval forces, including two destroyers and a cruiser, sat offshore during the 1932 Massacre, granting silent consent while the army slew some 30,000 people, this time the U.S. trained the butchers who turned out to be masters of the game.

Before Reagan took office, the U.S. government, from 1946 to 1979, sent some $16.7 million in U.S. military aid to El Salvador. When Reagan took the helm, the Salvadoran military received $82 million in military aid—*in the first year.*[32] And the U.S.-trained Salvadoran military proved they were worthy of their weapons by using them against anything that moved. They killed campesinos, labor leaders, students, mothers, fathers—and, oh yes—*Fathers*—men (and women!) of the cloth—and many, many children. They raped as if it were legal. They sowed the dragon's teeth of terrorism as their U.S. paymasters smiled down on them from on high, applauding their games of gore.

El Salvador spiraled downward into the nightmare of civil war, and the Salvadoran people were the net in the middle of this game of death, receiving the lion's share of the bleeding. During U.S. support for the Salvadoran military, American-trained troops attacked, raped, and shot to death nuns who protested the government's repression. When that failed to silence them, they slew a priest who was a prominent critic of the government's repression against the people.

During the previous American administration, the Catholic Archbishop of San Salvador (the capital), Oscar Romero, wrote to U.S. President Jimmy Carter, *Christian to Christian*—imploring him to cease U.S. aid to the military. Padre Oscar Romero would take to the pulpit to denounce the repression that was turning the country into a charnel house. In his last sermon, he said to the nation's military and police forces: "I beseech you, I beg you, I order you, in the name of God: *stop the repression.*"[33] The next day, Archbishop Romero had his answer.

He was assassinated. And the U.S. government's military aid not only continued, but, under Reagan, it continued to soar. This was the Cold War—but to the Salvadoran people, it was as hot as hell. Massacre followed massacre after massacre—with the well-armed government troops and police at the core of this war against the poor and the working class, working at the behest of the twenty-five who owned 60% of the nation's resources.

When assassinations didn't bring them the concessions they wanted, then the State turned to its ravenous death squads: *Escuadrón de la Muerte.* One such unit had a provocative slogan: "Be Patriotic—Kill a Priest." The CIA assisted such units by providing them with lists of suspected communists (no doubt, some priests were on the lists!).

Nor was there any serious question about why the Salvadoran people were tired of this state of poverty and repression. Salvadoran President Jose Napoleon Duarte (1980-'82; 1984-'88) knew very well why the people were so riled up, as shown by this exchange between him and a reporter for *The New York Times*, as William Blum reports:

> In December 1980, New York Times reporter Raymond Bonner asked Jose Napoleon Duarte "why the guerrillas were in the hills." Duarte, who had just become president of the ruling junta, responded with an answer that surprised Bonner: "Fifty years of lies, fifty years of injustice; fifty years of frustration. This is a history of people starving to death, living in misery. For fifty years the same people had all the power, all the money, all the jobs, all the education, all the opportunities."[34]

Damn. Who after reading that statement, from the president of the country, could dare to disagree? Well, the Fourteen Families could, as well as those in the White House. For they wanted to maximize profit—at all costs—which simply meant, to minimize payments to workers.

To stabilize El Salvador, and make it safe for business, these forces destabilized everything else. Schools. Churches. Union halls. Homes. Workplaces. Villages. The society was at war with itself and, remarkably, the State, more often than not, was on its heels. That's because many, many Salvadorans recognized the rank unfairness of it all. They saw the way that the wealthy elites treated them and spoke about them. They saw the way that the police looked at them. For many, many young men and women, the revolutionary road was the only real option. It was the only road to a kind of dignity that did not exist among the campesinos.

Young people joined the popular, guerrilla armies, and the State responded with its own brand of expertise. When one young State recruit questioned why he had to kill a child—an innocent child, who had done nothing—his ranking officer instructed him, "if we don't kill them now, they'll just grow up to become guerrillas."[35]

Massacre after massacre after massacre, and the war raged on. It was in the 1990s that the two sides sat down and signed peace pacts. By the cessation of this very, very Hot War, some 75,000 Salvadoran souls were lost, thanks to the military support of the Americans.

Tens of thousands of people.

If we take Reagan at his word (a dangerous thing to do considering the imperial record of America's political leaders), we may seriously consider that the immense number of people killed (more, for instance, than U.S. troops were killed during the decade-long Vietnam war) were but sacrifices to "protect" the "American Way of Life"(!).

For El Salvador, however, the long, bloody, shattering war led to that most dangerous of effects: ambiguity. Tens of thousands dead (out of a nation with a population of only about 6.5 million people!)—and when the guns were silenced by the promises of the politicians and the scribbling of pens on paper, what was won and what was lost? In the quiet of a suspicious peace, *The Washington Post* interviewed two combatants from the ruinous, devastating 12-year war. William Blum, himself an expert on the carnage, used that interview to paint two chilling portraits from this modern-day heart of darkness. Initially, Blum cites the case of Jose Salgado, who fought for the U.S.-backed government in El Salvador.

> Salgado enthusiastically embraced the scorched-earth tactics of his army bosses, the *Post* reports, even massacres of children, the elderly, the sick—entire villages. It was all in the name of beating back communism, Salgado says he remembers being told. But he's now haunted by doubts about what he saw, what he did, and even why he fought. A U.S.-backed war that was defined at the time as a battle against communism is now seen by former government soldiers and former guerrillas as less a conflict about ideology and more a battle over poverty and basic human rights. "We soldiers were tricked," says Salgado, "They told us the threat was communism. But I look back and realize those weren't communists out there we were fighting—we were just poor country people fighting poor country people." Salgado says he once thought that the guerrillas dreamed of communism, but now that those same men are his colleagues in business and politics he is learning that they wanted what he wanted: prosperity, a chance to move up in the world, freedom from repression.[36]

One of Salgado's opponents was guerrilla Benito Argueta, who, Blum writes, experienced a similar fall from the revolutionary faith. Indeed, the question is rather, did he ever have any? Blum notes:

> Former guerrilla Benito Argueta laments that the future didn't turn out as he'd hoped. Even though some factions of the coalition of guerrilla armies that fought in the civil war were Marxist, he said, ideology had

> nothing to do with his decision to take up arms and leave the farm where his father earned only a few colones for backbreaking work. Nor did ideology play a role in motivating his friends in the People's Revolutionary Army. He remembers fighting "for a piece of land, for the chance that my children might someday get to go to the university."[37]

To protect the sacred right of property over the sanctity of human life, the U.S. spent some $6 billion in weapons sales as well as the training of death squads. The Fourteen Families were very proud of such an investment in capitalism. For, their property was indeed protected (with the monetary and material aid of the United States), but the nation—i.e., the people of the country—were broken, terrorized, beaten down, and corrupted. People migrated from the lands of their birth and fled to places where some hope of peace and seemingly regular life could be lived, where children could be raised and educated. But Home, that place of sacred, sweet memory, would be erased from the land of the living—because the Fourteen Families, and their servants in the police and military forces, were fighting communism—and the U.S., the richest nation on earth, graciously helped reap a killing field.

In nations such as El Salvador, the nightmares of *norteamericanos* became the real lives lived by the little people on the imperial periphery. Presidents wanted to prove their toughness, so they issued decrees that sent tens of thousands of people to their graves. They armed death squads (and called them "Freedom Fighters"—as Reagan did of the Contras—master rapists, torturers, and child-slayers all), taught torture in their special schools for foreign soldiers, and employed the CIA to buy off, subvert, or steal elections—all to the greater glory of Capital. Of Democracy. Of Freedom.

Or whatever.

This may, at first glance sound somewhat cavalier—"whatever?" But the lives or deaths of millions depended on the arcane rhythms and cadences of the internal American political dynamics of who was soft and who was hard on communism. The frequencies, pitched to the choir of American paranoia, determined how often and how brutally the Americans would intervene in another nation's internal affairs. To an Empire, it seems, no country has affairs of which it cannot interfere.

In the nadir of the end of the term of U.S. President Jimmy Carter, a man who popularized the relevance of "human rights," his opponents on the right considered this the height of U.S. softness in the realm of American foreign policy. The Carter foreign policy team tried to counter such a perception by upping U.S. military aid to the region, despite consistent and conspicuous complaints from Salvadorans that such aid would only strengthen the forces of repression. In January 1981, Carter released some $10 million in military aid and sent additional advisers to deal with the growing rebel movements there. Two years thereafter, now a private citizen, Carter would be free to say, "I think the government in El Salvador is one of the bloodthirstiest in [the] hemisphere now."[38]

The Carter administration, bowing to press and public pressure, certainly helped this process into becoming so, but the Reagan administration, determined to prove how the GOP was tougher than the liberals, ran the tab in their efforts to defeat communism in America's backyard.

Yet as we have seen, the raging civil war in El Salvador actually had little to do with communism, and even less to do with the Soviet Union; for this resistance was homegrown, based upon a long and ugly history of oligarchic repression. But the Americans, drunk on the absinthe of the (so-called) Cold War, saw the Soviets everywhere, and through that projection they saw a simplistic world defined as "for or against, pro or con, black or white."

The words of Benito Argueta have a certain ring. He was, he said, "fighting for a piece of land," or perhaps, a "chance that my children might someday get to go to the university." The sadly tragic truth is that the resources of the United States are so vast, so globally unprecedented, that it could have fulfilled the demands of the working campesino classes with pennies, and furthered the better interests of the Salvadorans and the Americans, with no loss of life. But given the toxic nature of the American "liberal-conservative coalition" politics, the lure to war was an easier sell than the call to peace and justice.

The administration of Ronald Reagan is remembered as American arrogance writ large; it was a time of war, of terror, of widespread destruction, and of many deaths of Latin Americans. Although remembered by Republicans and their conservative cohorts with warmth and nostalgia as the "Reagan Revolution," it was, if anything, a profound counter-revolution. It was a political period designed to roll back the social gains of the '60s era, both domestically and abroad. And while Reagan turned an evil eye toward South America, he also tried to make a global attack work against all that he and his generation saw as a "threat" to U.S.

hegemony. To do so, it was necessary to "Sovietize" everything and every place. Cuba? The Soviets... Nicaragua? The Soviets... El Salvador? The Soviets... South Africa? The Soviets.

This monoscopic and simplistic view, which was invalidated by the internal realities of each country, was sold to Middle America as a War Against the Evil Empire, and Americans gobbled it up like burgers and fries.

In point of fact, the Soviets were rarely interlopers in the affairs of other states, primarily because they didn't want to expend the resources that such entanglements required, and, perhaps more importantly, they regarded their national security needs as superior to those of their allies or other members of the socialist bloc. Of course, a socialist bloc was, to be sure, not the Soviet bloc. The idea of "peaceful coexistence," embraced by many in the Kremlin, was an idea that allowed the Russians to give lip service to its ideals, while quietly allowing many "allies" to sink or fall under their own weight. Because Cuban premier Fidel Castro could read these signs, he and other members of the Central Committee were uncommonly critical of such Soviet failures, and none were as critical as the Argentine doctor, Ernesto "Che" Guevara. Clara Nieto makes precisely this point in her summary of Che's last public speech, before the Afro-Asian Solidarity Organization in Algiers, in February of 1965, where:

> [H]e accused the Soviet Union of being to some degree "an accomplice of imperialist exploitation," and denounced the "immoral character" of its treatment of the recently independent African nations. In particular, he pointed out the excessive requisites the Soviet Union set before the African nations in their "mutually beneficial" commercial agreements. Next to Fidel, Che was the most vigorous voice of the revolutionary government. In March, Fidel also criticized the Soviets for not aiding North Vietnam—a victim of United States aggression—more effectively and for not reacting with greater force to the United States bombings that had begun a month earlier.[39]

Words like these had a powerful sting among the Soviets, perhaps because it had the ring of truth. These attacks may have also convinced the Soviet Central Committee to join the Cubans in their bold and principled attempt to turn back the Afrikaners of the South African state, which laid siege to the southern African republic of Angola in August and September of 1975. According to Wayne

Smith, director of the U.S. State Department's Cuban Affairs Office during that period, the Nationalist South African government invaded Angola "with full U.S. knowledge."[40] Smith added, "No Cuban troops were in Angola prior to this intervention."[41]

In October 1975, MPLA (Movimento Popular de Libertação de Angola in Portuguese; People's Movement for the Liberation of Angola in English) leader Agostino Neto requested both Cuban and Soviet aid to repel the South Africans. Again, Clara Nieto:

> The next day Cuba launched Operation Carlota, and the Soviet Union began sending arms and advisers. A battalion of 18,000 Cuban soldiers arrived secretly by air and sea. At this point the South African troops were 15 miles from Luanda, and the United States was already giving arms and instructors to the Frente Nacional de Libertacao de Angola (FNLA: Angolan National Liberation Front) led by Holden Roberto, and to the Uniao Nacional para Independencia Total de Angola (UNITA: National Union for the Total Independence of Angola), headed by Jonas Savimbi.[42]

A month after the entry of the Cuban/Soviet forces, Portugal pulled out, and Neto proclaimed the independence of the People's Republic of Angola. More than 30 nations recognized this new African state. In December 1975, 36,000 Cuban soldiers and the Angolan Army engaged the South Africans on four fronts, forcing an Afrikaner retreat. Within four months the Cubans returned home. The Angolan triumph over the racists in Johannesburg (and U.S. support to the FNLA and UNITA) caused Fidel to gloat that it was an "African Giron" (the Spanish name for the Bay of Pigs). In fact, it was the Cuban efforts on the field of battle that proved to be the straw that forced the Afrikaners to sit down with the ANC and open Mandela's prison cell. In the absence of military power demonstrated by the Cuban-Angolan alliance, apartheid would've puttered on, perhaps for decades more.

The odiousness of the system of apartheid, and how repellent it seemed to hundreds of millions of Africans (and others) made it increasingly untenable, not just to the Afrikaners—but to their American allies and sponsors. This position actually long preceded the Angola invasion, as can be seen by a memo sent from U.S. Undersecretary G. Mennen Williams to U.S. Secretary of State Dean Rusk, July 12, 1963:

> The moral issue needs little elaboration. Apartheid is obnoxious not only to all colored peoples who are the majority of the world's population but to all civilized people as well. Votes in the UN are ample evidence of this. If we refused an arms embargo, and another Sharpeville massacre occurred, we would stand condemned in the eyes of most of the world.[43]

These words might sound enlightened, but, in fact, the U.S. role was, to say the least, duplicitous. For while it gave lip service to arms embargoes against South Africa, it also helped them achieve a nuclear weapons program. The record shows that the Americans prized their Cold War position vis-à-vis the Soviets over any qualms about morality.

The U.S. assistant Secretary for African Affairs, Nathaniel Davis, resigned in opposition to the U.S. policy of intervention in Angola supported by Secretary of State Henry Kissinger. Davis' idea of a diplomatic solution found no favor with either Kissinger, or his boss, President Gerald Ford (or, for that matter, his predecessor, Richard Nixon). Washington's position, as announced by Kissinger, was that the U.S. would not recognize the new, post-invasion, and repulsive government of Angola under the MPLA's Neto. That position placed the U.S. at odds with much of Africa, and other polities in the world, as shown by the following note of events following this conflict:

> *November 25, 1975*: Nigeria announces that it will recognize the MPLA as the legitimate government of Angola, citing South African involvement in Angola as the primary reason for this recognition. In a December 3 cable to Secretary of State Henry Kissinger, Donald Easum warns that continuing silence by the United States on South African involvement in Angola would discredit the United States in the eyes of many African countries and "provide ammunition for those who already accuse us of abetting South African intervention."[44]

This gives us some idea of the power of the Latin American revolutionary idea, indeed, at Cuba's initiation, and its global impacts. For decades, the South African forces were able to strike with virtual impunity at the so-called Frontline states (Angola, Mozambique, Zimbabwe, Botswana, and Namibia). Supported by the U.S., and its aversion to Black independence, with a robust (if exploitative) economy, the South Africans were able to field armed forces with the most potent of weapons—until the Angolans were supported by Cuba, and the armies struck them at Cuito Cuanavale.

The bottom-line: Cuba shook the world with Operation Carlota, and the events there helped greatly to close the door on the formal program of apartheid.

The Eagle and the Mouse

Cuba may be the largest island in the Caribbean, but, in truth it is a relatively small island, and, as history has shown us, small islands (such as Britain, for example) can have outsized impact on the world.

As regards to the outsized impact of small islands, when Cuba got into a conflict with the United States, i.e., when the Cuban rebels ousted a U.S./Mafia-supported dictator, Fulgencio Batista, the U.S. pulled out all the stops to reverse this historical measure—and tried to utilize assassinations to achieve what we would later call (openly!) "regime change." We cannot examine the history of Latin America without giving due consideration to the impact of the U.S.-Cuban conflict.

Cuba became the stage of superpower Grand Strategy in the Cold War, when it crafted its republic as an openly socialist state, which the U.S. found (and indeed, finds today) intolerable, since Cuba was situated in what was considered "the American Lake," and all too close for U.S. comfort. But, unbeknownst to most Americans, the world's other superpower, then-called the Soviet Union, was almost surrounded by states which pledged fealty to the Americans and their military instrument, the North American Treaty Organization (NATO): Turkey, Iran, and, some 50 miles away, Pakistan. But, clearly, in an imperial sense, what's good for the Goose doesn't necessarily go for the gander. For the U.S. resolved to punish the impudent Cubans, who had the audacity to arm themselves with "offensive" (as opposed to "defensive") weapons, sent by the Russians.

The Americans elected to militarily "embargo" the island, setting a ring of heavily armed naval vessels and Marines to close off the island from international commerce and interaction. Few in the West either noticed, or mentioned the U.S. armaments placed in Turkey, to Russia's southwest. Years later, in his memoirs, Russian leader Nikita Khrushchev would write:

> The Americans had surrounded our country with military bases and threatened us with nuclear weapons, and now they would learn just what it feels like to have enemy missiles pointing at you; we'd be doing nothing more than giving them a little of their own medicine... After all, the United States had no moral or legal quarrel with us. We hadn't given the Cubans anything more than the Americans

> were giving to their allies. We had the same rights and opportunities as the Americans. Our conduct in the international arena was governed by the same rules and limits as the Americans.[45]

Neither U.S. political leadership nor the media perceived it quite that way, and the only words to adequately cover the period were "all-out panic." From the White House, to the Pentagon, to the CIA, to the American media, panic was all encompassing. For here, for the first time since the Revolutionary War, America was threatened by weapons nearly as destructive as their own—held by *Cuh-Cuh-Communists!*

It was impossible. It was unthinkable. Yet, here it was. Here, on the doorstep of the Empire, like an unloved, unwanted, bastard child. When U-2 flights over Havana confirmed CIA suspicions that some forty nuclear weapons were on the island (despite Soviet diplomatic denials of such weapons), the highest levels of America's political and military hierarchies met in Executive Committee of the National Security Council (ExCom) to decide options.

"What shall we do?" they wondered. The options were few, and all carried considerable risk—notably the obvious risk of failure. The table rang with positions: an all-out attack on Cuba, varied military invasions, naval blockades, and the mythical "surgical strikes." Some called for secret diplomacy. Others, surprisingly, urged that the U.S. simply do nothing, for fear that the presence of such weapons would leak out into the public and cause widespread, maddening panic.

Those against the attack would seem surprising, given their public personae. Robert Kennedy, the pugnacious Attorney General, advanced precisely that option (of no attack), likening it to a "Pearl Harbor in reverse," for it would "blacken the name of the United States in the pages of history."[46] Kennedy reasoned that such an attack by a large country on a tiny nation would electrify all of Latin America and produce new Castros across the continent. That said, the U.S. mobilized more than 80,000 men and put several units of the military on red alert. A day later, John Kennedy broke the news in a nationally broadcast speech to the American people. He announced a quarantine of the island, and promised a "full retaliatory response" if Cuba attacked.

Before the speech, he had a special communiqué delivered to Khrushchev and the Kremlin, with the text of his remarks. Several days thereafter, the Soviet Embassy invited an American news correspondent to its offices to suggest a diplomatic way out. Generally, the grounds were that the Soviets would dismantle the weapons, and remove them, if the U.S. publicly declared it wouldn't invade the island, and it withdrew U.S. missiles from neighboring Turkey and Italy. Simultaneously, Soviet leader Khrushchev sent a similar message to the White House.

The odd man out, however, was Cuban President Fidel Castro, who was not informed of the secret notes between the two superpowers. He went to the Soviet Embassy in Havana to send a message that he expected an American attack between 24-to-72 hours. To forestall such an attack, Fidel wrote (having his words translated on the spot into Russian by embassy officials) that it was "the moment to eliminate such danger forever by an act of the most legitimate defense."

The letter reached Khrushchev within 48 hours, Moscow time, and it terrified him, for he interpreted the communication as proposing a first strike against the Americans. To douse the possibility of this nuclear fire, the Soviet chief hit the airwaves to announce a deal between the Soviets and the Americans, agreeing to nix any invasion plans of the Cubans, and to withdraw weapons from the Caribbean theatre. Fidel was livid, for he felt he had been "handled" by the U.S.S.R, while the big boys talked out the details that could have meant the destruction of his country. Perhaps here were spawned the seeds of discontent between the two nations, which allowed both Che and Fidel to criticize them publicly—especially during their African sojourns.

Nonetheless, the crisis passed, not with fire, but with anger, anxiety—and relief. And yet, a deal with an empire is a deal with the devil. For, amidst such unequal powers to the pact, one side may choose to interpret said deal in ways that favor their side. True, the U.S. has never reinvaded Cuba—but it has done everything short of it. It has sent in spies, provocateurs, biological agents of war, and (this it has admitted) tried to slay Fidel at least eleven times. And, less than twenty years after the crisis, the efforts of Cuba abroad forced one White House aide, (who would soon be U.S. Secretary of State) General Alexander Haig to proclaim, during a meeting: "Give me the word and I'll make that island a fucking parking lot!"[47] The pale faces sitting in the room went even paler at the prospect of nuking Cuba.

Cuba—little Cuba—has been a beacon of resistance. It has paid, and continues to pay, ungodly debts for this intransigence. Yet, when humanity was confronted with the vile face of a state officially organized under anti-Black racism, Cuba—

little Cuba—responded with the force of arms in defense of its Afro-Cuban nation.

In many ways, the history of Latin America can form a lens through which one views the wider, non-white world. For what they experienced in continental microcosm, much of the world has experienced in horrid macrocosm. Imperial wars, invasions, regime changes, support of venal, brutal dictators, economic exploitation and, as in the case of Japan—atomic desolation. With the exception of the latter, Latin America has had more than its share of pain, suffering, and mass death to please the investor class to the North.

A New World?

In the summer of 2015, after months of quiet diplomatic talks, the United States reestablished diplomatic relations with the Cuban government. Whaaaaaa?

A few months later in March 2016, Air Force One descended from the rainy skies over Cuba (skies that once ushered mankind to the brink of extinction) as an American president flew into Havana—the first U.S. president since Calvin Coolidge in 1928 to visit the island nation. African-American President, Barack Hussein Obama, tweeted, "Que bola? Just touched down here, looking forward to meeting and hearing directly from the Cuban people." Obama alit from his plane and descended to the tarmac with First Lady Michelle Obama and his two daughters. They smiled, shook hands, and greeted Cuba's President, Raul Castro Ruz. For real!

Obama casually strolled the streets of the Old City, with Cubans gasping in recognition. In Havana's Alicia Alonso Grand Theater, Obama held forth, trying to set a tone of calmness and reasonableness when he told the assembled throng:

> It is time, now, for us to leave the past behind. It is time for us to look forward to the future together. And it won't be easy, and there will be setbacks. It will take time. But my time here in Cuba renews my hope and my confidence in what the Cuban people will do. We can make this journey as friends, and as neighbors, and as family—together.[48]

Cuba's revolutionary lion-in-winter, Fidel Castro Ruz, caused more than a few chuckles when he wrote, shortly thereafter that, "I suppose all of us were at risk of a heart attack upon hearing these words from the President of the United States."[49]

In a lengthy letter to readers of the leading Cuban newspaper, *Granma* (entitled "Brother Obama"), the 86-year-old former President reminded the world of what was expected to be 'forgotten': "After a ruthless blockade that has lasted almost 60 years, and what about those who have died in the mercenary attacks on Cuban ships and ports, an airliner full of passengers blown up in midair, mercenary invasions, multiple acts of violence and coercion?"[50]

Another way to observe America's new obliquity with Cuba is to imagine a "relationship" between a violently abusive schoolyard bully and the new kid on the block, and after a long year of the new kid being punched, kicked, choked, and ridiculed, the bully suddenly throws his arm around the terrorized kid and says hey let's put all of that behind us, let's be friends, let's hang out. Can I buy you a Coke?

Yet, embassies are being built and dedicated in both countries, and as these words are being written, airlines and cruise ship companies, hungry for Caribbean profits, have signed up to carry U.S. *turistas* to the sunny, balmy isle. American corporate interests, slobbering for some of that swag that has tempted tourists from Europe for more than a decade, wanted in on the biggest island in the region. But, another reason is clear for this new explosion of interest in Havana.

Other Latin American states, many of which have moved leftward away from the *caudillos* (or military dictators) and their western imperial masters, began to disinvite Washington brokers to OAS and other hemispheric meetings. "There is a lot of talk that the purpose of opening up the relationship is to bring about change in Cuba, I don't think that's the case," suggests Kevin Casas-Zamora, the former vice-president of Costa Rica. "Obama is doing this not for Cuba's sake, but the US's sake, because this had become an embarrassment for the US—a major obstacle in the relationship with Latin America."[51]

Clearly, the Americans were being pushed out of Latin American interactions, as heads of state were demanding that Washington invite the Cubans into the fold. Despite its economic challenges, and the eternal enmity of the *norteamericanos,* many throughout the continent admired Fidel and the Cuban people for their bravery, their steadfastness, and their grace under superhuman pressures. Dr. Nelson Mandela, the late anti-apartheid leader and then-President of the new South Africa, visited Cuba before any country after his long and dreadful imprisonment. His words of praise still ring in Cuban ears:

> What other country can point to a record of greater selflessness
> than Cuba has displayed in its relation with Africa?[52]

Mandela (considered a terrorist from the late 1980s until 2008 by the U.S. government) was well aware of Fidel Castro and Cuba's support of Africa throughout the Cold War as the embattled Caribbean nation sent thousands of Cuban doctors, teachers, and construction workers to Africa. In fact, almost 30,000 African students studied in Cuba on full scholarships that were funded by the Cuban government. Mandela also acknowledged that the Cuban victory over the South African army in 1988 "destroyed the myth of the invincibility of the white oppressor… [and] inspired the fighting masses of South Africa… Cuito Cuanavale was the turning point for the liberation of our continent—and of my people—from the scourge of apartheid."[53]

As we've seen, Castro sent the dark, strong fruit of Cuban youth to fight against the hated apartheid regime of South Africa—and by so doing, made Mandela's freedom (and so many others) possible. They bled Cuban blood on the high, sacred altar of freedom, to bring new breath to African lives. At Freedom Park, outside Pretoria, more than two thousand names of Cuban soldiers who died in Angola from 1975 through 1988 are inscribed alongside the names of South Africans who perished during their own African liberation struggle.

But on that rainy day in March 2016, the Empire wasn't done overlooking its violent history with Cuba as Obama then played his own Africa card, telling the crowd, "We both live in a new world, colonized by Europeans. Cuba, like the United States, was built in part by slaves brought here from Africa. Like the United States, the Cuban people can trace their heritage to both slaves and slave-owners." Castro, hearing these words, suggested in his *Granma* response, "The native populations don't exist at all in Obama's mind."

Castro concluded his response to Obama's visit and words by underscoring Cuban pride and independence:

> Nobody should be under the illusion that the people of this dignified and selfless country will renounce the glory, the rights, or the spiritual wealth they have gained with the development of education, science and culture.
>
> I also warn that we are capable of producing the food and material riches we need with the efforts and intelligence of our people. We do not need the empire to give us anything. Our efforts will be legal and peaceful, as this is our commitment to peace and fraternity among all human beings who live on this planet.
>
> —Fidel Castro Ruz, March 27, 2016, 10:25 p.m.[54]

Eight months later, the man who rightfully tormented eleven U.S. presidents, who fought off American might, embargo, and assassination attempts with every breath he could muster for more than half a century, died of natural causes on November 25, 2016—exactly sixty years to the day when he along with Che Guevera, Raúl Castro, Camilo Cienfuegos, and eighty revolutionaries set sail from Mexico for Cuba on the yacht Granma. Together they envisioned a new world.

We shall see.

❖ ❖ ❖

10 No

We dedicate this ongoing and unfolding chapter (at the end of book one, two, and three) to the courageous women and men who have defied "civil obedience" to battle the forces of empire head on, unconditionally, and without regard for personal wealth, safety, or legacy. These individuals have looked the monster straight in the eye and said "No, not this time."

Our collection of defiant ones profiled at the end of each book, personal heroes of your authors, is not meant to be comprehensive but representative of those uncompromising insurgents who have inspired us both. They are exemplars that remain emblazoned in our psyche as audacious examples of valor, gallantry, heroism, and guts—and none of these brave individuals wore uniforms. Instead of protecting the ruling class using the tools and mechanisms of imperial power—money, guns, and violence—these Empire-busters used words, ideas, civil disobedience, and courageous action to fight back the beast. The Zapatistas explain it best: "Our words are our weapons." Howard Zinn echoes this spirit: "On the other side are formidable forces: money, political power, the major media. On our side are the people of the world and a power greater than money or weapons: the truth."

Cynics will frame these individuals, and others like them, as a collection of Don Quixotes on a noble but futile quest. Ultimately these detractors, these misanthropists, these guardians of the status quo, will frame and marginalize our freedom fighters as laughable characters, harebrained in their fight for peace and justice. They will ridicule their efforts and attack their character, painting images of, at best, hopeless romantics, and at worse, of outlandish buffoons. These "practical" critics will further define the actions of those on this list as vacant idealism bordering on insanity, and the nobility of their actions as utter folly. And if these demonizing efforts fail, the power system in place, historically and right now, will charge these miscreant rebels with criminal activities, and then finally with treason. Obedience to the gospel of the ruling class is how they render these "dreamers" as weak, impotent, and useless.

In a letter to a friend (of course not something he would ever weave into public speak), President John Kennedy wrote this telling line: "War will exist until the distant day when the conscientious objector enjoys the same reputation and prestige as the warrior does today."[1]

When Miguel de Cervantes wrote *El Ingenioso Hidalgo Don Quijote de La Mancha* (The Ingenious Gentleman Don Quixote of La Mancha) in the early 17th century, his work was viewed as a comedy, a farce. But following the French Revolution, the novel grew in popularity due to its essential theme that individuals can be right while the whole of society can be absolutely dead wrong. Returning to Howard Zinn, he frames the age-old manipulation this way:

> Civil disobedience is not our problem. Our problem is civil obedience. Our problem is that people all over the world have obeyed the dictates of leaders… and millions have been killed because of this obedience… Our problem is that people are obedient all over the world in the face of poverty and starvation and stupidity, and war, and cruelty. Our problem is that people are obedient while the jails are full of petty thieves… and the grand thieves are running the country. That's our problem.[2]

The essence of civil disobedience is the ability to live authentically in the face of injustice, and the first word spoken—whether engaging the murder machine, the economic rapists, the race and fear mongers, or the misogynists who cling to the systemic nature and destructive bias of a patriarchal society—must always be "no." Dick Gregory describes the importance of the word NO:

> If you look at the story of Jesus Christ, the one thing that keeps coming up was the word *NO*. I mean they said, *"Look man, we don't want to kill you. The big man came in and said, 'The Jews are crazy. We don't want to kill you. But just say that you are not the son of the Father."* Jesus said *NO*. He didn't get into any high-fiving or rapping. He just said NO. *"Let me see, can you just say—Christ says NO!"* Okay? NO got him killed.[3]

So on 2 November 1965, when Norman Morrison, a Baltimore Quaker, doused himself with kerosene outside Robert McNamara's Pentagon office and set himself on fire, he was saying NO. When Mary Harris "Mother" Jones—dubbed in 1902 as "the most dangerous woman in America"[4] for her numerous successes organizing mine workers against mine owners, who then led a children's march from Philadelphia to the New York home of President Theodore Roosevelt to protest the lax enforcement of child labor laws, she was saying NO. In the early morning hours of 28 June 1969, on Christopher Street in lower Manhattan, in a popular gay bar called the Stonewall Inn, the customers—en masse—finally screamed NO to the constant and illegal harassment by the Neanderthal New York City Police Department, and in a flash ushered in the modern LGBT movement (more recently expanded to LGBTQIA, a challenge to the status quo's nervous desire to keep things in neat, clean dichotomies, if ever there was one.)[5]

In 1970, at the Berkeley Community Theatre, during the height of the Vietnam War, a genius from Seattle screeched the howling notes that accompany–

> *...the rocket's red glare, the bombs bursting in air,*
> *Gave proof through the night that our flag was still there.*

At which point, Hendrix interjected whilst wailing his iconic Star Spangled Banner:

> *"The flag was still there, big deal."*

It was Jimi's way of saying NO.

Nat Turner said it. Chief Joseph said it. John Brown said it. Emma Goldman said it. Andrea Dworkin said it. Dalton Trumbo and Assata Shakur said it. Harvey Milk said it. Cesar Chavez and Dolores Huerta said it. Tecumseh and Sitting Bull said it. Celia Sanchez and Ruben Salazar said it. Gil Scott-Heron and Selma James said it. Arundhati Roy and Gary Webb said it. Bernadette Dohrn said it. Muhammad Ali and Vito Russo said it. Fred Hampton, Public Enemy, and Mario Savio said it. Allen Ginsberg and Lawrence Ferlinghetti said it. Sacco and Vanzetti said it. Daniel and Philip Berrigan said it. So did Sojourner Truth... as did Ellsberg, Manning, Greenwald, Snowden, and the entire Occupy Wall Street movement.

As well as all of those unsung and unknown warriors throughout history, those pugilists who stood toe-to-toe with Goliath and said "not now, not ever, no."

As did these two remarkable mutineers.

❖ ❖ ❖

Soldier for Freedom

Her name may be known, but few have written openly and honestly about her magnificent exploits. Perhaps that's because most of those who have written about her—historians, documentarians, and even her contemporaries—were men, and as such, they felt comfortable if she were somehow de-radicalized, made safe and palatable for the wider, whiter world of America. Indeed, a whiter shade of pale. But her life, which began in bondage and ended in the privation of "freedom" in the North, is a story the stuff of which legends are made.

In a slave cabin in 1820, she was born Araminta Ross, in Dorchester County, Maryland, but the world came to know her as Harriet—Harriet Tubman, one of the freest souls this world has ever birthed. She learned early how to say NO to the unhindered brutality, the savage usages, and the unbridled hatreds that were the abnormal norm of American slavery. And an early passion fired her life and lit her footsteps all her days on Earth.

Like many captives in the American South, she knew that the wider, white world was dangerous and even deadly to dark people like herself. She didn't learn this by seeing the terror so frequently practiced against others. She learned it in her own young flesh, even as a child. Black activist historian, Butch Lee, in her underground classic, *Jailbreak Out of History*, writes a military history of Tubman and the many forces that converged to make her life take the road less traveled. Lee details an early experience that scarred Harriet for life:

> At age five her childhood as we think of it ended, and she was rented to a white woman to do full-time domestic labor. The white woman believed in torturing Afrikans every day, and the small Harriet was lashed with a leather whip four times across her face and neck as an introduction before breakfast that first day. Harriet's first escape attempt (i.e., attempted prison break) came when she was seven years old. Caught by the latest white woman she had been rented

out to, while trying to steal a piece of sugar (forbidden to Afrikan children), Harriet outran the white woman and her rawhide whip:

> "By and by when I was almost tuckered out, I came to a great big pig-pen. There was an old sow there, and perhaps eight or ten little pigs. I was too little to climb into it, but I tumbled over the high part and fell in on the ground; I was so beaten out that I could not stir. And I stayed from Friday until the next Tuesday, fighting with those little pigs for the potato peelings and the other scraps that came down in the trough. The old sow would push me away when I tried to get her children's food, and I was awfully afraid of her. By Tuesday I was so starved I knew I had to go back to my mistress. I didn't have anywhere else to go, even though I knew what was coming."

Because attempting to escape was the second-most serious crime, Harriet was whipped senseless by the white man of the house. So, Harriet Tubman had become a full-time productive worker, had become familiar with daily violence and utmost danger, had committed crimes and stolen from white settlers, and had tried to escape (prison-break)—all by age seven. And this was not exceptional in any way, but common, a story shared by millions of New Afrikans."[6]

As Lee informs us, this was not rare, but a norm impressed upon the lives of so many of the oppressed that it seemed normal. Such brutality and such terrorism as this can only serve to produce two things: a servile, terrified being, or one so determined to be free, that death itself doesn't matter. Fortunately for us and our history, in the spirit of Tubman, it produced the latter. She was a woman who could not turn away and who would not turn away from any of the captives held in bondage in the massive American Slave system. In fact, when free herself, she would not rest until she became the unselfish instrument of freedom for a multitude of others.

We've noted that male historians, writers, and activists have tended to minimize and de-radicalize her immense accomplishments. One of the ways this was done was by using words that were code in a normative fashion that obscures their deeper meanings—for example, "Underground Railroad," "conductor," and the like. These were, in fact, secret organizations of men and women, some well armed to protect themselves from the ruthless violence of the American state—or equally, the militias of the hidebound South.

When she escaped to the North (circa 1849), she spoke at various public anti-slavery meetings despite the fact that a $40,000 bounty was placed on her head by various Southern state governments. Because various organizers knew the very real danger that she faced when she spoke at events, her presence was rarely advertised. When she arrived, quietly, she would be introduced as "Moses" or with another fictitious name. We must recall that the infamous Fugitive Slave Law was still in force, which meant that any former slave (in truth, any Black person) could be, on a virtual whim, seized, shackled, and sent back to the hell of American bondage and torture.

Soldier, Spy

Tubman knew the South, and what she didn't know, her wide ring of contacts provided. She was so revered and so famous that when the Negro spiritual, "Go Down, Moses", began to be sung in the plantation shacks, wise folk knew that it was a code meaning that she—General Moses—was near, and coming soon (and "comin' for to carry them home"). When North and South could no longer be reconciled, and the Civil War began in earnest, Tubman became an invaluable resource to northern commanders and generals, for she knew the lay of the land; even more, she knew the people. When the Northern forces wanted to strike a powerful blow against the Confederates in June of 1863, they chose her to open the way barred by what were then called "torpedoes"—mines buried in the Combahee River of South Carolina. Because she intimately knew the terrain, she knew where the mines could be found and disarmed. The raid went as planned, cutting off the supplies of the rebels, and scattering them in disarray. Harriet Tubman actually chose the commander of the mission, and then saw it through to its glorious fruition: the destruction of the lands, plantations, properties, and railroads of the Confederates—and more important to her, the liberation of hundreds of "contrabands"—slaves.

But, as in any war, both sides had their share of spies, and the *New York Tribune* listed the coming expedition, with its troop strength and composition (hundreds of Black forces), all under the command of a Colonel Montgomery. Fortunately for the North, however, the South believed its "torpedoes" made the Combahee River impregnable to Union attack. The night raid, Butch Lee argues, could have been just another such action lost to history, had not the Boston newspaper, *The Commonwealth,* ably reported it. Here is a reprint from the article that offers a contemporaneous report of this remarkable event:

> Col. Montgomery and his gallant band of 300 black soldiers, *under the guidance of a black woman* [emphasis in original], dashed into the enemy's country, struck a bold and effective blow, destroying millions of dollars worth of commissary stores, cotton and lordly dwellings, and striking terror into the heart of rebeldom, brought off near 800 slaves and thousands of dollars worth of property, without losing a man or receiving a scratch. It was a glorious consummation.
>
> After they were all fairly well disposed of in the Beaufort charge, they were addressed in strains of thrilling eloquence by their gallant deliverer... The Colonel was followed by a speech from the black woman, *who led the raid and under whose inspiration it was originated and conducted* [emphasis in original]. For sound sense and real native eloquence, her address would do honor to any man, and it created a great sensation.[7]

Three gunboats were overloaded with "contraband," four plantations were put to the torch, and six mills were burned. Harriet was thrilled beyond measure to see her people make it away from their place of historic bondage. She would later exalt:

> I never saw such a scene. We laughed and laughed and laughed. Here you'd see a woman with a pail on her head, rice-a-smoking in it just as she'd taken it from the fire, young one hanging on behind... One woman brought two pigs, a white one and a black one; we took them all on board; named the white pig Beauregard [a Southern general], and the black one Jeff Davis [president of the Confederacy]. Sometimes the woman would come with twins hanging around their necks; it appears I never saw so many twins in my life; bags on their shoulders, baskets on their heads, and young ones lagging behind, all loaded...[8]

While the Combahee River Raid was perhaps her most famous exploit, one could hardly forget her first profession, as a "Soldier for Freedom." Not for the army, nor for the U.S., but for her People. Her lesser-known exploits, while they may have involved fewer souls, were no less splendid or heroic. These daring acts, if found out, could have meant death and disaster to many people up and down the line of the "Underground Railroad." She therefore had to use special skills to avoid detection, to strengthen the hearts of her charges, and ultimately to succeed. Butch Lee writes:

> Her professional skill as a guerrilla, operating behind enemy lines in the Underground Railroad, is well documented. Season after season, in nineteen raids, she evaded and misdirected the Slaveocracy. Her always-changing tactics were like textbook lessons. Coming under suspicion, she would lead her escapees with forged papers onto a train going South, not North, then circle back. Disguises were sometimes used, disguising women as men—something Harriet herself did—or vice-versa. Once, knowing she might meet her former master in town, she dressed even more raggedy. And she carried an armful of live chickens. When she saw him, she "accidentally" let the birds loose. The former master passed by in amusement at the apparently hapless old Black woman—her face averted as she scrambled on the ground to catch her chickens.[9]

Like many of her era, she couldn't read nor write; but freedom burned in her heart and lit her spirit, and gave her a glow that impressed all in her presence. When she resolved, at the age of twenty-five, to make her break for liberty, she didn't do it idly or vainly. Her young flesh had tasted the lash since her toddling days, but freedom burned in her like mercury. She instinctually knew that she had only two choices left:

> I had reasoned this out in my mind; there was one or two things I had a right to, liberty or death; if I could not have one, I would have the other; for no man should take me alive; I should fight for my liberty as long as my strength lasted, and when the time come for me to go, the Lord will let them take me.[10]

That kind of passion for freedom could not be bridled, and in her lifetime, she became more a beacon of freedom than the towering Statue of Liberty looming in New York Harbor. But freedom had a cost. As Lee recounts, Tubman's time in the wilderness, escaping the vast Prison of the militarized, slave-drenched South, Harriet brooked no nonsense when it came to breaking free of this vast, repressive archipelago:

> Other times, when a slave would weaken during the difficult journey and want to go back, Harriet would simply put her pistol to his head and give him her only choices: "Dead niggers tell no tales."[11]

Suffice it is to say, she lost no charges, and the recalcitrant would discover that they had more energy than previously thought to walk that long road to freedom.

Harriet Tubman, one of the finest abolitionists the struggle ever produced, left life in her 92nd year, 1913, in Auburn, New York. Her remarkable life was the life of saying NO!—to slavery, to bondage, to brutality, and to the myth of white supremacy.

To freedom, her very life spelled another word: YES!

❖ ❖ ❖

Disturbing the Peace

June 16, 1970. The Associated Press headline announced: "17 Arrested Inside Pentagon." The lead read: "Seventeen antiwar protesters were arrested today as they tried to celebrate a 'mass for peace' inside the Pentagon." Almost five years earlier, in November of 1965, another headline blared a much harsher narrative, this one in *The Baltimore Sun*: "Baltimore Quaker With Baby Sets Self Afire, Dies In War Protest At Pentagon." Both actions—although dramatically different—were in kinship, forever linked by the criminal absurdity known as The Vietnam War.

And when it came to the ferocious bombardment of Southeast Asia, the links were everywhere. Then as now they were not hard to find. Norman Morrison, the Baltimore Quaker who drove to the Pentagon with his baby daughter Emily, handed off his precious one-year old to an unsuspecting bystander, doused himself with kerosene below Secretary of Defense Robert McNamara's office window, and then set himself ablaze. Self-immolation. His link? Thich Quang Duc—the Buddhist monk who in 1963 also famously self-immolated in protest of the viciousness of the war, in his case the persecution of Buddhists in South Vietnam by the corrupt government of American puppet president Ngo Dinh Diem.

Again, kindred spirits forever linked by their hatred of the war, by desperation, but above all, by love.

More links. In 1967, after Morrison's self-immolation and before the "mass for peace," we find what Norman Mailer chronicled as *The Armies of the Night*—a massive march on the Pentagon, one that started near the Lincoln Memorial and ended on the front steps leading to the front door of the Pentagon. Tens of thousands of protestors—a cross section of antiwar anguish—gathered at the giant rockpile that encased America's bureaucratic Howitzer. Hundreds upon hundreds were arrested, Mailer included, dragged away by federal marshals, along the way clubbing and kicking the passive demonstrators. Mailer writing in *The Armies of the Night*: "There is no greater impotence in all the world like knowing you are right and that the wave of the world is wrong, yet the wave crashes upon you."[12] Dissident Noam Chomsky, also arrested by federal marshals, wrote that, "the Washington demonstrations symbolized the transition 'from dissent to resistance.'"[13] Chomsky remembers the images:

> Almost at once, another line of soldiers emerged from somewhere... rifles in hand... We sat down... I had no intention of taking part in any act of civil disobedience, until that moment. But when that grotesque organism began slowly advancing—more grotesque because its cells were recognizable human beings—it became obvious that one could not permit that thing to dictate what one was going to do.[14]

On that same day, 21 October 1967, a feat of monumental symbolic theater—a mix of protest, performance, and ritual—was also undertaken by a splinter group, one led by Abbie Hoffman and Allen Ginsberg, who tried through chant and meditation to levitate the Pentagon in an attempt to exorcise its evil spirits. Mailer, who also witnessed this event, later wrote, "The new generation... had no respect whatsoever for the unassailable logic of the next step: belief was reserved for the revelatory mystery of the happening where you did not know what was going to happen next; that was what was good about it."[15]

Belief in the power of revelatory mystery is as akin to a man of the cloth as it is to a hippie of the bell-bottom. A few years later, the Pentagon was again the site of metaphysical protest. That AP story from 16 June 1970, continues, citing now from the *Pittsburgh Post-Gazette*: "Police moved in as the Rev. Malcolm D. Boyd, author and Episcopal priest, led the group in prayer on the Pentagon's shopping concourse crowded with government employees during the noon hour."

This wasn't Malcolm Boyd's first entanglement with the Empire and their oppressive behavior. In fact, his nonviolent public actions began in 1961 as one of the original Freedom Riders—those courageous men and women who traveled on buses throughout the Deep South to defy the evils of Jim Crow and demand immediate change. Violence and hatred followed the "Riders" everywhere. Klansmen attacked and burned buses and the cops were nowhere to be found—except possibly under white hoods. Birmingham, Alabama, police commissioner Bull Connor, together with his KKK sidekick, Sergeant Tom Cook, not to mention southern cops by the Dixie droves, made sport of their sadistic state-sponsored terrorism against the bus riders—behavior which the Blacks in the movement found all too familiar.

Firebombs, baseball bats, and pipes were the tools employed by angry white mobs throughout the South when teaching uppity Blacks and their "nigger-loving" compatriots a thing or two about which group was actually in charge. Clearly, lynching wasn't far behind and the good Rev. Malcolm Boyd fully understood the true-grit reality facing his ultimate decision to get on those Greyhound buses. But he did. Boyd remembers:

> I received a letter saying that around 20 Episcopal clergy, black and white, would participate in a public protest. We'd seek service at a segregated lunch counter and would be arrested following refusal. It was a bloody, agonized time. I felt considerable fear. Our group gathered in New Orleans at the YMCA where John Howard Griffin had stayed during the writing of his classic "Black Like Me." We were instructed in nonviolence by Martin Luther King Jr.'s staff. Yes, I prayed a lot. I knew clearly that my life was not in my own hands, but God's.[16]

> *We had most trouble, it turned into a struggle,*
> *Half way 'cross Alabam,*
> *And that 'hound broke down, and left us all stranded,*
> *In downtown Birmingham.*
>
> —Chuck Berry

Hurray for Hollywood

Malcolm Boyd's life navigated a remarkable path toward peace and justice. Born in

Buffalo, New York, in 1923, young Malcolm grew up a privileged kid on Riverside Drive in Manhattan. His father was a wealthy investment banker and his mother a top fashion model. The Great Depression obliterated their wealth and divorce ravaged their family. Malcolm and his mother ended up in Colorado. In high school, Malcolm began writing and the young transplanted New Yorker wrote a lot. He also began gravitating toward a more spiritual life. Both of these elements began weaving themselves together, setting the framework for his life's work. But first Hollywood and a shot at pictures.

He began producing television in the late forties and was elected the first president of the Television Producers Association of Hollywood. Malcolm then met the legendary Mary Pickford. They formed a partnership and went into business together. In fact Hollywood was being exceedingly good to Malcolm—he was nose-to-nose with fame, glamour, and serious wealth; but for Malcolm, it turned out to be strike one, two, and three. The trappings of Hollywood created emptiness. It might have been the first time he said "No!"

Espresso Love

Malcolm Boyd attended divinity school in Berkeley and then returned to New York City to pursue his post-graduate work at Union Theological Seminary. His spiritual work delivered him right into the firestorm of the civil rights movement, working closely with various groups including Martin Luther King, Jr., the Southern Christian Leadership Conference (SCLC), as well as the Student Nonviolent Coordinating Committee (SNCC). In 1965, Boyd penned a powerful book of political, social, and personal prayers entitled *Are You Running With Me, Jesus?* The book became a runaway national bestseller. A year later, he appeared for a month at the famed San Francisco nightclub "hungry i" with the headliner, Dick Gregory—comedian and fellow civil rights activist. Boyd read his prayers to the nightclub audience, engaging them in serious dialogue, and this rather "unique" event became an international sensation. "Malcolm Boyd is a latter-day (Martin) Luther," writes *The New York Times Magazine*, "or a more worldly (John) Wesley, trying to move religion out of 'ghettoized' churches into the streets where people are."[17]

Boyd's trailblazing style took him to college campuses and coffeehouses across America. Hailed as the "Espresso Priest," Boyd's spoken word dynamic made it onstage at the 1966 Newport Jazz Festival. Audiences were digging his brand of counterculture.

Take fire and burn away our guilt and our lying hypocrisies.
Take water and wash away our brothers' and sisters'
blood which we have caused to be shed.
Take hot sunlight and dry the tears of those we have hurt,
and heal their wounded souls, minds, and bodies.
Take love and root it in our hearts, so that community may grow,
transforming the dry desert of our prejudices and hatreds.
Take our imperfect prayers and purify them, so that we mean what we
pray and are prepared to give ourselves to you along with our words.
(from "We're praying for repentance")[18]

Along with many others, Boyd followed MLK's political arc through the 1960s as King rightly and successfully joined the civil rights movement with the antiwar movement. "He was vilified for that," Boyd told us, "both by the press and by those in the movement. But it was a natural and necessary connection. As King said, 'This madness must cease.'"[19]

> *Somehow this madness must cease. We must stop now. I speak as a child of God and brother to the suffering poor of Vietnam. I speak for those whose land is being laid waste, whose homes are being destroyed, whose culture is being subverted. I speak for the poor in America who are paying the double price of smashed hopes at home and death and corruption in Vietnam.*[20]
>
> —MLK, *The Trumpet of Conscience*

In 1965, Malcolm unofficially "came out" as a gay man with the publication of his poem-prayer entitled "This is a homosexual bar, Jesus." Twelve years later, in 1977, Boyd officially announced his homosexuality to the world. "At this point, you could throw your hands up and scream, because what do you do with a story like this?" he jokes. "Here's Malcolm Boyd—terribly controversial—and now on top of everything, he's a queer?"[21] The defiant Episcopal priest wrote about his life in the much-acclaimed book *Take Off the Masks*. In *Library Journal's* review of the book, they wrote: "A man reborn who learns to love himself, other people, and God, step by bloody step." Of course, the church, as it is apt to do, treated Boyd "like a leper," according to Rev. Fred Fenton of St. Augustine-by-the-Sea in Santa Monica.[22]

But back in the world of sane people, his courage and commitment to justice has never been questioned, and frankly can never be questioned—especially on that June day in 1970, in the belly of the beast. And make no mistake about it, the year 1970—up to the point Malcolm Boyd walked into the Pentagon—was a raging, rough and tumble period in the historic continuum of the Vietnam War. By mid-1970, with Nixon in office a year and a half and his so-called "secret plan" to end the war obviously nothing more than campaign rhetoric, the U.S. invaded Cambodia and this massive incursion set the American political landscape on fire. The expansion of the war revitalized the antiwar movement, which had weakened in the previous months, and the incursion triggered large demonstrations all across the country, especially on college campuses, culminating with the tragic shootings and killings at Kent State University on 4 May 1970.

Literally hours before Nixon and Kissinger invaded Cambodia, and with no end to the war in sight, Senators George McGovern and Mark Hatfield introduced an amendment to the Military Procurement Authorization Bill, that if passed, would prohibit the use of funds to finance American military operations in Southeast Asia after 31 December 1970—the end of the year. The McGovern-Hatfield Amendment was the first serious attempt by either the House or the Senate to reclaim from the Executive Branch the war-making and war-funding powers clearly granted to them by the United States Constitution. At the time, Washington D.C. was literally a cauldron of antiwar anguish—leading to McGovern's impassioned and historic speech to an overflowing senate chamber when he flogged and flayed his fellow senators by bellowing, "This chamber reeks of blood."

This is the same cauldron Malcolm Boyd entered when he walked inside the crowded Pentagon to say mass and offer the Eucharist—the body of Christ offered to sinners right at the gates of hell. We sat down with the Espresso Priest in a café near the Episcopal Cathedral Center in Los Angeles:

> **SV:** How did you get inside so easily?
> **MB:** *Remember, this is eons before 9/11. People weren't hysterical then.*
>
> **SV:** Before you offered the Eucharist, what was your sermon about?
> **MB:** *My thoughts centered around "if the salt has lost its flavor," which of course is Jesus' Sermon on the Mount.*

("You are the salt of the earth, but what good is salt if it has lost its flavor? It is then good for nothing, but to be cast out and trampled underfoot as worthless." Jesus, as remembered in Matthew 5:13)

> **SV:** Serious times.

MB: *Deadly times.*

SV: Must have been. You rolled out the Sermon on the Mount?
MB: *Not only was it serious and deadly, but very desperate. It was also an absurd time, clearly absurd. You were a bad guy if you opposed the war.*

SV: There were a lot of bad guys.
MB: *I wasn't sure if there would be an impact, but it had to be done.*

SV: I'm reminded of your good friend William Sloane Coffin's remark: "If what we're doing in Vietnam is right, what the hell is left to be called wrong."
MB: *That gets back to the absurdity of it all.*

SV: "You are the salt of the earth, but what good is salt if it has lost its flavor?" I guess this is about the integrity of man, maintaining integrity.
MB: *Of course.*

SV: Or lack thereof. Especially with, as Dylan called them, the masters of war.
MB: *When salt loses its integrity, the result is disintegration—a collapse of truthfulness. Without salt, the meat rots.*[23]

Suddenly, Pentagon security descended on the small peace mass. A guard with a bullhorn announces: "YOU'RE ALL UNDER ARREST." The clergy and laypeople that were quietly offering their government some grace—maybe even a chance for atonement—were instead treated to gendarmes and their arresting attitude of "Fuck this Jesus hippie shit, get in the wagon."

SV: What was the charge?
MB: *Disturbing the peace. (laughter)*

SV: The paradox is, as you said, absurd.
MB: *The contradiction was laughable. "Disturbing the peace" on a day when the bombing of Vietnam was at its height. The forty of us praying and having a very quiet peaceful mass, you know, "disturbing the peace?"—which is a little like we have to destroy the village in order to save it. I love the ironies that emerge.*

SV: D.C. police, Pentagon military police. Then what happens?
MB: *So we got on the police bus and I remember passing the White House and realizing that people like Dr. Billy Graham would be having*

> *lunch or dinner in a state of honor with the president. Many times. Something is wrong when you have a pro-war preacher shouldering up with those in power. You realize it's all about privilege.*[24]

This wasn't the beginning or the end of Boyd's outrage (along with many other concerned antiwar clergy) when it came to Billy Graham and other sanctimonious religious co-conspirators and their unwillingness to face the murder binge taking place in Asia. For these religious pitchmen, it's always about mass conversion of the flock and the subsequent membership (read: $$$). The simple concept of recognizing moral depravity just isn't part of their job description. In 1973, Boyd wrote about his fellow religious leaders' aversion to confronting the moral inequities of Vietnam:

> An activist and public relations-engendered drive seems to be in danger of treating living/breathing people as dehumanized conversion statistics [because it offered people] a packaged brand of personal comfort instead of calling them to repentance.
>
> Repentance? Yes, for racism, the rape of Indochina, and participation in a callous materialism that stands blind to poverty/deprivation whether across the city or halfway around the world...
>
> Can American Christianity plunge into a campaign to save souls without penitently taking a long, hard, slow look at the bodies of human victims of U.S. bombings in Indochina?[25]

Boyd recalls that his group completed the peace mass in a D.C. jail.

> **SV:** So the mass continued behind bars?
> **MB:** *Somebody had some bread and some wine... and a very nice adjunct to this, one of the guards who arrested us at the Pentagon showed up for a peace fellowship meeting and asked to join us. That's really how movements grow I think, isn't it? Because it's people. It isn't power at national or international levels. It's big issues with very small groups of very ordinary people.*[26]

Boyd ended our conversation painfully speaking about the missed opportunities for repentance—opportunities that continue to fall by the wayside through more imperial wars, poverty, and the fallacy of a "post-racial" America. His cadence was poetic and succinct, wisdom flowing effortlessly from his ninety years on this planet.

MB: *If we're going to anoint the canvas of America, then we must acknowledge the stains on that canvas. We must prophetically and courageously admit where the stains are rather than lie through our teeth. We must confess sins. But it's never enough to confess sins. That's cheap grace. We must change the direction. Repentance means changing direction.*

Malcolm Boyd, the priest who hung out in nightclubs, the iconoclast, is no doubt a revolutionary in every sense of the word. Throughout his long and courageous life, Boyd has made a habit of saying NO to the ruling power structures. From mounting imperialism to the vicious chains of racism and poverty, right through to the bigotry that has historically engulfed the LGBT struggle, Malcolm Boyd has clearly and distinctly said "NO."

On 15 June 1970, with the Vietnam War raging in the jungles of Southeast Asia, as well as in the streets of America, the quiet man with the heart of a lion walked inside the Empire's garrison, looked to the heavens, looked to hell, and said:

NO

❖ ❖ ❖

Endnotes

Foreword

1 Gary B. Nash, *The Unknown American Revolution*, Penguin, New York, 2006, pp. 2-3.

2 Fred Jerome and Rodger Taylor, *Einstein on Race and Racism*, Rutgers University Press, New Brunswick, NJ, 2005, pp. 16-17. *From text: "The all-black First Rhode Island Regiment was composed of thirty-nine freedmen and ninety-two slaves who were promised freedom if they served until the end of the war. They distinguished themselves in the Battle of Newport. However, the regiment was all but wiped out in a British attack at Yorktown."

3 David Stannard, *American Holocaust: The Conquest of the New World*, Oxford University Press, New York, 1992, p. 126.

4 James W. Loewen, *Lies My Teacher Told Me*, Simon & Schuster, New York, 1995, pp. 117-118.

5 John Perkins, interview with the authors, "Murder Incorporated Sessions," Street Legal Cinema, October 2006, transcript.

Prologue

1 The Bureau of Investigative Journalism, "Naming the Dead," Bibi Mamana, Villagers and local officials (The News); family and tribesmen (The News); family testimony (BBC Panorama, The Times, Express Tribune, Guardian, Guardian, ABC); witness and family testimony (Amnesty International); https://www.thebureauinvestigates.com

2 Chris Hedges, writing praise for Morris Berman, Why America Failed: The Roots of Imperial Decline, Wiley, John & Sons, Hoboken, New Jersey, 2011.

3 Michael Parenti, The Sword and the Dollar: Imperialism, Revolution, and the Arms Race, St. Martin's Press, New York, 1989, p. 64.

4 Charles Sullivan, "Manifest Destiny Rides Again," Counterpunch, February 12, 2003; http://test.counterpunch.org/2003/02/12/manifest-destiny-rides-again/ (Retrieved January 12, 2015)

5 Ibid.

6 Thomas Jimson, "Reflections on Race and Manifest Destiny," Center For World Indigenous Studies, 1999; http://cwis.org/GML/?post=1373 (Retrieved Jan 28, 2015)

7 Cornel West, Democracy Matters: Winning the Fight Against Imperialism, Penguin, New York, 2004, p.178.

8 Michael Parenti, "Making the World Safe for Hypocrisy," ZNet, July 3, 2011; https://zcomm.org/znetarticle/making-the-world-safe-for-hypocrisy-by-michael-parenti/ (Retrieved Jan 25, 2015)

9 Jimson, Reflections on Race and Manifest Destiny.

10 R.F. Pettigrew, Imperial Washington, Charles H. Kerr & Company, Chicago, 1922, p. 180.

11 Howard Zinn, The Zinn Reader: Writings on Disobedience and Democracy, Seven Stories Press, New York, 2009, p. 516.

12 Glenn Greenwald, "The Key War on Terror Propaganda Tool: Only Western Victims Are Acknowledged," The Intercept, April 24, 2015; https://theintercept.com/2015/04/24/central-war-

terror-propaganda-tool-western-victims-acknowledged/ (Retrieved January 11, 2017)

Chapter 1

1 Sidney Lens, *The Forging of the American Empire,* Thomas Y. Crowell Company, London, 1971, p. 166.

2 James Bradley, *The Imperial Cruise,* Little, Brown and Company, New York, 2009, p. 23.

3 Ibid., p. 24.

4 Ibid.

5 Tacitus, as quoted in Reginald Horsman, *Race and Manifest Destiny: The Origins of American Racial Anglo-Saxonism,* Harvard University Press, Cambridge, 1981, p. 12.

6 Bradley, p. 25.

7 Ibid.

8 Ibid., p. 26.

9 Ibid.

10 Ibid., p. 27.

11 Theodore Roosevelt, *The Winning of the West,* Vol. 4, The Knickerbocker Press, New York & London, 1908, p. 201.

12 John F. Kennedy, "City Upon a Hill," delivered to a Joint Convention of the General Court of the Commonwealth of Massachusetts, January 9, 1961.

13 Ronald Reagan, "Farewell Address to the Nation," Oval Office, January 11, 1989.

14 Mitt Romney, "Remarks in Manchester Following the New Hampshire Primary," Southern New Hampshire University, Manchester, January 10, 2012.

15 R.C. Winthrop, *Life and Letters of John Winthrop,* Ticknor and Fields, Boston, 1869, Vol. ii, p. 430.

16 C.S. Manegold, "New England's scarlet 'S' for slavery," *The Boston Globe,* January 18, 2010. http://www.boston.com/bostonglobe/editorial_opinion/oped/articles/2010/01/18/new_englands_scarlet_s_for_slavery/ (Retrieved January 23, 2015)

17 Anders Stephanson, *Manifest Destiny: American Expansion and the Empire of Right,* Hill and Wang, New York, 1995, p. 6.

18 Ibid., p. 11.

19 Ibid., p. 9.

20 Ibid., p. 10.

21 Ibid., p. 11.

22 John Rolfe, as quoted in Perry Miller, "The Religious Impulse in the Founding of Virginia: Religion and Society in the Early Literature," *The William and Mary Quarterly,* Third Series, Vol. 5, No. 4, Oct., 1948, pp. 492-522.

23 John Winthrop, as quoted in Michael Grunwald, *The Swamp: The Everglades, Florida, and the Politics of Paradise,* Simon & Schuster, New York, 2006, p. 32.

24 Ben Franklin, as quoted in Grunwald, p. 32.

25 Samuel Langdon, as quoted in *God's New Israel: Religious Interpretations of American Destiny,* Conrad Cherry, editor, Prentice-Hall, New Jersey, 1971, p. 99.

26 Ezra Stiles, as quoted in Cherry, p. 88.

27 Thomas Jefferson, "Second Inaugural Address," March 4, 1805.

28 Ward Churchill, *A Little Matter of Genocide,* City Lights, San Francisco, 1997, p. 211.

29 Reginald Horsman, *Race and Manifest Destiny: The Origins of American Racial Anglo-Saxonism,* Harvard University Press, Cambridge, 1981, p. 253.

30 Ibid.

31 Noam Chomsky, "U.S. Savage Imperialism, Part 4," *Z Magazine*, March 2, 2011. https://zcomm.org/zmagazine/u-s-savage-imperialism-part-4-by-noam-chomsky/. (Retrieved January 23, 2015) (From the source: "This series began with the December 2010 issue of *Z Magazine*. Parts one and two featured the text of Chomsky's talk; parts three and four are transcriptions of the Q&A that followed.")

32 Dr. James Horton, as quoted in Glenn Collins, "A Main Event in Old New York," *The New York Times*, September 27, 2005. http://www.nytimes.com/2005/09/27/arts/design/27slav.html (Retrieved January 23, 2015)

33 Ulrich Boser, "The Sorry Legacy of the Founders," *US News & World Report*, January 12, 2004.

34 Hal Rounds, as quoted in Trymaine Lee, "Tea Party Groups In Tennessee Demand Textbooks Overlook, U.S. Founder's Slave-Owning History," *The Huffington Post*, Jan 12, 2012; http://www.huffingtonpost.com/2012/01/23/tea-party-tennessee-textbooks-slavery_n_1224157.html (Retrieved January 23, 2015)

35 Richard Pryor, *...Is It Something I Said*, Warner Bros. Records, 1975.

36 Howard Zinn, *A People's History of the United States*, Harper Collins, New York, 2003, p. 33.

37 Boser, "The Sorry Legacy of the Founders".

38 W.E.B. Du Bois, *The Suppression of the African Slave-Trade to the United States of America 1638-1870*, Harvard Historical Studies, Longmans, Green, and Co., New York, 1896, Chapter 12, Section 92.

39 Leah Caldwell, "The New and Improved Thomas Jefferson, Enlightened Slave Owner," *The Awl*, March 19, 2012. http://www.theawl.com/2012/03/the-new-and-improved-thomas-jefferson-enlightened-slave-owner (Retrieved January 23, 2015)

40 Edward Rothstein, as quoted in Caldwell, "The New and Improved Thomas Jefferson, Enlightened Slave Owner".

41 Frederick Douglass, *The Essential Frederick Douglass*, Wilder Publications, Radford, 2008, p. 107.

42 Robert Jensen, "Jefferson's Crime: Not Mitigated by the Standards of Time," *The Black Commentator*, Issue 150, September 15, 2005. http://www.blackcommentator.com/150/150_jeffersons_crime.html (Retrieved January 23, 2015)

43 *American Icons: Monticello*, Studio 360 radio series, Originally aired October 22, 2010.

44 Ibid.

45 Ibid.

46 Ibid.

47 Ibid.

48 Ibid.

49 Ibid.

50 Ibid.

51 Zinn, p. 27.

52 Zinn, p. 28.

53 Douglass, p. 29

54 Paul E. Lovejoy, "The Impact of the Atlantic Slave Trade on Africa: A Review of the Literature," *The Journal of African History*, Vol. 30, No. 3, 1989, p. 368.

55 Karl Marx, *The Poverty of Philosophy: A Reply to M. Proudhon's Philosophy of Poverty*, International Publishers, New York, n.d.,

pp. 94-95.

56 Eric Williams, *Capitalism and Slavery*, University of North Carolina Press, Chapel Hill, 1944, p. 52.

57 Philip S. Foner, "The International Slave Trade," from *African Americans in the US Economy*, Cecilia Conrad, editor, Rowman and Littlefield Publishers, Lanham, MD, 2005, pp. 9-13.

58 David Brion Davis & Steven Mintz, *The Boisterous Sea of Liberty: A Documentary History of America from Colonization through the Civil War*, Oxford University Press, New York, 1998, p. 254.

59 C.L.R. James, "The Revolution and the Negro," *The New International*, Volume V, December 1939, Published under the name J.R. Johnson, pp. 339-343.

60 Ibid.

61 *Reports of Decisions in the Supreme Court of the United States, Volume 14*, Benjamin Robbins Curtis, Houghton and Company, Boston, 1855, p.158.

62 Andrew Burnaby, as quoted in *The American Spirit: United States History as Seen by Contemporaries, Vol. 1: To 1877*, 12th Edition, Wadsworth, Boston, 2010, p. 123.

63 Bradley, p. 28.

64 Ibid.

65 Thomas Jefferson, as quoted in Bradley, p. 28.

66 Ibid., p. 29.

67 Thomas Hart Benton, as quoted in Horsman, p. 90.

68 Ralph Waldo Emerson, *Essays and English Traits*, The Harvard Classics, P.F. Collier & Son, New York, 1909–14, p. 351.

69 Bradley, p. 31.

70 Josiah Nott, as quoted in Bradley, p. 33.

71 Josiah Nott, as quoted in Adam Dewbury, "The American School and Scientific Racism in Early American Anthropology," in *Histories of Anthropology Annual*, 3, 2007, Regna Darnell, Frederic Gleach editors, University of Nebraska Press, Lincoln, p. 141.

72 Lewis Henry Morgan, as quoted in Herbert Hovenkamp, "Social Science and Segregation before *Brown*," from *Critical White Studies: Looking Behind the Mirror*, Richard Delgado & Jean Stefancic, editors, Temple University Press, Philadelphia 1997, p. 204.

Chapter 2

1 Noam Chomsky, *Hegemony or Survival: America's Quest for Global Dominance*, Henry Holt and Company, New York, 2003, p. 236.

2 Cornel West, *Democracy Matters: Winning the Fight Against Imperialism*, Penguin Press, New York, 2004, p. 148.

3 Ibid.

4 Ibid.

5 Ibid., pp. 149-151.

6 Cornel West, interviewed by Don Edwards on "Every Church a Peace Church," YouTube, August 22, 2012. Uploaded by LivingPeaceChurch. https://www.youtube.com/watch?v=yTJMf-LxyH8 (Retrieved January 24, 2015)

7 Gore Vidal, "Gore Vidal and the Mind of the Terrorist," interview with Ramona Koval, Australian Broadcasting Corp. Radio National, November 2001.

8 Chris Hedges, "The Folly of Empire," *Truthdig*, October 14, 2013. http://www.truthdig.com/report/item/the_folly_of_empire_20131014 (Retrieved January 24, 2015)

9 Ibid.

10 Ibid.

11 Ibid.

12 Juvenal, *Satire 10*, "The Vanity of Human Wishes."

13 Barry Levinson, "Our Roman Circus," *The Huffington Post*, June 9, 2014. http://www.huffingtonpost.com/barry-levinson/our-roman-circus_b_5474552.html (Retrieved January 24, 2015)

14 Hedges, "The Folly of Empire".

15 Antonio Negri and Michael Hardt, *Empire*, Harvard University Press, Cambridge, 2000, pp. 301-303.

16 Virgil, *The Aeneid*, translated by Robert Fitzgerald, Random House, New York, 1983, p. 103.

17 Ibid., p. 105.

18 Mark Curtis, *Web of Deceit: Britain's Real Role in the World*, Vintage, London, 2003, p. 366.

19 Chalmers Johnson, *Nemesis: The Last Days of the American Republic*, Henry Holt and Company, New York, 2006, p. 10.

20 John Pilger, Forward to Curtis, *Web of Deceit: Britain's Real Role in the World*, p. x.

21 Hedges, "The Folly of Empire".

22 Ann Laura Stoler, *Haunted by Empire: Geographies of Intimacy in North American History*, Duke University Press, North Carolina, 2006, p. 12.

23 George W. Bush, State of the Union Address, January 20, 2004.

24 Chalmers Johnson, *DemocracyNow* interview, February 27, 2007. http://www.democracynow.org/2007/2/27/chalmers_johnson_nemesis_the_last_days (Retrieved Jan 24, 2015)

25 Ibid.

26 Ibid.

27 Ibid.

28 Nick Turse, "The Pentagon's Planet of Bases," *TomDispatch*, January 9, 2011. http://www.tomdispatch.com/blog/175338/ (Retrieved January 24, 2015)

29 Ibid.

30 "Secretive US military space shuttle lands itself at California base," *The Guardian*, Associated Press, June 16, 2012. http://www.theguardian.com/world/2012/jun/16/secretive-us-military-space-shuttle (Retrieved January 24, 2015)

31 Antony Barnett, "US planned one big nuclear blast for mankind," *The Guardian*, May 13, 2000. http://www.theguardian.com/science/2000/may/14/spaceexploration.theobserver (Retrieved January 24, 2015)

32 Ibid.

33 United States Space Command, "Vision for 2020," self-published pamphlet, 2002.

34 Ibid.

35 Ibid.

36 Ibid.

37 Ibid.

38 Jonathan Granoff and Craig Eisendrath, "United States—Masters of Space? The US Space Command's 'Vision for 2020,'" Global Security Institute, December, 2005, p. 2. http://www.worldacademy.org/files/The_US_Space_Command_Vision_for_2020.pdf (Retrieved January 24, 2015)

39 United States Space Command, "Vision for 2020".

40 Ibid.

41 Noam Chomsky, "We Own the World," *ZNet*, January 1, 2008. http://www.

chomsky.info/articles/20080101.htm (Retrieved January 24, 2015)

42 David Foster Wallace, *A Supposedly Fun Thing I'll Never Do Again*, Back Bay Books/ Little, Brown and Company, New York, 1997, p. 17.

43 David Hambling, "Science Fiction Inspires DARPA Weapon," *New Scientist*, April 22, 2008. http://www.newscientist.com/blog/technology/2008/04/science-fiction-inspires-darpa-weapon.html (Retrieved January 24, 2015)

44 Roland Dante, "5 Famous Sci-Fi Weapons That They're Actually Building," *Cracked*, July 11, 2008. http://www.cracked.com/article_16477_5-famous-sci-fi-weapons-that-theyre-actually-building.html (Retrieved January 24, 2015)

45 Eric Adams, "Rods from Gods," *Popular Science*, June 1, 2004, http://www.popsci.com/scitech/article/2004-06/rods-god (Retrieved Jan 24, 2015) Jonathan Shainin, "Rods from Gods," *The New York Times*, December 10, 2006. http://www.nytimes.com/2006/12/10/magazine/10section3a.t-9.html (Retrieved January 24, 2015)

46 Dante, "5 Famous Sci-Fi Weapons That They're Actually Building".

47 Shainin, "Rods from Gods".

48 Noam Chomsky, "Militarizing Space," *International Socialist Review*, Issue 19, July-August 2001.

49 Ibid.

50 Arms Control Association Press Conference, December 13, 2002. http://www.armscontrol.org/node/2515 (Retrieved January 13, 2015)

51 Ibid.

52 John Perkins, *The Secret History of the American Empire*, Plume Publishing/ Penguin, New York, 2007, pp. 4-5.

53 Ibid., p. 5.

54 Ibid.

55 Seth Mydans, "Across cultures, English is the word," *The New York Times*, April 9, 2007. http://www.nytimes.com/2007/04/09/world/asia/09iht-englede.1.5198685.html (Retrieved January 24, 2015)

56 Perkins, p. 5.

57 Ibid.

58 Ibid., p. 6.

59 Ibid,

60 John Perkins, *Confessions of an Economic Hit Man*, Plume Publishing/Penguin, New York, 2004, p. xi.

61 John Perkins, interview with Amy Goodman, *DemocracyNow*, November 9, 2004. http://www.democracynow.org/2004/11/9/confessions_of_an_economic_hit_man (Retrieved January 24, 2015)

62 Ibid.

63 Ibid.

64 John Perkins, interview with the authors, "Murder Incorporated Sessions," Street Legal Cinema, October 2006, transcript.

65 Michael Parenti, interview with the authors, "Murder Incorporated Sessions," Street Legal Cinema, October 2006, transcript.

66 Perkins, "Murder Incorporated Sessions".

67 Parenti, "Murder Incorporated Sessions".

68 Gallup International (in collaboration with the BBC), http://www.wingia.com/web/files/services/33/file/33.

pdf?1422107011 (Retrieved January 24, 2015)

69 Gallup International, http://www.wingia.com/web/files/news/139/file/139.pdf (Retrieved Jan 24, 2015)

70 William Blum, "Overthrowing other people's governments: The Master List," williamblum.org, February, 2013. http://williamblum.org/essays/read/overthrowing-other-peoples-governments-the-master-list (Retrieved January 24, 2015)

71 David Swanson, *War is a Lie*, published by author, Charlottesville, VA, 2010, p. 32.

72 Coleman McCarthy, "The Consequences of Covert Tactics," *The Washington Post*, December 13, 1987.

73 Ibid.

74 Ibid.

75 White, Pauline Lubens, Geraldine Gorman, & Amy Hagopian, "The Role of Public Health in the Prevention of War: Rationale and Competencies," October 28, 2013, American Journal of Public Health, June 2014, Vol. 104, No. 6. http://ajph.aphapublications.org/doi/abs/10.2105/AJPH.2013.301778

76 Ibid.

77 David Swanson, "Public Health Experts Identify Militarism As Threat," *WarIsACrime*, May 15, 2014. http://warisacrime.org/content/public-health-experts-identify-militarism-threat (Retrieved January 24, 2015)

78 Ibid.

79 APHA, "The Role of Public Health in the Prevention of War".

80 Ibid.

81 Jill Lepore, "The Force," *The New Yorker*, January 28, 2013.

82 APHA, "The Role of Public Health in the Prevention of War".

83 Xiaoping Yang, Robert North, and Carl Romney, "Worldwide Nuclear Explosions," Science Applications International Corporation, Center for Monitoring Research, Arlington, VA & Paul G. Richards, Lamont-Doherty Earth Observatory, and Department of Earth and Environmental Sciences, Columbia University, Palisades, NY, August, 2000. https://www.ldeo.columbia.edu/~richards/my_papers/WW_nuclear_tests_IASPEI_HB.pdf (Retrieved January 24, 2015)

84 President Ronald Reagan, as quoted in Richard Reeves, *President Reagan: The Triumph of Imagination*, Simon & Schuster, New York, 2005, p. 265.

85 Noam Chomsky, "Rogue States Draw the Usual Line," *Agenda* magazine interview, May, 2001. http://www.chomsky.info/interviews/200105--.htm (Retrieved January 24, 2015)

86 Ibid.

87 Sam Dillon, "Harvard Chief Defends His Talk on Women," *The New York Times*, January 18, 2005.

88 Lawrence Summers, as quoted in William Blum, *Rogue State: A Guide to the World's Only Superpower*, Common Courage Press, Maine, 2000, p. 6.

89 Mark Selden and Alvin Y. So, *War & State Terrorism*, Rowman & Littlefield, Maryland, 2004, p. 4.

90 Noam Chomsky, "International Terrorism: Image and Reality," http://www.chomsky.info/articles/199112--02.htm#n3, originally published in *Western State Terrorism*, Alexander George, editor, Routledge, December, 1991. (Retrieved

January 24, 2015)

91 Donna Jo Napoli as quoted in Oliver Libaw, "How Do You Define Terrorism?," *ABC News*, October 11, 2011. http://abcnews.go.com/US/story?id=92340 (Retrieved Jan 24, 2015)

92 John Perkins, "Murder Incorporated Sessions".

93 Tariq Ali, interview with the authors, "Murder Incorporated Sessions," Street Legal Cinema, October 2006, transcript.

94 Ibid.

Chapter 3

1 David Stannard, *American Holocaust: The Conquest of the New World,* Oxford University Press, New York, 1992, pp. 3-4.

2 Bernal Diaz del Castillo, *The Discovery and Conquest of Mexico,* 1517-1521, as quoted by Stannard, p. 4.

Chapter 4

1 David Stannard, *American Holocaust: The Conquest of the New World,* Oxford University Press, New York, 1992, p. 66.

2 "Christopher Columbus: Extracts from Journal," Medieval Sourcebook, Fordham University, http://www.fordham.edu/halsall/source/columbus1.asp (Retrieved Jan 22, 2015) (What is titled "The Diary of Christopher Columbus" also served as a log of his journey intended to be read by the Spanish monarchy—hence his reference to "Your highnesses".)

3 Stannard, p. 95.

4 Wahunsonacock (Powhatan), as quoted in *Great Speeches by Native Americans,* Bob Blaisdell, ed., Dover, Mineola, NY, 2000, p. 4.

5 Stannard, p. 62.

6 Stannard, pp. 98-99.

7 Ibid., p. 4.

8 Ibid., p. 92.

9 Bartolomé de Las Casas, as quoted in Stannard, p. 70.

10 de Las Casas, as quoted in Stannard, p. 81.

11 William L. Sherman, *Forced Native Labor in Sixteenth Century Central America,* University of Nebraska Press, Lincoln, 1979, pp. 315-316, as quoted by Stannard, p. 85.

12 Stannard, pp. 69-70.

13 Stannard, pp. 113-114.

14 William Bradford, as quoted in Stannard, p. 114.

15 Stannard, p. 115.

16 Ibid.

17 William Apes, as quoted in *Great Speeches,* pp. 94-95.

18 *The World Almanac and Book of Facts,* Sarah Janssen, editor, World Almanac Books, New York, 2012, p. 566.

19 Stannard, p. 120.

20 Thomas Jefferson, as quoted in Stannard, p. 120.

21 Ibid.

22 Stephen Ceasar, "Tucson students confront loss of their Chicano studies class," *Los Angeles Times,* January 11, 2012.

23 *World Almanac,* pp. 476-477.

24 James W. Loewen, *Lies My Teacher Told Me,* Simon & Schuster, New York, 1995, pp. 117-118.

25 Ben Franklin, as quoted in Loewen, p. 109.

26 Ibid.

27 Andrew Jackson, as quoted in Loewen, p. 122.

28 John G. Burnett, as quoted in *Voices of a People's History of the United States*, Howard Zinn & Anthony Arnove, editors, Seven Stories Press, New York, 2004, pp. 144-145.

29 Ibid., p. 145.

30 James Bradley, *The Imperial Cruise: A Secret History of Empire and War*, Back Bay/ Little, Brown & Co., New York, 2009, p. 40.

31 Alexis de Tocqueville, as quoted in Stannard, p. 123.

32 Tatanka Yotanka (Sitting Bull), as quoted in *Great Speeches*, p. 175.

33 Blackfoot, as quoted in *Great Speeches*, pp. 142-143.

34 Josiah Nott, as quoted in Bradley, p. 33.

35 Stannard, pp. 129-130.

36 Ibid.

37 Ibid., p. 132.

38 John Chivington, as quoted in Stannard, p. 131.

39 Robert Bent, as quoted in Stannard, pp. 132-133.

40 Stannard, p. 133.

41 Ibid., p. 134.

42 *World Almanac*, pp. 442-443.

43 L. Frank Baum, as quoted in Stannard, p. 126.

44 Stannard, p. 268.

45 Stannard, p. 86, citing Nathan Wachtel, *The Vision of the Vanquished: The Spanish Conquest of Peru Through Indian Eyes, 1530-1570*, translated by Ben & Sian Reynolds, The Harvester Press, Sussex, 1977, p. 114.

Chapter 5

1 Alexandre Popovic, The Revolt of African Slaves in Iraq in the 3rd/9th Century, Markus Weiner Publishers, Princeton, N.J., 1999 (1976), p. 20.

2 Ibid., p. 20.

3 Ibid., fn. 15, p. 30.

4 Ibid., pp. 40-41.

5 Ibid., p. 69.

6 Jalal Chijeel, as quoted in Aamer Madhani, "Obama's Rise Inspires African Iraqis in Politics", *USA Today*, January 19, 2009.

7 Khalid Majid, as quoted in Madhani, "Obama's Rise Inspires African Iraqis in Politics".

8 David Stannard, *American Holocaust: The Conquest of the New World*, Oxford University Press, New York, 1992, pp. xi, 61.

9 Ibid., p. 181.

10 Mary Frances Berry and John W. Blassingame, *Long Memory: The Black Experiences in America*, Oxford University Press, New York, 1982, p. 7.

11 W.E.B. Dubois, *The World and Africa*, International Publishers, New York, 1947, pp. 257-258.

12 Thomas Jefferson, as quoted in Lerone Bennett, *Forced into Glory: Abraham Lincoln's White Dream*, Johnson Publishing, Chicago, 1999, p. 3.

13 Stannard, p. 150.

14 J.A. Rogers, *Africa's Gift to America*, Helga Rogers, New York, 1961, p. 45, as quoted in Ishakamusa Barashango, *Afrikan People and European Holidays: A Mental Genocide, Book 1*, IVth Dynasty Publishing Co./Barashango & Assoc., Washington, D.C., 1979, p. 25.

15 Stannard, p. 151.

16 James Bradley, *The Imperial Cruise: A Secret History of Empire and War*, Little, Brown & Co./Back Bay, New York, 2009, p. 29.

17 Berry & Blassingame, p. 195.

18 Otto E. Huiswood, as quoted in Berry & Blassingame, p. 196.

19 George M. Stroud, *George M. Stroud's Slave Laws: A Sketch of the Laws Relating to Slavery in the Several States of the United States of America*, Imprint Ed., Baltimore, 2005 (1856), pp. 31-32.

20 Ibid., pp. 33-34.

21 Ibid., pp. 66-67.

22 Ibid., p. 66.

23 Chief Justice Roger B. Taney, *Dred Scott v. Sanford*, 60 U.S. 393 (1857).

24 Theodore Parker, as quoted in Howard Zinn and Anthony Arnove, *Voices of a People's History of the United States*, Seven Stories, New York, 2004, pp. 177-179.

25 Frederick Douglass, as quote in Zinn, Arnove, pp. 184-185.

26 Ibid., p. 186.

27 Philip S. Foner, "A Tribune of His People," introduction to *Frederick Douglass On Slavery and the Civil War: Selections From His Writings*, Dover, Mineola, N.Y., 2003 p. 1.

28 Frederick Douglass, *Frederick Douglass On Slavery and the Civil War*, pp. 9-10.

29 Ibid., pp. 14-15.

30 Lerone Bennett, Jr., *Forced into Glory: Abraham Lincoln's White Press*, Johnson Publishing, Chicago, 1999, p. 35.

31 Trymaine Lee, "In Rediscovered Letter from 1865, Former Slave Tells Old Master to Shove It", *Huff Post/Black Voices*, Feb. 1, 2012, http://www.huffingtonpost.com/2012/02/01/in-recently-discovered-le_n_1247288.html (Retrieved January 5, 2015)

32 Frederick Douglass, as quoted in Lerone Bennett, *The Shaping of Black America*, Johnson Publishing Co., Chicago, 1983, p. 207.

Chapter 6

1 *The World Almanac & Book of Facts: 2012*, Sarah Janssen, editor, World Almanac Books, New York, 2012, p. 657. (The World Almanac was number one on *The Washington Post* bestseller list as recently as November 27, 2011.)

2 Howard Zinn, *Howard Zinn Speaks*, Anthony Arnove, editor, Haymarket Books, Chicago, 2012, p. 102.

3 Thomas Hutchinson, as quoted in *Voices of a People's History of the United States*, 2nd, Howard Zinn and Anthony Arnove, editors, Seven Stories Press, New York, 2004 (2009), pp. 80-81.

4 Zinn, *Howard Zinn Speaks*, p. 242.

5 Ibid.

6 Joseph Clarke, as quoted in Zinn, Arnove, *Voices*, pp. 94-95.

7 *Great Dates in United States History*, Andre Kaspi, editor, Facts on File, New York, 1994, p. 27

8 Henry Knox, as quoted in Zinn, Arnove, *Voices*, p. 104.

9 Alexander Hamilton, as quoted in Jerry Fresia, *Toward an American Revolution: Exposing the Constitution & Other Illusions*, South End Press, Boston, 1988, pp. 3, 177.

10 *The Concise Columbia Encyclopedia*, Third Edition, Columbia University Press, New York, 1994, p. 373.

11 Fresia, *Toward an American Revolution*, p. 20.

12 Gouverneur Morris, as quoted in Fresia, *Toward an American Revolution*, p. 28.

13 Plough Jogger, as quoted in Zinn, Arnove, *Voices*, p. 104.

14 Joseph Plumb Martin, as quoted in Zinn, Arnove, *Voices*, p. 96.

15 Ibid., p. 99.

16 Zinn, *Howard Zinn Speaks*, p. 146.

17 Herbert Aptheker, *American Negro Slave Revolts*, International Publ., New York, 1943, p. 22.

18 Zinn, *Howard Zinn Speaks*, pp. 242-243.

19 Fred Jerome and Rodger Taylor, *Einstein on Race and Racism*, Rutgers University Press, New Brunswick, NJ, 2005, pp. 16-17. *From text: "The all-black First Rhode Island Regiment was composed of thirty-nine freedmen and ninety-two slaves who were promised freedom if they served until the end of the war. They distinguished themselves in the Battle of Newport. However, the regiment was all but wiped out in a British attack at Yorktown."

20 Zinn, *Howard Zinn Speaks*, p. 242.

21 Aptheker, p. 213.

22 Lord Dunmore (John Murray) as quoted in Gary B. Nash, *The Unknown American Revolution*, Penguin, New York, p. 2006, p. 162.

23 Lund Washington, as quoted in Nash, *The Unknown American Revolution*, p. 162.

24 Edward Rutledge, as quoted in Nash, p. 166.

25 Nash, p. 166.

26 John Adams, as quoted in Nash, p. 65.

27 Woody Holton, *Forced Founders: Indians, Debtors, Slaves, & the Making of the American Revolution in Virginia*, University of North Carolina Press, Chapel Hill, NC, 1999, pp. 153-154.

28 Nash, p. 162.

29 Ibid., p. 163.

30 Lord Dunmore, as quoted in Nash, p. 163.

31 Holton, p. 158.

32 Philip Fithian, as quoted in Holton, p. 158.

33 Nash, pp. 164-166.

34 Janet Schaw, as quoted in Nash, p. 165.

35 Nash, p. 161.

36 Ibid.

37 Nash, pp. 165-166.

38 Ibid., p. 231.

39 Ibid., p. 428.

40 Peter Fontaine, as quoted in Holton, p. 6.

41 Nash, p. 173.

42 Ibid., p. 175.

43 Joseph Brant, as quoted in Nash, p. 176.

44 Nash, pp. 247-248.

45 Blacksnake, as quoted in Nash, p. 253.

46 Nash, p. 255.

47 Lord Shelburne, as quoted in Nash, p. 381.

48 Ibid., pp. 2-3.

49 Ibid., pp. 39-40.

50 Ibid., p. 40.

51 Ibid., p. 57.

52 John Adams, as quoted in Nash, p. xvi.

Chapter 7

1 Anders Stephanson, *Manifest Destiny: American Expansion and the Empire of Right*, Hill and Wang, New York, 1995, p. 107.

2 Ibid.

3 Gore Vidal, *Imperial America*, Nation Books, New York, 2004, p. 47.

4 John A. Crow, *The Epic of Latin America*, University of California Press, Berkeley, 1992, p. 675.

5 Thomas Jefferson, as quoted by Crow, *The Epic of Latin America*, pp. 675-676.

6 James Monroe, "Seventh Annual Message," December 2, 1823, *The American Presidency Project*; http://www.presidency.ucsb.edu/ws/?pid=29465 (Retrieved January 12, 2015)

7 Dexter Perkins, *A History of the Monroe Doctrine*, Little Brown, New York, 1955, pp. 30-31.

8 Ibid., p. 68.

9 Jay Sexton, *The Monroe Doctrine: Empire and Nation in Nineteenth-Century America*, Hill and Wang, New York, 2011, p. 4.

10 William Blum, *Killing Hope: U.S. Military and CIA Interventions Since World War II*, Common Courage Press, Maine, p. 89.

11 Martin Hass, review of Gretchen Murphy, *Hemispheric Imaginings: The Monroe Doctrine and Narratives of U.S. Empire*, H-LatAm, H-Net Reviews, October, 2007; http://www.h-net.org/reviews/showrev.php?id=13796 (Retrieved January 12, 2015)

12 Gretchen Murphy, *Hemispheric Imaginings: The Monroe Doctrine and Narratives of U.S. Empire*, Duke University Press, Durham & London, 2005, p. 120.

13 Ibid., p. 27.

14 U.S. Department of State, Office of the Historian, *Milestones: 1801-1829*, "Monroe Doctrine, 1823"; http://history.state.gov/milestones/1801-1829/Monroe. (Retrieved January 12, 2015)

15 Murphy, p. 14.

16 "The Monroe Doctrine," Teaching American History Project (TAHPDX), Portland State University; http://www.upa.pdx.edu/IMS/currentprojects/TAHv3/Monroe_Doctrine.html (Retrieved January 12, 2015)

17 Murphy, p. 120.

18 Pat Hudson, "The Workshop of the World," BBC History, 2011, online; http://www.bbc.co.uk/history/british/victorians/workshop_of_the_world_01.shtml (Retrieved January 12, 2015)

19 "The Monroe Doctrine," TAHPDX, Portland State University.

20 Rolf Hobson, *Imperialism at Sea: Naval Strategic Thought, The Ideology of Sea Power, and the Tirpitz Plan, 1875-1914*, Brill Academic Publishing, Boston, 2002, p. 63.

21 Clara Nieto, *Masters of War: Latin America and U.S. Aggression*, Seven Stories Press, New York, 2003, p. 18.

22 Ibid.

23 Ibid.

24 Ward Churchill, *A Little Matter of Genocide: Holocaust and Denial in the Americas 1492 to the Present*, City Lights Books, San Francisco, 1997, p. 147.

25 Charles Sullivan, "Manifest Destiny Rides Again," *Counterpunch*, February 12, 2003; http://test.counterpunch.org/2003/02/12/manifest-destiny-rides-again/ (Retrieved January 12, 2015)

26 James Bradley, *The Imperial Cruise*, Little, Brown and Company, New York, 2009, pp. 113-114.

27 Andrew J. Bacevich, "What's an Iraqi Life Worth?" *The Washington Post*, July 9, 2006, citing Michael R. Gordon and

Gen. Bernard E. Trainor, *Cobra II*, Vintage Books, New York, 2006; http://www.washingtonpost.com/wp-dyn/content/article/2006/07/07/AR2006070701155_pf.html (Retrieved January 12, 2015)

28 David E. Stannard, *American Holocaust: The Conquest of the New World*, Oxford University Press, New York, 1992, p. 120.

29 Ibid.

30 Library of Congress, Thomas Jefferson Exhibition, "The West"; http://www.loc.gov/exhibits/jefferson/jeffwest.html (Retrieved January 12, 2015)

31 Stannard, p. 120.

32 Ibid.

33 Ibid.

34 Noam Chomsky, interview with the authors, "Murder Incorporated Sessions," Street Legal Cinema, 2007.

35 "Letter to King Ferdinand of Spain, describing the results of the first voyage," American Studies at the University of Virginia; http://xroads.virginia.edu/~hyper/hns/garden/columbus.html (Retrieved January 12, 2015)

36 Michael Parenti, interview with the authors, "Murder Incorporated Sessions," Street Legal Cinema, 2007.

37 Charles Sullivan, "Manifest Destiny Rides Again".

38 Ibid.

39 Ibid.

40 Thomas Jefferson, *Notes on the State of Virginia, Query XIV*, 1787, as compiled by the University of Virginia American Studies Program; http://xroads.virginia.edu/~hyper/JEFFERSON/ch14.html (Retrieved January 14, 2015)

41 Ibid.

42 Robert Jensen, *The Heart of Whiteness: Confronting Race, Racism and White Privilege*, City Lights, San Francisco, 2005, pp. 41-42.

43 Ibid, p. 42.

44 Ibid, pp. 42-43.

45 Bill Moyers interview with Sissela Bok, "Now with Bill Moyers," July 2, 2004; www.pbs.org/now/transcript/transcript327_full.html (Retrieved January 12, 2015)

46 Jensen, pp. 41-43.

47 Henry Wiencek, "The Dark Side of Thomas Jefferson," *Smithsonian Magazine*, October, 2012; http://www.smithsonianmag.com/history/the-dark-side-of-thomas-jefferson-35976004/ (Retrieved January 12, 2015)

48 Ibid.

49 Henry Louis Gates, "The Curse on Haiti," *The Root*, January 25, 2010; http://www.theroot.com/articles/history/2010/01/pat_robertson_was_wrong_the_curse_on_haiti_came_from_thomas_jefferson.html (Retrieved January 12, 2015)

50 Ibid.

51 Ibid.

52 James W. Loewen, *Lies My Teacher Told Me*, Simon & Schuster, New York, 1995, p. 121.

53 David Brion Davis, *Challenging the Boundaries of Slavery*, Harvard University Press, Cambridge, 2003, p. 76.

54 Henry Wiencek, "The Dark Side of Thomas Jefferson".

55 Ibid.

56 Ibid.

57 Robert McColley, *Slavery and Jeffersonian Virginia*, University of Illinois Press, Champaign, IL, 1964, pp. 3-4.

58 David Brion Davis, *The Problem of Slavery in the Age of Revolution, 1770-1823*, Oxford University Press, Oxford, 1999, p. 184.

59 Churchill, p. 219.

60 Ibid., p. 218.

61 John S. D. Eisenhower, *So Far from God: The U.S. War With Mexico, 1846-1848*, Random House, New York, 1989, p. 44.

62 Reginald Horsman, *Race and Manifest Destiny: Origins of American Racial Anglo-Saxonism*, Harvard University Press, Cambridge, 1981, p. 158.

63 Ibid., p. 1.

64 Vidal, pp. 44-45.

65 Ulysses S. Grant, *Personal Memoirs of U. S. Grant, Complete*, Project Gutenberg, Chapter III; http://www.gutenberg.org/files/4367/4367-h/4367-h.htm (Retrieved January 12, 2015)

66 Ibid.

67 "'Gloriously Fighting a Glorious Cause'": Tennesseans in the war with Mexico, 1856-1848", Tennessee State Library and Archives; http://www.tennessee.gov/tsla/history/guides/guide13.htm (Retrieved January 14, 2015)

68 Frederick Douglass, "Texas, Slavery, and American Prosperity: An Address Delivered in Belfast, Ireland, on January 2, 1846," Belfast *News Letter*, January 6, 1846 in *The Frederick Douglass Papers: Series One –Speeches, Debates, and Interviews*, John Blassingame, editor, Yale University Press, New Haven, 1979, Vol. 1, p. 118.

69 Noam Chomsky, "How the U.S.-Mexico Border Is Cruel by Design," *Alternet*, October 28, 2013; http://www.alternet.org/economy/noam-chomsky-americas-suburban-nightmare-and-how-us-mexico-border-cruel-design (Retrieved January 12, 2015)

70 Ibid.

71 Steve Earle, "Transcendental Blues," Indieblu Music, 2004.

72 Howard Zinn, "The Power and the Glory: Myths of American Exceptionalism," *Boston Review*, June 1, 2005; http://bostonreview.net/BR30.3/zinn.php (Retrieved January 12, 2015)

73 Noam Chomsky, "History of U.S. Rule in Latin America," speaking at the Massachusetts Institute of Technology, December 15, 2009, recorded by *International Socialist Review* and *Socialist Worker*, posted by "PHubb," December 19, 2009; https://www.youtube.com/watch?v=NKwJI9axblQ (Retrieved January 12, 2015)

74 Gore Vidal, "Theodore Roosevelt: American Sissy," *The New York Review of Books*, August 13, 1981.

75 Theodore Roosevelt, as cited by Wolfgang Mieder in *The Politics of Proverbs: From Traditional Wisdom to Proverbial Stereotypes*, University of Wisconsin Press, Madison, WI, 1997, p. 147.

76 Bradley, p. 204.

77 Theodore Roosevelt, "Fourth Annual Message," December 6, 1904, The American Presidency Project; http://www.presidency.ucsb.edu/ws/index.php?pid=29545 (Retrieved January 12, 2015)

78 David Nakamura, "Obama invokes Teddy Roosevelt in speech attacking GOP policies," *The Washington Post*, December 6, 2011.

79 Sam Bradley, "Theodore Roosevelt and Progressivism," *1984 Recurring*, August 27, 2012; http://1984recurring.wordpress.com/2012/08/27/theodore-roosevelt-and-progressivism-a-progressive-president/ (Retrieved January 12, 2015)

80 Howard Zinn, *A People's History of the United States*, Harper Collins, New York, 2003, p. 349.

81 Mumia Abu-Jamal, *We Want Freedom*, South End Press, Cambridge, 2008, p. 18.

82 Zinn, pp. 349-350.

83 Gabriel Kolko, *Triumph of Conservatism*, Simon & Schuster, New York, 2008, pp. 2-3.

84 Zinn, pp. 350-354.

85 Noam Chomsky, "Presidential 'Peacemaking' in Latin America," *In These Times*, January 5, 2010; http://inthesetimes.com/article/5375/presidential_peacemaking_in_latin_america (Retrieved January 12, 2015)

86 Vidal, *Imperial America*, p. 51.

87 Brooks Adams, as quoted in John Carlos Rowe, *Literary Culture and U.S. Imperialism*, Oxford University Press, New York, 2000, p. 189.

88 Mark Twain, *Mark Twain, a Biography, Volume III Part 1, 1900-1907*, Classic Literature Library, eBook, p. 24.

89 Nikita Khrushchev, as quoted in "U.S. Stand Against Reds in Cuba Has Its Roots in Monroe Doctrine," *The New York Times*, April 19, 1961.

90 Charles Sullivan, "Manifest Destiny Rides Again".

91 Daniel P. Erikson, "Requiem for the Monroe Doctrine," *Current History*, Volume 107, Issue 706, p. 58.

92 Nieto, p. 15.

93 Noam Chomsky, interviewed by David Barsamian, *How the World Works*, Arthur Naiman, editor, Soft Skull Press, Brooklyn, NY, 1986-2011, p. 10.

94 Ibid.

95 Ibid.

96 Ibid., p. 11.

97 George Kennan, as quoted by Chomsky in *How the World Works*, pp. 11-12.

98 Chomsky, *How the World Works*, p. 12.

99 George Kennan, as quoted by Chomsky in *How the World Works*, p. 12.

100 Ibid., p. 13.

101 Nieto, p. 25.

102 Noam Chomsky, *American Power and the New Mandarins*, The New Press, New York, 2002 (1967), p. 332. (Chomsky quotes Walt Rostow, economist, political theorist, and Lyndon Johnson's Special Assistant for National Security Affairs.)

103 Michael Parenti, *Against Empire*, City Lights Books, San Francisco, 1995, p. 91.

104 Nieto, p. 81.

105 *UN Yearbook 1962*, New York, pp. 104-105; *Everyman's United Nations, 1945-1963*, UN, New York, p. 178.

106 Noam Chomsky, "A Century Later," *Peace Review*, September, 1998;

http://www.chomsky.info/articles/199809--.htm (Retrieved January 12, 2015)

107 Ronald Reagan, as quoted in Gerald Boyd, "Reagan Terms Nicaraguan Rebels 'Moral Equal of Founding Fathers,'" *The New York Times*, March 2, 1985.

108 Nieto, pp. 395-396.

109 Max Boot, "What the Heck is a Neocon?", *The Wall Street Journal*, Op-Ed,

February 6, 2007; http://www.cfr.org/world/heck-neocon/p5343 (Retrieved January 12, 2015)

110 Max Boot, Interviewed by Ben Wattenberg, *America, Quo Vadis? Part 1, Think Tank with Ben Wattenberg*, PBS, original broadcast April 12, 2007.

111 Murphy, p. vii.

112 Murphy, p. viii.

113 Glen Ford, "The Ultimate Logic of a Society Built on Mass Murder," *Black Agenda Report*, December 21, 2012; http://blackagendareport.com/content/ultimate-logic-society-built-mass-murder (Retrieved January 12, 2015)

Chapter 8

1 David Stannard, *American Holocaust: The Conquest of the New World*, Oxford University Press, New York, pp. 3-4.

2 James Bradley, *The Imperial Cruise: A Secret History of Empire and War*, Back Bay/ Little, Brown & Co., New York, p. 63.

3 Ibid.

4 Frederick Merk and Lois Bannister Merk, *Manifest Destiny and Mission in American History: A Reinterpretation*, Harvard University Press, Cambridge, 1963, p. 123; also Noam Chomsky, *Hopes and Prospects*, Haymarket Books, Chicago, 2010, p. 160.

5 Bradley, p. 64.

6 Colonel Ethan Allen Hitchcock, as quoted in Howard Zinn & Anthony Arnove, *Voices of a People's History of the United States*, Seven Stories Press, New York , 2004, pp. 155-156.

7 Ibid., p. 158.

8 William Loren Katz, *Black Indians: A Hidden Heritage*, Simon Pulse, New York, 1986, pp. 47-48.

9 Frederick Douglass, as quoted in Zinn & Arnove, pp. 149-150.

10 Ulysses S. Grant, *Personal Memoirs of U. S. Grant, Complete*, Project Gutenberg, Chapter III; http://www.gutenberg.org/files/4367/4367-h/4367-h.htm (Retrieved January 12, 2015)

11 Anders Stephanson, *Manifest Destiny: American expansions and the Empire of Right*, Hill & Wang, New York, 1995, pp. 36-37.

12 *The World Almanac and Book of Facts*, Sarah Janssen, editor, World Almanac Books, New York, 2012, p. 610.

13 Colonel Ethan Allen Hitchcock, as quoted in Zinn & Arnove, pp. 155-156.

14 Michael Parenti, *The Assassination of Julius Caesar: A People's History of Ancient Rome*, The New Press, New York, 2003, p. 16.

15 Ibid., p. 17.

16 Stephanson, p. 3.

17 Ralph Waldo Emerson, as quoted in Stephanson, p. 53.

18 Theodore Parker, as quoted in Stephanson, p. 54.

19 Clara Nieto, *Masters of War: Latin America and U.S. Aggression*, Seven Stories Press, New York, 2003, p. 18.

20 John Calhoun, as quoted in Bradley, p. 64.

21 Nieto, p. 19.

22 Zinn & Arnove, p. 161.

Chapter 9

1 *Bartlett's Familiar Quotations*, 17th ed., Little, Brown & Co., New York, 2002 (1882), p. 376.

2 Robert Olds, as quoted in Clara Nieto, *Masters of War: Latin America and U.S. Aggression (From the Cuban Revolution*

Through the Clinton Years), Seven Stories Press, New York, 2003, p. 11.

3 Howard, Zinn, *A People's History of the United States*, Harper Collins, New York, 2003, p. 408.

4 Nieto, p. 18.

5 Walter Lippman, as quoted in Nieto, p. 22.

6 James Bradley, *The Imperial Cruise: A Secret History of Empire and War*, Little, Brown Co., New York, 2009, pp. 80-81.

7 Nieto, pp. 33-34 (Campesinos is a Spanish term meaning the peasantry.)

8 Zinn, p. 439.

9 Nieto, p. 54.

10 Zinn, p. 440.

11 Ibid.

12 Nieto, p. 38 (citing fn.17: *Bohemia*, Havana, Feb. 15, 1959).

13 Nieto, pp. 78-79.

14 Nieto, p. 59.

15 Eric Thomas Chester, *Rag-Tags, Scum, Riff-Raff and Commies: The U.S. Intervention in the Dominican Republic, 1965-66*, Monthly Review Press, New York, 2001, p. 17.

16 Ibid., pp. 16-17.

17 Ibid., p. 80.

18 Ibid., pp. 272-273.

19 Nieto, p. 100.

20 Ibid., p. 101.

21 Ibid., pp. 182-183.

22 Ibid.

23 Ibid., p. 108.

24 Ibid., pp. 108-109.

25 Allen Dulles, as quoted in Chalmers Johnson, *Dismantling the Empire: America's Last Best Hope*, Metropolitan Books, New York, 2010, p. 75.

26 Ibid.

27 Michael Parenti, *The Face of Imperialism*, Paradigm Press, Boulder, CO, 2011, p. 8.

28 Nieto, pp. 116-117.

29 Ibid., p. 117.

30 Ibid.

31 Ronald Reagan, as quoted in William Blum, *Killing Hope: U.S. Military and C.I.A. Interventions Since World War II*, Common Courage Press, Monroe, ME, 2004, p. 352.

32 Zinn, p. 590.

33 Oscar Romero, as quoted in Blum, p. 355.

34 Blum, p. 353.

35 Ibid., p. 359

36 William Blum, *America's Deadliest Export: Democracy; The Truth About U.S. Foreign Policy and Everything Else*, Zed Books, London/New York, 2013, p. 200.

37 Ibid., p. 201.

38 Jimmy Carter, as quoted in Blum, *Killing Hope*, p. 357.

39 Nieto, p. 208.

40 Blum, *Killing Hope*, p. 254.

41 Ibid.

42 Nieto, p. 218.

43 G. Mennen Williams, as quoted in *South Africa and the United States: The Declassified History*, Kenneth Mokoena, ed., The New Press, New York, 1992, Doc. 3, p. 3.

44 Ibid., p. 20 (citing *Message to Nigerian Foreign Minister*, 11/29/75; *South African Involvement in Angola*; *MPLA Visit to Lagos*, 12/3/75).

45 Nikita Khrushchev, as quoted in Blum,

Killing Hope, p. 185.

46 Robert Kennedy, as quoted in Nieto, p. 83.

47 Alexander Haig, as quoted in Nieto, p. 455.

48 Remarks by President Obama to the People of Cuba, March 22, 2016, whitehouse.gov

49 Fidel Castro, *Brother Obama,* Granma, March 28, 2016.

50 Ibid.

51 Dan Roberts, *Obama lands in Cuba as first US president to visit in nearly a century,* The Guardian, March 21, 2016.

52 Nelson Mandela, as quoted in Piero Gleijeses, *Visions of Freedom,* University of North Carolina Press, Chapel Hill, NC, 2013, p. 526.

53 Ibid., p. 519.

54 Fidel Castro, *Brother Obama,* Granma, March 28, 2016.

Chapter 10

1 John F. Kennedy, as quoted in Arthur M. Schlesinger, Jr., *A Thousand Days: John F. Kennedy in the White House*, Houghton Mifflin Company, Boston, 1965, p. 88.

2 Howard Zinn, *Failure to Quit: Reflections of an Optimistic Historian*, South End Press, Cambridge, MA, 2002, p. 45.

3 Dick Gregory, interviewed in *One Bright Shining Moment: The Forgotten Summer of George McGovern*, documentary film, Stephen Vittoria, director, Street Legal Cinema, 2005.

4 Elliott J. Gorn, *Mother Jones: The Most Dangerous Woman in America*, Hill and Wang, New York, 2001.

5 David Carter, *Stonewall: The Riots that Sparked the Gay Revolution*, St. Martin's Press, New York, 2004, p. 2.

6 Butch Lee, *Jailbreak Out of History: The Re-Biography of Harriet Tubman*, Stoop-Sale Books, Brooklyn, NY, 2000, p. 9.

7 Ibid., pp. 74-75.

8 Ibid., p. 76.

9 Ibid., pp. 55-56.

10 Harriet Tubman, as quoted in Lerone Bennett, Jr. *Before the Mayflower: A History of Black America,* Johnson Publishing Company, Chicago, 2003 (1962), p. 154.

11 Lee, p. 56.

12 Norman Mailer, *The Armies of the Night*, Penguin, New York, 1968, p. 176.

13 Noam Chomsky, "On Resistance," *The New York Review of Books*, December 7, 1967; archived at http://www.nybooks.com/articles/archives/1967/dec/07/on-resistance/ (Retrieved February 12, 2015)

14 Ibid.

15 Mailer, p. 86.

16 Malcolm Boyd, interview with the authors, December, 2013.

17 Gary Yerkey, "Malcolm Boyd brought Christianity into the streets to promote civil rights," *Christian Science Monitor*, May 10, 2013; http://www.csmonitor.com/World/Making-a-difference/2013/0510/Malcolm-Boyd-brought-Christianity-into-the-streets-to-promote-civil-rights (Retrieved February 12, 2015)

18 Malcolm Boyd, *Are You Running With Me, Jesus?*, Cowley, Cambridge, MA, 2006 (1965), p. 103.

19 Malcolm Boyd, interview with the authors, December, 2013.

20 Martin Luther King, *The Trumpet of Conscience*, Beacon Press, Boston, 1967, p. 31.

21 Pat McCaughan, "Malcolm Boyd at 90: Still writing, still 'running,' still inspiring," Episcopal News Service, June 7, 2013; http://episcopaldigitalnetwork.com/ens/2013/06/07/malcolm-boyd-at-90-still-writing-still-running-still-inspiring/ (Retrieved February 12, 2015)

22 Michael B. Friedland, "Giving a Shout for Freedom, Part III" from a paper presented at the Sixties Generation conference, March 1993, Fairfax, VA; http://www2.iath.virginia.edu/sixties/HTML_docs/Texts/Scholarly/Friedland_Boyd_03.html (Retrieved Feb 12, 2015)

23 Malcolm Boyd, interview with the authors, December, 2013.

24 Ibid.

25 Malcolm Boyd, "Responding to Suffering," *American Report*, March 26, 1973, as quoted in Friedland, "Giving a Shout for Freedom, Part III".

26 Malcolm Boyd, interview with the authors, December, 2013.

Credits

The Imperial Cruise: A Secret History of Empire and War by James Bradley, copyright © 2009. Reprinted by permission of Little, Brown, and Company, a division of Hachette Book Group, Inc.

Excerpts from *The Unknown American Revolution: The Unruly Birth of Democracy and the Struggle to Create America* by Gary B. Nash, copyright © 2005 by Gary B. Nash. Used by permission of Viking Books, an imprint of Penguin Publishing Group, a division of Penguin Random House LLC. All rights reserved.

Clara Nieto, excerpts from *Masters of War: Latin America and U.S. Aggression from the Cuban Revolution Through the Clinton Years.* Copyright © 2003 by Seven Stories Press. Reprinted with the permission of The Permissions Company, Inc., on behalf of Seven Stories Press. www.sevenstories.com

From *A People's History of the United States: 1492–Present* by Howard Zinn. Copyright ©1980 by Howard Zinn. Reprinted by permission of HarperCollins Publishers.

Copyright © 2011 by Noam Chomsky, David Barsamian, and Arthur Naiman, from *How the World Works.* Reprinted by permission of Counterpoint.

From *Rag-Tags, Scum, Riff-Raff, and Commies: The U.S. Intervention in the Dominican Republic 1965-1966,* Eric Thomas Chester. Copyright © 2001, Monthly Review Press.

Excerpt from *Are You Running With Me, Jesus* by Malcolm Boyd. Copyright © The Rowman & Littlefield Publishing Group. Reprinted by permission.

Passages from Bill Bigelow's article Grenada: Remembering a Lovely Little War first appeared as part of the Zinn Education Project "If We Knew Our History" series. www.zinnedproject.org

Photograph of the Rev. Malcolm Boyd courtesy of The Archives of the Episcopal Church.

Books by Mumia Abu-Jamal

Live from Death Row
1996, Harper Perennial

Death Blossoms
1997, Plough Publishing House

All Things Censored
2000, Seven Stories Press

Faith of Our Fathers:
An Examination of the Spiritual Life of African and African-American People
2003, Africa World Press

We Want Freedom
A Life in the Black Panther Party
2004, South End Press (new edition, 2016, Common Notions)

Jailhouse Lawyers:
Prisoners Defending Prisoners v. the USA
2009, City Lights Publishers

The Classroom and the Cell:
Conversations on Black Life in America with Marc Lamont Hill
2011, Third World Press

Writing on the Wall:
Selected Prison Writings of Mumia Abu-Jamal
2015, City Lights Publishers

Have Black Lives Ever Mattered?
2017, City Lights Publishers

Documentary Films by Stephen Vittoria

One Bright Shining Moment
The Forgotten Summer of George McGovern
2005, First Run Features

Mumia: Long Distance Revolutionary
2013, First Run Features

Index

F

G

J

K

L

M

S

T

U

V